The Anti-Slavery Project

PENNSYLVANIA STUDIES IN HUMAN RIGHTS

Bert B. Lockwood, Jr., Series Editor

A complete list of books in the series is available from the publisher

The Anti-Slavery Project

From the Slave Trade to Human Trafficking

Joel Quirk

PENN

UNIVERSITY OF PENNSYLVANIA PRESS

PHILADELPHIA

Published by
University of Pennsylvania Press
Philadelphia, Pennsylvania 19104-4112
www.upenn.edu/pennpress

Printed in the United States of America on acid-free paper
10 9 8 7 6 5 4 3 2 1

Library of Congress Cataloging-in-Publication Data
ISBN 978-0-8122-4333-8

For Pat Quirk and June Forbes

Contents

The Anti-Slavery Project

Where slavery is legally recognized one can tell who is a slave, but how does one describe the situation of people who seem to be exactly like slaves but who, in the eyes of the law, cannot be so because the law says nobody can be legally enslaved.

—Jonathon Derrick, *Africa's Slaves Today*, 1975

The whole problem is still before us, as urgent and uncertain as it has ever been. It is not solved. What seemed a solution is already obsolete. The problem will have to be worked through again from the start. Some of the factors have changed a little. Laws and regulations have been altered. New and respectable names have been invented. But the real issue has hardly changed at all.

—Henry Nevinson, *A Modern Slavery*, 1906

[O]nly that which has no history is definable.

—Friedrich Nietzsche, *On the Genealogy of Morals*, 1887

In January 2004, the *New York Times* once again found itself embroiled in a controversy concerning one of its reporters. The journalist in question was not named Jayson Blair, or Judith Miller, but was instead Peter Landesman, who had just published a *New York Times Magazine* cover story entitled "The Girls Next Door" exploring the increasingly topical issue of human trafficking. In his article, Landesman made the dramatic claim that the United States had "become a major importer of sex slaves."[1] To support this conclusion, he drew on a variety of figures, including an estimate from Kevin Bales, president of Free the Slaves, which suggested that between 30,000 and 50,000 sex slaves were being held in captivity at any given point in time. Like any good investigative reporter, Landesman had covered considerable ground putting together his material, moving back and forth between Eastern Europe, Mexico, and the United States, and interviewing a wide range of specialists. The picture that emerged was not pretty. Poverty stricken east European women were reported to have been tricked into emigrating, only to be "sold into sexual bondage." In Mexico, one source spoke of 15 major organizations and 120 associated factions, serving as "wholesalers: collecting human merchandise and taking orders from safe houses and brothels in the major sex trafficking hubs in New York, Los Angeles, Atlanta and Chicago." Young Mexican girls were reported to have been abducted or seduced, brutally broken in, and forced to have sex with "20 to 30 men a day."[2] Government officials were said to be complicit, indifferent, or overworked, allowing elaborate criminal networks to make tremendous profits.

Landesman's article was by no means atypical. Other newspapers and magazines have been regularly publishing similar stories since the mid-1990s. What was unusual was the persistent controversy it provoked, as various critics repeatedly challenged the reliability of Landesman's sources. One of the strongest indictments came from media critic Jack Shafer at *Slate.com*, who immediately denounced Landesman's supporting evidence: "Where it is not vague, it is anecdotal. Where it is anecdotal, it is often anonymous, too. And where it is not anecdotal or vague it is suspicious and slippery."[3] With the passage of time, three main lines of critique emerged. The first concerned the overall scale of the problem. How could we know how many slaves there were? Could estimates provided by Bales and others be justified? The second concerned Landesman's corroborating evidence. How much faith should we place in lurid anecdotes from various third parties? Was it legitimate to generalize from the potentially suspect stories of Landesman's two main sources, who were both young trafficking victims?[4] The final line of critique concerned hidden political subtexts. To what extent were activists "blinded by their agenda"?[5] Had Landesman been echoing right wing ideologues, or stirring moral panic?[6] Had other forms of forced labor been left out of the equation?[7] These questions resulted in the *New York Times* revisiting the article multiple times, culminating in a lengthy response from their new ombudsman, Daniel Okrent, who concluded that the "inflamed" article suffered from "rhetorical problems," but nonetheless retained a substantial core.[8] Landesman vigorously defended his reporting, crossing swords with critics such as Jack Shafer on a number of occasions. A fictional movie based on his 2004 article, entitled *Trade*, was formally launched at United Nations headquarters in New York in September 2007. Heated debates over the classification and quantification of human trafficking continue to this day.

This minor controversy is an imperfect microcosm of a major problem. All of the participants in this often fractious dispute were in general agreement that various forms of human bondage remained an ongoing problem, both in the United States and elsewhere. The main points at issue were their overall scale and distribution, and the extent to which broader generalizations could be extrapolated from anecdotal stories of individual abuses. This is a recurring problem. If we extend our gaze to other parts of the globe, it quickly becomes apparent that stories of large-scale suffering and severe exploitation can be found on nearly every continent. In Brazil, tens of thousands of slave laborers have been trapped in bondage by rural landowners, stretching mobile anti-slavery units recently established by the Brazilian government.[9] In Uganda, the Lord's Resistance Army has abducted upward of 20,000 children over many years, forcing them into sexual slavery and forced labor.[10] In North Korea, hundreds of thousands of enslaved prisoners have endured inhuman conditions for decades within an elaborate network of labor camps.[11] In countries like Britain, Malaysia, and Saudi Arabia, privileged elites continue to confine domestic servants in virtual slavery.[12]

How should these various practices be classified? Is the term slavery an appropriate designation, or would some other frame of reference be more suitable? What types of legal and analytical criteria should be employed in making this determination? These conceptual challenges are further compounded by the illicit character of most of the practices in question. While criminal prosecutions and other sources of information offer some guidance, relatively few cases of human bondage find their way into the public domain, making it difficult to determine the scale and distribution of many practices. Attempts to classify various problem areas also tend to be complicated by complex variations in individual experience, which can sometimes make it difficult to draw a clear-cut distinction between "severe" and "every-day" exploitation. Our answers to these questions have important implications for attempts to quantify the issues involved. How many "slaves" are there? How do we know? No one expects these types of questions to be easy, but even the most tentative and sensationalized figures regularly take on a life of their own. This can in turn further complicate our capacity to move beyond particular cases, and thereby situate the various examples outlined above within a shared frame of reference. What do these otherwise disparate cases share in common? On what terms can they be legitimately brought together?

The conceptual ambiguities surrounding these various forms of human bondage have important political ramifications. The problem is not that there are no answers to these types of questions, but that there are many competing answers of varying quality and credibility. At an institutional level there is official agreement. Every state in the world has now legally abolished slavery, but once we penetrate this veneer a more partisan picture quickly emerges. No government wants to be seen to be condoning slavery, and state officials have proved to be particularly adept at using these ambiguities to deflect their critics. This usually means insisting that the practices in question are *not* slavery, but belong in some other category. In many settings, it is not always clear where responsibility begins and ends, since the abuses in question are perpetrated by various individuals, yet are also facilitated by official complicity and indifference. In such cases, governments tend to be both a major part of the problem and the most obvious potential solution, as relevant laws need to be enforced, perpetrators brought to justice, victims rehabilitated, and preventive measures introduced. Wherever problems persist, we also encounter a widespread tendency to blame official failings on a lack of resources, rather than a lack of commitment. Without a clear institutional target (legal slavery) and a simple, singular solution (legal abolition), it can be difficult to mobilize political constituencies to combat various forms of human bondage.

The Anti-Slavery Project

These complex issues do not exist in a historical vacuum, but instead represent the most recent phase in an evolving political project that began in the mid-eighteenth century, with the emergence of an organized anti-slavery movement. In stark contrast to their modern counterparts, these anti-slavery pioneers had little problem identifying who the slaves were, or how they differed from non-slaves, because slavery was a clearly demarcated legal category with a venerable historical pedigree. This profile meant that slave systems were relatively vulnerable to political challenge, because it allowed opposition to be channeled around a definitive overall goal: legal abolition (of either slave trading or slavery itself). It was not always clear how this goal was to be realized, but there was usually little doubt about what ultimately needed to be done. With the passage of time, the politics of anti-slavery regularly boiled down to one basic question: was slavery legally sanctioned or legally prohibited?

Historical and contemporary slavery are usually treated as independent fields of study. There is an immense literature concerned with the history of transatlantic slavery in general, and the United States in particular, a smaller yet still substantial literature concerned with the history of slavery and abolition in other parts of the world, and a rapidly expanding literature concerned with contemporary forms of slavery.[13] The published works of most historians of slavery and abolition have tended to bypass contemporary problems entirely. When the topic does come up, it usually takes the form of a brief postscript which takes the form of a passing observation that the struggle against slavery has not yet conclusively ended.[14] A comparable story applies when it comes to recent works on contemporary slavery, which rarely go beyond brief allusions to the immediate events that led to the abolition of transatlantic slavery.[15] This has resulted in an informal separation between past and present, which has indirectly obscured the historical roots of a variety of contemporary problems.

The primary goal of this book is to integrate these different topics into a coherent whole. This is reflected in my four primary research questions, which are as follows:

- What were the underlying causes that led to slavery being redefined as a crime against humanity, rather than a legitimate institution?
- How were anti-slavery measures introduced in various parts of the globe?
- What were the strengths and weaknesses of the legal abolition of slavery as an institutional solution?
- On what terms can we connect the history of slavery and abolition to more recent discussions of contemporary forms of slavery?

To help address these questions, I turn to the concept of an "Anti-Slavery Project." The Anti-Slavery Project concept is designed to offer a framework for integrating a range of issues and events that have tended to be regarded as separate and self-contained episodes. As an analytical framework, the Anti-Slavery Project refers to both an ongoing task, or undertaking, which has gone through a number of different phases, and to a distinctive form of historical projection, which has seen an inherited image of transatlantic slavery invoked as an unofficial yardstick against which various forms of human bondage have been evaluated.

Organized anti-slavery first emerged in the mid-eighteenth century in response to the severe and systematic abuses associated with transatlantic slavery. The anti-slavery cause has subsequently experienced a number of different incarnations over the past two and a half centuries. The Anti-Slavery Project offers a framework for analyzing this gradual evolution. By describing anti-slavery in terms of a project, I aim to capture the long-term process of reinvention and redefinition that has been a core feature of organized anti-slavery over the centuries. As we shall see, the political horizons of anti-slavery have constantly shifted in response to changing circumstances, with cumulative reflections on the strengths and weaknesses of previous outcomes and events in turn provoking further mobilizations around new political goals. This does not mean, however, that this sequence of events was predetermined. There were many points along the way where things could have gone very differently. It would also be a mistake to ascribe a common set of purposes to the various protagonists involved.

The Anti-Slavery Project does not refer to a teleological process, or to a self-conscious political platform, but is instead conceived as an analytical tool that can help to illuminate a variety of connections and associations between historical practices and contemporary problems. In order to develop this concept farther, it is necessary to take into account an additional series of analytical distinctions: (1) legal abolition versus effective emancipation; (2) strict equivalence versus sufficient similarity; and (3) analytical category versus evocative concept. Each of these formulations captures a key aspect of the underlying relationship between legal abolition and more recent concerns about contemporary forms of slavery. These distinctions not only help to develop the concept of the Anti-Slavery Project, they also lay much of the intellectual groundwork for the core arguments of later chapters.

Legal Abolition Versus Effective Emancipation

In its most basic form, the term "project" refers to a complex task, or undertaking, which usually involves a number of different phases. In this context, the concept of an Anti-Slavery Project offers a necessary corrective to a widespread tendency to assume that the problem of slavery came to an end at some indeterminate point in the past. Over the past two and a half centuries, organized anti-slavery has been in a state of constant flux. The pioneers of British anti-slavery were initially preoccupied with slavery in their own country, but when legislation abolishing the slave trade was passed in 1807 interest turned to other countries, resulting in a major popular campaign in 1814–1815. When the British Parliament abolished slavery in 1833, the treatment of ex-slaves similarly emerged as a political issue. These evolving priorities were not only rooted in specific victories, they also reflected a partial recognition of their limitations. The legal abolition of slavery is commonly viewed as a historical endpoint, but in both of these examples the next phase in the struggle is critical to the overall efficacy of the initial goal: if slavery were to expand in other countries, or simply persist under another name, this would call into question the realization of the original goal.

To make sense of this evolving political horizon, we need to make a distinction between legal abolition and effective emancipation.[16] If slavery is renounced, but proprietary claims and extreme forms of exploitation persist under other headings, what does this say about the effectiveness of legal abolition? If the legal abolition of slavery has proved to be ineffective or incomplete, what other measures are required? From this vantage point, effective emancipation does not represent a static, singular standard, but instead constitutes a set of evolving political aspirations and ethical expectations. In this context, the concept of emancipation can be best understood as a "politically contingent idea around which people . . . discuss what to do next in politics."[17] In the aftermath of the legal abolition of slavery, the Anti-Slavery Project has become more ambitious and demanding. The legal abolition of slavery typically involved an official change in status, with slaves receiving no compensation and little or no support. Effective emancipation now includes issues such as prevention, restitution, rehabilitation, further institutional reform, and larger concerns about social justice.

This distinction between legal abolition and effective emancipation has important implications when it comes to the difficult task of defining and demarcating slavery. There are two main challenges facing historical efforts to formulate a universal definition of slavery: developing a definition of slavery that captures key variations among a wide range of historical slave systems; and developing a definition that consistently distinguishes between slavery and related forms of bondage, such as serfdom, helotage or pawnship.[18] The most common approach to defining slavery rests on the idea of slaves as human property, with masters exercising a legal right to personal ownership. This focus on property is usually understood in terms of a combination of largely unfettered authority and extreme treatment, with the exceptional degree of personalized control that masters exercised over their slaves going hand in hand with consistently high levels of institutionalized brutality, psychological abuse, and economic exploitation. This familiar approach works relatively well in some settings, such as transatlantic slavery, but can struggle in other historical contexts.[19]

This concentration on property represents one of two main approaches to defining slavery.[20] As part of his seminal comparative study, *Slavery and Social Death* (1982), Orlando Patterson famously defined slavery as "*the permanent, violent domination of natally alienated and generally dishonored persons.*"[21] According to Patterson, efforts to define slavery exclusively in terms of proprietary claims are fundamentally misguided, because such claims can also apply to other practices and institutions, from serfs to professional athletes.[22] He instead defined slavery in terms of particularly severe forms of coercion, social and genealogical isolation, and distinctive forms of sociopolitical dishonor.[23] In Patterson's view, slavery is as much a social as an interpersonal relationship, as interactions between master and slave are bound up in broader relations between slaves and societies. This theme has also been taken up by Claude Meillassoux, who observes that "one captive does not make slavery." For Meillassoux, slavery can be best understood as a far-reaching system that needed to be constantly renewed through enduring conflicts between civilizations, as captured individuals were withdrawn from their native social milieu and desocialized, depersonalized, and desexualized, acquiring an "alien" status within their new host society.[24]

Most efforts to define slavery have revolved around historical settings where slavery was a legal institution, but this approach is ill-suited to contemporary practices, since slavery has now been legally abolished across the globe. This change introduces a new set of definitional challenges. The main point at issue here has been an enduring divide between legal injunctions and actual practices. If enslavement has continued to be a major problem in the absence of official recognition, on what grounds can we meaningfully distinguish slavery from comparable forms of exploitation? In an institutional environment where slavery has been legally abolished, the key question has gradually become which (of many) practices and institutions are sufficiently similar to legal slavery that they can be legitimately placed on the same footing.

This is a complex exercise, which remains open to interpretation and manipulation. If we follow the approach favored by scholars such as Patterson or Meillassoux, very few contemporary practices would qualify as slavery, since slavery is much more than individual ownership, but instead entails the natal alienation of slaves from an entire social and institutional order. In the vast majority of cases, this social order was fatally disrupted by legal abolition. This was often far from instantaneous. Individual master/slave relationships sometimes survived for decades, even generations, but the institutional status of slavery has proved to be less secure. There are now very few places in the world today where slavery exists as a fully fledged institution. The real sticking point, however, is how we approach this achievement. If an enduring social order expires, but its more heinous characteristics continue under different designations, or through illicit activities, is it still feasible to claim that it has effectively come to an end? In this context, procedural distinctions between "classical" slavery and other forms of bondage have become increasingly difficult to sustain.

Strict Equivalence Versus Sufficient Similarity

To make sense of this dilemma, we need to make a further distinction between two ideal types: strict equivalence and sufficient similarity. Strict equivalence maintains that forms of human bondage should be equated with slavery only in cases of close correspondence. It accepts that similarities exist, but nonetheless insists that similarity should not be confused with equivalency. This can be contrasted with sufficient similarity, which places other examples of bondage alongside slavery on the basis of familial resemblance. It accepts that the practices in question are not always identical, yet maintains that they still share sufficient features in common to be placed on the same footing. Both ideal types are inherently comparative, with transatlantic slavery typically serving as a key yardstick. Strict equivalence was the dominant approach until (at least) the mid-twentieth century, providing a foundation for (among other things) political campaigns against colonial labor abuses in the Congo Free State and Portuguese Africa. The concept of strict equivalence is most effective when it can be used to describe an entire category of persons. Problems arise, however, when only a subset of involved persons can be plausibly described in such demanding terms, as is often the case when it comes to child labor, servile marriage, or sex work. In such circumstances, strict equivalence requires case by case evaluation, where it can be difficult to say when particular experiences "cross a line" and can therefore be legitimately described as slavery.

Sufficient similarity offers a way out of these complications by giving pride of place to analogous *practices* and *institutions*, rather than equivalent *cases*. With this crucial move, slavery splinters into *different forms*, which can be formally accorded *equal importance*. This less exacting model has become increasingly prominent in recent times, building on a crucial precedent established by the 1956 United Nations Supplementary Convention on the Abolition of Slavery. For many modern observers, classical slavery has ceased to be a singular, exceptional category, but has instead come to be regarded as one of many forms of contemporary slavery. In this political environment, it has become increasingly difficult to determine where slavery begins and ends. In a 1991 fact sheet published by the United Nations Centre for Human Rights, slavery was linked to an extensive list of abuses:

> In addition to traditional slavery and the slave trade, these abuses include the sale of children, child prostitution, child pornography, the exploitation of child labour, the sexual mutilation of female children, the use of children in armed conflicts, debt-bondage, the traffic in persons and in the sale of human organs, the exploitation of prostitution, and certain practices under *apartheid* and colonial régimes.[25]

Despite its length, this statement captures only some of the issues involved. Other major themes include forced labor for the state, "cult" slavery, servile marriage, domestic servitude, "honor" killings, and abuses inflicted on migrant workers, prisoners, indigenous peoples, and street children. These are rarely discrete categories, but instead regularly overlap. Trafficked persons are often caught in debt bondage. Child labor can also involve forced labor for the state. In the face of such diversity, it is not always easy to identify a coherent rationale that links them together. This uncertainty is further exacerbated by a widespread tendency to describe various practices as "slavery," yet not say how this status was determined.[26] In many cases, slavery ceases to be an analytical category and instead becomes an *evocative concept*.

Analytical Category Versus Evocative Concept

At this juncture, I turn to a quite different understanding of the Anti-Slavery Project, which is concerned with historical *projection*. This refers to a widespread tendency to invoke an inherited image of transatlantic slavery as a key benchmark, or baseline, against which various forms of human bondage have been consistently conceptualized and classified. As we shall see in the next chapter, the pioneers of organized anti-slavery were able to successfully frame slavery as an unconscionable evil that was outside "normal" (i.e., legitimate) practices and institutions. There were many facets to their overall case, but there were two themes in particular that stood out: the *ownership of human beings* and *extreme dominion and exploitation*. For anti-slavery pioneers, it was both the legal right to buy, sell, and own other human beings, and the extreme brutality, mortality, and debasement that rendered transatlantic slavery fundamentally unacceptable. Over the past two and a half centuries, this triad of ownership, exploitation, and transatlantic slavery has consistently served as a key yardstick against which other practices have been evaluated. This is chiefly applicable to three main problem areas: legal slavery, post-abolition shortcomings, and analogous practices.

In the case of legal slavery, it is not uncommon for people to mistakenly declare that legal slavery came to an end in the nineteenth century. This is epitomized by a recent collection on contemporary slavery, which begins with the erroneous claim that slavery was "outlawed in Britain and in the rest of the world in the nineteenth century."[27] Similar sentiments can be found in a 2001 International Labour Organization (ILO) report on forced labor.[28] This is extremely problematic. The legal abolition of slavery was not confined to the Americas, or to the nineteenth century, but extended to most corners of the globe, encompassing millions of slaves in Africa, Asia, and the Middle East. This larger story has been consistently overshadowed by a narrow focus on selected aspects of transatlantic slavery, fostering a parochial orientation that not only distorts our understanding of anti-slavery by reducing a global phenomenon to a regional event, but also has consequences for our capacity to evaluate the historical roots of contemporary problems. To correct this imbalance, we need to examine how legal abolition came about in various parts of the globe. This means confronting uncomfortable links with European imperialism. For centuries, European agents had either tacitly accommodated or actively exploited the slave systems of other civilizations. This slowly began to change in the nineteenth century, as anti-slavery was harnessed to imperial expansion, colonial conquest, and the "standard of civilization."

Ownership, exploitation, and transatlantic slavery served as critical benchmarks throughout this period. To justify numerous delays in the course of abolition, political elites of all stripes would frequently seek to distinguish the "mild," or "benign," slavery practiced within their jurisdictions from the horrors associated with transatlantic slavery. This disingenuous stance may well have been appropriate in some cases, but was not tenable as a blanket characterization. In colonial Africa, European powers heavily invested in the concept of "domestic" slavery, a somewhat amorphous category that nonetheless dominated official pronouncements and public debate. In this popular scheme, domestic slaves would be distinguished from "trade" slaves and the plantation slaves of the Americas. From this starting point, an expedient approach to legal abolition became responsible and desirable policy, since "domestic" slavery was at worst a minor evil and at best a positive good. In the later years of colonial rule there was a further round of conceptual gymnastics. Official declarations that slavery had ceased to be an ongoing concern, or was limited to diminishing pockets or "vestiges," tended to be heavily dependent on how slavery was defined.

None of these machinations would have been necessary if slavery had remained a legitimate institution. From its inception, the Anti-Slavery Project has created political complications and economic costs that could otherwise have been easily avoided. The main aim of much of this maneuvering was not to maximize gains, but to minimize losses, using a combination of delay, deflection, and dilution. This long-running rearguard action did not end with legal abolition, but would inform subsequent debates over "suitable" replacements. In the aftermath of legal abolition, there was often an urgent need to find effective substitutes for positions that would previously have been occupied by slaves. By espousing a minimalist understanding of anti-slavery, political authorities in various parts of the globe routinely sanctioned a range of highly coercive practices. These assorted instruments were by no means new, but they nonetheless took on additional importance once slavery had ceased to be a legitimate source of labor. In recent times, "free" labor has come to be regarded as natural, rather than exceptional, but when slavery was abolished it was often by no means clear that free labor would be adequate or effective, so authorities consistently resorted to other means.

The most prominent examples of this dynamic involved indentured migration, bonded labor, and forced labor for the state. Indentured migration saw millions of workers from Asia, Africa, India, and the Pacific being transported to many parts of the globe to toil under restrictive work contracts for extended periods. Bonded labor was particularly prominent in the Indian subcontinent and Latin America, where it proved to be a popular alternative to slavery in the aftermath of legal abolition. Forced labor took place in most colonial jurisdictions, as millions of workers were pressed into service on public and private projects, often enduring horrific treatment and high mortality for little or no reward. In some cases, these workers closely followed in the footsteps of their slave forebears. In Africa, it was not uncommon for European traders to buy slaves and then disingenuously rebrand them as indentured laborers. In other cases, such as Peru, Malaya, or Fiji, links with slavery were more tangential, as workers were recruited from places such as India, China, and Japan. A similar story applies to forced and bonded labor. In colonial Africa, slaves and ex-slaves were often the first to be pressed into service, but rapacious demands for labor would inevitably impact on a broader cross-section of "native" society. In both colonial and post-colonial India, bonded labor incorporated both former slaves and other vulnerable and marginal groups.

When forced, bonded, and indentured labor aroused controversy and political scandal, stylized images of ownership, exploitation, and transatlantic slavery consistently served as evaluative benchmarks. When critics charged that specific practices marked a continuation of slavery by another name, what they were usually suggesting was that they were just as horrific as (inherited images of) transatlantic slavery, further obfuscating the divide between analytical category and evocative concept. Tragically, these charges frequently proved to be ineffective. Complicit officials would point to institutional safeguards that ostensibly guarded against abuses, and routinely dismiss negative reports as "isolated incidents" or "politically motivated" slurs. In such circumstances, slavery was regularly invoked by both critics and apologists, with the later emphasizing differences, and the former emphasizing similarities. When anti-slavery is framed as a bounded obligation, other forms of labor can end up being legitimated on the grounds that they represent a "step up" from slavery, and can thus be construed as either lesser evils or positive improvements. When anti-slavery is framed as an expansive obligation, other forms of behavior can end up being tarnished by association, as evocative images of suffering and deprivation are used to challenge their overall legitimacy.

By the mid-twentieth century, the stage was set for a further reconfiguration. At this point, slavery had been legally abolished in all but a handful of Arabian polities, and officially sanctioned forced labor was in decline following the end of the Second World War. In this political environment, anti-slavery advocacy increasingly concentrated on analogous practices and institutions. This dynamic was set in motion by a key precedent established by the 1956 Slavery Convention, and has now come to incorporate the diverse range of practices listed above. One of the most revealing aspects of this ongoing transformation has been a gradual merging with allied political agendas, as anti-slavery has come to overlap with closely related themes such as human rights, wartime abuses, child labor, sexual exploitation, and human development. In this context, reports of slavery frequently end up as one component of a larger catalogue of human rights abuses. It is also clear, however, that slavery contin-ues to carry political and ideological connotations that can set it apart from other issues. During the second phase of the Sudanese civil war (1983–2005), government sanctioned slave raids emerged as a major international issue, yet wartime enslavement was only a small component of a much larger cataclysm that involved the deaths of upwards of two million people. In a world where systematic human rights abuses remain all too common, slavery continues to be a powerful tool for political mobilization. It is not overly surprising, there-fore, that "forms" of slavery have proliferated over time, as the anti-slavery banner has been taken up by a wide range of activists.[29] As forms of slavery have proliferated, it has become increasingly difficult to determine whether slavery is being invoked in literal (actual slavery) or rhetorical (a far looser metaphorical association) terms.

This issue finds expression in the use of references to "new," "modern," "contemporary," or "twenty-first-century" slavery. These additions help to distinguish current problems from inherited images of transatlantic slav-ery, while working to retain the political and ethical urgency slavery evokes. This popular move is by no means unwarranted or illegitimate, but it has also tended to be accompanied by an informal separation between past and present, whereby the history of slavery is held to have little or no bearing on current issues. This is reflected in a widespread tendency to attribute the rise of the "new" slavery to recent innovations, such as economic globaliza-tion. As we shall see, this has contributed to an incomplete diagnosis of the causes of—and solutions to—a variety of contemporary problems. When we designate a problem a species of slavery, we are not only making an empirical claim about the subject at hand, but also invoking a preexisting ethical argu-ment for uncompromising action to correct unconscionable evil. This overall line of argument is unlikely to be politically compelling—or at least not as compelling as it could be—when references to "slavery" lack a solid historical foundation. By situating contemporary forms of slavery within a larger his-torical trajectory, the Anti-Slavery Project offers a way of bringing together a range of otherwise isolated issues within a common frame of reference.

The Plan of the Book

This book favors a "big picture" approach. I do not propose to offer a detailed analysis of a specific issue or sequence of events, but instead aim to use historical inquiry to illuminate various connections and associations between past and present. To this end, I have divided my argument into three distinct sections. In the first section, I examine the historical events that led to the legal abolition of slavery throughout the globe. In the second section, I focus on links between historical and contemporary slavery. In the third and final section, I examine some of the main forms of contemporary slavery currently in operation today.

The first section is entitled "The British Empire and the Legal Abolition of Slavery." Using the history of British anti-slavery as an analytical focal point, I explore the primary mechanisms that were behind legal abolition in a variety of historical contexts. This focus on the British Empire chiefly stems from the decisive role of British anti-slavery in the international history of the Anti-Slavery Project, starting with the Congress of Vienna and continuing with international campaigns in Africa, the Americas, the Middle East, and Asia. Events in France, Haiti, the United States, and Latin America all played important roles in the early history of anti-slavery, but their analytical value is more narrowly circumscribed. The Civil War was an extremely traumatic event for the United States, as millions of slaves were freed at tremendous cost, but at an international level this worked to *consolidate* and *extend*, rather than *inspire*, an international trend.[30] The primary catalyst for this trend came from Britain.

In Chapter 1, "A Short History of British Anti-Slavery," I examine the origin and subsequent evolution of the British anti-slavery movement. After opening with an introductory survey of the historical dimensions and distinctive features of transatlantic slavery, I go on to examine the contingent sequence of historical events that led to popular mobilization against slavery in Britain. My primary argument here is that the political achievements of British anti-slavery were not based on a rejection of the prevailing order, but on its moral redemption. Two main themes will be highlighted here. The first theme revolves around the construction of slavery as a compelling political problem that was both stark and solvable. The second theme revolves around the acute problems that slavery posed for evolving conceptions of national virtue and religious exceptionalism within Britain.

In Chapter 2, "British Anti-Slavery and European International Society," I explore the British government's unwelcome efforts to internationalize anti-slavery in Europe, Africa, and the Americas. In this environment, initial anti-slavery measures usually had more to do with political expediency than philosophical conviction, but they would nonetheless have important cumulative effects. Over time, anti-slavery would come to be construed as a further expression of the inherent superiority of European "civilization." Throughout this process, official commitments to the Anti-Slavery Project primarily revolved around what anti-slavery was held to symbolize about the distinctive virtues (or vices) of particular communities. In an age of imperial expansion, most non-European elites were similarly unconvinced by anti-slavery, but nonetheless ended up reluctantly adopting institutional reforms in an effort to secure their civilized credentials and sovereign status. In this context, taking action against a bounded and "exceptional" evil such as slavery did not necessarily preclude other "normal" activities, such as colonial conquest. These themes are continued in Chapter 3, "British Anti-Slavery and European Colonialism," where I trace the halting progress of legal abolition under colonial jurisdictions. In this setting, colonialism and anti-slavery were not contradictory, but complementary, reflecting ideologies of benevolent paternalism that created an obligation to "civilize" various "inferior" peoples languishing in earlier stages of human development. Having exploited or otherwise accommodated the slave systems of other civilizations for centuries, European powers cautiously introduced a variety of limited anti-slavery measures. Despite the extravagant claims that often accompanied conquest, colonial rulers were slow to fulfill their official commitments. Anti-slavery rhetoric frequently concealed a multitude of grievous sins, but it also regularly created problems that could otherwise have been avoided if slavery had remained an entirely legitimate institution.

The second section, "Linking the Historical and Contemporary" considers underlying linkages between past and present. In Chapter 4, "The Limitations of Legal Abolition," I argue that the legal abolition of slavery constituted an imperfect change in official status, rather than a historical endpoint. By focusing on various responses to legal abolition, I aim to identify a number of enduring issues and calculations that continue to have a major influence on more recent practices. The main points at issue here are the (micro-) economic attractions of coercive labor techniques, the enduring influence of various forms of social hierarchy and patriarchy, the continuing significance of various forms of negotiation and contestation, and the continuing role of governments in sanctioning and supporting various forms of human bondage. In Chapter 5, "Defining Slavery in All Its Forms," I go on to argue that the emergence of the category of contemporary forms of slavery can be best understood as the most recent phase in an evolving response to the historical limitations of the legal abolition of slavery. The main focal point here is the status of slavery under international law, and the allied activities of a series of expert groups established by both the League of Nations and the United Nations. From this starting point, I argue that the shift from strict equivalence toward sufficient similarity can be primarily traced to evolving answers to two interrelated questions: what "counts" as slavery when slavery has no official standing? and what additional steps beyond legal abolition need to be taken to combat outstanding problems?

The final section is entitled "Contemporary Forms of Slavery." It consists of three thematic chapters. While many issues could have potentially been included here, I have selected three practices that have been at the forefront of contemporary debates: classical slavery, bonded labor, and human trafficking. In Chapter 6, "Classical Slavery and Descent-Based Discrimination," I examine a small number of cases where the historical categories of master and slave have continued to have a major influence on contemporary life. The main focus here is Saharan Africa in general, and Mauritania, Niger, and Sudan in particular. The first two cases represent a continuation of colonial shortcomings. The later involves a return to wartime enslavement. In stark contrast to the top-down dynamic that typically defined legal abolition, these cases have been primarily driven by domestic activists and nongovernmental organizations. Despite qualified progress, effective emancipation remains elusive, reflecting the continuing influence of underlying structural problems.

In Chapter 7, "Slaves to Debt," I examine the enduring issue of debt-bondage, which has long been identified as sharing many features in common with classical slavery. This is the one form of contemporary slavery that has been consistently measured in millions, rather than tens of thousands. The main focus here is the Indian subcontinent, where legal abolition precipitated a gradual reconfiguration of longstanding models of bondage, with prevailing slave systems being recast as debt-bondage. After decades of inaction, governments in the region have belatedly tightened laws against bonded labor, but effective emancipation remains an ongoing challenge. In this context, discussion of debt-bondage is inevitably caught up in larger issues of caste, poverty, demography, and inequality. In Chapter 8, "Trafficked into Slavery," I take up the topical issue of trafficking in persons. Trafficking is most commonly associated with sexual servitude, having grown out of earlier "white slavery" campaigns, but the concept has recently been extended to cover virtually all forms of contemporary slavery. This represents a mixed blessing, as other problem areas tend to be overshadowed by specific concerns with border protection, prostitution, and organized crime. In taking up these various themes, I argue that these ongoing problems mark the most recent phase in a larger historical trajectory, and that the lessons, legacies, and strategies of earlier contests over historical slave systems have important ramifications for current events.

Caveats and Cautions

Before going farther, it is important to acknowledge that this book remains subject to a number of limitations and preoccupations. While most of these limitations are best left to future critics, there are three themes that need to be briefly addressed here. First, and perhaps most significantly, it is important to acknowledge that certain consequences flow from my decision to begin the historical narrative with the political campaigns that culminated in legal abolition. This decision was primarily made on pragmatic grounds, since a book of this type must invariably prioritize some topics over others, but it nonetheless has consequences for how we think about the history of slavery. In any discussion of slavery and abolition, it is essential to keep in mind that both slavery and enslavement were practiced for thousands of years without arousing significant political opposition. I have discussed some of the main characteristics of a number of pre-abolition slave systems at various stages over the course of this book, but any references to slavery tend to be immediately followed by references to abolition. For thousands of years there was just slavery and no abolition. Focusing on more recent events runs the risk of obscuring this essential fact.

The decision to focus on legal abolition also has important ramifications when it comes to other human rights issues. In any discussion of slavery, it is difficult to avoid thinking in terms of an implicit hierarchy, whereby practices and institutions that fall short of slavery end up as lesser evils, and perhaps even positive goods. Working in a sweatshop in Brazil, Mexico, or the Philippines may not be ideal, but it is still likely to appear preferable to life in a North Korean gulag, or as a sex slave in Uganda. Problems quickly arise, however, when discussion of anti-slavery ends up at least tacitly normalizing otherwise unsavory structures and situations, and the underlying economic dynamics that allow them to take place. According to one popular estimate, there are currently around 27 million slaves in the world today.[31] This appears to be a significant figure at first glance, but it needs to be placed alongside the just over a billion people currently estimated to be living on less than one U.S.

dollar a day, with 2.6 billion, 40 percent of the world's population, living on less than two dollars a day.[32] Focusing on contemporary slavery should not mean diminishing (and perhaps indirectly legitimating) the plight of a much larger number of people who also face tremendous burdens. When slavery is placed at the center of discussion, global patterns of poverty, inequality, and exploitation tend to end up at the margins of discussion, running the risk of obscuring other systematic abuses.

The third and final theme to be addressed here concerns the way we conceptualize change. On this front, it is not uncommon to encounter claims that the scale of contemporary slavery greatly exceeds that of transatlantic slavery.[33] Behind such statements is a tacit claim that nothing much has changed, and that things are perhaps no better now than in the past. This position is not sustainable. As we shall see, these types of statements bypass historical slave systems in Africa, the Middle East, and elsewhere, and thus end up sidestepping essential parts of the history of slavery and abolition.[34] In any comparison between past and present, it is also necessary to include the wide range of practices that we now designate as slavery, and not just persons who were then legally classified as such. If we were to extend current definitions of slavery backward through time, it would quickly become necessary to reclassify many common historical practices as forms of slavery.

The global prevalence of human bondage has substantially declined since the mid-twentieth century (primarily because of the end of Nazi era abuses, colonial forced labor schemes, and the decline of Communist gulags and slave systems in Africa and the Middle East), yet most recent commentators have tended to overlook this global trend because their primary frame of reference remains transatlantic slavery.[35] By any reasonable standard, organized anti-slavery has proved to be highly successful, just not quite as successful—or final—as has sometimes been assumed. It does not necessarily follow, however, that the legal abolition of slavery was all but inevitable. There is no question that major changes have taken place, but it would be a mistake to conclude that these changes constituted part of a linear or teleological process. The first steps toward the legal abolition of slavery first emerged in the mid-eighteenth century. The final stages of the legal abolition of slavery took place in the second half of the twentieth century. Throughout this process, there was a consistent pattern of delay, deflection, and dilution. These strategies may not amount to much in macro-historical terms, since slavery was eventually abolished, but their cumulative *human* cost was astronomical. When slavery was abolished in Sierra Leone in 1928, the colony had been under British jurisdiction for over a hundred years. Every decade abolition was delayed ensured that tens of thousands of individuals lived out their lives as slaves.

The obvious response to this line of argument is to highlight resistance, weakness, and cost. With even the best will in the world, the Anti-Slavery Project will always be a long-term proposition that requires complex institutional, economic, and social adjustments. In such circumstances, it can be very difficult to determine how long is too long. Do we celebrate modest changes when they finally take place, since there is no guarantee they will occur at all, or should we lament the time taken for even qualified progress to occur? The ultimate goal of organized anti-slavery—ending slavery in all its forms—has yet to be realized, but there should also be little doubt that things have improved since the mid-eighteenth century.

PART I

The British Empire
and the Legal Abolition of Slavery

Chapter 1

A Short History of British Anti-Slavery

Slavery and enslavement have existed in a number of different guises throughout recorded history. This pedigree raises a number of difficult and contentious issues. If slavery represents a self-evident wrong, as current legal and moral opinion maintains, why did all of the world's major religions and civilizations sanction slavery and slave trading for thousands of years? If enslavement represents a clear-cut "crime against humanity," why was it repeatedly endorsed by leading philosophers, theologians, and jurists from every corner of the globe? These types of questions are understandable, but misleading. If we start with the contemporary assumption that slavery is an obvious wrong, the key question becomes *when*, and not *if*, this status would come to be belatedly recognized. If we further assume that the end of slavery was all but inevitable, it becomes easy to mistakenly conclude that individual historical slave systems were not really that significant—or dynamic—in the first place.[1] In any discussion of slavery and abolition, it is essential to keep in mind that slavery is the historical norm, and organized anti-slavery is the historical anomaly. Framed in these terms, the emergence and subsequent success of the Anti-Slavery Project constitutes a truly remarkable development. Rather than being surprised that slavery has displayed such resilience, we should instead be surprised at how much has recently been accomplished.

This chapter examines the early history of the British anti-slavery movement. This begins with an introductory survey of the historical dimensions and distinctive features of transatlantic slavery. From here, I go on to explore an intellectual sea change in attitudes toward slavery in European political culture during the eighteenth century. This sea change laid the groundwork for later political developments, but it did not in itself constitute a direct threat to the ongoing viability of transatlantic slavery. The transition from intellectual revolution to political movement was inaugurated by a national petition campaign against the slave trade in 1787, which elicited an unprecedented response from the British public.[2] Since this remarkable popular response to anti-slavery ideas was vital to its political success, I explore in some detail the underlying causes of this breakthrough. Weaving together a number of different strands, I argue that Britons' unprecedented support for anti-slavery can be traced to the advancement of a new set of claims that appealed to prevailing conceptions of religious virtue and national identity. The chapter concludes with an analysis of the Parliamentary contests surrounding the abolition of the slave trade in 1807, and the abolition of slavery in 1833. By the end of these protracted contests, anti-slavery was firmly ensconced at both a social and an institutional level. This new consensus not only represented a remarkable turnaround in British attitudes toward slavery, it also had major international consequences.

Historical Starting Points

For the vast majority of recorded history, various forms of slavery could be found in political communities in Africa, the Americas, Asia, and Europe. In all these communities, slavery was widely regarded as a natural, venerable, and fairly unremarkable part of the prevailing social order.[3] In most instances, slavery also represented a key source of wealth and property, ensuring that political and economic elites were consistently among the most prominent raiders, traders, and holders of slaves. Their long-term activities were in turn legitimated and imperfectly regulated by laws that codified both master-slave and slave-society relations.

Until relatively recently, legal discussion of slavery primarily focused on the terms under which slaving could be legitimately practiced. The two main themes animating these discussions were the conditions under which enslavement could legitimately occur, and the conditions under which slaves could be traded, treated, and manumitted (freed). Most historical slave systems developed elaborate legal and ethical injunctions against enslaving compatriots of the same religion, caste, race, or place of origin.[4] These injunctions were not always absolute or strictly adhered to, but they nonetheless represent a key illustration of the importance of social membership in determining who could be legitimately enslaved. Some historical slave systems also included mechanisms for enslaving social insiders, but in such cases enslavement was usually viewed as a legitimate punishment for "fallen" individuals who had either been convicted of serious social transgressions, or who were unable to discharge their debts.[5] As a general rule, enslavement was an intergenerational burden, which required elaborate rules governing the inheritance of slave status.

Resistance to particular acts of enslavement has occurred throughout history, with the most overt strategies being rebellion, flight, and suicide. It is clear, however, that a majority of slaves at least partially reconciled themselves to their status, and instead chiefly focused on improving their lives *as* slaves. Prior to the emergence of organized anti-slavery, slave resistance does not appear to have constituted a politically significant challenge to slavery as a general institution, but instead found expression in more parochial challenges to either personal enslavement or the enslavement of compatriots. When slaves successfully rebelled, escaped, or obtained their freedom, they sometimes went on to acquire slaves of their own.[6] Europeans who were appalled by the enslavement of their compatriots in North Africa and the Middle East had few qualms about being members of societies that supported the enslavement of millions of Africans through transatlantic slavery.[7] Despite this universal opposition to specific instances of slavery, most communities at most times considered at least some portion of humanity to be legitimate candidates for enslavement. On this point, even objections to the "wrong" types of people being enslaved were often colored by a pragmatic recognition that there was often little that could be done about "illegitimate" cases.

Organized anti-slavery first emerged in western Europe and northern America in the second half of the eighteenth century. Before this period, there appear to have been few—if any—politically significant challenges to slavery as a general institution.[8] The key intellectual and political developments in the early history of anti-slavery took place in the British and French empires and (after 1776) in the United States of America. Like other European participants in transatlantic slavery, these states practiced an especially severe form of economically driven and racially defined slavery that had important legal and social antecedents in both Roman and Medieval practice.[9] In order to understand the emergence of political opposition to slavery at this historical juncture, we first need to briefly explore i) the distinctive features of transatlantic slavery relative to other historical slave systems, and ii) the distinctive features of eighteenth-century European political and intellectual culture.

Unlike many historical slave systems, transatlantic slavery was organized around a legally defined demarcation between slave and non-slave. This legal model was reinforced by an imperfect yet extremely powerful association between slavery and race. This association was so strong that free Africans in the Americas were often assumed to be slaves unless they could prove otherwise.[10] This ensured that slaves were consistently treated as a clear-cut, readily identifiable category of persons in public discourse. This sharp demarcation can be contrasted with forms of slavery practiced in most parts of Asia and Africa, which regularly involved a variety of evolving and overlapping variations in status, which were rarely compatible with European categories of slave and non-slave, black and white, or free and unfree.[11]

While all historical slave systems involved systematic human rights abuses, commercial imperatives and this strong racial and legal distinction had the consequence that transatlantic slavery involved unusually heavy burdens, with slaves enduring severe punishments, tenuous family relationships, high mortality, extreme workloads, and comparatively high barriers to obtaining their freedom. For David Eltis, this amounted to "exploitation more intense than had ever existed before."[12] While life was by no means easy for the white working poor of Europe or the Americas, the hardships that black slaves endured set them apart from all but the most piteous. This was not always the case in slave systems in other parts of the globe, where the lives and lifestyles of slaves varied significantly from (materially) well-off to wretched. While the latter situation was usually preponderant, there were often major variations in the roles different slaves performed, and thus corresponding differences in their relative material comfort and (reflected) social standing.

One illustration of the analytical and political implications of this dynamic is provided by Ehud Toledano, who argues that Ottoman responses to British pressure for abolition in the mid-nineteenth century were significantly influenced by the political elite's attachment to kul-harem, or "elite" slavery.[13] These slaves were housed in harems or worked as functionaries, soldiers, or administrators. While elite slaves undoubtedly experienced a significant amount of exploitation and vulnerability, their material circumstances can be favorably contrasted with both black domestic slaves and much of the general population. One of the main reasons political elites resisted external pressures was that they considered Ottoman slavery comparatively "benign." Toledano argues that this assessment was largely built on a conflation of kul-harem and domestic slavery, with their familiarity with the former blinding elites to the miseries of the latter. Since there were clearly worse fates than being a kul-harem slave, it was difficult to formulate a strong case for general abolition on humanitarian grounds, because other groups in society could suffer equivalent, or even greater, physical and social hardships. These themes are echoed by Igor Kopytoff, who notes that the "placement of a slave as 'politically and socially at a lower level than the mass of the people' would have surprised many a Grand Vizier or Janissary."[14]

A somewhat similar situation prevailed in much of South East Asia and India.[15] In his discussion of slavery in Thailand, Burma, and (to a lesser extent) Cambodia, Anthony Reid argues that the "ordinary man" faced three realistic alternatives in earning a living: bondage to the king as part of the corvee system; bondage to a monastery or religious foundation; or private bondage or slavery to the upper class. The first of these alternatives is said to have been the most onerous.[16] In India, slaves often came from intermediate castes because particular roles were not meant to be performed by people of "impure" standing:[17] "unlike slaves in the West, slaves in India did not necessarily belong to the lowest rung of society."[18] Since these slaves were often symbols of status and consumption, their level of material comfort and (reflected) social standing were in many respects superior to that of lower castes. In places such as the Indian subcontinent, the economics of slavery sometimes involved expenses incurred pursuing other goals, such as prestige, consumption, warfare, or reproduction, rather than commercial enrichment. These noncommercial roles saw slaves forced into service as bureaucrats, concubines, retainers, sailors, soldiers, and sacrifices.

The racial and economic foundations of transatlantic slavery made it possible to approach slaves as *a homogeneous group whose individual fates were primarily determined by their shared status.* In places such as the Middle East, India, and South Asia, other intervening variables such as caste, work duties, vested authority, and gender roles played a greater role in determining the fortunes of individual slaves. One of the major implications of these variations was that slaves did not always stand out as unusually or uniquely oppressed compared with other members of their community. In the case of transatlantic slavery, there was an unusually strong correlation between slave status and severe hardship which imbued the divide between slave and non-slave with a distinctive social and political resonance. Slavery could be plausibly characterized as "peculiar," or aberrant, because it evoked images of misery, deprivation, and exploitation that were removed from the everyday expectations and experiences of the wider community.

Transatlantic slavery was also embedded within a distinctive political and intellectual environment. One of the key features of eighteenth-century European political discourse was a collective belief—at least among elites—that human progress was both possible and desirable. For most of human history, slavery appeared as a permanent, unalterable fact of life, somewhat akin to warfare, famine, or disease. This (realistic) appraisal was often sustained and reinforced by a more general pessimism about the prospects of fundamental change. When anti-slavery pioneers began to disseminate their ideas, their endeavors were indirectly facilitated by a larger sociopolitical environment that regarded significant improvements to the prevailing status quo as possible, desirable, and, in more extreme cases, inevitable. This belief in human progress was not specifically concerned with slavery, but was bound up in a larger worldview that appears to have been relatively open (at least intellectually) to a range of proposals for sweeping reform. The transition from abstract idealism to political struggle and legislative action would not have taken place without various political actors determining that anti-slavery proposals were not simply desirable, but also *feasible*. Belief in the possibility of fundamental change was a necessary (but not sufficient) condition of this transition.[19]

Another important feature of this historical period was the premium placed on personal freedom (or liberty) in public, political, and intellectual discourse. Modern commentators often assume that human beings have an innate desire for individual freedom. This viewpoint has been challenged on several fronts. One influential argument comes from Orlando Patterson, who has observed that "for most of human history, and for nearly all of the non-Western world prior to Western contact, freedom was, and for many still remains, anything but an obvious or desirable goal."[20] In hierarchical, communally oriented societies where power is personalized and complex patronage networks define interpersonal relationships, individual freedom tends to be associated with isolation, uncertainty, and vulnerability.[21] Noting that few non-Western societies had a word for freedom, as the term is currently understood, prior to contact with the West, Patterson argues that the particular importance attached to individual freedom in European culture is a direct legacy of the distinctive ideological and legal practices that characterized Greco-Roman slave systems.[22] The notion that freedom should be enjoyed equally is a recent innovation, but the more longstanding understanding of individual freedom as a preeminent value to which people (should) aspire was clearly an important progenitor of organized anti-slavery.

This veneration of freedom was also connected to highly stylized commitments to the foundational values of rights, reason, and the individual. These commitments would also play a significant role in shaping the terms on which opposition to transatlantic slavery was both formulated by activists and taken up within British society. The language of (negative) rights presumes that individuals (ought to) have a range of innate or quasi-contractual entitlements that circumscribe the legitimate scope of external authority. For Britain and the United States, a public discourse of rights was an established and historically embedded feature of political life. In France, more radical variants of this discourse provided a major component of the intellectual foundations of the 1787 revolution. Within each of these states the language of rights was regularly invoked in discussions on the ways in which different types of persons or groups could (or should) be treated, with the concept of informed consent often serving as a key benchmark.[23] Many prominent arguments for fundamental reform were founded on a perceived dissonance between contemporary practices and foundational values. This does not mean, of course, that the latter were always politically triumphant, since competing and contradictory orientations, interpretations, and positions also sought a place on the political agenda. My point is not that these commitments automatically trumped other considerations, but rather that they were prominent components of a distinctive milieu that influenced appraisals of what was politically plausible and ethically desirable in ways that may not have been feasible in other historical contexts, or for other historical slave systems.

Britain, Transatlantic Slavery, and an Intellectual Revolution

African slaves played an indispensable role in the colonization of Europe's "New World." Between 1501 and 1866 around twelve and a half million slaves embarked from Africa to the Americas via the infamous Middle Passage.[24] This multinational trade supplied European émigrés with the labor they desperately needed to develop newly conquered territories. Commercial considerations dominated this complex triangular network. The main economic motor of transatlantic slavery was Europe's insatiable demand for sugar, which led to the expansion of plantations across the New World.[25] When indentured Europeans and enslaved "Indians" proved insufficient, the planters and miners of the New World turned to Africa, where indigenous elites provided European traders with slaves who had been captured, conquered, or condemned in exchange for currency and commodities such as weaponry and textiles.[26] Until its forcible suppression, the transatlantic slave trade experienced three centuries of sustained and often rapid growth.[27]

The transatlantic slave trade reached its peak in the second half of the eighteenth century. The Portuguese were preeminent in the sixteenth and seventeenth centuries, supplying both their own nationals and Spanish settlers. By the beginning of the eighteenth century the British, French, and Dutch had all acquired Caribbean colonies and established themselves as major slave traders. This increase in national involvement and productive potential significantly increased demand for African slaves. Over the course of the eighteenth century, an estimated 6,494,619 slaves were embarked from ports in Africa. British slave traders are held responsible for 2,545,297 of this total. This was more than any other state.[28] British traders not only supplied their own colonies in the Caribbean and North America, but also transported significant numbers of slaves to other European territories. As both the premier slave trader of the Atlantic world and a major slave holder, Britain had considerable economic and political interests in the perpetuation and ongoing expansion of slavery. Prior to the loss of the United States in the 1770s, "the British Dominions encompassed the largest slave system in the Americas. Of the two and a half million human chattels in the New World, more than one third were the property of the subjects of George III."[29]

The early history of anti-slavery takes place on many fronts, encompassing early moves, both local and national, in the United States,[30] abortive radicalism in revolutionary France combined with rebellion in Saint Domingue,[31] cautious reforms in Denmark,[32] and the political tumult surrounding independence in Spanish America.[33] It is not my intention to delve into all of these expansive topics. This book is chiefly concerned with changes over time, rather than variations between historical cases.[34] From this standpoint, the British anti-slavery movement provides a natural starting point, because of its decisive influence on larger international trends. British slave traders were at the forefront of transatlantic slavery in the eighteenth century, and key economic indicators pointed toward further growth.[35] Instead, domestic political agitation forced a remarkable turnaround. Having earlier consolidated its position as the premier slaver of the Atlantic world, Britain abruptly emerged as the foremost international opponent of slavery. As a leading maritime power and an emerging industrial powerhouse, Britain advanced this new agenda in various ways, culminating in reluctant anti-slavery agreements with elites across the globe. Events in France, the United States, and Latin America were undoubtedly profoundly important, but they ultimately did not have the same global ramifications as developments in Britain.

The horrors of slavery may now seem self-evident, but for early pioneers anti-slavery was an impressive feat of both imagination and mobilization. Eighteenth-century audiences "could look back on slavery and slave trading as institutions accepted and practiced from time immemorial."[36] Powerful vested interests meshed with centuries of received wisdom, rendering slavery a somewhat unpleasant but otherwise unalterable fact of life.[37] In this inhospitable enviroment, intellectual arguments against slavery emerged through "an extraordinarily interplay between the ideas of the European continent, America, Scotland and England."[38] There were both philosophical and theological strands to anti-slavery thought. Since similar conceptions of rights, reason, and progress had an important influence on the development of both strands, they frequently proved to be complementary. One of the most striking features of this break with the past was its breadth. According to Roger Anstey, "Nearly every school of thought which dealt with ethical problems had, from about the middle of the century, come up with specific condemnations of slavery sometimes persuasively encapsulated in a corpus of moral or legal philosophy."[39]

When the leading thinkers of the continental Enlightenment such as Montesquieu, Rousseau, Raynal, Turgot, and Condorcet denounced slavery as a direct affront to liberty, virtue, reason, individual rights, and natural law, it was largely their stature as eminent scholars, not necessarily the depth and sophistication of their treatments of slavery, that shaped how educated elites thought about the institution.[40] Montesquieu's discussion of slavery in the L'Esprit des lois (1748), while fairly short and somewhat ambiguous, had an especially pronounced influence on the development of anti-slavery thought in both England and Scotland.[41] Other intellectuals who embraced Montesquieu's conceptual framework helped refine his treatment of slavery. Prominent voices included James Beattie, George Wallace, William Blackstone, William Paley, and Edmund Burke. As the intellectual case against slavery was cumulatively developed, traditional justifications such as the right of capture, biblical sanction, and the Aristotelian dictum of natural roles were systematically challenged. The Scottish Enlightenment played a particularly significant role in the development of anti-slavery thought.[42] The works of the moral philosopher Francis Hutcheson (1725, 1755) had an influence on subsequent discussion of slavery in Britain that paralleled Montesquieu. In addition to the works of scholars such as Hutcheson, there was Adam Smith's influential argument in *The Wealth of Nations* (1776) that slavery was an inefficient labor system because slaves had no real incentive to apply themselves.

The theological strand of anti-slavery thought has a somewhat longer pedigree and is generally more strident and systematic. When religious condemnation of slavery began to surface in the late seventeenth and early eighteenth centuries, it drew inspiration from broader theological trends that placed particular emphasis on divine providence, personal obligation, and the transformative powers of moral conduct. It was the Quakers, a nonconformist religious sect founded by George Fox in the mid-seventeenth century, who were chiefly responsible for the early development of theological anti-slavery arguments. In 1688, a small group of Germantown Quakers presented a petition condemning slavery to a regional meeting in Pennsylvania. While the petition had an extremely limited audience and no immediate impact, it marked the beginning of an internal dialogue over the morality of slavery that helped lay the intellectual foundations for a concerted political challenge. From the mid-eighteenth century onward, ongoing internal debates led to increasingly stringent injunctions against slave holding and trading for Quakers on both sides of the Atlantic.[43]

A Philadelphian Quaker named Anthony Benezet made a key contribution here. Benezet was not the first religious figure to oppose slavery, but he was one of the most systematic and influential. His published works, political activities, and personal correspondence had a profound influence on the actions and outlooks of abolitionists in the Anglo-Saxon world.[44] At the heart of his religious case against slavery was a conviction that the institution was fundamentally incompatible with "the plainest Precepts of the Gospel, the dictates of reason, and every common sentiment of humanity."[45] Once slavery had been identified as sinful, a strong belief in divine providence helped ensure that opposition to slavery was framed as a religious obligation that had important implications for divine favor.[46] From this vantage point, abolishing slavery was integral to both personal and national redemption. While Benezet played an important role in developing these themes, his works also highlighted the deleterious effects of the slave trade on western Africa, the way slavery debased both master and slave, and the parallels between transatlantic slavery and disputes between Britain and its American colonies. This synthesis of religion, empiricism, and philosophy appealed to many different audiences. In the second half of the eighteenth century non-Quakers on both sides of the Atlantic became involved in anti-slavery as authors, activists, and supporters.[47] Other key religious figures in this embryonic abolitionist movement were John Woolman, Benjamin Rush, Granville Sharp, John Wesley, and Jack Ramsay.

The diverse works of these anti-slavery pioneers collectively amounted to an intellectual revolution in attitudes toward slavery. By decisively breaking with centuries of entrenched orthodoxy, these pioneers laid a philosophical foundation for the political struggles that followed. In most instances the intricacies of the individual arguments were somewhat less important than the image of slavery they collectively conveyed. By 1780, slavery had been repeatedly and systematically denounced as contrary to reason, liberty, natural law, morality, and, perhaps most important, both the Christian faith and national virtue. The devastating impact of slave trading on Africa, the destruction of family life, and the mutually degrading relationship between master and slave were widely regarded as fundamental flaws. While such arguments were undoubtedly a decisive first step, they did not in themselves constitute a politically significant challenge to either slave trading or slave holding. It is clear, for instance, that "The philosophical critique of slavery was predominantly, though not exclusively, moderate and reformist in its implications or even purely speculative and theoretical."[48] Since slavery tended to be one of many topics that philosophers considered, their works were in no way a strident call to political action. Although the Quakers were more vocal and better organized, they were a small, politically marginal group.[49] While anti-slavery ideas had been either taken up or independently advanced by elements within British society,[50] there were few signs that this modest transfusion of ideas constituted an immediate threat to slavery as an institution. While important steps had been taken, the characteristics and consequences of this intellectual revolution are probably clearer in hindsight than they were to most contemporaries.

In his influential analysis of the early history of British abolition, Chris Brown has persuasively shown that diffuse anti-slavery sentiments and "isolated moralists" could be found in many parts of the British Empire by the early eighteenth century. For the most part, however, this "anti-slavery sentiment lay dormant, inert and ineffective ... sufficient to raise moral doubts but unable to stimulate political action."[51] According to Brown, this state of affairs was undermined from the 1760s onward by the political upheaval that led to the American Revolution. The "War of Independence" (1775–1783) that followed not only divided colonial slavery in two separate jurisdictions,[52] it also resulted in a "crisis of British liberty."[53] During this time of profound ideological anxiety and political reappraisal, slavery rapidly acquired new political and ethical dimensions as part of debates over the morality and legitimacy of the British Empire as whole. In the aftermath of defeat and the loss of the thirteen colonies, anti-slavery would come to be construed as a symbolic test of both moral worth and national virtue: "To a people that wished to think of themselves as Christian, moral and free, the abolitionists presented an opportunity to express their reverence for 'liberty, justice and humanity' . . . at little cost to themselves."[54]

The Abolitionist Breakthrough, 1787–1792

British Quakers presented the first public petition against the slave trade to Parliament in 1783. The petition was politely ignored. Subsequent lobbying of British elites made some headway, but did not amount to a political breakthrough.[55] When the Quaker-dominated Committee for the Abolition of the Slave Trade (henceforth London Committee) formed in May 1787,[56] there were few indications that a sea change was imminent.[57] This newly formed organization confirmed an important tactical decision to exclusively focus on the abolition of the slave trade.[58] Earlier anti-slavery literature had usually condemned both slavery and the slave trade. While the right of Parliament to regulate commerce was widely accepted, attempts to abolish slavery were likely to provoke strenuous objections regarding the sanctity of private property.[59] Making a distinction between trading and holding allowed the committee to avoid—or at least postpone—a direct challenge to one of Britain's most hallowed institutions, while also concentrating attention on the truly barbaric conditions experienced by Africans forced to endure the Middle Passage.[60] This move undoubtedly enhanced the political prospects of anti-slavery, but it also meant that the ready supply of labor provided by the trade was publically blamed for the larger evils associated with slavery.[61] This shift in emphasis led to arguments that ending the slave trade would produce a gradual amelioration in slave conditions in the Americas, since it would be in the interest of Caribbean planters to treat them more humanely in the absence of fresh reserves.

The London Committee actively solicited the support of sympathetic reformers throughout Britain, disseminating numerous pamphlets condemning the slave trade. While the Quakers continued to play an important role, the key figure in efforts to develop an anti-slavery network was a committed evangelical named Thomas Clarkson.[62] In the summer of 1787, Clarkson undertook a tour of northern England to gather information on the slave trade. During this tour an unexpected development in the town of Manchester radically altered the politics of anti-slavery. Throughout his tour Clarkson encouraged the formation of regional abolition societies, and encouraged these societies to petition Parliament.[63] In December 1787, a committee based in Manchester organized a petition against the slave trade that collected a remarkable 10,639 signatures. This unprecedented figure constituted around 20 percent of the local population and, perhaps more important, around two-thirds of the men who were eligible to subscribe.[64] Petitions were a well-established and politically effective form of popular agitation in eighteenth-century Britain.[65] The Manchester abolitionists also advertised their petition in major newspapers, echoing Clarkson's call for regional petitions. In late January 1788, the London Committee began to be informed by regional correspondents that petitions were being organized in towns across the country.[66] By May more than 100 petitions dealing with the slave trade had been received by the House of Commons. This was over half the total number of petitions received in this session of the House. While popular responses were strongest in northern England, it is clear that towns across Britain participated in the campaign. Smaller counter petitions defending slavery were limited to the comparatively small number of locations that had a direct interest in the perpetuation of the slave trade. This primarily meant Liverpool and, to a lesser extent, Bristol.

This campaign not only revealed an unexpected reservoir of anti-slavery sentiment, it helped establish a national network of abolitionist groups. The Manchester petition, "like almost all of its 15,000 sequels during the next 50 years, based demands for action on the offensiveness of such a traffic to humanity, justice and national honour."[67] It did not include detailed legislative proposals. Prior to the petition campaign the London Committee had been working closely with a Member of Parliament named William Wilberforce, also a committed evangelical, about raising the issue in Parliament. Wilberforce had long been a close confidant of William Pitt, the British prime minister. Pitt supported ending the slave trade, but was unable to make abolition government policy because his cabinet was collectively in favor of continuing the trade.[68] Working in concert, Wilberforce, Pitt, and the London Committee sought to translate significant popular support into legislative action. Convinced that additional information would strengthen the case for abolition, they had Pitt appoint a Privy Council Committee to examine the transatlantic slave trade.

This committee was the first of a number of official investigations into slavery. These investigations "embodied the spirit of the Scientific Enlightenment. They gave expression to the desire to question traditional assumptions, to gather a multitude of facts, to weigh evidence, and to reject unprovable claims, including those arising from humanitarian zeal."[69] Throughout these investigations Clarkson played an indispensable role in procuring important witnesses and information, yet the picture that emerged does not appear to have conclusively favored either side. While the horrors of the slave trade were brought into the public spotlight in an unprecedented way, the economic and political importance of slave trading was also highlighted.[70] What ultimately made these investigations politically salient was their role in informing both public and Parliament. By sharpening the terms of public and political discourse, they not only raised awareness of the issues involved, but also helped turn anti-slavery into a known quantity whose feasibility—if not desirability—was widely accepted.

When the Privy Council Committee finally reported in April 1789, the abolitionists had lost much of their earlier momentum.[71] In May a motion calling for the House to consider abolition was passed without direct challenge. Despite the lengthy and comprehensive report of the Privy Council, the defenders of the trade successfully lobbied for additional hearings. The merchants and planters of the British West Indies were well organized and had excellent political connections.[72] Despite the increasingly unpopular nature of slavery, they enjoyed substantial support in Parliament and at court. By successfully insisting on further hearings, proslavery forces helped delay the vote until April 1791. In the lead-up to this vote Wilberforce and his colleagues had concentrated their energies on elites and allowed active public support to decline. When the vote was finally taken, more than three years after the initial petition campaign, the abolitionists lost decisively 88 to 163.

This defeat provoked further public agitation. In late 1791 and early 1792 the London Committee orchestrated a national petition campaign that produced 519 petitions from all corners of Britain. Seymour Drescher has calculated that this was the "largest number ever submitted to the House on a single subject or in a single session," with between 350,000 and 400,000 signatures.[73] These petitions almost exclusively involved men. This unprecedented public response was encouraged by speaking tours and public meetings, the publication of large numbers of abolitionist tracts and icons, and the further growth of local committees. One of the most striking (albeit largely economically ineffective) displays of public support came in the form of public boycott of slave-produced sugar. According to Thomas Clarkson's history of the period, approximately 300,000 people were involved at the height of the boycott.[74] While the proslavery lobby devoted considerable resources to publicly challenging the abolitionists, they were unable to significantly undermine the general impression of a national anti-slavery consensus, at least at the level of public opinion.[75]

Both sides had grounds to be confident when Wilberforce reintroduced a motion for the abolition of the slave trade in early 1792. The proslavery lobby had the precedent of their earlier victory, while anti-slavery parliamentarians were buoyed by their renewed public support. The ultimate result of the debate that followed was an unexpected compromise, as Wilberforce's motion was modified in favor of *gradual* abolition. Despite objections from abolitionists, this amendment was passed 193 to 125.[76] After further debate a new bill calling for the end of the trade by 1796 passed the House of Commons,[77] but before any further action could be taken international events precipitated a radical shift in the prevailing political climate. In 1793 revolutionary France declared war on Britain. While the Parliamentary abolitionists and most of their supporters were moderates, revolutionary ideals appealed to some of their more radical compatriots. The radical turn taken by the French Revolution, and the related impact of the unprecedented slave rebellion of Saint Domingue, quickly led to widespread distrust of popular(ist) political activity.[78] The ideals and the tactics of the abolitionists were fatally tainted. The Parliamentary campaign also stalled, with the conservative House of Lords indefinitely delaying consideration of earlier bills. It is difficult to say what would have happened if events in France had not intervened. While the abolitionists were certainly close to their legislative goal, victory was by no means assured.[79]

It is important to place these early legislative failures in a larger historical context. While slavery and slave trading continued to enjoy both legislative sanction and substantial elite support, the terms of public and political discourse had been radically and unexpectedly altered by the remarkable success of the campaigns of 1787/88 and 1791/92. British participation in transatlantic slavery had always enjoyed institutional and public support. By the end of 1792, only the institutional component remained substantially intact. Although proslavery positions continued to resonate in particular circles, the petition campaigns had demonstrated that there was effectively a public consensus in favor of ending the slave trade.[80] What had been previously regarded as a natural, venerable, and fairly unremarkable part of the prevailing political order was now widely considered both illegitimate and immoral in British society. An influential synopsis of this transition comes from Drescher, who states that: "it was the mobilization of public opinion which ushered in the consciousness that one was in a new period in the history of slavery; not in the sense of the inauguration of an era of uninterrupted victories but in the sense that the terms of public discourse about the institution in Britain were dramatically and forever altered."[81]

There was also a corresponding shift in collective appraisals of the political feasibility of abolitionist ideas.[82] Many prominent abolitionists had been fairly pessimistic about their immediate political prospects prior to 1787. The changing attitudes of prominent politician and leading intellectual Edmund Burke provides a good demonstration of this sea change. Burke had formulated a plan for the gradual abolition of slavery in the early 1780s, but he decided against publication because he feared being politically exposed for a cause that had limited prospects of success.[83] Once a reservoir of anti-slavery support was revealed, Burke offered his strong support for abolition. Anecdotal evidence suggests that Burke's earlier assessment was shared by the well-organized West India interest, who appear to have considered early manifestations of abolitionist sentiment to be more annoying than alarming.[84] Two of the major groups that opposed abolition, the West India interest and the political elite of Liverpool, only began major proslavery agitation in February 1788.[85]

Explaining the Breakthrough

In May 1792, Sir Manule Romilly wrote that

> the cause of the negro slaves is at present taken up with much warmth in almost every part of the kingdom as could be found in any matter in which the people were personally and immediately interested. Innumerable petitions for the abolition have been presented to Parliament and (what proves men's zeal more strongly than petitions) great numbers have entirely discontinued the use of sugar. All persons, and even the West Indian planters and merchants, seem to agree that it is impossible that the trade should last many years longer.[86]

Having documented the sequence of events that led to this unexpected state of affairs, I now raise the more difficult question of why Britons collectively responded to anti-slavery appeals in such a remarkable way.

Until the mid-twentieth century, most historians of British anti-slavery presented the abolition of slavery as a straightforward humanitarian triumph over sectional commercial interests.[87] One (in)famous example here is *The British Anti-Slavery Movement* (1933). Its author, Reginald Coupland, offered a celebratory history of British activism that narrowly focused on Parliamentary debates, the virtues of abolitionists leaders, religious inspiration, and the contributions of other eminent figures.[88] By framing slavery as an obvious wrong whose time was almost inevitably passing, Coupland effectively marginalized longstanding British involvement in transatlantic slavery. Despite the fact that transatlantic slavery had been practiced for centuries without political opposition, Britons were expected to be in favor of legal abolition *unless* their self interest dictated otherwise. Responsibility for slavery was attributed to sectional economic and political interests, rather than British society as a whole.

This self-congratulatory formula was overturned by the publication of *Capitalism and Slavery* in 1944. Its author, Eric Williams, focused on the primacy of economic interests in shaping the rise and fall of British slavery. According to Williams, the legal abolition of slavery could be primarily traced to the economic transition from mercantilism to laissez faire capitalism, with an economically declining monopoly being destroyed by powerful capitalists to advance their strategic interests.[89] In this line of argument, humanitarian sentiments and popular support appear as "one of the greatest propaganda movements of all time."[90]

By challenging established conventions, Williams played a critical role in setting the agenda for future research, as many scholars would subject his provocative arguments to detailed historical analysis. Over time, a number of serious problems with his work would be identified.[91] One line of critique focused on the actions of key political actors, who were revealed to have behaved in ways that directly contradicted Williams's position.[92] A second line of critique focused on the economics of abolition. One of the central planks of Williams's book was his claim that British slavery was in economic decline during the late eighteenth century. The publication of Seymour Drescher's *Econocide: British Slavery in the Era of Abolition* (1977), persuasively undercut this line of argument, as Drescher demonstrated that British slavery was not a moribund, declining institution, but a profitable endeavor with favorable future prospects. Accordingly, "overproduction, structural weakness, and imperial insignificance played no role in the decision to abolish."[93] This conclusion has cast grave doubts about the capacity of economic interests to explain British anti-slavery, to the point where "few scholars now rely heavily on economic paradigms to explain the ending of slavery."[94] By forcibly suppressing the slave trade when it was at its peak, British elites incurred a range of substantial penalties, yet secured no equivalent material tradeoffs.

These critiques of Williams helped to sharpen new research into the sociological dynamics driving British anti-slavery. Two main lines of inquiry can be identified here. On the one hand, we find a concerted effort to explore the actions, outlooks, and backgrounds of anti-slavery reformers. Unlike earlier celebrations of a small group of abolitionist "Saints," this approach attempts to place anti-slavery within a broader reforming impulse. On the other hand, we find renewed interest in the causes of public support for anti-slavery. This has involved sustained analysis of both prevailing notions of rights, liberty, and identity, and the political institutions that governed the exercise of legitimate authority.

Most prominent abolitionist leaders were evangelical Christians. The term evangelical has been generally employed "to describe those Protestants who believe that the essential part of the gospel consists in salvation by faith through the atoning death of Christ."[95] The British evangelical movement experienced significant growth in both the established and nonconformist churches in the latter half of the eighteenth century. This "great awakening" was defined by a high degree of social and political dynamism.[96] Instead of being understood as an introspective, self-contained process, scriptural analysis and religious reflection were explicitly connected to a divinely inspired agenda for moral and social reform.[97] Having faith that their activities reflected God's plans, British evangelicals pursued their goals with conviction and perseverance, providing a committed core for more diffuse anti-slavery sentiments. Anti-slavery leaders would also frame the struggle against slavery in absolute terms. While Wilberforce was not always the most effective leader, his adamant refusal to moderate his goals ensured that legal abolition, and not the more realistic compromise of ameliorative reform, was the only goal the movement was prepared to accept.[98]

The struggle against slavery can be best understood as a prominent feature of a broader reforming impulse. This impulse included free trade, missionary activity, temperance, international peace, and the reform of manners and morals. According to David Turley, reformers chiefly focused on groups of persons "subject to harsh and brutal treatment and regarded as less than fully human by those who exercised power over them."[99] These groups included slaves, prisoners, the insane, and poverty-stricken children. Evangelicals advocated the reform of institutions geared toward suppression and control in the belief that individuals who were unjustly oppressed would benefit from greater autonomy to improve their physical and spiritual lives. Anti-slavery was the most successful component of this larger agenda.

The anti-slavery leadership was predominantly middle class in origin. While it is now generally accepted that capitalist interests were not at the vanguard of the anti-slavery movement,[100] class nonetheless remains a key analytical benchmark. In his seminal works on the history of slavery and abolition, David Brion Davis has observed that anti-slavery served a key ideological function for the British establishment and an expanding bourgeoisie, helping to legitimate both Parliamentary governance and the moral foundations of liberal capitalism.[101] Some elements of this argument have been challenged, especially in relation to links between capitalism and anti-slavery, but this does not necessarily detract from the more general point that this core relationship between anti-slavery, ideology, and political institutions was hugely important.[102] It is clear, however, that there are limits to class-based analysis. Detailed analysis of petition campaigns has revealed that the anti-slavery movement consistently enjoyed significant levels of support from a broad cross section of British society.[103] This widespread support suggests that differences between classes may have been at least partially overshadowed by what various classes *shared* in common.

On this point, a useful point of departure is provided by James Walvin, who observes that "the years when the British slave empire emerged and prospered were also the years when political life in Britain was characterized by a long, protracted, vocal and insistent struggle for a wide range of political and social rights."[104] At the heart of these ongoing struggles within British society was a distinctive conception of national and religious identity. In her influential discussion of nationalism and modernity, Liah Greenfield argues that British society coalesced around a unique conception of national identity in the sixteenth and seventeenth centuries. During this period both subnational (local identities and allegiances) and supranational (kinship ties among European ruling elites) attachments were at least partially overshadowed by a distinctive conception of nationality that idealized Britons' singular devotion to individual liberty, the exceptional character of their political institutions, and the virtues of Protestantism, which were largely embodied in the Church of England.[105]

Competing appeals to religious authority, national virtues, and "traditional" rights were central to political and intellectual discourse throughout the early modern era. This is captured by Harry Dickinson, who identifies "a profound and prolonged debate throughout the eighteenth century between those who were confident about the existence of English liberties and those who believed that the people did indeed have an historic claim and a natural right to liberty but were being denied their just deserts by a corrupt administration."[106] This protracted debate was primarily concerned with the *application* of commonly accepted principles, helping to sustain a distinctive national identity and political vocabulary that would help to shape how slavery was conceptualized and discussed.

Despite numerous inconsistencies and shortcomings, there is ample evidence to suggest that most Britons genuinely believed that they enjoyed unique rights and freedoms that circumscribed the scope of legitimate political authority.[107] Within this ideological complex, slavery was routinely presented as the antithesis of British liberty. Many situations of perceived injustice and oppression were regularly characterized as slavery, or no better than slavery.[108] Peoples subjected to arbitrary and unrepresentative political authority were widely seen as being less than free.[109] Of particular importance here was the principle of individual consent. Political authority was held to be legitimated by a quasi-contractual relationship between governors and governed. Labor relations, however coercive, were held to involve "voluntary" contractual agreements.[110] Placed alongside these highly stylized concepts of political authority and labor relations, slavery appeared in an especially unfavorable light.

What it meant "to be a Christian in a Christian nation . . . was integral to Briton's everyday lives."[111] To be Christian (Protestant) and British was to be "fully" human. It was generally accepted that Britons and, more broadly, Europeans were owed ethical and political obligations that non-Britons, or non-Europeans, were not.[112] This familiar dynamic was at the heart of the transatlantic slavery. Since slaves from Africa were not Christian Europeans, it had long been accepted that they could be legitimately treated in ways that compatriots could not. Some of the causes and consequences of this divide between (a British/European) Self and (a non-British/European) Other have been taken up by David Eltis, who has calculated that it could have been more cost-effective to secure colonial labor requirements from *within* Europe by enslaving other Europeans. The fact that there were no efforts to enslave large numbers of compatriots offers a key demonstration of the politics of social membership.[113]

Most modern commentators have tended to view organized anti-slavery in cosmopolitan and egalitarian terms. While British anti-slavery undoubtedly had cosmopolitan *effects*, it does not automatically follow that public support for anti-slavery reflected a cosmopolitan *orientation*. There were, of course, some enlightened individuals who embraced human equality, but these were the exception, not the rule. It would be one thing to be in favor of better treatment, and another thing to be committed to universal equality. Millions of Britons repeatedly signed anti-slavery petitions, but few considered African slaves their equals.[114] How could they be? Britons enjoyed divine favor, unique liberties, singular religious virtues, and exceptional institutions. The key to the remarkable popular success of anti-slavery was not the withering away of distinctions between insider and outsider, but the emergence of a new conception about what it meant to be a true British Christian.

For centuries, Britons had defined themselves in terms of their unique liberties and religious virtues. Organized anti-slavery would construct a symbolic challenge to this self-image. It asked, in effect, how a "civilized" Christian nation with an innate love of liberty could sanction a heinous system of government-supported exploitation. These tensions may appear to be clearcut in retrospect, but there was no serious contradiction between liberty, religion, and slavery so long as British virtues were understood as a set of rights and orientations that only Britons enjoyed.[115] This formula had been perfectly compatible with slavery, as "unfit," "undeserving." or "inferior" peoples could be consigned to their fate.

The Anti-Slavery Project successfully challenged this enduring status quo by turning the treatment of slaves into a symbolic referendum on British virtue and British exceptionalism. Other nations may have had no problems with slavery, but Britain was not like other nations. For William Wilberforce, Britain was "A nation, which besides the unequalled degree of true civil liberty, had been favored with an unprecedented measure of religious light, with its long train of attendant blessings."[116] Despite these unique blessings, Britain had fallen from grace, leaving "a foul blot on our national character, and a crying sin in the sight of heaven."[117] If Britons valued individual freedom so highly, why had they denied it to others? If voluntary consent was a core principle, why had they purchased millions of slaves and forced them to work? If arbitrary authority was so onerous, why had they sanctioned a system of unconstrained dominion? If religious virtue distinguished Britons from others in the eyes of God, why had they contravened (a new version of) scripture? In sum, if slavery was the antithesis of British liberty, why had Britons sanctioned what they had historically regarded as "the vilest and most degraded social and political institution"?[118]

Anti-slavery activists also benefited from their capacity to convince the British public that transatlantic slavery was a manageable problem that was both *stark* and *solvable*. As we have seen, the highly exploitative and racially defined character of transatlantic slavery created a distinctive environment in which slaves were viewed as a homogeneous group whose individual fates were primarily determined by their shared status. This created a window of opportunity in which to develop a compelling argument that slaves who endured the Middle Passage (and later slaves on plantations in the Americas) were subject to a set of severe abuses that starkly separated them from other social and economic groupings. Unlike the working poor, who could be rebuffed for "idleness" or "depravity," it was difficult to hold slaves responsible for their predicament. Their suffering, torment, abuse, and debasement could be solely attributed to an institution sanctioned by Parliament, the symbolic embodiment of British liberty. Equally important, the defenders of transatlantic slavery could be reduced to "base" economic interests, setting up a principle versus profit dynamic in which national honor and religious virtue would be juxtaposed against commercial interests. This does not mean, however, that anti-slavery represented a "natural" reaction to the worst form of exploitation imaginable. If transatlantic slavery inspired natural revulsion, why would this reaction take centuries to manifest itself? The key issue was not simply the inherent cruelties of transatlantic slavery, but the ideological problems these cruelties posed for British national and religious identity. Segments of British society also experienced severe hardships, but they did so as "consenting" freemen, who were held responsible for their own destiny.

Another political advantage that helped to facilitate popular support for British anti-slavery was the existence of a straightforward legislative solution around which to rally support: "since slavery was a legal status and slaving a regulable trade, both were susceptible to 'solutions' by parliamentary vote."[119] British abolitionists enjoyed a huge advantage over most other (potential) causes because they were able to concentrate their energies on a clear institutional target (legal slavery) and a clear legislative solution (legal abolition). This can again be contrasted with the plight of the British underclass, which was not only complicated by issues of individual culpability, but was also less amenable to decisive solutions. Much like war and disease, poverty was widely viewed as a problem that could not be solved, only ameliorated, and even then there was limited agreement on how (or even whether) this should be accomplished. In many ways, the physical and psychological distance between "saviors" and "saved" indirectly enhanced the appeal of anti-slavery, as the issues at stake were largely defined by stylized and symbolic arguments rather than direct personal experience.[120]

Parliamentary Legislation and Social Consolidation

There were two main stages in the development of the Anti-Slavery Project in Britain. The first stage involved the initial expression and gradual consolidation of anti-slavery at a social level. The second stage involved the integration of anti-slavery into political institutions and government policies. This pattern was highly unusual. Prior to the legal prohibition of the slave trade in 1807 and the abolition of most forms of colonial slavery in 1833, numerous displays of popular support had revealed overwhelming public support for legal abolition. This makes Britain one of a handful of cases (alongside the northern United States and, to some degree, Haiti, France, and Brazil) where strong popular support predated major legislative reforms.[121] This does not mean, however, that public agitation led inexorably to legislation.[122] Although popular support undoubtedly played an indispensable role in placing anti-slavery on the political agenda, many members of Parliament were yet to be convinced, particularly when it came to the abolition of the slave trade. While opposition was strongest among those with economic interests in slavery, only a fairly small group of Parliamentarians fell into this category. Since a similar number of Parliamentarians were committed abolitionists, both groups were forced to appeal to their peers for support. Proslavery forces in Britain found it difficult to mount a compelling defense of slavery on moral grounds, but they did make a number of compelling political and economic counterarguments.[123]

The case against the abolition of the slave trade was built around three overlapping themes. The first theme emphasized the economic and political importance of slavery to the Empire. In an era where Britain retained relatively few colonies and had recently lost major territories in the Americas, the British West Indies were widely regarded as the Empire's most important overseas possessions.[124] This prominence was largely based on the significant contribution of the West Indian sugar industry to the British economy. There was therefore a compelling argument to be made that the abolition the transatlantic slave trade—itself of substantial economic significance—would greatly undermine the productivity of West Indian colonies, and was thus directly contrary to the national interest. The second theme was concerned with the

international consequences of abolition. If Britain were to unilaterally withdraw, there was every reason to expect that their international rivals would
take advantage of new commercial opportunities. According to one contemporary critic (1790), ending "the trade by one nation would not prevent it
amongst others, nor in the least benefit the Africans. If those who suggest this
notion be sincere, it proves their *total* ignorance of the character of nations,
and of the habits and practices of the world."[125] This not only meant that other
states were likely to derive economic benefit from British withdrawal, it also
meant that the humanitarian benefit of abolition would be hugely compromised by increased trading by British rivals.[126] This underlying logic was not
easy to refute.[127] The final theme was concerned with property rights. One
of the overarching concerns of the landed oligarchs who dominated British
politics was the sanctity of personal property. While this concern was partly
based on self-interest, it was also a reflection of the larger importance attached to the sanctity of private property within society as whole. Despite
regular denials, there was justified suspicion that the dispute over the slave
trade concealed a broader desire to abolish slavery itself. From here, debates
over the slave trade would become a matter of general principle in which the
integrity of property rights was held to be at stake. These concerns only grew
in political importance when the focus shifted to slavery itself in the 1820s.

This brief survey demonstrates that political opposition to the abolition
of the transatlantic slave trade was not reducible to self-interested support for
narrow economic and political interests. Many of Britain's political elite opposed abolition not only because it was contrary to their self-interest, but also
because of its dubious merits as a piece of public policy.[128] The political salience of these issues is illustrated by the fact that: "the loose anti-abolitionist
alliance included the king and royal family; the admirals of the navy; leading
commercial interests in London, Liverpool and Bristol; and above all, many
landed proprietors who feared any innovation that might weaken the empire,
raise taxes, or set a precedent for more dangerous reforms."[129] While the abolitionists occasionally sought to rebut these pragmatic objections, their overall case mainly rested on other concerns.[130] If debates over abolition had been
confined to calculations of national interest, it is difficult to envisage how that
abolition could have taken place.

After the initial breakthrough of 1787–1792, the anti-slavery cause faltered in a political climate dominated by the war with France. Despite some
close votes, Wilberforce was unable to secure passage of a bill abolishing the
slave trade through Parliament.[131] The London Committee was increasingly

dormant and there was limited scope for popular mobilization.[132] While anti-slavery remained on the agenda, there were few indications that a legislative breakthrough was imminent. It is not easy to pinpoint what finally broke this deadlock. There was no one decisive factor, but many factors working in combination, including international events, tactical shifts, and changes in the composition of Parliament.

During the early nineteenth century, the association between anti-slavery and revolution ended with the installation of Emperor Napoleon Bonaparte.[133] The now longstanding war with France and its allies had also brought about gradual changes in the composition of the transatlantic slave trade, with the British indirectly securing a virtual monopoly on the trade through their wartime maritime dominance. As part of military operations in the Caribbean and elsewhere, the British had conquered a number of sugar colonies. As the (temporary) rulers of these colonies, the British government had to decide whether to sanction their involvement in transatlantic slave trading. Since further investment in slaves was likely to undermine Britain's older colonies, slave trading to these territories was widely viewed as contrary to the national interest.[134] In a time of peace, any restrictions would have meant other nations increasing their share of the trade, but in wartime there was no danger of immediate competition. Following intense pressure from Wilberforce, an ailing Pitt issued an Order in Council in 1805 prohibiting the supply of slaves to these conquered colonies. This order did not have the force of legislation, but it also aroused little political opposition.[135]

There were concurrent changes in the composition of the Parliament during this period. Wilberforce introduced motions for the immediate abolition of the slave trade in 1797, 1798, 1799, and 1802. While none of these motions were passed by the House of Commons, a May 1804 bill met success, passing three readings by a significant margin.[136] The bill later failed in 1805, but this unexpected result indicated growing support for abolition. During this same period, West Indian planters may have alienated some supporters by illegally trading with merchants from the United States.[137]

In early 1806, the "Ministry of Talents" took office following the death of Pitt. The key figures in the ministry were Lord William Grenville (Prime Minister), Charles Fox (Foreign Secretary), and Lord Henry Addington (Home Secretary). Grenville and Fox were staunch abolitionists. While Addington's opposition to general abolition meant anti-slavery could not be made a government measure, his fortunes rapidly declined after taking office, which diminished his objections.[138] In close consultation with Wilberforce and the other abolitionists, Grenville had a bill introduced on March 31, 1806, that proposed the legal abolition of the slave trade to both foreign and conquered territories. The bill was presented as a supplement to Pitt's Order in Council. Couched in the language of the national interest and political expediency, it eventually passed both houses of Parliament by significant margins. With one stroke, more than two-thirds of the British slave trade was legally abolished.[139] Only a month after the passage of the 1806 bill banning the foreign slave trade, Parliament endorsed by a significant margin a symbolic resolution calling for the total and immediate elimination of the slave trade. This was followed in early 1807 by the introduction of a bill that mandated total abolition. Support for the slave trade all but evaporated during this period. The 1807 bill was passed by an overwhelming majority, 283 to 16 in the House of Commons and 100 to 36 in the House of Lords. Unlike the earlier bill, this sequence of votes was justified entirely on humanitarian grounds. The ostensible rationale for ending the foreign slave trade—the economic protection of the British West Indies—was effectively undercut by a universal ban depriving these territories of new slaves.

Grenville's political advocacy as prime minister was pivotal to this rapid turnaround. He and many members of his cabinet lobbied fiercely for the passage of the 1807 bill, applying considerable pressure to uncommitted members, particularly in the House of Lords.[140] These endeavors built on the growing support evident in the narrow defeat of 1805. The impact of the abolition of the foreign slave trade in 1806 is harder to quantify. The fact that over two-thirds of the slave trade had already been abolished clearly made total abolition a less daunting proposition. The political stakes involved in subsequent bills were drastically reduced, making them easier to support and harder to resist. It is clear, however, that there was a decisive reservoir of support that was not dependent on national interest arguments. The fact that Britain's economic rivals were unable to exploit abolition meant that the international consequences of ending transatlantic slave trading were effectively delayed until the (then uncertain) end of the Napoleonic Wars.

While there was clearly a shift in favor of the abolitionists in the early years of the nineteenth century, Grenville's individual contribution was also hugely important. In the hands of a different prime minister, the outcome might have been very different. It is clear, however, that the vote of 1807 was informed by larger popular(ist) forces that helped to define the political environment in which Grenville and others operated. Despite the exorbitant long-term costs of the decision to abolish the slave trade, both state and society maintained their formal support for the anti-slavery cause. If anti-slavery had not enjoyed broad-based popular support, British political elites may well have attempted to renounce the 1807 legislation and restore slave trading. Instead, the 1807 legislation was repeatedly celebrated as a major national accomplishment, resulting in regular displays of public self-congratulation, which included King George being repeatedly praised for his key role in ensuring abolition (despite his earlier opposition) during the Royal Jubilee in 1809.[141]

Anti-slavery ceased to be a major political issue in the years that followed 1807. There was a general recognition that it would take time to ascertain whether an end to the trade would force West Indian planters to treat their slaves more humanely, as the abolitionists had maintained. In the lead-up to the Congress of Vienna of 1814–1815, popular anti-slavery activity resulted in a tremendous display of public support for ending the international slave trade, but slavery within the British Empire was no longer a major object of concern. This began to change with low-level contestation over the Registration Act of 1819, but was not until the early 1820s that the campaign for the abolition of slavery within the British Empire began in earnest.

Fortified by a new generation of leaders, abolitionists were able to quickly reestablish an extensive national network, led by a newly formed Anti-Slavery Society, and employing the now traditional techniques of petitions, tours, meetings, and tracts.[142] By the 1820s there was a general recognition that the abolition of the slave trade had not improved the treatment of slaves in British colonies. Instead, conditions may well have deteriorated.[143] This required a new understanding of the "problem" of slavery, in which inhuman abuses were attributed to unredeemable flaws in slavery as a general institution. As before, support for anti-slavery came from a broad cross section of society. It also included the active involvement for the first time of a substantial number of predominantly middle-class women.[144] The ease with which the campaign shifted from slave trading to slave holding confirmed that popular antipathy was not confined to the slave trade. The initial goal of the abolitionist leadership was gradual emancipation, reflecting widespread agreement that slaves were not yet "ready" for freedom.

The political dynamics surrounding this new campaign are particularly revealing. From the outset, Parliamentary debate over slavery concentrated on the *terms* and *timing* of legal abolition. When Thomas Buxton, the Parliamentary leader of the campaign, first broached the issue of gradual emancipation in Parliament in 1823, the government quickly responded by committing itself to a policy of gradual amelioration and eventual emancipation. Successive governments maintained this general policy, resulting in a series of legislative directives to relevant Colonial authorities designed to improve slave conditions.[145] Even the West Indian interest nominally endorsed the principle of slave emancipation, and instead strategically argued that it would take an extremely long period to "prepare" slaves for freedom.[146] While the abolitionists were never entirely satisfied with official policies, it would take time to ascertain whether they were having an influence on colonial practices. From 1825 onward, dissatisfaction with the pace of reform (and the spoiling tactics of colonial authorities) led growing numbers of abolitionists to embrace immediate emancipation.

The emancipation campaign built on the tactics, support, and organizational base of earlier campaigns. There were, however, a number of key differences between 1787 and 1823. Perhaps the most important change was the way in which slavery was conceptualized and discussed within British society. In many respects, the abolitionists found themselves preaching to the converted. They were not compelled to prove from first principles that slavery in the British Empire was wrong, but could safely assume that most people already shared their general viewpoint. From 1826 onward, the abolitionists challenged Parliamentary candidates to publicly declare their support to abolition, ensuring that few politicians were prepared to oppose their cause. A parallel shift occurred among religious institutions. By 1830, "The Quakers, the Church of England, Ireland and Scotland, the Catholics and a plethora of dissenting churches had all come out enmass against slavery."[147] These popular and institutional endorsements confined opposition to defensive (yet still highly effective)[148] maneuvering over the terms and timing of legal abolition.

The case against slavery was based around themes that were fully developed in the second half of the eighteenth century. Slavery was regularly denounced as unchristian and inhuman, as an arbitrary and inherently corrupt institution, and as a national affront that compromised both core values and divine favor. The fact that none of these claims were considered particularly radical or unreasonable provides a further demonstration of the profound ideological shift that had occurred within British society. Another theme that became increasingly prominent as the campaign progressed was the idea that slave labor was less efficient than free labor. While this line of argument had been developed by Adam Smith in the 1770s, it had not been a significant part of the campaign against the slave trade.[149] Despite a lack of compelling evidence, this link between slavery and liberal capitalism would become an enduring, albeit sometimes problematic feature of anti-slavery. The notion that free labor was economically superior not only reflected a broader commitment to liberal capitalism within British society, it added an important public policy dimension to the campaign. The relative efficiency argument enabled the abolitionists to claim that emancipation was likely to benefit both planters and slaves, and that conservative planters were simply unable to recognize their own interests. This argument played a decisive role in deflecting concerns about the political and economic costs involved in emancipation.[150] It also further encouraged the increasingly popular characterization of slavery as a historical anachronism, which was no longer viable due to inexorable moral and economic trends.[151]

This process culminated in the early 1830s, with two massive public campaigns in 1830–1831 and 1832–1833. The immediate catalyst for these campaigns was a somewhat belated decision to press for immediate abolition. This brought Parliamentary abolitionists in line with many provincial anti-slavery societies, which had moved toward immediate abolition in the late 1820s.[152] This shift reflected a general consensus that the West Indian planters and their sympathizers had successfully frustrated previous reforms, and that there was limited space for moral and economic improvement while slavery persisted. This left immediate abolition as the only acceptable option, but the Parliamentary abolitionists retained enough of their previous commitment to gradualism to endorse a fairly lengthy period of "apprenticeship" after abolition. Throughout this period, "abolitionism was self-confident, incomparably supported, and convinced that emancipation was but a matter of time."[153] The 1831 campaign was overtaken by a political crisis over the reform of Parliament, but its deferment enabled the passage of the Great Reform Act of 1832, which bolstered legislative support.[154] When the campaign resumed in late 1832, the national response was overwhelming, with 5,000 petitions and just under one and a half million signatories. One in five males over the age of fifteen are said to have participated in this campaign, with a substantial number of women adding their signatures.[155] A further catalyst came from a major slave rebellion in Jamaica in December 1831. This called into question the stability of the status quo, leading to arguments that immediate emancipation was required to dampen simmering unrest.[156] This was not the first such rebellion; there had been others in Grenada (1795), Barbados (1816), and Demerara (1823), leading to fears that slaves would take matters into their own hands if emancipation was drawn out indefinitely.

Unable to confront these multiple challenges, the West India interest increasingly focused on ensuring ample compensation and a continued supply of labor. There was considerable sympathy for these positions within Parliament and the legislation proposed by the government in May 1833 sought to accommodate the interests of slave owners.[157] Not everyone was convinced that the slaves were "ready" for legal freedom, and there was solid support for the principle of compensation. The planters received the exorbitant figure of twenty million pounds compensation for the loss of their legal property, and provisions were made for a period of apprenticeship, a new category of servitude that was similar to slavery in many important respects. Parliamentary abolitionists challenged both the amount of compensation and the terms of apprenticeship, but did not strongly challenge their general legitimacy.[158] More radical elements within the anti-slavery movement strongly challenged and ultimately repudiated this moderate position. These radical elements centered on the Agency Committee, an organization started as an adjunct of the Anti-Slavery Society in 1828, which rejected any form of compensation. The fact that a substantial minority of the anti-slavery movement were able to reject legislation that conferred freedom on around 800,000 slaves on a matter of principle is a testament to a remarkable change in attitudes toward slavery.[159] Prior to 1787, the abolition of British slavery had appeared hopelessly unrealistic. The abolition of the slave trade in 1807—probably the single most important event in the early history of anti-slavery—occurred within a unique political environment after two decades of frustration. By 1833, success would be at least partially measured by the terms on which abolition was accomplished, rather than by whether or not the ultimate goal was attained.

Concluding Remarks

The post-1833 era was defined by a combination of political fragmentation and social consolidation. After a successful national campaign against the abuses of the apprenticeship system in 1838, the era of popular antislavery mobilization came to a close. The anti-slavery movement continued to play an important role in British politics, but it would never again capture the imagination of the British people to the same degree. Anti-slavery efforts continued at an international level, but abolitionist leaders found it difficult to unite around a clear political strategy that satisfied their related commitments to pacifism and free trade. Despite the declining fortunes of organized anti-slavery in the 1840s, the Anti-Slavery Project continued to enjoy high levels of support from both state and society: "What had begun as the seemingly impractical proposals of a few eccentrics had become the subject of grave legislative arrangements and had now attained the status of unquestioned assumptions."[160] By the mid-nineteenth century, anti-slavery was a deeply embedded and highly stylized component of British culture, achieving the status of an inherited orientation handed down from generation to generation without critical engagement.[161] Throughout the nineteenth and twentieth centuries, "Factual accounts, fictional stories, historical lessons and even lessons from geography were all dangled before the young as proof of their country's superiority."[162] Centuries of British complicity in transatlantic slavery were almost entirely set aside.

The achievements of British anti-slavery were not based on a rejection of the prevailing social order, but on its moral redemption. Two main themes can be identified here. The first theme involves the construction of slavery as a compelling political problem that was both stark and solvable. Unlike many problem areas, transatlantic slavery displayed a number of distinctive characteristics that facilitated (but did not in themselves necessitate) political mobilization. From the late eighteenth century onward, the severe abuses that characterized transatlantic slavery would be primarily traced to a clear-cut, highly exploitative, and racially defined institution that could be legally abolished—and therefore ostensibly ended—through a singular act of Parliament. The second theme concerns the acute problems slavery posed for longstanding models of British exceptionalism. For centuries, Britons had been congratulating themselves on their religious virtues and innate love of liberty. There was no automatic contradiction between these cherished ideals and transatlantic slavery as long as being "exceptional" also meant leaving "lesser" peoples to their fate. The Anti-Slavery Project challenged this longstanding formulation by turning the horrific treatment of African slaves into a symbolic referendum on British national identity, and thereby provoked an unprecedented public response from a broad cross section of British society. This unprecedented popular support was cosmopolitan in effect, but it was not cosmopolitan in orientation. Having once been "the world's greediest and most successful traders of slaves . . . the British had shifted to being able to preen themselves on being the world's foremost opponents of slavery. This . . . extraordinary revolution . . . revealed as much if not more about how the British thought about themselves, as it did about how they saw black people on the other side of the world."[163]

Chapter 2

British Anti-Slavery and European International Society

The British Parliament's 1807 decision to outlaw slave carrying by British subjects had profound international consequences. Having supported transatlantic slave trading for centuries as a central pillar of colonial projects in the Americas, British governments in the nineteenth century pursued a range of policies designed not only to end slavery in British territories, but also to restrict the slave systems of other political communities. This global campaign proved to be difficult, expensive, and divisive. In places untouched by organized anti-slavery, both slavery and enslavement continued to be regarded as politically legitimate and economically valuable, much as they had been in Britain in previous centuries. International contests over slavery and abolition not only aroused substantial vested interests, they also inflamed popular sentiments. Political elites throughout the globe were suspicious that anti-slavery masked other strategic goals, and were reluctant to embrace policies that were both politically unpopular and economically perilous. Many governments resisted external pressure for anti-slavery legislation for decades, but once they finally succumbed they quickly followed Britain's example by celebrating their anti-slavery credentials and downplaying their earlier misdeeds. These individual decisions to first restrict and then eventually abolish slavery had important cumulative effects, leaving governments that continued to legally sanction slavery increasingly isolated from their international peers.

This story can told in a number of different ways. In this chapter, I focus on the macrohistorical relationship between British anti-slavery, European "civilization," and the global expansion of European political authority during the age of high imperialism. Drawing on a growing literature concerned with the history of European international society, I argue that the globalization of the Anti-Slavery Project usually involved one of three main paths; popular mobilization, armed conflict, and external pressure. In the vast majority of jurisdictions, the legal abolition of slavery was driven by external pressures, rather than domestic popular agitation. For most governments faced with international pressures, the main point at issue was not so much slavery per se, but instead what slavery came to symbolize about the "backward," or "un-civilized" status of their communities. In order to develop this line of argument, I have divided this chapter into four sections. The first section uses the concept of international society to analyze the key features of the Eurocentric international order within which global contests over slavery and abolition took place. The second section focuses on Britain's campaign to build an anti-slavery consensus in Europe, and the attendant consequences of this campaign for evolving models of civilization. In the third section I extend this argument by arguing that the international history of anti-slavery advocacy can be primarily traced to evolving ideologies of European exceptionalism, rather than a commitment to human or racial equality. In the final section I use this argument to analyze the relationship between the legal abolition of slavery and the expansion of European political authority during the nineteenth and early twentieth centuries.

European International Society in the Age of High Imperialism

The concept of international society can be understood as both a set of theoretical claims and a historical category.[1] The theoretical strand involves a distinctive image of international order, where common interests, institutions, and orientations (or the lack thereof) are held to play a central role in shaping relations between political communities. This image is commonly associated with the "Grotian Tradition," which is held to occupy a middle ground between "Machiavellian" power politics and "Kantian" utopianism.[2] From this vantage point, an international society is said to exist: "when a group of states, conscious of certain common interests and common values, form a society in the sense that they conceive themselves to be bound by a common set of rules in their relations with one another, and share in the working of common institutions."[3] This formula has both institutional and sociological dimensions.

At an institutional level, scholars have emphasized the mediating role of a small number of core institutions, such as the balance of power, diplomacy, and international law, which help to maintain a fragile yet nonetheless identifiable international order. At a sociological level, scholars have emphasized the mediating influence of shared values, orientations, ideologies, and cultural identities in shaping relations between different political communities.[4]

Historical analysis of international society starts with the premise that there have been different *kinds* of society, which have evolved with the passage of time. Framed in these terms, the concept of international society offers a framework for exploring the main principles and procedures that have defined relations between communities at various stages in history.[5] The primary focal point here has been the history of European international society, which in turn has a major bearing on the composition and future direction of our current international order.[6] Two main lines of inquiry can be identified within the existing literature. One line of inquiry has focused on changes *within* Europe, where scholars have identified a series of transformations in the foundations of political authority, such as the transition from medieval Christendom to sovereign statehood.[7] The second line of inquiry has focused on the outward *expansion* of European authority, starting with the Iberian conquests of the fifteenth century.[8] This chapter favors an integrated approach, which holds that transformations within Europe helped to shape—and were in turn shaped by—relations with the world at large.[9]

Of particular importance here are historical boundaries of civilizational membership and related conceptions of Self and Other.[10] During the early modern period, European international society was chiefly defined in terms of a shared religious identity (Christian) and common heritage (Roman/Medieval). This shared collective identity was reflected in key institutions, such as distinctive forms of diplomatic exchange, treaty agreements, and mutual recognition, which applied to relations within Christendom, but did not usually extend to relations with non-Christians.[11] This institutional and ideological nexus did not do away with conflict within Europe, but instead helped to legitimate principles and procedures that both partially codified and imperfectly regulated relations between European political elites.[12]

European relationships with cultural and religious outsiders would be constructed on quite different terms.[13] One of the main determinants of historical patterns of cross-cultural exchange has tended to be the relative strengths of the parties involved. From the fifteenth century onward, the Ottoman Empire played a major role in European politics, yet stood apart from

European international society. As long as the Ottomans enjoyed regional primacy, Europeans largely conformed to their principles and practices.[14] This dynamic changed following the decline of the Ottoman Empire, and by the nineteenth century Ottoman rulers were forced to conform to unfamiliar European models. This was also true elsewhere. Until the nineteenth century, elites in Africa and Asia regularly dealt with European interlopers from a position of strength.[15] The major exception was in the "New World," where a combination of political manipulation and demographic catastrophe led to the cumulative deaths of tens of millions of indigenous peoples throughout the Americas.[16] While European enclaves were established elsewhere during the early modern era, the main thrust of colonial expansion in most parts of Africa and Asia came in the nineteenth century.[17]

The global conquests that took place during this period were made possible by the rapid accumulation of an unprecedented level of military, economic, and organizational superiority.[18] While European peoples had previously enjoyed advantages in particular areas, the nineteenth century ushered in a new era of material dominance. This greatly reduced both the material costs and political risks of colonial expansion.[19] These advances were reflected in ideologies of civilization and European superiority. In previous centuries, the divide between Europeans and non-Europeans had been primarily articulated in the language of cultural values, with Europeans favorably contrasting their rationalism and religious virtue with the values of pagans, infidels, and unenlightened peoples.[20] During the nineteenth century differences between peoples were increasingly framed in terms of technological attainment and racial difference.[21] This found expression in evolving ideologies of civilization, which saw Europeans arrogantly divide the world into "civilized," "barbarian," and "savage" peoples on the basis of racial, technological, and administrative criteria.[22]

These models of European superiority were reinforced by—and legitimated through—international institutions. Of particular importance here is the evolution of nineteenth-century European international law, which saw a new attachment to "rules that had been agreed upon by sovereign states, either explicitly or implicitly, as regulating relations between them."[23] During the early modern era, Europeans had routinely reached agreements with authorities in many parts of Africa and Asia that required them to work within (or around) local institutions.[24] The legal positivists of the nineteenth century tended to downplay or disregard these earlier agreements, and instead prioritized relations between civilized, sovereign states.[25] In this new institutional order, "non-European states were excluded from the realm of international law, which now made a distinction between civilized states, which were sovereign and possessed full personality, and noncivilized states, which were not properly members of the 'family of nations' and hence lacked complete personality."[26]

In a sharp break with historical precedent, nineteenth-century Europeans unilaterally determined the ideological and institutional standards that all non-Europeans were now required to adhere to, and forcibly established their preferred models of political authority using their superior capabilities. In the vast majority of cases, this translated into aggressive wars of conquest, which saw much of the globe come under various forms of colonial rule by the early twentieth century. During this period, we also find the consolidation of the "standard of civilization," which held that non-European elites could ensure sovereign recognition and equal status under international law by meeting certain criteria, such as the protection of "basic" rights, maintenance of an effective bureaucracy, and adherence to European legal principles and diplomatic practices.[27] For the handful of non-European governments lucky enough to escape direct colonization, this meant radically overhauling their political institutions.[28] In most cases, sovereign recognition came only after extended periods where European diplomats and traders exercised a key role in the internal affairs of non-European governments, including the collection of revenues and the exercise of judicial authority.

The global history of the legal abolition of slavery is closely connected to this larger trajectory of European political expansion and allied models of civilizational superiority. Two main dynamics can be identified here. The first dynamic revolved around a cumulative change in public and political attitudes toward slavery *within* the European world, with British pressure serving as a decisive catalyst. The second dynamic revolved around the globalization of anti-slavery legislation (on paper, if not always in practice) as consequence of the outward *expansion* of European authority. From the mid-nineteenth century onward, anti-slavery formed a prominent part of self-congratulatory efforts to distinguish between "civilized" and "uncivilized" peoples, and thereby helped to further legitimate European expansion. In this environment, it is tempting to reduce anti-slavery rhetoric to "window dressing" for other political and economic interests. This perspective is not entirely without merit, since there were certainly cases that fit this mold, such as King Leopold's activities in the Congo, but it does not hold as a blanket description. Anti-slavery advocacy was rarely a cost-free exercise. The main burden of the international campaign fell on Britain, but the Anti-Slavery Project also created costs and complications for other European governments. Ending slavery was never a singular unshakable goal where no effort was spared, but it would have been easier to adopt an official policy of noninterference, or to directly take advantage of the various commercial opportunities presented by non-Europe slave systems in other parts of the world.

Anti-Slavery and the Evolution of European International Society

The passage of the 1807 bill abolishing the British transatlantic slave trade created a major conundrum for the British government. Unless other foreign carriers could be convinced to withdraw, it was unlikely that British legislation would substantially reduce the volume of transatlantic slave trading. Some states, such as Denmark and the United States, took independent action to legally end their relatively minor transatlantic trades,[29] but major slavers such as France, Spain, and Portugal were reluctant to abolish what they continued to regard as a legitimate and profitable traffic. Prior to the 1807 legislation, Britain's share of the transatlantic slave trade had increased to a virtual monopoly due to the Napoleonic Wars. Other carriers were concerned that they had used this opportunity to restock their colonies and were now seeking to undercut their rivals. This marked the beginning of an enduring pattern in the international politics of anti-slavery, where British diplomats maintained that they were driven by humanitarian concerns, yet other actors remained justifiably suspicious of their motives. These disputes over slavery and abolition also involved more fundamental disagreements. Thanks to the success of the British anti-slavery movement, the British government was officially committed to the abolition of an institution that—with a few notable exceptions—the rest of the world continued to regard as entirely legitimate, socially necessary, and economically valuable. These conflicting viewpoints were not resolved through philosophical debate, but on the basis of more pragmatic political calculations.

As the preeminent power of the nineteenth century, Britain had considerable diplomatic and political capital with which to advance its new anti-slavery agenda.[30] Following the passage of the 1807 bill, British diplomats made repeated attempts to persuade other governments to follow their lead. Other European carriers were rarely convinced by anti-slavery arguments, yet they still found it necessary to accommodate British overtures for political reasons. By the latter stages of the Napoleonic Wars the British government had accumulated considerable diplomatic and financial leverage over its continental allies. By the end of the Congress of Vienna (1814–1815), Holland, Sweden, Portugal, Spain, and France had all taken (sometimes symbolic) steps against the slave trade.[31] British diplomats attempted to develop robust international mechanisms against slave trading during negotiations in Vienna, but had to settle for a symbolic declaration denouncing the trade as "repugnant to the principles of humanity and universal morality."[32] The British anti-slavery movement had sought to influence the outcome of the Congress through a domestic petition campaign, which collected an unprecedented 750,000 signatures, and through appeals to continental elites.[33] British activists and diplomats looked to Prussia, Austria, and Russia, who had no interests to protect, but discovered that they were unwilling to expend energy on their cause.[34] While British hegemony was sufficient to place anti-slavery on the international agenda, obtaining effective cooperation proved to be a more difficult proposition.

Instead of accepting that the traffic in slaves would continue as long as a viable market existed and the legitimacy of slavery was widely accepted, the British government devoted tremendous resources to anti-slavery diplomacy. By the mid-nineteenth century, Britain stood at the apex of a complex array of bilateral and multilateral anti-slavery agreements, which included political authorities in parts of coastal Africa, most of Europe, and nearly all of the Americas.[35] The importance of British diplomacy was such that "No country in the world in this era signed a treaty containing antislave provisions to which Britain was not also a party."[36] These agreements provided a platform for the second dimension of the campaign, which saw the British navy devote considerable resources to suppressing illegal slave trading.

These suppression efforts initially focused on the Atlantic Ocean, but later extended to the Indian Ocean and the Red Sea. The main focal point of suppression efforts was the western coast of Africa. British sailors regularly detained illegal slave ships, but the effectiveness of their efforts was severely undermined by legal disputes over the "right of search," which meant that slavers flying specific flags could not be prosecuted, or could only be prosecuted in limited circumstances defined by international treaties. Traders of many nationalities exploited these loopholes by acquiring flags and registration papers that offered greatest protection.[37] By the 1840s, the British navy had been supplemented by vessels from the United States, France, and Portugal. For the

French and U.S. governments, these commitments were a politically useful means of neutralizing demands for intrusive searches,[38] as their squadrons could legally apprehend only vessels flying their own colors.[39]

Naval suppression was not particularly successful. Around three million slaves left Africa for the Americas after British abolition, with perhaps two-thirds of these being moved illegally.[40] The British blockade interdicted around 160,000 slaves. Of the approximately 7,750 ships involved, an estimated 1,635 were captured, with approximately 85 percent being detained on British orders.[41] These captures came at tremendous financial cost. David Eltis has calculated that by "any reasonable assessment of profits and direct costs, the nineteenth-century costs of suppression were certainly bigger than the eighteenth century benefits."[42] Chaim Kaufman and Robert Pape estimate that the campaign absorbed an average of 1.8 percent of national income over a sixty-year period. They illustrate the magnitude of this commitment by contrasting this figure with modern development aid, which averaged 0.33 percent among Organisation for European Economic Co-operation (OECD) countries between 1975 and 1996.[43] Neither of these calculations takes into account of the opportunities that were forgone as a result of British withdrawal. Having established themselves as the premier slavers of the Atlantic world during the eighteenth century, British nationals would have been well placed for further expansion if organized anti-slavery had not intruded.[44] The idea that British capitalists orchestrated the legal abolition of slavery to advance their commercial interests is extremely difficult to sustain.[45]

The volume of slaves trafficked to the Americas steadily increased following the end of the Napoleonic Wars. A combination of British diplomatic pressure and outright bribery led to the transatlantic trade being first restricted and then legally abolished in France (1814, 1815), Portugal (1810, 1815, 1817), Spain (1814, 1817, 1820), and Brazil (1822, 1826, 1830), yet a substantial trade continued with the support of authorities in these countries for many decades.[46] The illegal trade involved vessels flying other flags, most notably the flag of the United States, which was unwilling to concede the right to search. French slave trading ended only in the 1830s, after twenty years of tacit government support.[47] This left the Spanish Caribbean and the newly independent state of Brazil as the two main destination regions. The volume and price on arrival of slaves continued to grow in both regions during the 1840s.[48] This was a source of growing frustration and disillusionment for British elites, who responded by adopting a range of dubious but ultimately successful policies.

By the late 1840s widespread frustration within Britain over the limited success of the naval campaign translated into a Parliamentary campaign for withdrawal of the naval squadron on the grounds that it was increasing the horrors associated with the slave trade and had little chance of achieving its overall goals. This campaign was primarily backed by free traders, but also received support from Parliamentary abolitionists philosophically opposed to the use of force. This came to a head in a key vote in the winter of 1850, where both the prime minister and foreign secretary threatened to resign if Parliament voted to remove the squadron. This intervention proved to be decisive and the bill was defeated.[49] What ultimately ended this controversy, however, was the successful application of a more combative approach. The groundwork for this policy was laid in 1845, with the passage of the Aberdeen Act, which directed the British navy to treat Brazilian slave traders as pirates. This in turn followed a precedent established by the Palmerston Act of 1839, which authorized the British navy to seize slave traders operating under Portuguese colors. This effectively coerced the Portuguese government into signing a new treaty (1842) against the slave trade.[50] The legal rationale behind these Acts was extremely tenuous, and they justifiably aroused considerable resentment in both Portugal and Brazil.

In the late 1840s the British government turned to the Aberdeen Act to justify an increasingly aggressive naval campaign off the Brazilian coast, which culminated in the navy destroying a number of slave ships anchored within Brazilian harbors in early 1850. This dramatic action not only stemmed from decades of frustration with Brazilian complicity in a flourishing trade that had then been illegal for twenty years, it also reflected a pressing need to placate domestic critics in Britain. This intervention had an unexpected influence on Brazilian politics. For the first time, the Brazilian government took decisive steps to halt the slave trade, which dramatically collapsed in the face of sustained pressure.[51] The end of the Brazilian trade was a major turning point that not only validated the operations of the British navy, it also left the Spanish Caribbean as the only remaining destination for slave traders. The closure of this final branch of the trade proved to be a similarly protracted process, with an illegal traffic persisting for nearly fifty years. The decisive moment came in 1861, when the outbreak of civil war compelled the United States to finally accept the right of search. Following an aggressive naval campaign in the Caribbean and a more proactive approach by Cuban authorities, the transatlantic slave trade finally came to an end in the late 1860s.

In the last chapter, I suggested that the 1806/7 legislation ending British involvement in the slave trade was probably the single most important event in the larger history of British anti-slavery. The suppression of the transatlantic slave trade played a similar role in most parts of Europe. For European powers involved in transatlantic slavery, the decision to abolish the trade meant officially accepting (if only symbolically initially) that slavery was a problem to be addressed, rather than a legitimate institution. The end of maritime trading placed severe constraints on the long-term demographic and economic prospects of most slave systems in the Americas. With the notable exception of the United States, the slave populations of the New World were rarely self-sustaining and thus required a regular influx of slaves from Africa to maintain overall numbers. The closure of the transatlantic trade usually resulted in demographic stagnation or decline, bringing to an end centuries of sustained expansion.[52] In many cases the end of the trade signaled a gradual deterioration in the economic fortunes and, in some cases, the relative economic importance of related slave systems. None of these developments made the legal abolition of slavery inevitable,[53] but they did play a more qualified role in making abolition politically and economically feasible. This led to an environment where the cumulative weight of previous anti-slavery commitments helped channel political discourse toward procedural questions of *when* and *how* the abolition of slavery should occur, rather than *if* it should occur at all.

Unlike the abolition of the transatlantic slave trade, where Britain exercised a preponderant role, the legal abolition of slavery occurred in a variety of different ways. In most parts of Latin America, where slavery was generally of moderate importance, slavery was slowly phased out following the violent struggle for independence.[54] Denmark and Sweden ended colonial slavery in the late 1840s. The Dutch belatedly abolished slavery in their Caribbean colonies in 1863.[55] These were primarily elite decisions, where there was little public engagement. The French government legally freed around a quarter of a million slaves in 1848, following in the wake of revolutionary turmoil and increasing—yet still fairly modest—popular agitation. Events in 1847–1848 ended a protracted, predominantly low-key contest over the terms and timing of abolition that mirrored debates elsewhere in Europe.[56] In the United States, slavery famously came to an end in 1865, following decades of popular struggle and increasing polarization, ending in a catastrophic civil war.[57] Each of these decisions had important cumulative effects, leaving remaining holdouts increasingly isolated within civilized society.[58] The last bastion of New World slavery was Brazil, where an elite-driven decision to gradually

end slavery in 1871 was followed by a dramatic period of popular mobilization in the 1880s, culminating in the "Golden Law" of 1888.[59] During this
period slavery was increasingly viewed as a national embarrassment, as Bra-
zilians were humiliated by "references to their country as the last Christian
nation that tolerated slavery, on a level with 'backward' African and Asiatic
slaveholding societies."[60]

Three main paths to the legal abolition of slavery can be identified during this period. The first path revolved around popular mobilization against
slavery. As we saw in the last chapter, this path is chiefly applicable to Britain,
where the abolition of both the slave trade and slavery can be primarily traced
to decades of public engagement that saw a popular anti-slavery consensus
emerge *prior* to the passage of key legislation. This path had fainter echoes
elsewhere, most notably in the northern United States and at times in France
and Brazil, but it was peculiarly British in intensity and duration. The second
path revolved around armed conflict. This path is chiefly applicable to Haiti
(San Domingue) and the United States, where the ending of slavery occurred
through revolution and war, with consequent losses of blood and treasure.[61]
In the century after 1787, more enslaved people of African descent living in
the Americas were liberated through violent conflict than by popular mobilization. Here, as elsewhere, the collective actions of both slaves and ex-slaves
would play an indispensable role, as slaves took advantage of the narrow opportunities to challenge their situation through fight, force of arms, and other
forms of contestation and negotiation.[62]

The third path revolved around external pressures. This path is primarily applicable to continental Europe, where legal abolition was not defined
by domestic mobilization, but was instead set into motion through British
intervention. On this point, I turn to the work of Seymour Drescher, who
has demonstrated that anti-slavery in continental Europe usually received
little or no popular support prior to key legislative changes.[63] With the partial exception of France, anti-slavery societies in mainland Europe comprised
small elite groups with at best modest political influence. Unlike Britain and
the northern United States, there were no large-scale petitions, outpourings
of anti-slavery tracts, mass mobilizations, public meetings, or boycotts. Outside of periodic public outrage at the overbearing British, public opinion was
rarely aroused, leaving vested interests and political elites to grapple with cumulative external pressures. In these circumstances, legislative enactments
against slavery were primarily dictated not by pressure from below, but by
political elites reluctantly responding to external influences. In most parts of

the European world, popular anti-slavery attitudes only deepened and solidified after (and often long after) involvement in transatlantic slave trading and even related slave systems had come to an end. It is clear, however, that this belated (and therefore fairly passive) support was symptomatic of a larger transformation.

Until the mid-eighteenth century, slavery was routinely characterized as a progressive institution that spared the lives of captives who would otherwise have been slain, and thereby paved the way for their cultural and religious redemption.[64] The political success of anti-slavery severed this link between slavery and progress.[65] By the second half of the nineteenth century, most Europeans had instead come to regard slavery as a regressive anachronism from an earlier stage in human development. As more and more European states legally abolished slavery, the *absence* of slavery came to be viewed as normal, rather than exceptional. Centuries of complicity in transatlantic slavery would in turn be recast as "abnormal" or, to coin a new nineteenth-century phrase, "peculiar."[66] To make sense of this dynamic, I look to Bernard McGrane's analysis of social evolution. According to McGrane, nineteenth-century European thought was characterized by a "peculiar valorization of time, i.e., its belief that civilization progresses, developing through stages from the primitive to the advanced."[67] This social anthropology established a new basis for ethnographic evaluation, which saw "barbarian" and "savage" peoples from outside Europe redefined as representatives of stages in human history that Europeans had ostensibly progressed beyond. By the second half of the nineteenth century, slavery had come to be similarly construed as a (somewhat regrettable) feature of an earlier, a less-developed stage in social evolution.

In this new formulation, the abolition of slavery no longer appeared as a discrete event, but instead came to be construed as a key example of the unique achievements and advanced standing of both European civilization and modern Christianity. At this juncture, it is important to distinguish between two different understandings of "civilization."[68] In one variant, civilization can be used to describe a variety of supranational cultural identities, which can each be described as distinctive civilizations.[69] In the second variant, civilization can be used to more narrowly describe the unique virtues ostensibly displayed by a singular, superior community, which is in turn distinguished from "backward" or "barbarous" practices elsewhere.[70] This variant can contain a qualified inclusive dimension, which holds that "uncivilized" peoples can gradually acquire superior virtues through emulation and adaptation. In this version of civilization social divisions are not immutable, but can (and should) be ameliorated by adhering to superior yet nonetheless universally applicable models.

Both of these variants involved evolving forms of collective identification and social differentiation. By the second half of the nineteenth century, most Europeans had come to regard the abolition of slavery as a key illustration of the exceptional virtues of European civilization. Framed in these terms, the legal abolition of slavery not only offered confirmation of progress within the European world, it would also be invoked as a prominent example of the "superior" values that set European civilization apart from peoples in other parts of the globe. From this vantage point, the legal status of slavery would come to represent a symbolic yet still politically significant litmus test of national and civilizational honor. This meant different things in different contexts. European governments were already (self-)defined as "civilized," so legal abolition meant reaffirming a preexisting status. Non-European powers were already (externally) defined as "uncivilized," so the status of slavery came to be implicated in larger efforts to establish their credentials to skeptical outsiders.

European Imperialism, Colonialism, and the Globalization of Anti-Slavery

The close association between European imperialism, colonialism, and anti-slavery raises many complex and contentious issues. Many critics have tended to define European encounters with non-European peoples primarily in terms of a series of bloody, sometimes genocidal, encounters, followed by economic exploitation, political oppression, and social discrimination. While these critiques have offered compelling indictments of systemic abuses, they have also had a tendency to dismiss the ideological agenda at the heart of the imperial project by reducing European convictions to "little more than a hypocritical attempt to elevate base motives with high-sounding clichés about the European destiny to better the condition of humanity."[71] From this standpoint, anti-slavery can be reduced to little more than a disingenuous pretext that concealed vested political and economic interests.[72] While there is no doubt that the extravagant, self-serving, and often hypocritical rhetoric that accompanied European imperialism often bore little or no resemblance to actual practices, this does not mean that anti-slavery advocacy can be easily dismissed as an elaborate smokescreen.

Until the nineteenth century, European diplomats and traders who encountered slave systems in other parts of the world either adopted a policy of noninterference, or sought to harness local slave systems to their own ends. European encounters with non-European slave systems were not confined to transatlantic slave trading in western and southeastern Africa, they extended to the Indian Ocean and various parts of Asia and the Middle East. The Dutch were particularly active in the Indian Ocean in the seventeenth century, developing an elaborate transcontinental slave trading network that drew slave labor from three interlocking and overlapping circuits; East Africa, South Asia, and South East Asia.[73] The French, Portuguese, Spanish, and British also engaged with enduring slave systems in the Indian Ocean World during the early modern era.[74] Unless European Christians were the ones being enslaved,[75] European traders and diplomats appear to have had few problems accommodating slavery in India, Africa, and Central, East, and South East Asia.

This enduring pattern of cross-cultural accommodation and adaptation came to an end during the nineteenth century. The Anti-Slavery Project not only successfully challenged the status of European slave systems and transatlantic slavery, it also called into question the legitimacy of venerable slave systems in other parts of the world. This shift took place at a time when European elites had recently acquired an unprecedented technological and military advantage over their counterparts elsewhere. If organized anti-slavery had emerged within Europe during the sixteenth or seventeenth centuries, European powers would not have had sufficient capabilities to directly challenge most external slave systems. By the second half of the nineteenth century the balance of power had decisively shifted, paving the way for the globalization of anti-slavery through colonial conquest and imperial imposition.

This profound transformation cannot be easily reduced to either strategic calculations or economic interests. From a strategic standpoint, the most pragmatic course of action would have been to continue a hands-off approach. Taking action against slavery routinely created costs and complications that could otherwise have been avoided if relevant governments had been prepared to sanction slavery as a legitimate institution. From an economic standpoint, the most pragmatic course of action would have been either to officially sanction non-European slave systems, or, alternatively, to attempt to harness slavery to European economic interests. Taking action against slavery not only meant forgoing a series of potential economic opportunities, it could also mean expending blood and treasure on anti-slavery measures. In the vast majority of cases, both strategic calculations and economic interests found expression in various efforts to minimize costs, rather than maximize gains. While there is no question that the implementation of anti-slavery commitments frequently left a great deal to be desired (leaving ample scope for charges that anti-slavery advocacy should have gone faster and further), this does not entirely negate the fact that it can often be difficult to identify compelling strategic reasons for taking up anti-slavery in the first place.[76]

If the legal abolition of slavery poses problems for critics of Western imperialism, does it alternatively offer ammunition for imperial apologists? On this front, there is a strong case to be made that the Anti-Slavery Project is primarily a European invention. One influential example of this line of argument comes from David Eltis, who observes that "In no non-western countries did abolition emerge independently as official state policy, and no non-western intellectual tradition showed signs of questioning slavery per se, as opposed to questioning the appropriateness of slavery for specific groups."[77] Since there is a plausible case to be made that the legal abolition of slavery would not have occurred without European intervention, it would appear to belong among other "benefits" identified by imperial apologists, such as "stability" and "development."[78] However, this approach begins to break down when anti-slavery advocacy is deployed to validate more general claims about the relatively "benign" character of European imperialism. At the heart of this line of argument is an intuitively plausible proposition: if Europeans were responsible for the legal abolition of slavery (and potentially other public goods), then perhaps the imperial order they established was not as heinous or self-serving as critics suggest. However appealing this argument might appear at first glance, it runs into severe problems when placed alongside European involvement in the enslavement of tens of millions of African and Native Americans, the annihilation of numerous indigenous peoples, the appropriation of vast territories through bloody conquest and systematic repression, numerous massacres in many corners of the globe, long-term economic exploitation, and the widespread use of forced labor well into the twentieth century.[79] This brings us to an apparent contradiction. How can we reconcile the fact that European powers pushed for the legal abolition of various slave systems, while simultaneously engaging in a range of unsavory and highly reprehensible practices?

In the previous chapter, I argued that the unprecedented success of British anti-slavery can be ultimately traced to the construction of a compelling problem that was both stark and solvable. This involved slavery being successfully framed as a unique and exceptional evil, while many other forms of suffering and maltreatment were tacitly excluded and sometimes indirectly legitimated. From this vantage point, there was no automatic contradiction between being formally committed to legal abolition while simultaneously sanctioning other exploitative practices. This dualism is evident when it comes to the international politics of anti-slavery. When European powers cautiously pressed for legal abolition, they believed they were acting against an exceptional evil that was antithetical to civilized society. Being opposed to slavery did not necessarily preclude other "normal" activities, such as colonial conquest, the liquidation of "native" peoples, or forced labor. All of these activities involved systematic abuses, but only one was viewed as being wholly illegitimate.

To help make sense of this state of affairs, I turn to Richard Price's analysis of the construction of chemical weapons as a unique and exceptional category over the course of the twentieth century. Price has no doubt that chemical weapons can cause "horrible suffering," but he observes that "most if not all other weapons share similarly dubious properties." It is not immediately obvious that being "torn apart by burning shrapnel," which is a normal part of conventional warfare, is any less horrific than being killed by chemical weapons, yet the latter has come to be accorded an exceptional status owing to a complex chain of historical events.[80] Over the course of the nineteenth century, slavery and enslavement came to be accorded a similarly exceptional status, while the overall legitimacy of other more conventional yet nonetheless problematic practices remained relatively unscathed.[81]

In order to better understand the construction of slavery as an exceptional category, we need to explore the underlying motivations driving anti-slavery advocacy. In the previous chapter, I argued that British anti-slavery was cosmopolitan in effect, but not (for the most part) cosmopolitan in orientation. Two of the main ingredients in this argument were national honor and religious virtue. As "God's first children," Britons distinguished themselves from outsiders on the grounds of superior religious virtue and a unique love of liberty. When the British public expressed unprecedented support for anti-slavery, they were effectively reaffirming these stylized values. After the passage of the key bills of 1807 and 1833, there were tremendous outpourings of self-congratulatory sentiment, which saw legal abolition hailed as a national accomplishment that both redeemed and further consolidated British values.[82] Having reaffirmed their exceptional character, Britons went on to contrast their leading role in the anti-slavery cause, often epitomized by the noble work of the royal navy, with the perfidious conduct of other powers, such as Spain, Portugal, or Brazil, who condoned a flourishing illegal trade for decades despite their treaty commitments. This juxtaposition would be invoked to provide further confirmation that Britain stood at the vanguard of European civilization and at the forefront of progress.[83]

This enduring nexus between anti-slavery and collective honor and identity not only played a key role in Britain, it also made a central contribution to anti-slavery globally. To make sense of this complex relationship, it is important to take into consideration two different (yet not entirely separate) perspectives on the underlying motivations behind anti-slavery activism. In the first perspective, anti-slavery can be chiefly understood in terms of a (proto-) egalitarian commitment to human or racial equality.[84] There is no doubt that this perspective has helped motivate anti-slavery activism, particularly in more recent times, but this does not necessarily mean that it was the sole—or even primary—driving force behind anti-slavery agitation in the eighteenth or nineteenth centuries. There were undoubtedly some enlightened figures who were committed to equality, particularly among activists in the United States, but they were the exception, not the rule. The European world of the eighteenth and nineteenth centuries was deeply hierarchical, reflecting entrenched cleavages based on sex, class, race, religion, and civilization. Much like other political campaigns from this era, the Anti-Slavery Project called for better treatment of a depressed category of persons, but this did not automatically require human equality, only a more limited commitment to sufficient commonality.[85] This distinction between equality and commonality has tended to be lost amid a widespread tendency to project recent models of human equality backward through time.

This brings us to the second perspective on the underlying motivations behind anti-slavery activism, which is chiefly concerned with what (anti-) slavery came to signify, or otherwise symbolize, about the distinctive virtues (or vices) of particular communities. This perspective connects anti-slavery to ideologies of benevolent paternalism, where peoples who considered themselves blessed with "superior" sensibilities/opportunities were held to be duty bound to assist those who were unable or unwilling to help themselves. It is no coincidence that the famous slogan "am I not man and brother," was attached to an image of a kneeling African slave raising his chained arms in a desperate plea.[86] This stylized relationship did not take place between equals, but between a helpless supplicant and "civilized" benefactor.

This orientation became even more important from the mid-nineteenth century onward. Even if we accept, if only for the sake of argument, the more familiar idea that anti-slavery was primarily motivated by a historically anomalous commitment to human equality, there are few indications that this commitment survived the subsequent development of essentialist models of human difference, such as scientific racism and social Darwinism. Racial arguments appear to have been of marginal importance in the early history of British anti-slavery,[87] but following the end of the apprenticeship system in 1838 many Britons rapidly turned to racial models to explain the subsequent "failure" of legal action. By the late 1840s, it was clear that their "mighty experiment" was not living up to previous expectations. Sugar production was in decline in most parts of the British Caribbean, as ex-slaves favored small holdings over plantations, and displayed little inclination to embrace idealized British social mores. This dispiriting state of affairs would be widely attributed to the innate inferiority of African peoples,[88] and epitomized an increasing emphasis on the causes and consequences of racial categories.[89] This in turn had important implications for evolving ideologies of European superiority. If racial categories reflected unalterable dispositions, as increasingly dominant pseudoscientific theories maintained, there was little to be done to bridge divisions between racial groupings. Caucasian Europeans were both biologically and technologically endowed with "superior" qualities and capacities that effectively meant they were morally entitled to rule over "inferior" peoples.[90]

It may seem somewhat surprising, in light of these developments, that no European power took formal steps to restore legal slavery.[91] If the Anti-Slavery Project had been primarily animated by a commitment to human equality, one could have reasonably inferred that the increasing prominence of essentialist models would have overthrown the underlying rationale for retaining and further extending anti-slavery policies. The most likely candidates for (re) enslavement were black Africans, who occupied the bottom of European racial hierarchies, receiving extremely unflattering and highly pessimistic characterizations.[92] The fact that slavery was not officially reintroduced, and further steps were taken to ensure legal abolition in other parts of the globe, strongly suggests that the Anti-Slavery Project was driven by far more than a commitment to human equality. Anti-slavery advocacy was not contingent on favorable conceptions of the Other, but reflected more durable conceptions of a virtuous Self. Racial theories would offer further confirmation of European exceptionalism, but shift explanations for non-European inferiority away from mutable environmental factors toward more enduring physiological traits.[93] In this hierarchical ideological environment, it would have been relatively easy to envisage a return to slavery, but for the now firmly entrenched notion that anti-slavery paternalism extended to all peoples, despite their obvious inferiority. This idealized worldview concealed a range of grievous sins, but restoring slavery would have demolished its ideological foundations.

This series of arguments go at least some way to resolving the apparent tension between anti-slavery advocacy and European imperialism. In recent times, the "modern tendency to see colonial conquests as violent and bad, and emancipation as gentle and good, has obscured their ideological relationship."[94] Instead of being viewed as antithetical forces, anti-slavery and imperial expansion can be best understood as overlapping expressions of deeply entrenched models of European superiority. In intra-European settings, rivals would seek to advance or defend their standing as civilized powers. In extra-European settings, these divisions were partially subsumed by a common European identity and a common civilizing mission. This relationship is usefully summarized by Joseph Miller, who observes that "Once the campaign shifted to non-Western slavery, otherwise divided Europeans could find a common cause, at least superficially, in suppressing [slavery]."[95] From a strategic standpoint, the Anti-Slavery Project was a political and economic inconvenience. From a normative standpoint, it was a core component of a larger ideological complex, which would most visibly manifest itself in an unprecedented expansion of European authority. By 1914, Europe occupied "roughly 85% of the earth as colonies, protectorates, dependencies, dominions, and commonwealths."[96] This new political authority played an indispensable role in bringing about legal abolition throughout the globe. In the reminder of this chapter, I concentrate on anti-slavery measures introduced by rulers who were not subjected to direct colonial authority. In the chapter that follows, I go on to consider the legal abolition of slavery in territories under European colonial rule.

Anti-Slavery and the Expansion of European International Society

Faced with external pressures to take action against slavery, non-European elites initially responded in much the same way as their European counterparts: delay, deflection, and reluctant and symbolic concessions. While these reactions may be comparable, the context in which they took place varied markedly. Within the European world, debates over slavery revolved around sovereign states who were recognized members of international society. European states who continued to sanction slavery had their credentials as civilized states called into question, but this did not fatally undermine their sovereign prerogatives. For non-European elites, the status of slavery tended to be bound up in the aforementioned "standard of civilization," which made sovereign equality contingent on extensive institutional reforms. During this period European powers routinely intervened in the internal affairs of non-European rulers.[97] Taxes and tariffs were regularly decided or collected by European agents. Exemptions from the jurisdiction of local institutions were common. Moreover, European embassies and vessels regularly offered (at least qualified) sanctuary to escaped slaves.[98] In exceptional cases, they even acquired a legal right of consular manumission.[99] These regular intrusions offered a focal point for political anger and resentment. Bringing relevant institutions in line with the "standard of civilization" offered a way for political elites to challenge European intrusions as unwarranted and illegitimate, and to hopefully demonstrate that negative portrayals of their societies were inappropriate and unfounded.

In this bifurcated international order, the status of slavery frequently impinged on broader efforts to defend both political autonomy and collective honor. The primary focus of anti-slavery agitation occurred in Africa and the Middle East, but also included independent polities in Asia, such as Thailand and China.[100] From the early nineteenth century onward, British diplomats entered into various agreements with non-European elites restricting or legally abolishing slave-trading and slave-holding within various jurisdictions.[101] This multifaceted campaign included treaties with African rulers mandating an end to their involvement in transatlantic slavery, overlapping restrictions on the Ottoman (1847, 1854, 1857, 1880) and Egyptian slave trade (1854, 1877), prohibitions on maritime imports into Persia (1848, 1851/52, 1882) and Madagascar (1817, 1820, 1865), and treaties (1822, 1839, 1845/47, 1873, 1876) with the "Sultan" of Zanzibar that initially restricted and then ultimately abolished slave trading.[102] To garner British support, the Bey of Tunis went as far as legally declaring the abolition of slavery itself in 1846.[103] These anti-slavery agreements with non-European elites tended to be constructed on quite different terms to similar treaties between European states. The British were not only reluctant to officially recognize those involved as sovereign equals, they sought to maintain exclusive responsibility for enforcement when it came to issues such as the right of search. According to Edward Keene, "The main reason why African, Arab and Muslim rulers got a worse deal than even the weakest and most reluctant European and American state was because the British saw the former as 'barbarians,' while they saw the latter as belonging to the 'family of civilized nations.'"[104]

In the vast majority of cases, these anti-slavery measures appear to have had (at least initially) a limited effect on established practices and procedures.[105] Some traders found it necessary to operate in a more covert fashion, or shift to alternate routes, but for most of the nineteenth century these legal restrictions would selectively subdue, rather than effectively conclude. Various rulers primarily responded to anti-slavery overtures out of political necessity, or on the basis of strategic calculations, and frequently lacked both the capacity and inclination to consistently uphold their commitments. In many respects, these responses were broadly comparable to the failures of the French, Portuguese, and Brazilian governments to honor their legal obligations during the first half of the nineteenth century. Primary responsibility for preventing illegal maritime traffic again fell on the British navy, which engaged in a protracted and often frustrating campaign covering the east coast of Africa, the Red Sea, the Persian Gulf, and parts of the Mediterranean.[106]

This campaign resulted in regular captures and periodic lulls along particular routes, but it could not prevent the transportation of hundreds of thousands of slaves over many decades. According to Pier Larson, around 1,312,000 slaves were involved in the external slave trades of Africa and Madagascar between 1801 and 1900. This total represents around half of an estimated 2,604,000 slaves transported between 1501 and 1900. This pattern is in keeping with larger regional trends, which saw slave systems in many parts of Africa and the Middle East reach their historical zenith *after* the emergence of organized anti-slavery. Larson's nineteenth-century total can be further divided into 492,000 for the Red Sea, 618,000 for East Africa, and 202,000 for Madagascar.[107] In both the Red Sea and Persian Gulf, modest maritime slave trading persisted until at least the mid-twentieth century.[108]

Throughout this period the status of slavery was caught up in a familiar balancing act between international and domestic constituencies. British diplomats secured reluctant concessions rooted in political expediency, but gained few genuine adherents. Writing on Anglo-Ottoman disputes over slavery, Ehud Toledano observes that

the Ottoman government, acting to accommodate its British ally, operated without an ideological support that would justify such a policy or endow it with meaning. For those who carried it out, this was change without genuine motivation, reform without conviction, a putting things right without accepting that they were indeed wrong.[109]

In a period when the Ottoman elites were struggling to maintain control over much of their empire, they were understandably reluctant to intrude on an institution that was supported by substantial economic interests and sanctioned by social and religious conventions.[110] In 1855–1856, the Ottoman government faced a rebellion in the Hijaz (now part of Saudi Arabia), in which the prospect of the abolition of the slave trade served as a rallying point for opposition to Ottoman rule. Order was eventually restored, but the status of slavery remained a sensitive issue for many years, with local authorities making no attempt to restrict the trade until the late 1870s.[111] Elsewhere in the Empire, restrictions on the slave trade proved to be fairly ineffective, but by no means entirely irrelevant.[112] It was only in the late nineteenth century, following the "Scramble for Africa" and the emergence of a more proactive approach, that slave trading gradually declined to little more than a trickle.[113] In the absence of a viable trade, slavery itself often ceased to be demographically sustainable, precipitating a "slow death" over many decades.[114]

The Turkish Republic that emerged out of the ashes of the Great War was one of a small group of communities to escape direct colonization. In most cases, nineteenth-century contests over slavery were overtaken by colonial conquest, suggesting that the anti-slavery measures adopted by non-European rulers did little to inhibit or otherwise prevent European military aggression. Escaping colonization required a combination of good fortune, military accomplishment, diplomatic maneuvering, and favorable geopolitics. The introduction of anti-slavery measures ultimately did little to hold back the tide. By the early twentieth century, European colonial expansion was mostly complete (notwithstanding a final iteration involving the League of Nations mandate system). As we shall see in the following chapter, the task of abolishing slavery passed to colonial authorities. In the international arena, there remained around a dozen independent polities that continued to sanction slavery.

For rulers in these communities, slavery was increasingly recognized as a national embarrassment, which significantly affected their international reputation. The key sticking point, however, was not so much slavery per se, but what slavery was held to symbolize about the retrograde qualities of their entire communities. In an age of European dominance, slavery and "backwardness" were inextricably linked. Political elites were acutely aware that broader evaluations of their societies were bound up in the status of slavery, and that any aspirations they might have to become (or appear) "civilized," or "modern," required action against slavery. This was compounded by the cumulative effects of earlier anti-slavery measures, which concentrated discussion around a small number of increasingly isolated cases. For rulers in these communities, anti-slavery was often caught up in enduring contests between political reformers and social conservatives, with the former taking up the cause as one aspect of a more general commitment to wider reforms, and the latter mounting a similarly wide-ranging defense of the status quo. Issue-specific groups do not appear to have played a major role on either side of these political debates. Much like most of continental Europe in the first half of the nineteenth century, there were no mass mobilizations against slavery along the lines of the British anti-slavery movement.

These political and ideological tensions are particularly evident in international debates over the status of slavery in Abyssinia (Ethiopia). In 1896, Abyssinia inflicted a major defeat on Italian invaders and thereby cemented its unique status as the only African polity to (then) escape European conquest. Having maintained their independence by force of arms, Abyssinian elites found themselves in a somewhat precarious diplomatic position, where encroachment, intervention, or partition could plausibly come from Italy, Britain, or France. In this inhospitable environment, slavery emerged as a major international issue. According to British anti-slavery activists, the slave population of Abyssinia stood at around two million (of an estimated population of ten million). The depredations of slave-raiders, including repeated incursions into neighboring territories, attracted particular notoriety.[115]

In a bid to placate their European critics, Abyssinian rulers repeatedly proclaimed restrictions on slave trading.[116] This once again resulted in a divide between policy and practice, as slaving continued with limited regard for the ineffective, half-hearted efforts of the weak central government. In keeping with larger trends, European observers tended to portray slavery as a symptom of the "backward" condition of Abyssinia as a whole. An illustrative example of this general tendency comes from British anti-slavery advocate Noel Buxton, who observed that, "It was surprising to find ourselves in a country the uniqueness of which lies in the fact that, though it is Christian, its social life reposes on the institution of slavery. Slavery accords with the absence of conditions associated with what we should call government. The state machinery is little more than medieval."[117] In this formula, the presence of slavery becomes a peculiar anomaly, which can be explained by the presence of a "medieval" political infrastructure belonging to an earlier phase in human development. Having displaced Brazil as the "last" Christian country to sanction slavery, Abyssinia would provoke considerable international debate following the end of the Great War.

A key moment came in 1923, when Abyssinia applied for membership to the League of Nations. This followed a sustained period of adverse publicity regarding slavery that culminated in formal discussions within the League focusing on slavery in Abyssinia.[118] League membership offered international confirmation of Abyssinia's sovereign status and a formal affirmation of its territorial integrity. Much was expected of the League during this period, and Abyssinian rulers were not alone in thinking that membership would provide some protection against foreign incursion. In the diplomatic exchanges that followed, slavery proved to be major issue. Opposition was fiercest in Britain, where the government deemed Abyssinia "unfit" for membership and repeatedly emphasized the problem of slavery in pressing its case.[119] This ultimately proved to be an unsustainable position. Abyssinia was officially admitted in late September 1923 on the proviso that it would "observe the St. Germain Arms Convention of 1919, provide the council with information on slavery, and consider League recommendations on obligations under the covenant."[120] This consolidated Abyssinian slavery into a persistent international issue that would occupy anti-slavery activists, diplomats, and League of Nations agencies for over a decade.[121] In an effort to diffuse international pressure, Abyssinian elites issued a number of proclamations that reaffirmed earlier prohibitions, and required slaves to be freed following their master's death. Other measures included symbolic acts of manumission, the establishment of anti-slavery agencies, and the publication of lists of slaves who had been freed and traders who had been prosecuted. These measures were not entirely inconsequential, but their overall effect was limited by the fact that slaving continued to be viewed as both profitable and legitimate.[122]

This deadlock was broken by the Italian invasion of 1935. In keeping with historical precedent, the Italian government turned to anti-slavery to help validate their activities. Here, as elsewhere, the status of slavery was linked to the "backward" nature of Abyssinia as a whole.[123] The Italians maintained that their bloody conquest (which included the use of chemical weapons) was warranted, or at least excusable, given the country's "uncivilized" condition, which rendered European tutelage both desirable and necessary. The abolition of slavery was presented as one of the benefits of Italian occupation, forcing their European critics to confront arguments that they had previously used to support their own conquests. In this respect, it was not so much the substance, but the timing of the Italian action that set it apart from their European peers.[124] When Abyssinia regained its independence in the early 1940s as part of British campaigns against Italian territories in Africa, it proved to be politically impossible to uphold slavery, and the newly restored Emperor Haile Selassie moved to abolish the institution in 1942. This decree marked a symbolic turning point, but it was some years before political authority could be reestablished, and reports of small-scale slaving in the Horn of Africa continued well into the second half of the twentieth century.[125]

Viewed from a contemporary perspective, the final stages in the struggle against legal slavery acquire a certain inevitability, creating the impression that any lingering resistance was swept away by an all but inexorable tide. This is somewhat misleading. While rulers in Afghanistan (1923), Nepal (1926), and Iran (1929) legally abolished slavery in the 1920s, political elites in the Arabian peninsula generally refused to consider legal abolition until after the Second World War.[126] Throughout this period there were few indications that regional elites were prepared to prohibit slavery, as opposed to prohibiting maritime slave trading. For contemporary activists and government agents, the deeply rooted character of Arabian slavery pointed toward a prolonged continuation of the prevailing status quo, rather than imminent change. As the paramount power in the region, the British government repeatedly faced awkward questions about the status of slavery under its auspices. It is clear, however, that external pressures could not be entirely set aside. Following the end of the Second World War, United Nations delegates from both Yemen and Saudi Arabia felt obliged to issue false declarations that there was no slavery within their jurisdictions.[127]

The key regional holdout was Saudi Arabia, which emerged as both the largest state in the peninsula and the home of the two holiest sites of the Islamic faith. These sites were not only of tremendous symbolic and religious importance, they served as a long-standing destination for slave traders, with trading in slaves forming part of (or, once the trade was legally abolished, sometimes being concealed under) pilgrimages to Mecca. In 1962, the status of slavery in Saudi Arabia was caught up in a series of larger events, with an ailing king being sidelined by his brother during a time of regional turmoil. On November 6, 1962, this new regime proclaimed the legal abolition of slavery.[128] This abrupt decision followed in the wake of repeated criticism from Egypt and newly independent states in Africa, with the latter expressing concerns about their citizens being enslaved.[129] Saudi legislation was preceded by anti-slavery measures in Bahrain (1937), Kuwait (1949), and Qatar (1952), and overlapped with piecemeal reform in wartorn Yemen. Oman formally abolished slavery following a coup d'état in 1970.[130] In 1972, the Arab League, keen to put the embarrassments of the not too distant past behind them, audaciously reported to the United Nations that "Slavery has never been an issue in the Arab world, for by their nature and ethics, the Arab community reject slavery and similar practices."[131]

Information on post-abolition developments in many of these territories has proved difficult to obtain. Official responses to requests for information from international organizations rarely go beyond curt denials or brief statements setting out relevant laws.[132] As we shall see in following chapters, other sources of information often take the form of anecdotal claims, incidents, and experiences that can be hard to corroborate and difficult to generalize. This does not mean, however, that we should conflate legal abolition and effective emancipation. Colonial laws prohibiting slave systems in Africa and Asia rarely precipitated an abrupt and decisive conclusion, but instead marked a more qualified turning point in which slave populations underwent a period of gradual decline frequently measured in decades. It seems that the countries listed above followed a roughly comparable pattern, which was sometimes facilitated by official compensation schemes for slave owners, as was the case in Nepal, Qatar, and Saudi Arabia,[133] and hampered by the fact that relevant political authorities often exercised limited or qualified control over parts of their territories.

Once slavery had been legally abolished, non-European rulers followed historical precedent in highlighting their commitment to anti-slavery and downplaying both earlier resistance and external influence, but this posture had limited salience. By the time of the League of Nations, anti-slavery could no longer be plausibly characterized as a distinctive value or singular virtue, and instead came to be construed as a more elementary standard that all states had (or should) endorse. In this context, the image of slavery as a historical anachronism had particular resonance. The presence of slavery among non-European peoples had helped confirm broader characterizations of various communities as trapped in an earlier phase in human history. In the aftermath of legal abolition, this association would be rapidly inverted. Political elites in places such as Saudi Arabia and Abyssinia were keen to relegate slavery to an earlier phase in their country's historical development, which was now in no way connected to either its current character or future prospects.

Once slavery was confined to the past, the Anti-Slavery Project was no longer widely regarded as an ongoing issue, leaving limited space for difficult questions about the continuation of various slave-like practices. Throughout the history of anti-slavery, political elites have been quick to declare slavery to be a thing of the past, but these declarations have rarely captured the full extent of the issues involved, leaving many problems unresolved in the aftermath of legal abolition.

Concluding Remarks

The ideological integrity of European international society was severely tested on multiple fronts between 1914 and the 1960s. The first great test was the Great War. This conflict not only involved unprecedented sacrifices of blood and treasure, it posed a profound challenge to entrenched ideologies of moral and racial superiority. In the aftermath of the Great War, these pretentions were further shaken by the political achievements of fascism and communism, which fractured European unity into contending worldviews. This culminated in an even greater military conflict and the horrors of the Holocaust. At the same time that the European world was being torn apart from within, it was being challenged from without. In what has been aptly described as a "revolt against the West," popular campaigns in Asia, Africa, and the Middle East successfully challenged the ideological foundations of European imperialism and colonialism.[134] This far-reaching revolt culminated in dramatic moves toward racial equality, decolonization, and self-determination. By the 1960s, the institutional and ideological dualism that had long been at the heart of European international society had largely (but not entirely) collapsed, with numerous postcolonial states securing international recognition of their sovereign status.[135] None of these newly independent states displayed any inclination to reverse the unpopular anti-slavery measures introduced under colonial rule in the not too distant past. As we shall see, there were still places where slavery persisted unofficially, but it was no longer feasible to unapologetically endorse slavery at an international level. This is emblematic of a much larger trend. Once measures legally abolishing slavery have been introduced, they have rarely been reversed.[136]

With a handful of important exceptions, the initial impetus for the legal abolition of slavery throughout the globe primarily came from external actors and influences, rather than internal mobilization. This typically involved anti-slavery being reluctantly embraced out of political expediency in the face of significant domestic opposition. It is not overly surprising, therefore, that many political elites initially failed to effectively uphold their official commitments, allowing both slavery and slave trading to continue in many jurisdictions for decades after legal abolition. In most parts of the world, significant popular support for anti-slavery only emerged after—and often long after—key legislative measures had been introduced, and even then support for anti-slavery frequently had more to do with questions of collective honor and identity than a more principled commitment to human equality. It should be clear, moreover, that the construction of slavery as a bounded, exceptional category would remain compatible with other more conventional yet otherwise reprehensible practices, such as colonial conquest and related abuses. For a small group of political communities who were fortunate enough to escape direct colonization, the legal abolition of slavery ended up being implicated in larger efforts to defend political autonomy and collective honor. For ruling elites, (being seen to be) taking action against slavery represented a symbolic yet nonetheless significant test of their civilized credentials and communal virtue. This would be one of two main paths whereby slavery was abolished in Africa, Asia, and the Middle East. The second path involved the direct exercise of colonial authority. It is here that I now turn.

Chapter 3

British Anti-Slavery
and European Colonialism

On the one hand, we have the legal abolition of slavery, which has been repeatedly acclaimed as a great moral victory. On the other, we have European colonialism, which has been repeatedly denounced as a vast criminal enterprise. What should we make of the close historical connection between subjects that provoke such diametrically opposed reactions? In the last chapter, I argued that this otherwise perplexing relationship can be primarily explained in terms of the construction of slavery as a bounded, "exceptional" category, which was distinguished from other "normal" practices, such as colonial conquest, and the pervasive influence of an evolving relationship between anti-slavery and collective honor and identity, which saw the status of slavery feature prominently in more general appraisals of the "civilized" credentials of governments throughout the globe. This second theme is particularly important, because it helps to explain why European political elites maintained and further extended their official commitments to anti-slavery during the age of High Imperialism. If the Anti-Slavery Project had been primarily animated by a commitment to human equality, as some modern commentators have mistakenly suggested, it is difficult to imagine how it would have survived the growth of essentialist models of human difference, such as scientific racism, which posited a deep and insurmountable divide between "superior" Europeans and "inferior" peoples elsewhere. Once these themes are taken into account, it should become apparent that colonialism and anti-slavery were not contradictory, but were in fact complementary, contributing to a larger ideological worldview that not only legitimated colonialism, but also maintained that European "superiority" conferred a paternal obligation to "civilize" lesser peoples languishing in earlier stages of human development.

This chapter aims to develop this overall argument by examining some of the main issues and events associated with the legal abolition of slavery under colonial rule. To help make sense of this far-reaching topic, I have organized my remarks into four distinct sections, focusing on (1) the relationship between anti-slavery, precolonial incursions, and "informal" empire; (2) the ideological relationship between anti-slavery and colonial conquest; (3) the main categories and compromises that characterized legal abolition under colonial jurisdiction; and (4) subsequent tensions between official anti-slavery commitments and various colonial labor practices. This analysis concentrates on colonial Africa in general, and British rule in Africa in particular. Africa was not the only region where colonial authorities encountered slavery. Longstanding slave systems also proved to be a substantial challenge for the Dutch in Indonesia,[1] the Russians in Central Asia (Turkestan),[2] the Americans in the Philippines,[3] the French in Indo-China,[4] and the British in South East Asia, the Indian subcontinent, and elsewhere.[5] It was Africa, however, that attracted particular interest in anti-slavery circles over the course of the nineteenth and early twentieth centuries.

This not only reflected the final stages of the transatlantic slave trade, which continued illegally until the 1860s, but also reflected an ambitious program of social and economic reform based on a troika of Commerce, Christianity, and Civilization. Despite the extravagant rhetoric that accompanied the colonial "Scramble" during the later stages of the nineteenth century, European powers were reluctant to take decisive action once colonial conquest had actually taken place, resulting in a "slow death" for slavery that was frequently measured in decades, rather than years. By the end of colonial rule, "classical" slavery in Africa was much diminished although not entirely suppressed, but this unprecedented transformation would in turn be hugely compromised by the widespread use of other highly coercive labor practices.

Commerce, Christianity, and "Informal" Empire in Africa

As we saw in the previous chapter, the Anti-Slavery Project is a relatively new addition to the history of European imperialism and colonialism. When Iberian forces embarked on the conquest of their "New World" in the sixteenth century, they quickly turned to slavery (both African and Native American) to develop their overseas empires. Other European powers followed their example with tragic consequences. More modest colonial ventures in parts of Asia, such as the Portuguese in Goa, or the Dutch in Indo-China, also made use of regional slave systems.[6] The fact that anti-slavery played virtually no role in European colonialism during the early modern era means that we should be cautious about overstating its more recent influence. Organized anti-slavery added a new dimension to a preexisting template, and thus profoundly influenced the lives of millions of people, but the colonial and imperial projects that facilitated legal abolition continued to be primarily driven by other political, economic, and ideological considerations. If organized anti-slavery had never materialized, there would have been no shortage of other justifications or motivations for colonial conquests in Africa, Asia, and the Pacific. Framed in these terms, the main point at issue is the way in which the addition of anti-slavery helped to (re)shape the terms and timing of colonial rule. It is not feasible to talk of anti-slavery being a primary cause of colonialism.

The early history of the Anti-Slavery Project primarily impacted established colonies. This was not only an issue in the Caribbean, which was a key focal point in early contests over colonial slavery, but extended to territories in other parts of the globe. Prominent examples of this dynamic include British-ruled Cape Colony, which was covered by the 1833 emancipation act (leading to a "Great Trek" inland by disgruntled slave owners),[7] and British India, which first moved to end the legal status of slavery in 1843.[8] When the French abolished slavery in 1848 a variety of territories were affected, including colonies in Algeria and Senegal, much to the displeasure of local slave-owners.[9] Unlike anti-slavery legislation in the Americas, most of these measures applied to non-European slave systems, raising difficult questions about whether administrators were willing—or able—to combat forms of slavery practiced by their "native" subjects. The introduction of anti-slavery measures also tended to complicate relations with neighboring rulers, particularly when it came to the return of fugitive slaves and cross-border trading.[10] In order to reduce political tensions, both British and French administrators in West Africa introduced an artificial distinction between colonies and protectorates in order to restrict the geographic scope of their anti-slavery obligations.[11]

In the mid-nineteenth century, colonial rule in Africa was largely confined to a series of coastal enclaves in West Africa, growing settlements in South Africa and Algeria, and older Portuguese holdings in Angola and Mozambique.[12] The vast majority of the continent remained under the authority of African elites, raising difficult questions about how slave populations in the interior could be effectively reached. As we have already seen, the British government secured various treaties with political elites along the African coast, and rulers in Zanzibar, Egypt, and the Ottoman Empire, but primary responsibility for enforcing these treaties usually fell on the British navy, leaving slavery in large parts of Africa untouched. For most of the nineteenth century, European efforts to combat slavery in the interior found expression as part of more general attempts at long-term socioeconomic transformation, which aspired to remake and/or redeem Africa according to European behavioral models. Key examples of these ambitious efforts included the growth of "legitimate" commerce, the proselytizing efforts of missionaries, the formation of settlements for ex-slaves in places such as Sierra Leone and Liberia, and the disastrous Niger Expedition of 1841.[13]

The history of "legitimate" (i.e., nonslave) commerce is bound up in the final stages of transatlantic slavery. In the decades that followed Britain's renunciation of the slave trade, transcontinental trade in agricultural products such as palm oil, timber, gum, and groundnuts increased markedly along the West African coast.[14] "Legitimate" trade was routinely invoked as a vehicle for socioeconomic reform in Africa, which would indirectly promote European ideals and orientations.[15] For much of the nineteenth century, commerce was presented as a platform for supplementing—and perhaps even supplanting—naval interdiction efforts by establishing alternative branches of commerce that would undercut the transatlantic slave trade, or even slavery in Africa.[16] This approach was misguided on multiple levels. In the Bight of Biafra, to take but one prominent example, British vessels moved from trading in slaves to trading in palm oil, but their counterparts in Africa routinely "engaged in both trades simultaneously."[17] Even more problematic, however, was the contribution of "legitimate" commerce to a massive expansion of the use of slave labor in many parts of West Africa.

This new political economy is usefully summarized by Paul Lovejoy and David Richardson, who observe that "expanding production of commercial crops, whether for export overseas, as in the case of gum arabic and palm oil, or consumption within West Africa, as in the case of kola nuts, grain and cotton, provided a major impetus to slavery within Africa."[18] A key component of this process involved the integration of increasing numbers of slaves into regional production networks.[19] This transition has been much debated. Some scholars maintain that the shift to "legitimate" commerce signaled an important break with the past that facilitated the emergence of "new men," and thus posed "acute problems of adaptation for the traditional warrior entrepreneurs who had co-operated so profitably with European slavers during the days of the Atlantic Trade."[20] Others contend that established elites (at least for the most part) successfully adapted to the suppression of the overseas slave trade, and that the problems associated with adaptation have been either misrepresented or overstated.[21] There is, however, one major point where there remains substantial agreement: the marked growth in slavery and enslavement across much of Africa.

The scale of this transformation is encapsulated by Patrick Manning, who notes that "the last half of the nineteenth century was the period in which slavery expanded to its greatest extent in Africa."[22] In many parts of the continent the expansion of slavery was bound up in an aforementioned increase in the use of slave labor. This was by no means a uniform phenomenon. There were some places where slavery was not particularly significant, or demand for slaves remained relatively constant.[23] There were also important variations in the timing of—and reasons for—the growth of slavery. In most cases, however, the primary catalyst for expansion stemmed from increasing demand for various agricultural products (and their transportation):

> Palm oil came first from the Bight of Biafra and then from the whole Western Coast; peanuts came from Senegambia; and cloves came from Zanzibar to India. In Angola after 1850, exports of ivory, beeswax, and rubber arose through a similar dependence on slave labor.[24]

This process was indirectly facilitated by European industrialization, which significantly reduced the cost of producing manufactured goods and improved naval transportation.[25] Production methods in Africa ranged from small-scale ventures to large-scale plantations, with the latter evoking comparisons with plantations in the Americas.[26] The central role of slavery in many parts of Africa has led to discussion of a "slave mode of production," which can in turn be traced to the cumulative influence of centuries of involvement in complex slaving networks linking Occidental, Oriental, and African peoples.[27]

Warfare, commerce, and slavery proved to be a potent combination. Over the course of the nineteenth century, much of the interior of West Africa was consumed by a series of devastating holy wars, or jihads, which saw the emergence of new sites of political authority, the most notable of which was the

Sokoto Caliphate, where slavery played a decisive socioeconomic role.[28] Hundreds of thousands of Africans were enslaved during this period. In many communities, slaves came to represent between one-third and one-half of the total population. These new slaves featured in the development of large-scale plantations, but these ventures were often geared toward local requirements, rather than overseas trade. In keeping with historical precedent, slaves occupied a variety of other roles, such as soldiers, bureaucrats, concubines, and domestic servants.[29] This acceleration of slaving activities can be linked to growing demand for slaves in North Africa and the Middle East. This not only resulted in an increase in the volume of the Trans-Saharan trade, it also contributed to the parallel growth of slavery in Eastern and Central Africa.[30]

Another major focal point was the island of Zanzibar, which formed part of a longstanding pattern of Arab engagement in many parts of Eastern Africa. By the early nineteenth century, the island's Omani rulers had established a major commercial hub, which claimed (at least nominal) political authority over significant portions of the neighboring mainland. Slavery was at the heart of this achievement. Plantations prospered in Zanzibar, the adjacent island of Pemba, and on various coastal sites.[31] Zanzibar's other major source of income came from the slave trade, where peoples enslaved in Central Africa were taken to the coast and transported by the thousands in dhows to sites in the Middle East. The British navy waged a long and often frustrating campaign against this traffic, but made few inroads into the African interior until the late nineteenth century.[32] Overland slave routes flourished in this permissive environment, contributing to depopulation in parts of Central Africa.[33]

Europeans often had little or no knowledge of many of these developments. The dark continent rhetoric that characterized the discussion of Africa in this period not only reflected a set of claims about the "barbarous" customs of its inhabitants, it also reflected a collective recognition that much of Africa remained shrouded in mystery. European attempts to shed light on the continent would be chiefly framed in terms of the three Cs: Commerce, Christianity, and Civilization.[34] Commercial activity usually took the form of transactions with coastal middlemen, or exchanges with peoples adjacent to colonial outposts. The task of penetrating the interior chiefly fell on explorers and missionaries. Neither of these groups were exclusively concerned with slavery, but they nonetheless came into frequent contact with enslaved Africans, and thus constituted a key source of (mis)information for audiences in Europe. Famous explorers such as David Livingstone and Henry Stanley were especially prominent. Their exploits were followed closely in Europe, their published works attracted widespread interest, and their evaluations carried considerable weight.[35] In travel accounts from this period, slavery featured prominently as part of more general appraisals of Africa. Two overlapping images of slavery in Africa can be briefly highlighted here. In the first image, slavery was depicted as an emblem of the more general "savagery" or "backwardness" of African peoples. In the second image, slavery was depicted as a "blight" or "burden," which saw countless atrocities inflicted by amoral slavers and thus required European intervention to combat a terrible affliction. These stylized images both reflected and reinforced the underlying paternalism of Europe's self-appointed "civilizing" mission.[36]

Christian missionaries described slavery in Africa in comparable terms,[37] but found that their operations required compromise and collaboration where slavery was concerned. Missionary activity often revolved around African rulers, in the hope that elite conversion would have a transformative affect on whole communities. This approach proved to be particularly successful in Buganda, but often proved ineffectual in other settings.[38] African elites primarily focused on the political and material (dis)advantages associated with European missions, rather than theological issues, and were reluctant to embrace doctrines such as monogamy, which could jeopardize their political and social standing.[39] Most conversions instead occurred at the other end of the social spectrum. In many settings, slaves and ex-slaves were central to the development of Christianity in Africa. Some missionaries expediently purchased slaves in order to gain converts or, in the case of Sudan, "wives."[40] Others built congregations by welcoming ex-slaves freed by the British navy,[41] or by providing havens for fugitives.[42] The latter would be a contentious issue, souring relations with neighboring groups, undermining proselytizing efforts, and even risking armed retribution.[43] Other missions adopted a more pragmatic approach, favoring better treatment of slave populations while steering clear of confrontation.[44] For the most part, however, missionaries were widely—and correctly—viewed as hostile to both slavery and enslavement. This was particularly the case in Eastern Africa, where disputes over fugitive slaves sparked a series of violent confrontations with distraught slave owners, contributing to open warfare between Afro-Arab slavers and European agents.[45]

Missionaries had some success providing different options and opportunities for some slaves and former slaves, but their efforts affected only a small portion of enslaved Africans. It is unsurprising, therefore, that the tremendous scale of slavery in Africa overshadowed whatever qualified progress was being made. This is captured in a bleak assessment from the Jesuit missionary Richard Clarke, who concluded in 1889 that

> Commercial activity has not succeeded in substituting legitimate trade for the nefarious traffic in human chattels, nor in persuading the native chieftains that it is more profitable to carry on pacific barter with the European merchant than to capture slaves and sell them to the Arab dealer. Missionary effort has penetrated into the heart of Africa, but it is almost powerless in the presence of the Moslem marauder.[46]

When it came to slavery, missionaries probably had more success promoting anti-slavery within Europe than in bringing about reform in pre-colonial Africa.

Graphic accounts of the horrors of African slavery were widely circulated across Europe in the second half of the nineteenth century.[47] Many of these reports came from missionaries, who routinely sought to validate their activities by highlighting the "barbarous" aspects of African life, such as slavery, polygamy, and cannibalism.[48] The work of Cardinal Lavigerie, the French head of the Catholic missionary group the White Fathers, proved to be especially influential here.[49] The White Fathers established many missions in Central Africa, but struggled to operate in a hostile environment where slaving was rampant.[50] This was a growing source of frustration for Lavigerie, who embarked on "a one-man crusade to inform the western world of the horrors of a traffic which he held responsible for his troubles in Africa."[51] In 1888, Lavigerie conducted an extensive tour of Europe, making strident denunciations of the horrors of the slave trade that were well received by both press and public. His campaign gave new life to organized anti-slavery, leading to the creation of numerous anti-slavery groups and raising the profile of existing organizations. In Britain, Lavigerie's campaign helped to revive the fortunes of anti-slavery activists who had lost much of their earlier momentum. In continental Europe, the cause of African slaves received an unprecedented degree of public interest. Unlike prior contests over transatlantic slavery, which were defined by external pressures and elites, Lavigerie's crusade helped to generate significant (albeit mostly short-lived) popular support for anti-slavery across Europe.

Like many who came before him, Lavigerie proved to be better at diagnosing the problem than formulating specific solutions. His preferred strategy called for a force of European volunteers to take up arms against slavers, but this faltered in the face of national cleavages, funding problems, and the pace of international events. Lavigerie's immediate political legacy was the Brussels Conference of 1889–90, a high-profile international forum dedicated to slavery in Africa. After much wrangling, conference delegates endorsed a convention obliging signatories to take modest steps against the slave trade in Africa.[52] From a political standpoint, the most significant outcome of Brussels was not the specific text of the agreement, but was instead its more general role in providing further legal and ideological ammunition for colonial conquest. When the pace of colonial conquest in Africa accelerated rapidly toward end of the nineteenth century, it followed closely in the wake of the failure of various anti-slavery schemes in Africa and overheated anti-slavery rhetoric in Europe.

The mid-nineteenth century is frequently characterized as a period of British global hegemony. This description does not work particularly well within Europe, where British influence was circumscribed by other Great Powers, but it does have considerable resonance in many other parts of the globe, where a combination of naval dominance and commercial preeminence underwrote British dominion.[53] British hegemony has often been loosely divided into formal and informal empire. The former refers to cases where British agents exercised formal legal authority, such as in India or Australia. The latter is a more diffuse concept, which represents an attempt to come to terms with imperial influence over the operations of ostensibly independent territories. The informal dimension of empire was first highlighted by John Gallagher and Ronald Robinson in their classic exposition on the "imperialism of free trade," which maintained that British empire should not be reduced to direct colonial authority, but also embraced to informal dominion in much of Africa, Latin America, East Asia, and the Middle East.[54] In all of these regions, Britain has been described as having "an 'empire' of effective control without formal responsibility."[55] This informal empire is usually connected to British policies toward market access and market domination, supported by naval supremacy, military force, and economic leverage. Yet the concept of informal empire—much like that of imperialism—can plausibly cover a wide range of relationships and varying degrees of authority.[56] It is generally agreed that Britain enjoyed a preeminent position in places such as China, Brazil, and the Levant, but the magnitude and composition of their regional standing remains open to differing interpretations.[57]

Britain's informal empire is traditionally held to include parts of pre-colonial Africa.[58] For much of North Africa—Egypt in particular—anti-slavery intervention emerged as a byproduct of a more general pattern of British influence. In other regions, this relationship was reversed, with anti-slavery playing a major role in the development of informal empire. This is particularly evident in West Africa, where Britain's multipronged campaign against maritime slave trading included an impressive naval presence, the construction of an elaborate treaty network, and the consolidation of coastal enclaves such as Sierra Leone and Lagos. Of particular importance here was the prospect— and periodic practice—of blockade and bombardment by the royal navy, which established Britain as a major regional power.[59] The resources deployed to secure this status were not reducible to the economic value of "legitimate" commerce, and were not justified by any overarching strategic imperative.[60] A comparable story can be told in Eastern Africa, where "British influence in Zanzibar, dominant thanks to the exertions of Consul Kirk, placed the heritage of Arab command on the mainland at British disposal."[61] This position was similarly bound up in a long running campaign against the East African slave trade, which again fell on the British navy.[62]

Anti-slavery not only provided a major catalyst for informal empire in Africa, it also exposed some of the limits of British hegemony. The concept of informal empire evokes an image of unchecked power, which tends to understate the practical constraints on effective authority.[63] When it came to slavery in pre-colonial Africa, British agents consistently fought an uphill battle characterized by repeated failures and compromises. Their exertions are most apparent in an array of anti-slavery agreements forced on reluctant elites, but enforcing these agreements proved to be a different matter entirely. For much of the nineteenth century, British agents and their counterparts in continental Europe sought to combat both slavery and enslavement in Africa using indirect methods, but they ultimately made limited headway. Buoyed by a variety of factors, slavery in Africa reached its historical zenith. As we shall see, the main factor that brought this growth to an end was the rapid (and largely unexpected) expansion of colonial authority in Africa from the late 1870s onward.

Anti-Slavery and the "Scramble" for Africa

In the late nineteenth century, European powers collectively embarked on an unprecedented land grab. By the time of the Great War, Abyssinia and (at least nominally) Liberia remained the only independent polities in Africa. For centuries, European activities had been confined to commercial relationships and a limited number of colonies and trading posts. The pace of these operations had quickened in the nineteenth century, but there were few indications that such a fundamental change was imminent.[64] Yet when we place developments in Africa alongside those in other parts of the world, the Scramble emerges as an extension and escalation of comparable ventures in Oceania, Central Asia, the Far East, North America, and the Indian subcontinent.[65] Considered in this light, the partition of Africa can perhaps be best understood as the most prominent example of a larger global trend.[66]

Enormous energies have been devoted to detecting the underlying forces behind the Scramble for Africa. This has resulted in the identification of many contributing factors, rather than a singular overarching cause. Some scholars have highlighted the influence of issues within Europe, including nationalist sentiments, economic dynamics, Great Power politics, populist displacement, and commercial maneuvering. Others have concentrated on developments in Africa itself, including frontier turmoil, economic dislocation, military adventurism, the opportunism of chartered companies, and the strategic ramifications of Egyptian annexation.[67] All of these factors can in turn be linked together using a punctuated equilibrium model, which builds on the idea that there were a series of key tipping points that in turn precipitated a more general shift to rapid colonial expansion.[68] It clear, moreover, that underlying structural changes, such as the pace of technological innovation and the distribution of material capabilities, also made a significant contribution.

The main purpose of this brief snapshot is to situate anti-slavery within a larger historical complex. It is not my intention to adjudicate between competing perspectives. Among the many factors that contributed to the Scramble for Africa, the influence of the Anti-Slavery Project is apparent in three main spheres. First, there is the aforementioned contribution of anti-slavery to the contours of informal empire. British agents secured a major portion of the territorial spoils in Africa. When the Scramble began in earnest in the 1880s, the cumulative effects of previous anti-slavery campaigns helped to ensure that Britain was well placed to secure new colonies on both sides of the continent. Second, there is the way in which anti-slavery was routinely invoked to justify and legitimate particular policies. This was a widespread phenomenon that acquired salience with the British bombardment of Lagos in 1851 and continued until the Italian conquest of Abyssinia in 1935. It was also a theme that was universally embraced throughout Europe. Britain was again at the forefront of this larger trend. Numerous acts of colonial expansion were at least partially justified on anti-slavery grounds, from the conquest of the Sokoto Caliphate in Northern Nigeria, to Anglo-Egyptian campaigns in the Sudan.[69] This was not only a matter of providing a justification for specific wars of conquest, but also proved useful when it came to individual policy preferences, such as the Anglo-German naval blockade of Eastern Africa in 1890,[70] or British funding for the Ugandan railroad.[71] For most European diplomats and adventurers anti-slavery convictions were (at best) of secondary importance, but they proved to be a useful cloak for policies that were chiefly driven by other considerations.

The final contribution of anti-slavery is rooted in prevailing ideologies of European civilization. The Scramble for Africa saw European powers engage in a complex mix of competition and collaboration. However misguided they might appear in hindsight, calculations of strategic advantage were undoubtedly an integral part of the often elaborate political maneuvering that characterized colonial rivalry in Africa. It is equally clear, moreover, that nationalist rivalries, together with an overarching compulsion to maintain international prestige, played an indispensable role in securing support for colonial ventures within Europe. Yet alongside these competitive calculations, we also find an unusual degree of collaboration and cohesion. This is particularly evident in numerous bilateral and multilateral agreements that were used to establish ground rules, assign spheres of influence, and demarcate boundaries. Unlike earlier colonial rivalries in the Americas, protracted military confrontations consistently involved warfare against Africans, rather than conflict among Europeans.

Europeans may have divided along national lines in their interactions with each other, but they conceived their relations with the peoples of Africa in terms of a common civilization, which included many nationalities. When considering the relative merits of peoples and practices in a continent dominated by other faiths, traditional cleavages between Protestants and Catholics were at least partially subsumed under a mutual commitment to Christianity. When it came to Afro-European relations, Europeans endorsed a shared vision of Africa, in which a benighted and backward continent would be gradually reformed by the enlightened agents of the preeminent civilization in the world. They may have preferred their national grouping (or religious faction) to play a prominent (or even paramount) role in bringing civilization to Africa, but they also viewed their endeavors as part of a collaborative enterprise, involving laudable contributions from other European powers.[72]

This helped to imbue the Scramble for Africa—and colonialism more generally—with a degree of coherence and conviction, suggesting that there was more at stake than small-minded squabbles and territorial aggrandizement. Following Livingstone, Lavigerie, and others, European audiences embraced evocative images of the exploits of unscrupulous slavers as a powerful symbol of the divide between "civilization" and "barbarity." As we saw in previous chapters, being officially committed to anti-slavery not only represented a symbolic referendum on collective honor and identity, it was also bound up in allied models of benevolent paternalism and the protection of "lesser" peoples. When the Scramble for Africa rapidly divided the entire continent into colonial fiefdoms, few Europeans doubted that colonialism would be a boon for Africa. For societies weaned on the idea that their shared civilization was the pinnacle of human progress, it was difficult to come to any other conclusion. Unfortunately, this endorsement was often little more than an article of faith, resulting in an enduring divide between expectations in Europe and practices in Africa.

Colonial Rule and the "Slow Death" of Slavery in Africa

The history of slavery and abolition in colonial Africa raises a series of difficult questions, which require us to once again cautiously navigate between condemnation and celebration. This does not involve a retroactive balance sheet, which attempts to weigh overall positives and negatives, but instead raises the more difficult issue of how organized anti-slavery, however compromised, nonetheless persisted alongside concurrent patterns of colonial exploitation and abuse. As we have already seen, the easiest way to resolve this conundrum is to question the sincerity of anti-slavery commitments. Colonial Africa offers considerable ammunition for this type of argument. The three main issues here are the rhetorical use of anti-slavery to justify colonial conquest, widespread complicity in the continuation of slavery for extended periods under colonial rule, and the introduction and/or expansion of other highly coercive labor practices. In the Congo Free State and other parts of Equatorial Africa, anti-slavery ultimately proved to be little more than a rhetorical shield for a vast criminal enterprise, which led to the deaths of millions of Africans in the pursuit of rubber profits.[73]

To help make sense of this troubling historical record, it is necessary to return to the construction of slavery as a bounded, "exceptional" category.

In colonial Africa, European administrators and other apologists used two main strategies in order to minimize the scope of their anti-slavery obligations. Both strategies were heavily reliant on how slavery was (re)defined. In the first strategy, colonial authorities sought to justify a cautious and/or complicit approach to slavery by insisting that "domestic" slavery in Africa was actually "benign" or "mild," and that slaves should be regarded as akin to "servants," "serfs," or "family retainers," rather than downtrodden beasts of burden.[74] These categories may have been applicable to a minority of cases, but they ultimately provided a highly distorted picture of conditions endured by most slaves in Africa.[75] Some officials took this strategy to its logical conclusion by suggesting that those involved were not actually slaves at all.[76] Others maintained that there was little difference between slave and non-slave. This stylized formula is exemplified by a British submission to the League of Nations, which stressed that "it is very difficult to draw any precise distinction in the matter of rights and privileges between domestic slaves and the free born."[77] By deliberately minimizing the serious human rights abuses that were integral to slave systems in Africa, colonial administrators were able to call into question the construction of slavery as a bounded, "exceptional" category.[78]

When the main axis of comparison revolved around slavery and other "native" practices, Europeans maintained that there was little difference between slave and free. When the axis of comparison revolved around slavery and labor practices used by colonial agents, they instead favored a quite different approach, which was based on a sharp distinction between slavery and other forms of compulsion and coercion employed by Europeans in Africa. This was the second major strategy used by colonial rulers to dilute their anti-slavery obligations. During the early decades of colonial rule there were often few substantive differences between indigenous slavery and forced labor under colonial direction, yet European authorities insisted on making a clear demarcation between the two categories. This not only involved once again (selectively) treating slavery as a bounded category, it also meant invoking slavery to legitimate other practices on the grounds that they represented progress toward European models of wage labor. This strategy often relied on the wording of labor legislation that frequently bore little or no resemblance to practices in the field.

By using these twin strategies, colonial authorities sought to minimize the risks involved in confronting powerful slave-owning elites, while simultaneously justifying various colonial labor practices. It is worth emphasizing, however, that anti-slavery would not be entirely cast aside on either of these fronts. Here, as elsewhere, colonial anti-slavery policies were frequently geared toward minimizing costs, rather than maximizing gains. By taking action against slavery, however qualified, colonial agents often endured economic costs and political complications that could otherwise have been avoided if they had been prepared to unapologetically sanction slavery. As we shall see in the final section of this chapter, anti-slavery rhetoric would be periodically invoked as a rhetorical tool for critics of colonial abuses. However much European authorities insisted on differences between slavery and colonial labor practices, there were also alternative voices that emphasized similarities.

In many cases, the slow pace of reform can be at least partially attributed to long-term resistance by elites in Africa, who continued to regard slavery as a legitimate and valuable institution. This resistance was particularly effective in cases where European authority was relatively weak. For much of the nineteenth and early twentieth century colonial rule was very much a work in progress. The conquest of Africa proved to be a protracted affair, which often continued long after colonial jurisdiction had been officially declared. In some regions armed resistance continued well into the twentieth century. European authority did not emerge suddenly, but was consolidated gradually. Hamstrung by money and manpower shortages, administrators frequently relied on local intermediaries, who retained varying degrees of authority and autonomy. The qualified and often fragmentary nature of European rule, particularly during the early history of colonialism, was one of the main reasons colonial agents invariably adopted a cautious and even complicit approach toward slavery. The Scramble for Africa brought millions of slaves—and at least tens of thousands of masters—under colonial jurisdictions.[79] The Anti-Slavery Project was an alien intrusion, which risked antagonizing powerful vested interests, challenging substantial economic assets, and inflaming popular sentiments. In these circumstances, some form of accommodation was almost inevitable. The result that followed was aptly characterized as a "slow death" for slavery, which ultimately took place over many decades.

Throughout this period, European invaders of all nationalities embraced a further distinction between raiding and (large-scale) slave trading, which was seen as a menace to order and stability, and slavery itself, where a more circumspect approach was preferred, with a view to minimizing social "disruption."[80] The ravages inflicted by slave raiders—and the plight of their shackled captives—had long been identified as the most abhorrent feature of slavery in Africa. For colonial administrators, these continuing depredations constituted a source of instability, an impediment to economic development, and a challenge to European pretentions to supreme authority.[81] Unlike slavery, which was regularly characterized as relatively benign, slave raiding and large-scale trading were overt, unambiguous enterprises, where delay and equivocation were harder to rationalize or conceal. Since the continued viability of slavery depended on supplies of new slaves, which could be only partially met by new births among existing populations, measures to end the slave trade could be presented as a decisive blow against slavery itself.[82] Advocates of a gradualist approach to existing slave populations would use this logic to support their claims that the demography of slavery rendered a more proactive policy unnecessary, or even undesirable.

This does not mean, however, that the advent of colonial rule marked a definitive end to either raiding or trading. Where colonial authority was particularly weak, slavers operated largely unchecked.[83] In some cases, European powers tacitly condoned slaving by securing treaties that exempted particular regions from raiding parties.[84] For the most part, however, the consolidation of colonial rule gradually diminished, but did not entirely suppress. By the time of the First World War "open raiding and large-scale dealing had ceased in colonial Africa."[85] While large slave markets were closed, there were some regions where a smaller, clandestine trade (and even occasional raids) continued under colonial rule for decades. In northern Nigeria, regular patrols along trade routes persisted until the 1930s, leading to arrests for illegal slave trading and the rescue of captive slaves. One of the distinctive features of this clandestine trade was the predominance of adolescents and women, who were seen as more amenable to concealment and socialization into new roles.[86] Similar stories can be told in other parts of the continent.[87] In some settings, "marriage," "redemption," or "adoption" helped conceal slave trading.[88] While the intensity of these activities receded over time, periodic reports of illicit slave trading continued into the second half of the twentieth century.

Colonial authorities were much more cautious where slavery itself was concerned. In some cases, such as Senegal (1848) and Zanzibar (1897), slave owners were offered modest compensation when slavery was legally abolished. For the most part, however, there were few resources available to recompense disgruntled masters. These fiscal limitations exacerbated an already highly sensitive issue. Slave owners were predominantly concentrated in the upper echelon of society, and thus constituted a key constituency whose support was integral to the overall fortunes of colonial rule. European concerns about political and social unrest over slavery were by no means unwarranted. Anti-slavery measures played prominent roles in several popular revolts, including Britain's humiliating defeat by Mahdist forces in Sudan.[89] In addition to reservations about antagonizing slave owners, administrators also expressed concerns about the responses of the slaves themselves. These included anxieties about vagrancy, economic dislocation, and the demands of former slaves on the public purse.

Despite these misgivings and the conservative inclinations of colonial agents, European intervention cautiously paved the way for the gradual decline of slavery in Africa. As we have seen, the overall tenor of colonial policy revolved around the concept of "domestic" slavery, which dominated official pronouncements and public discussion of slavery. The concept of domestic slavery was based on a distinction between "trade" slaves, who endured an unhappy existence characterized by capture, transit, isolation, and sale, and the plantation slaves of the Americas. The first axis distinguished domestic slavery from the more overt forms of violence and degradation associated with capturing, transporting, and marketing slaves.[90] The second axis established a distinction between the heinous forms of exploitation popularly associated with slavery in the Americas, and the ostensibly favorable treatment held to exemplify "domestic" slavery.[91]

This formula stressed the integrative aspects of slavery in Africa, where many long-serving slaves, or their descendants, could be gradually incorporated into the familial and social networks of their master, and were thus said to be relatively contented with their personal circumstances. Within this ideological framework, the gradual abolition of domestic slavery would be widely endorsed as both responsible and desirable. Recent scholarship has challenged the concept of domestic slavery on a number of fronts, ranging from questions about whether slavery in Africa was especially benign, to deeper conundrums regarding the imposition of European categories on African practices, where complex gradations in status were common.[92] These questions in turn form part of larger debates, involving various attempts to come to terms with the complexity of—and records pertaining to—the history of human bondage in Africa. It is not my intention to enter into these debates here. In this forum, the main point of interest is the way particular categories helped to shape the political and conceptual horizons of colonial rule. From this vantage point, it should be evident that colonial efforts to (re) define slavery were far from objective or disinterested.

European governments repeatedly invoked the distinctive features of domestic slavery to justify a circumspect approach toward slavery, thereby turning expedient compromise into responsible policy. Over the course of the late nineteenth and early twentieth centuries, the legal abolition of slavery was proclaimed in many territories, including British territories in the Gold Coast (1874), Egypt (1895), Sudan (1900), Nigeria (1901), Kenya (1907), and Sierra Leone (1928).[93] It would be misleading, however, to take these dates as marking a definitive end to slavery. In keeping with larger historical precedents, administrators turned to gradualist models such as "free birth laws" or "apprenticeship" schemes, which were designed to bring about gradual change while minimizing disruption and dissent. As we shall see in following chapters, the most popular model was pioneered by the British in India, and involved renouncing slavery as a legal status. In theory, this allowed slaves who were dissatisfied with their circumstances to leave, or otherwise renegotiate their terms of service, because their masters could no longer rely on the state to uphold their prerogatives. Officials were not required to take a proactive approach to liberation, but instead placed the onus on slaves to signal their discontent. Supporters of this model tended to downplay the influence of countervailing forces, such as the limits of colonial authority, the psychological, sociological, and religious dimensions of enslavement, the role of local institutions supportive of slave ownership, and even the regular return of fugitives by colonial agents. When slaves continued to serve their masters, this was disingenuously presented as a personal choice that could be chiefly attributed to the "benign" character of domestic slavery, rather than a lack of viable alternatives or effective surveillance.

The gradualist approach favored by colonial agents ensured that slaves consistently played a decisive role in their own emancipation. This is captured by Patrick Manning, who observes that "If the slave trade in Africa was suppressed mainly through the actions of European conquerors, the actual freeing of slaves was primarily an achievement of the slaves themselves."[94] In most cases, this involved a protracted process of low-key contestation, which could span decades, or even generations, and typically resulted in a renegotiation of both master-slave and slave-society relations. This often meant that the fortunes of individual slaves varied markedly, based on whether or not it was feasible for slaves to relocate or remain, or to pursue legal emancipation or reach some kind of informal accommodation.

For every permutation there could be further variation. Slaves who remained with their masters often established new terms of service, but at varying rates and on varying terms. Slaves who relocated could end up forging new communities, returning to their place of origin, or being caught up in colonial labor practices that were comparable to the enslavement they had sought to escape. These endeavors are explored in further detail in the following chapter. At this juncture, it is sufficient to offer the more general observation that the end of slavery in Africa was a highly variegated process, and that it could often be difficult to determine when slavery ended and other forms of service began. In most parts of the colonial Caribbean, the legal abolition of slavery involved an identifiable population that experienced a uniform change in status according to a clear timetable. In colonial Africa, the end of slavery involved an indeterminate population, a series of qualified proclamations that often went unenforced, and regular gaps between colonial policies and substantive practices.

In this ambiguous environment, the parameters of enslavement emerged as a critical issue, because the way in which slavery was officially defined played a key role in determining the scale and severity of the problems at hand. As we have seen, colonial officials consistently sought to minimize the scope of their anti-slavery obligations. At the beginning of colonial rule, this involved sympathetic descriptions of domestic slavery and further statements about how slaves were "free" to leave if they desired. In the later stages of colonial rule, the focus of these efforts shifted to defining slavery out of existence entirely. This translated into sweeping declarations that slavery had ceased to be an ongoing concern, or was limited to diminishing pockets, or "vestiges," which were nearer to serfs, or servants, than slaves. In some cases, these conceptual gymnastics came close to suggesting that individuals should be not classified as slaves—regardless of their circumstances—simply because slavery was no longer legally recognized.[95] Few allowances were made for slaves who were not treated well, who were not free to leave their masters, and who had generally experienced little or no change in personal circumstances. By the 1920s and 1930s slave populations in Africa were no longer measured in millions, but there continued to be a sizeable minority of slaves who had experienced little or no change. Rather than addressing this situation, most colonial officials were content to redefine slavery out of existence.

It was not unusual for forces within Europe, both in and outside government, to take the lead in advocating further action against slavery over the objections of "men on the spot" in Africa, who tended to favor a more conservative approach. These metropolitan pressures not only provided the initial impetus behind legal abolition, they had an influence on events decades after slavery had been officially prohibited. The history of colonial Africa is replete with cases where legal prohibitions on slavery went unenforced.[96] This placed colonial agents in an awkward position. Since it was politically difficult (whatever their private inclinations)[97] for colonial officials to defend slavery as a legitimate institution, they were regularly forced to support its continuation on a semi-clandestine basis.[98]

The grandiose rhetoric that accompanied the Scramble for Africa—together with the larger "civilizing" mission on which it was ostensibly based—provided a platform for difficult questions about whether or not colonial powers were living up to their paternalistic "responsibilities."[99] In the specific case of anti-slavery, periodic challenges to colonial policies came from a variety of sources, including anti-slavery groups, media sources, selected government officials, and various agencies within the League of Nations and the International Labour Organization. These voices were seldom powerful or particularly numerous, but they nonetheless had a sporadic influence on the tempo of colonial operations, most notably when it came to the introduction of new anti-slavery legislation or the emergence of a more proactive approach to anti-slavery enforcement.

The work of the League of Nations Advisory Committee of Experts on Slavery provides an excellent illustration of this larger historical trend. Spearheaded by British diplomat George Maxwell, the Committee had considerable success during the 1930s when it came to uncovering differences between rhetoric and practice in British colonial territories. Cutting through the various euphemisms surrounding "slavery" within colonial discourse, Maxwell obliged reluctant colonial bureaucrats to produce detailed reports, rather than vague generalizations.[100] His most startling revelations came in northern Nigeria, where an official census calculated that there remained 121,005 slaves "still living in their previous mode" after three decades of British rule.[101] This figure was still questionable (a more recent estimate starts at 390,000), but it nevertheless provided an important catalyst for reform.[102] Similar stories of individual activism and public exposure can be found in other parts of colonial Africa.[103] In Sudan, to take another prominent example, British administrators were reluctantly forced into a more combative approach to slavery following strident denunciations of their informal support for Sudanese slave owners by Major P. G. Diggle in the early 1920s.[104] In the British colony of Sierra Leone, the legal abolition of slavery belatedly occurred in 1928 following adverse publicity in Britain surrounding a court decision upholding the right of slave owners to use "reasonable" force to recover fugitive slaves.[105] Throughout the colonial period individual activism and public scandal helped to provide momentum to anti-slavery policies that were otherwise prone to stagnation.

The contribution of these relatively small-scale endeavors should not be overstated. There were many instances where official proclamations that slavery had come to an end went all but unquestioned. Faced with political pressure and public scandal, colonial authorities usually responded with legal reforms or more proactive activities that altered the *pace* of change, yet nonetheless left gradualist models in place. In a number of cases, the focus of political critique was not the status of African slave systems, but was instead the systematic labor abuses perpetrated by colonial agents. Once the focus shifted to colonial abuses, there was usually less scope for either political critique or legislative reform.

Colonial Rule, Forced Labor, and "Slavery in All but Name"

Colonial policies toward slavery in Africa placed a premium on order and stability, resulting in a protracted transition that saw the terms and timing of anti-slavery policies consistently diluted by a range of countervailing factors. There is no question (particularly with the benefit of hindsight) that far more could have been to combat slavery in Africa. It is important, however, not to overstate this line of critique. When we consider the previous history of European colonialism in the Americas during the early modern era, the fact that European agents in Africa took even qualified steps to bring slavery to an end is quite remarkable. Throughout the nineteenth and early twentieth centuries, administrators in Africa could have avoided a variety of costs and complications by unashamedly endorsing slavery as a legitimate, long-term institution. From a purely strategic standpoint, the most logical course of action in many circumstances would have been to regulate slavery to prevent "excesses," such as indiscriminate slave raiding, but otherwise leave local slave systems largely intact. In fact, "There was no reason of pure economics why slavery should not continue, hitched on to capitalism."[106] During the nineteenth century, Zanzibar emerged as the world's premier source of cloves. This profitable trade relied on slave plantations and thus ran afoul of British anti-slavery efforts, constricting the island's economic prospects. By officially renouncing slavery, colonial powers not only created a series of headaches they could have otherwise avoided, they once again constrained their capacity to openly employ African slaves in the pursuit of various economic opportunities.

This does not, however, mark the end of the equation. Colonial authorities may well have taken qualified action against slavery in Africa, but they were also responsible for the parallel introduction and/or further expansion of a variety of other highly coercive labor practices. This relationship between anti-slavery and colonial forced labor raises difficult questions about whether anti-slavery ended up paving the way for other institutions that were essentially the same as—or even worse than—local slave systems. The issues at stake here are usefully summarized in a 1900 report by a British anti-slavery activist, who observed that

> We have done much to stop the stealing of blacks in the African interior for sale in the slave markets on the coast, . . . but we are increasing, instead of lessening, our appliances for bringing under bondage to ourselves, a bondage often more irksome to them than the older slavery, those whom we take credit for having rescued.[107]

Here, as elsewhere, the key sticking point was the terms and conditions under which labor was recruited, conducted, and remunerated.

Colonial officials consistently presented coercive labor practices as an unfortunate necessity, which stemmed from acute labor shortages, urgent public requirements, and the need to moderate the inherent limitations of "native" peoples. The language of regrettable necessity proved to be highly malleable. In the early years of colonial rule, it was regularly invoked to justify the widespread use of forced labor on public works, such as railways or porterage, where mortality rates tended to be scandalous and wages poor or nonexistent.[108] It also regularly featured during times of conflict, including localized wars of colonial conquest and the larger tumult of the two world wars.[109] During the First World War millions of Africans were forced into service using crude coercive techniques. As porters, African laborers transported great burdens considerable distances for meager rewards. Tens of thousands died on the battlefield, and of disease, starvation, and exhaustion.[110] As conscripted soldiers, Africans fought on fronts in Africa, western Europe, and the Middle East.[111] As a general rule, these burdens fell hardest on slaves or ex-slaves. This usually involved either fugitive slaves being forced into service or slaves being dispatched by their masters to satisfy quotas, or call ups.[112]

These activities were portrayed as "public goods," which were rooted in vital public interests. In this respect, they were insulated against wholesale condemnation, despite periodic scandals over mortality rates and working conditions, by an almost universally accepted division between public and private purposes.[113] Since there was general agreement that coercion could be legitimately employed in at least some circumstances, political discourse tended to gravitate toward procedural issues, such as when compulsion was appropriate, and the types of safeguards that were necessary to guard against abuse. This was typically framed as a matter of finding an appropriate "balance" between two legitimate concerns: the public interest and "native" welfare. Colonial critics periodically objected to the practical terms on which this balance was struck, but their voices tended to be moderated by their acceptance of the overall legitimacy of the principles on which colonial policies were ostensibly based. Further complicating matters here were ideological commitments to free labor and racial difference, which tended to restrain criticism of colonial policy.[114]

Public scandals over various labor practices were a regular feature of colonial rule.[115] One of the most disturbing features of these scandals was a recurrent gulf between the horrendous abuses that eventually provoked public or official comment, and the modest procedural reforms that were presented—and widely accepted—as "solutions" to the problem at hand.[116] Critical voices could sometimes have a moderate influence on the pace of change, but they tended to leave established models in place, thereby ensuring that any balance was consistently weighted in favor of colonial interests. This standpoint eventually found expression in a series of international conventions. As part of the 1926 Slavery Convention, which is considered in more detail in Chapter 5, parties are obliged to "take all necessary measures to prevent compulsory or forced labour from developing into conditions analogous to slavery," but this injunction would be qualified by "transitional provisions" calling for the "progressive" eradication of forced labor for non-public purposes. The Convention also included provisions for "adequate remuneration" and "competent central authorities," suggesting that forced labor was legitimate in at least some circumstances.[117]

These themes were refined in the subsequent Forced Labour Convention of 1930, which begins with a modest commitment to ending compulsion "within the shortest possible period," yet the bulk of the Convention is devoted to codifying a series of "conditions and guarantees" that establish when forced labor is permissible and the types of terms on which it should ideally be conducted. This second theme is evident in provisions dealing with age, health, taxation, transportation and length of service. The most significant restriction contained in the Convention revolved around a key distinction between public and private purposes, which called on signatories to completely suppress forced labor "for the benefit of private individuals, companies or associations."[118] This proved to be a thorny issue for many colonial powers, including the Portuguese and French, who failed to ratify the Convention many years.[119]

Coercion was rarely confined to public works, but also applied to numerous commercial ventures and questionable partnerships between private interests and public officials.[120] These would be primarily rationalized by an extension of the "regrettable necessity" model, where labor shortages and the "lazy," "backward," and "child-like" character of native peoples would be offered up as part of a more expansive rationale for compulsion. In French West Africa, colonial policy would be belatedly framed in terms of "civilization through coercion," where forced labor was presented as a "disciplining" and "educative" influence that would "protect the native against his own nature,"[121] and promote a "higher" work ethic. [122] To this end, the colonial state engaged in a range of highly questionable activities, from large-scale coercive recruitment for private enterprises; forms of military conscription for nonmilitary purposes; and compulsory cultivation of various crops, which were subsequently purchased for very small sums. This could result in a self-reinforcing cycle. Since Europeans of all stripes were generally unwilling to offer attractive wages in markets where potential laborers had other options and inclinations, they found it difficult to secure sufficient workers to satisfy their requirements. Faced with endemic shortages, administrators endorsed various forms of coercion, locking reluctant "natives" into highly unfavorable long-term arrangements enforced with threats of criminal sanctions. Being misused and poorly compensated, workers had few incentives to apply themselves, leading to misguided charges that they were unwilling to work.[123] Their experiences led to regular desertions and triggered widespread attempts to avoid further recruitment. In some cases, potential laborers fled to neighboring colonies.[124]

Once colonial labor practices became the main focus of inquiry, discussion of slavery no longer referred to African slave systems, but returned to the more familiar iconography of transatlantic slavery. When colonial labor practices were described as "slavery," or "slavery in all but name," it was the slave plantations of the Americas that served as the principal point of departure, not the "mild" forms of African slavery that were reported to be dying an inexorable death. In this formula, slavery was effectively equated with hard physical labor under onerous conditions in pursuit of commercial gain.[125] There was, however, one arena where there was substantial overlap. Throughout the colonial period there were numerous reports of African forced laborers making unfavorable comparisons between the "slavery" introduced by Europeans and earlier African systems.[126]

These types of comparisons introduce a series of complex analytical and political questions, which remain with us to this day. From an analytical standpoint, we encounter the enduring problem of identifying the point where specific practices descend into "conditions analogous to slavery." From a political standpoint, we encounter the even greater challenge of demonstrating that the line between slavery and service should be *drawn at one point, but not another*. These are clearly complex, subjective issues, which therefore remain open to interpretation and manipulation. In colonial Africa, this situation was further complicated by gaps between formal policies and actual practices, which meant that colonial policies often looked less objectionable on paper than they were in practice. This not only presented an analytical problem, since it could be difficult to catalog the illicit, semi-clandestine character of many facets of colonial rule,[127] it also presented a political problem, since defenders of the status quo were able to routinely dismiss reports of abuse as exceptional events or isolated incidents that were in no way representative of otherwise legitimate policies. Contrary information could be hard to obtain and was often anecdotal or impressionistic, and thus remained vulnerable to countercharges of sensationalism and political duplicity. Critics of colonial labor policies had to contend with nationalist sentiments, antipathy toward foreign interference, and the fact that all European powers were implicated in various forms of abuse, and were thus reluctant to challenge their peers for fear of having their own records questioned. On the surface, there were various safeguards against "slave-like" practices, covering a range of issues from recruitment and remuneration, to length of service and overarching purpose.[128] These safeguards may not have been enforced, but their existence nonetheless complicated efforts to mobilize political opposition against colonial abuses.

In order to further understand colonial labor practices, we need to make an additional distinction between the methods used to recruit workers, and the conditions on which their labor was extracted. When it came to recruitment, colonial authorities resorted to a variety of direct and indirect models.

Direct recruitment typically involved crude forms of "man catching," where many communities were forcibly uprooted and dispatched to labor on various colonial projects. Indirect recruitment involved a variety of somewhat more sophisticated strategies based around vagrancy laws, taxation/monetary policies, and penal sanctions and land distribution. These measures frequently had similar consequences to more overt forms of compulsion, but they were rarely conceived in the same terms. In places such as British South Africa and Portuguese São Tomé, colonial authorities made extensive use of elaborate labor recruitment schemes that saw hundreds of thousands of workers transported considerable distances to labor in mines and on plantations. These schemes theoretically relied on individuals consenting to long-term work contracts, but in practice they were usually based on either outright coercion or varying degrees of deception.[129]

On the other side of the coin, we have the conditions on which labor was performed, which could be similarly variegated when it came to remuneration, length of service, mortality, and working environment. Within this context, general working conditions served as a key referent, but the dividing line between slavery and service was once again complicated by wide variations in experience. When it came to recruitment and terms of service, discussion of slavery was primarily reserved for practices that occupied the most extreme end of a multifaceted spectrum, based on varying degrees of consent, coercion, conduct, and compensation. There were many circumstances where the language of slavery was ill-suited to the complexities of labor relations. In a number of settings (especially in urban areas) the "labor question" tended to be framed in terms of migration, "detribalization," and the growth of collective action and unionization, relegating slavery to a subordinate theme that was periodically invoked to highlight especially crude forms of exploitation.

There were two notable cases where colonial labor practices resulted in a large-scale political mobilization using the language of anti-slavery. The first case involved the Congo Free State, where a multinational contingent under King Leopold of Belgium engaged in numerous crimes against humanity over many decades, provoking a sustained political opposition under the leadership of a British activist named E. D. Morel. This protracted campaign successfully documented widespread, systematic abuses, including harrowing accounts of severed limbs, brutal murders, hostage-taking, and death and destruction on a massive scale. This resulted in thousands of public meetings on both sides of the Atlantic, and eventually led to the Congo being discussed in the highest circles of government.[130] The second case involved Portuguese

Africa, where enduring tensions between Britain, Portugal, and British anti-slavery activists finally erupted in the early twentieth century over labor recruitment in Angola for cocoa plantations on the neighboring islands of São Tomé and Principe.[131] Critics charged that this was little more than slave trading by another name, and that the "labor contracts" that governed life on the plantations provided a cloak for perpetual servitude. For British journalist Henry Nevinson, this amounted to "Modern Day Slavery." Following a trip to Portuguese Africa, he argued that slavery had been "driven to take subtler forms, against which gun-boats have hitherto been powerless."[132] Nevinson's 1906 book of the same name helped to spark widespread popular interest in Britain (but not other European states), leading to a 1909 cocoa boycott by British chocolate manufacturers.[133]

Both of these high-profile anti-slavery campaigns resulted in widely celebrated reforms. King Leopold was eventually divested of the Congo Free State and replaced by the Belgian government, and the Portuguese introduced new regulations and temporarily halted labor recruitment. From the perspective of the abused Africans involved, these reforms involved (at best) qualified improvements, rather than a decisive break with the past. The Belgian government continued to use forced labor, albeit on a lesser scale, and the Portuguese persisted with forced labor schemes into the 1960s and 1970s. This pattern is consistent with other lower-profile scandals over labor practices in other more powerful colonial powers. Throughout the colonial period, there was a widespread tendency to reduce systematic abuses to deviations, temporary aberrations, and isolated incidents. Most colonial agents approached forced labor as a legitimate enterprise (that potentially needed minor procedural modification), rather than a symptom of the fundamental brutality of colonial rule as whole.

Concluding Remarks

Over the course of more than three and a half centuries, around twelve and a half million slaves were subjected to the horrors of the Middle Passage linking Africa to the Americas. When Britain embarked on its belated campaign to end transatlantic slave trading in the early nineteenth century, an entirely new international dynamic was set in motion. Instead of being a legitimate vehicle for commercial interests, slavery in Africa was gradually redefined as a problem to be corrected. As we have seen, British efforts to address this newly discovered problem took a variety of forms, starting with a protracted period of intra-European contestation, and continuing with ongoing exchanges with non-European elites. In Africa, as in other parts of the globe, the British government pursued its unpopular agenda through a combination of bribery, coercion, political maneuvering, and indirect models of socioeconomic reform such as "legitimate commerce." Backed by the royal navy, this anti-slavery campaign had some moderate success curbing maritime trading in slaves, but it did little to affect the lives of millions of slaves in the interior of Africa prior to the 1870s and 1880s. Building on sensational reports by missionaries and explorers, European audiences came to view slavery in Africa as both an emblem of the "backward" state of the continent and an affliction to be exorcised by paternal intervention by European civilization.

Following the rapid conquest of Africa in the late nineteenth century, colonial administrators found themselves ruling over both large numbers of slaves and large numbers of potentially disgruntled masters. The expansion of colonial authority ended large-scale slaving, but administrators were reluctant to take decisive action to liberate existing slave populations. They instead placed the onus on slaves to take matters into their own hands, resulting in a series of protracted contests in which the fortunes of individual slaves often varied markedly. In this environment, official attempts to define and demarcate slavery would have important political ramifications, starting with the concept of domestic slavery, an ostensibly mild form of servitude that was distinguished from the horrors commonly associated with transatlantic slavery. This framework was initially employed to rationalize a conservative approach to ending slavery, but it later found expression in disingenuous claims that residual slave populations were not really slaves at all, but more akin to servants or serfs. By the 1930s, European colonial powers were regularly proclaiming that slavery had effectively come to an end within their respective jurisdictions in Africa.

These colonial proclamations were often heavily reliant on how slavery was (re)defined. The problem was not that there had been no change, since countless slaves had gradually forged new options and opportunities, but that few allowances were made for a substantial minority of slaves who had experienced little or no change. As we have seen, these definitional issues extended to other labor practices, where colonial authorities made a concerted effort to dilute their anti-slavery obligations in order to legitimate the continuation of various forms of forced labor. According to numerous colonial apologists, (at least) most forms of coercion and compulsion were sufficiently different from slavery to be regarded as legitimate. According to a much smaller number of colonial critics, (at least) some of these practices were sufficiently similar to slavery to be regarded as a serious problem. At the heart of both of these approaches we encounter a common problem: how can we define and demarcate slavery in an environment where slavery no longer has any legal standing?

PART II

Linking the Historical and Contemporary

Chapter 4

The Limits of Legal Abolition

The legal abolition of slavery has often been presented as a historical endpoint, fostering a misleading impression that the passage of anti-slavery legislation marked a decisive break with the past. This sharp periodization is reflected in a widespread tendency to organize popular histories of anti-slavery around a series of transformative dates—such as 1833 in Britain or 1888 in Brazil—which are celebrated as key moments when slavery ostensibly ceased to be an ongoing concern in specific jurisdictions. These complacent narratives have helped to conceal a variety of complex and enduring issues. Instead of signaling a conclusive end to the problems at hand, the legal abolition of slavery usually marked (at best) a qualified reconfiguration of entrenched socioeconomic cleavages, with former slave owners and their sympathizers seeking to defend their earlier prerogatives and investments, and slaves and ex-slaves seeking to carve out new options and opportunities in the face of continued opposition. These protracted contests over the boundaries of freedom and coercion were further complicated by various forms of government intervention, which saw public officials attempt to reconcile their anti-slavery obligations with a variety of economic interests and ideological agendas. From this vantage point, legal abolition can be best understood as a qualified first step, rather than a historical endpoint.

This chapter explores some of the principal dynamics that have shaped global responses to the legal abolition of slavery. Four central themes will be highlighted: (1) the boundaries of freedom; (2) the economics of exploitation; (3) negotiation and contestation; and (4) the search for "suitable" replacements. The first theme is concerned with the boundaries of freedom in post-abolition societies, and the continuing role of coercion and constraint in shaping various options and opportunities. The second theme is concerned with the underlying economic calculations that informed the actions and outlooks of both policymakers and former slave owners. Of particular importance here is a widespread lack of faith in "free labor." The third theme to be considered is the indispensible contribution of slaves and ex-slaves in contesting the established terms of both master-slave and slave-society relations. This offers a necessary corrective to a lingering tendency to imagine slaves as passive beneficiaries of humanitarian campaigners and great emancipators. As we shall see, many of the substantive advances associated with legal abolition were not passively received from above, but were instead bravely secured from below. With the fourth and final theme, I reflect on global efforts to identify suitable replacements for roles previously occupied by slaves. The main focus of this inquiry is the global expansion of indentured migration schemes following legal abolition. Here, as elsewhere, we encounter difficulties firmly distinguishing between slave and non-slave. By exploring each of these themes, the chapter gradually develops an overall picture of the historical limitations of legal abolition. This picture will in turn provide a foundation for the chapter that follows, where I argue that an evolving appreciation of these limitations has been the primary catalyst behind the gradual emergence of the category of contemporary forms of slavery.

The Boundaries of Freedom and Coercion

In order to evaluate post-abolition practices, we must first unpack the meaning of freedom. The familiar juxtaposition between slavery and freedom is particularly unhelpful here, because it establishes a binary opposition between two sharply demarcated categories. Taken to its logical conclusion, this polarized (and often highly ideological) formula tacitly suggests that transition from one category to the other involved a fundamental break with the earlier status quo. This can end up concealing underlying continuities between pre- and post-abolition practices. When it comes to the practical dimensions of the "freedom" associated with legal abolition, it is necessary to take into account a number of countervailing factors. In thinking about these issues, it is important to emphasize that "Legislation before and after abolition did not compensate the slaves . . . for their past exploitation, economic or otherwise."[1] This meant that most former slaves had relatively few resources (i.e., land, money, or social capital) from which to fashion new lives in the aftermath of legal abolition.[2] It is clear, moreover, that the experience of long-term enslavement could have enduring psychological and sociological consequences, creating complex patterns of personal deference and self-subordination that could further constrain post-abolition activities.

This suggests that a more qualified view of freedom is required. To help make sense of the issues at stake, it is necessary to make a distinction between two quite different models of freedom. In the first model, freedom can be understood in terms of individual autonomy, or "freedom from constraint." The legal abolition of slavery officially removed one set of institutional constraints, yet opportunities for autonomous action continued to be constrained by a much larger combination of institutional regimes, the (mal)distribution of resources, and established patterns of behavior. In the second model, freedom can alternatively be understood in terms of isolation, uncertainty, and vulnerability. Presented in particularly stark terms, this can be framed in terms of "freedom to starve." This second understanding of freedom offers a valuable insight into why former slaves in many countries sought to renegotiate their terms of service from within the social and economic orbit of their (former) masters.[3] Severing all ties with the life that they had previously known represented a drastic and rather uncertain step from the perspective of many slaves and former slaves.

In addition to these considerations, we need to keep in mind that the legal abolition of slavery was nearly always a tentative and highly qualified process. There were two main reasons for this widespread pattern. The first was that many of the policy-makers involved were not genuinely convinced that abolition was morally or economically desirable—or that slave-owners' rights should be overthrown—yet they nonetheless initiated qualified reforms in response to a variety of predominantly external pressures. The second reason revolved around additional apprehensions over the likely consequences of abolition. These ranged from specific concerns about labor supplies and the prospect of economic dislocation, to more general reservations about social and political unrest emanating from either newly freed slaves or disgruntled former masters.[4] One prominent example of this general point of view can be found in Frederick Lugard's famous work, *The Dual Mandate in Tropical Africa* (1922). To justify his conservative approach to ending slavery while governor general of colonial Nigeria (1914–1919), Lugard repeatedly emphasized the dangers of "sudden emancipation," which he maintained would have risked dislocating "the whole social fabric. Men wholly unaccustomed to any sense of responsibility and self-provision would be thrown to the streets to fend for themselves. Slave concubines would become prostitutes. Masters, albeit with money in their pockets, would be ruined; industry would be at a standstill."[5]

These reservations and apprehensions ensured that the legal abolition of slavery was usually structured around a variety of gradualist models. The three most popular models proved to be (1) "free birth" laws, where those born after a specific date attained their freedom;[6] (2) "apprenticeship" programs, where servitude continued in modified form for a specified number of years;[7] and (3) what is commonly known as the "Indian model," where masters (at least theoretically) no longer had formal recourse to the law to uphold slave status, yet nonetheless informally maintained many (if not all) of their established prerogatives. In territories where the "Indian model" was introduced it regularly proved difficult to distinguish between slave and ex-slave, owing to the complex variations in status involved.[8] Each of these models helped to ensure that "freedom" was rarely a glorious, uninhibited condition, but instead involved long-term personal and political contestation.

For the vast majority of slave-holders, the legal abolition of slavery represented an unwarranted attack on a legitimate and highly valuable institution. The characteristics and consequences of this perspective are usefully summarized by Robert Ross, who observes that: "Slavery was not abolished anywhere as a result of the slaveowners collective munificence but was always imposed on them by some outside force. The slaveowners reaction was to attempt to minimize the consequences of emancipation and to re-establish, as far as possible, the status quo ante."[9] These efforts to uphold the previous status quo typically involved both economic interests and ideological agendas. From an economic standpoint, efforts to uphold earlier prerogatives can be chiefly attributed to a desire to protect assets and investments associated with established slave systems, and to minimize the additional costs of securing replacements for roles that would have otherwise have been performed by slaves. In the first case, these efforts primarily concentrated on former slaves. This is particularly evident in many parts of Africa, Asia, and the Middle East, where qualified laws and questionable enforcement usually resulted in a "slow death" characterized by protracted periods of low-key contestation between (ex-)masters and (ex-) slaves. In the second case, these efforts to defend economic interests extended beyond slave status to incorporate other social groupings.

The ideological side of the equation is harder to pin down. To help make sense of this topic, I follow Paul Lovejoy in using the concept of ideology as a way of capturing the complex array of intersubjective ideals and communal orientations that helped to situate slavery within a larger social order.[10] From this vantage point, the roles of both master and slave can be connected to underlying forms of social hierarchy and self-identification.[11] For (elite) slaveholders, personal deference and elevated social recognition were nothing less than their rightful due, since this was the natural order of things. Similarly, inferiority and dependency could be the natural lot of a slave. The legal abolition of slavery (at least officially) brought an end to the formal dimensions of this relationship, but could not (at least immediately) overturn its ideological foundations. When former slave owners sought to defend their prerogatives, they were not only protecting their economic fortunes, they were protecting their "rightful" standing within a larger social order. In many parts of the globe, it was not uncommon for slaves and ex-slaves to attach considerable importance to established relationships, however exploitative, and to the culture and community into which they had previously been socialized. This was not simply a matter of a lack of viable alternatives, but also reflected deeper questions of personal identity and social membership.[12]

The influence of ideology extends to allied models of collective honor and benevolent paternalism. As we saw in previous chapters, the legal abolition of slavery usually had little to do with a cosmopolitan commitment to human or racial equality, but can instead be primarily traced to more parochial questions of collective honor and identity. This not only had profound implications for the political dynamics surrounding legal abolition, it also had a further influence on post-abolition practices. When slavery was legally abolished in colonial Africa, the increasing use of forced labor was routinely justified by pointing out the innate limitations of "native" peoples. If Africans had been regarded as equals, various forms of coercion and compulsion would have been far more controversial (yet perhaps still not wholly illegitimate). The Anti-Slavery Project did not do away with ideological cleavages and social hierarchies, but instead introduced a qualified claim that even peoples at the bottom of the social and racial pecking order should not be officially enslaved. As long as this standard was (ostensibly) satisfied, differential forms of status, treatment, and entitlement were widely regarded as entirely legitimate. In this environment, policymakers found it relatively easy to introduce various forms of discrimination and selective treatment that would now be antithetical to the egalitarian sensibilities of a more modern audience. This far-reaching dynamic incorporated relationships *between* communities, such as European colonizers and "native" peoples, and relationships *within* communities, such as caste distinctions in India or racial differences in the United States. The vast majority of former slaves found themselves in "inferior" groups within these social hierarchies, ensuring their "freedom" was circumscribed by both social disabilities and discriminatory policies.

The preceding analysis has highlighted a number of core issues that had a profound influence on post-abolition practices throughout the globe. While these general themes can be found wherever slavery was legally abolished, their specific influence would be mediated by a variety of more case-specific considerations. On this front, it is important to emphasize that legal abolition usually involved one of three trajectories. In the first trajectory, legal abolition involved a uniform change in status according to a clearly defined timetable under the direction of a powerful central authority. This meant that there was a clear separation between slave and ex-slave, and the transition between categories was relatively clear-cut. This trajectory is most apparent in the colonial Caribbean, and included both Britain (1833) and France (1848). In the second trajectory, the passage of legal abolition was bound up in armed conflict or rebellion, and therefore involved a more variable process that saw some slaves escape from their masters, or take up arms, while many of their peers remained in bondage. This meant that the categories of slave and ex-slave were more fluid, but this ambiguity was usually clarified (one way or the other) once the conflict ended. This historical pattern could be found in Cuba, Haiti, the southern United States, and many parts of Latin America. In the final variant, legal abolition involved the introduction of (qualified) laws that were (at best) only partially enforced by weak central authorities, thereby ensuring that slavery and other servile relationships continued decades after legal abolition. This meant that it was often very difficult to clearly distinguish between slave and ex-slave. This trajectory could be found in most parts of Africa, Asia, and the Middle East.

Another variable that had a major influence on post-abolition outcomes was the relative socioeconomic importance of slavery prior to legal abolition. This issue can be best understood in terms of a stylized distinction between "slave societies" and "societies with slaves."[13] The concept of a slave society refers to a community where slavery played an especially dominant socioeconomic role. This can be juxtaposed with societies with slaves, where slavery was part of the prevailing order, but was not central to the organization of society. In slave societies—such as the southern United States or the Sokoto Caliphate—legal abolition involved reconfiguring the foundations of both economy and society. For societies with slaves—such as Mexico or Egypt—

legal abolition proved to be much less of an adjustment, because the main centers of economic and social life lay elsewhere. One of the main points at issue here was the link between slave labor and commercial activity. In societies with slaves, it was not uncommon for slaves to occupy a variety of noncommercial roles, such as soldiers, sacrifices, bureaucrats, and concubines. It proved easier to reconfigure these noncommercial roles than to replace the contribution of slave labor in slave societies.

The Economics of Exploitation

The legal abolition of slavery presented a series of profound economic challenges for slave societies. Once slavery was officially abolished, both former slave owners and policy-makers were compelled to cultivate alternative means of securing labor on favorable commercial terms. In responding to this challenge, political and economic elites in many jurisdictions regularly displayed a notable lack of faith in the competitive advantages of "free labor." This widespread lack of confidence runs against the grain of modern economic theory, which is predicated on the idea that slave labor is less efficient than free labor. This idea has a long and complex history.[14] Its most famous advocate was Adam Smith, who maintained that "the experience of all nations . . . demonstrates that the work done by slaves, though it appears to cost only their maintenance, is in the end the dearest of any."[15] Smith attributed this state of affairs to the fact the slaves had few incentives to apply themselves, and thus required the threat of violence to work beyond what was necessary for their own subsistence.

Smith offered no conclusive economic data to support his argument, but this did not prevent it from being (somewhat belatedly) taken up by the British anti-slavery movement as part of their anti-slavery campaign in the 1820s.[16] As we saw in Chapter 2, the success of organized anti-slavery brought about profound changes in the way in which slavery tended to be conceptualized and discussed over the course of the nineteenth century. This chiefly found expression in a form of historical inversion, whereby the absence of slavery came to be viewed as "normal" rather than remarkable, together with a widespread belief that slavery constituted a (somewhat regrettable) feature of an earlier phase in human development. From here, it was easy to take the further step of treating slavery as an archaic economic system that had invariably come to an end because it was unable to compete with the more modern alternatives offered by liberal capitalism.[17] Taken to its logical conclusion, this economic reductionism suggested that legal abolition was actually in the interests of the slave-holders themselves, if only their judgment had not been clouded by irrational attachments.

There are a number of historical and analytical problems with the general idea that free labor is more efficient than unfree labor. There may very well be macro-economic advantages to organizing an entire economy around free labor, but it does not necessarily follow that free labor will always be preferable for employers at a micro-economic level. In situations where labor supplies are limited, or the work on offer is relatively unattractive, prospective workers tend to acquire considerable bargaining power.[18] This may be good for workers, and even for the economy as a whole, but there may also be cases where slavery (or other forms of bondage) represents an attractive alternative for individual employers. This is chiefly an issue when it comes to situations requiring repetitive manual labor, rather than situations that require a more advanced skill set, or significant autonomy and flexibility. By assuming that free labor is always preferable, modern economics offers limited tools for understanding and evaluating the types of calculations that would come to define post-abolition practices.

One famous test of the economic efficiency of slave labor versus free labor occurred in the mid-nineteenth century. When the British government abolished slavery in the 1830s, it was initially hoped that the transition to free labor would improve sugar production in the Caribbean, but in most cases legal abolition moved the plantation economy backward, not forward. On islands where the ratio between land and labor favored former masters, such as Barbados and Antigua, some sugar planters were able to maintain earlier productivity levels, as many former slaves had few alternatives to the plantation. On islands where productive land was abundant, such as Jamaica and Trinidad, ex-slaves enjoyed a stronger bargaining position, resulting in relatively favorable wages, working conditions, and the growth of independent cultivation. By the early 1840s, large numbers of British planters were finding it difficult to compete with slave-grown produce from Brazil and Cuba. When protective duties on sugar were removed in 1846, many planters were forced into bankruptcy. Their rapidly declining fortunes were regularly cited by slave owners in Brazil, Cuba, and the United States as conclusive evidence of the economic absurdity of attempting to bring slavery to an end.[19]

This sequence of events can be at least partially explained in terms of two key variables: the use of the gang labor system and the prevailing ratio between available labor and available land. One of the most onerous features of slave plantations in the Americas was widespread use of the gang labor system, which demanded arduous exertion from dawn to dusk according to relentless production cycles, backed by the "discipline" of the whip and other cruel punishments. The legal abolition of slavery resulted in a dramatic decline in the use of gang labor on plantations in most parts of the Americas, because former slaves were now able to pursue less demanding and more rewarding employment.[20] The collapse of the gang labor system was one of the main reasons why many British planters found it difficult to compete with their slave-owning counterparts in Brazil.

In order to explain why some Caribbean planters weathered the legal abolition of slavery better than others, we also need to take into account the way in which the available supply of land influenced labor market conditions. In situations where there was a surplus of productive land, former slaves had more opportunities to earn a living, and thus enjoyed a relatively favorable position from which to negotiate wages and working conditions. In situations where land was scarce, former slaves had fewer alternatives, and were thus in a weaker bargaining position when it came to (re)negotiating terms of service.[21] In some cases, planters were even able to persist with gang labor. Prior to the massive population growth of the mid-twentieth century, there were many parts of the globe where arable land was abundant and labor was scarce. This may help to explain why political and economic elites displayed limited faith in free labor following legal abolition. This lack of confidence tended to be reflected in post-abolition responses. Rightly or wrongly, political and economic elites in the Americas, Africa, and elsewhere consistently interfered in labor markets in ways that are now completely antithetical to modern conceptions of free labor.

In its most recent incarnation, the concept of free labor is predicated on the idea that voluntary contractual agreements should determine wage and work rates, and that penalties for breach of contract should be limited to monetary damages.[22] While this formula is best understood as an idealized benchmark against which concrete practices can be evaluated and measured, it is still striking both how far and how regularly labor systems in post-abolition societies deviated from this basic template. As we saw in the previous chapter, this was a major issue in colonial Africa, where European invaders forced millions of Africans into service for both private and public purposes on highly unfavorable terms. Comparable practices can be found in many other parts of the globe. Throughout the nineteenth and early twentieth century, both former slaveowners and policy-makers regularly turned to other forms of coercion and compulsion to secure labor on their preferred terms. A useful snapshot of this dynamic comes from Frederick Cooper, who observes that:

> Never . . . has a slave community regretted its freedom . . . But emancipation—in the southern United States, in the Caribbean, in Brazil, and in parts of Africa as well—has been a time of disillusionment as well as joy . . . in case after case, a particular class . . . kept land from the eager hands of ex-slaves and vigorously applied the instruments of state and the law to block ex-slaves' access to resources and markets, to restrict their ability to move about, bargain or refuse wage labor, and to undermine their attempts to become independent producers.[23]

Many strategies were developed in pursuit of these goals, including forced labor schemes, taxation in the form of labor, draconian labor "contracts," forced recontracting, indentured labor schemes, debt-bondage, restrictions on movement and land ownership, penal sanctions for vagrancy or breach of contract, and even a legal obligation to work for others.[24]

These strategies were not unheard of prior to legal abolition, but they nonetheless took on much greater significance once slavery was no longer regarded as a legitimate policy option. While the scope and severity of individual policies varied between jurisdictions, they nonetheless shared sufficient features in common to strongly suggest that coercion and compulsion were widely regarded as the most effective means of maximizing labor productivity in the aftermath of legal abolition. If free labor had represented the most efficient alternative, these interventions would not have been necessary, since indirect environmental pressures should have been sufficient to advance various economic goals. It is possible that the policy-makers involved simply miscalculated the best strategy, but if this was the case we would expect to encounter subsequent efforts to correct their initial error by embracing free labor. This is not borne out in the historical record. Most of the involuntary labor practices that were introduced or expanded in response to legal abolition persisted for decades. Some lasted nearly a century.[25] As we saw in previous chapters, political and economic elites were often strong defenders of legal slavery. They later developed similar attachments to other forms of coercion, control, and questionable migration schemes.

The preceding discussion builds on a conventional distinction between free and coerced labor. While this distinction establishes a useful framework, it does not necessarily follow that they represent stable, mutually exclusive categories. As Robert Steinfeld has persuasively shown, this distinction is based on a historically contingent understanding of labor types that progressively assumed a fixed, immutable character during the twentieth century.[26] Focusing on Britain and the United States, Steinfeld argues that the traditional view of free labor as a system of "voluntary" agreements enforced by monetary penalties for breach of contract conceals recent changes in the boundaries of "free" and "unfree" over the last two centuries. Until at least the mid-eighteenth century, indentured labor was categorized as "free" because the terms and conditions of service initially stemmed from (ostensibly) voluntary agreements. Once a labor contract had been signed, employers in Britain and the United States had a legal right to imprison workers if they did not meet their obligations. Until the nineteenth century, the prospect of penal sanctions was consistently employed to compel employees to labor for the duration of their contracts, which could be measured in years. This not only illustrates the recurring problem of maintaining a sharp distinction between free and coerced, it also suggests that the behavioral models that underpin free and coercive labor regimes may not be as mutually exclusive as has sometimes been supposed.

Free labor depends on subsistence pressures (i.e., food and shelter) and pecuniary interests (i.e., monetary rewards) to compel individuals to reach "voluntary" work agreements. When people are desperate and lack bargaining power it is not uncommon to find these voluntary arrangements taking place on highly unfavorable terms, with workers enduring poor pay and terrible working conditions in order to maintain a tenuous livelihood. In its most extreme form, this dynamic can result in vulnerable individuals volunteering to become slaves to ensure their continued survival.[27] On such occasions, the language of "free choice" can end up being stretched to the point of incoherence. When it comes to differences between free and unfree, the logic of indirect environmental pressures tends to be contrasted with the more direct forms of intervention that are commonly associated with involuntary labor. This typically involves varying combinations of physical coercion, institutional compulsion, and restrictions on movement. This conventional distinction between environmental pressures (legitimate) and physical compulsion (illegitimate) undoubtedly has political and analytical utility, but it does not necessarily follow that these different forms of pressure are either qualitatively different or fundamentally incompatible. As the example of self-enslavement makes clear, environmental pressures and coercive practices do not always represent natural alternatives. There can also be times when they are complementary.

This connection between environment and coercion is particularly salient when it comes to many of the practices that fall under the rubric of contemporary forms of slavery. One of the key ingredients of modern global capitalism has been a "race to the bottom," which has seen many employers take advantage of poverty, inequality, population growth, and vulnerability in order to depress wages and working conditions. Many examples of contemporary slavery take this logic one step further by combining environmental pressures with additional coercive techniques. This means that victims of contemporary slavery—especially forced prostitution—regularly produce unusually high economic returns for their masters. By using coercion to restrict movements and further extend workloads, "employers" can reduce returns to "workers" to an absolute minimum while demanding exceptional exertions under unpleasant and unhealthy conditions.[28] In keeping with historical precedents, such as the gang labor system, this dynamic is chiefly applicable to situations requiring strenuous, repetitive labor, where those in bondage can be compelled to work harder, longer, and for less than potential alternatives. From this vantage point, the chief economic logic behind both post-abolition practices and contemporary forms of slavery is an individual desire for greater profits, and/or lesser costs, that might otherwise be available using other methods. This has far-reaching implications. If involuntary labor practices enjoy—or are even perceived to enjoy—competitive advantages over other practices, this has a major impact on efforts to bring them to an end, since the beneficiaries of these activities can be expected to have a vested economic interest in continuing human bondage.

Negotiation and Contestation

The preceding analysis should leave little doubt that the legal abolition of slavery consistently left a great deal to be desired from the perspective of slaves and former slaves. It is important, however, not to go to the other extreme of concluding that it was essentially meaningless, or of no consequence to those involved. There were definitely some cases where legal abolition (at least in the short-term) resulted in little or no substantive gains, but in most cases legal abolition was associated with a variety of qualified yet still consequential improvements in overall levels of consumption, family integrity, economic remuneration, and personal autonomy and movement, together with a decline in some of the more heinous aspects of slavery, such as public auctions, the gang labor system, widespread slave raiding, and the horrors of transcontinental slave trading. In order to make sense of these qualified gains, we need to take into account the indispensible contribution of slaves and ex-slaves—both pre- and post-abolition—in bravely securing moderate gains in the face of tremendous obstacles. This usually involved (ex-)slaves challenging the authority of their former masters through force of arms, forging new lives and livelihoods outside their masters control, and renegotiating their previous terms of service in a variety of ways.

These various forms of contestation or negotiation can be traced to behavioral models that predated the legal abolition of slavery. Over the last century, scholars of slavery have generated a rich and extensive literature examining the global history of slave resistance.[29] This literature has persuasively demonstrated that slaves were not simply passive victims, but were instead active agents who challenged their predicament using a variety of strategies. These strategies can be roughly divided into two main themes. On the one hand, we have overt acts of resistance, such as rebellion, flight, and even suicide, which revolve around slaves seeking to escape from enslavement entirely.[30] On the other hand, we have more subtle forms of "day-to-day resistance" that saw slaves pursue a number of different strategies in order to improve their lives while still enslaved. This theme is not confined to insubordinate acts such as stealing, sabotage, or shirking, but also extends to the qualified development of personal relationships, economic spaces, and cultural, religious, and social ties in the face of tremendous obstacles.[31] In theory, slaves were passive extensions of their masters. In practice, they were proactive agents who resisted their inhuman predicament.

These various forms of resistance had profound implications for post-abolition practices. As we have already seen, the legal abolition of slavery represented (at best) an imperfect change in official status, rather than a point of demarcation between qualitatively different eras in human relations. Once this is recognized, the long-term personal and political struggles that followed legal abolition can be reconceptualized as an extension and at least partial reconfiguration of earlier efforts by slaves—both individually and collectively—to contest their lived experiences of enslavement. On some notable occasions, such as the spectacular rebellion in (what became) Haiti, these collective efforts took the form of armed resistance. On other occasions, the legal abolition of slavery was defined by a series of long-term personal contests between individual masters and slaves. At both extremes—and in various combinations in between—slaves and former slaves took advantage of relatively small windows of opportunity to pursue new lives and livelihoods.

One of the most important consequences of legal abolition was the (at least partial) relaxation of the severe constraints on physical movement that usually applied to most slaves.[32] This not only made it feasible for many slaves to leave their masters in order to pursue other opportunities, both local and further afield, it introduced a new bargaining chip for slaves and former slaves seeking to renegotiate their existing terms and conditions of service. Here, as elsewhere, we encounter significant variations between individual cases. Some slave populations, or even specific individuals within slave populations, generally found it easier to move than others. As a general rule, former slaves in the Americas endured fewer restrictions on movement than their counterparts in Africa. It frequently took great courage for slaves to sever ties from their former masters in territories where legal abolition was at best only partially enforced. Not every attempt to break ties was successful, but there were also a number of occasions where slaves left their masters in large numbers.

The most notable example of this theme is the Banamba "exodus," which occurred in West Africa during the 1900s. The exodus is estimated to have involved between 800,000 and 900,000 slaves, and thereby transformed qualified anti-slavery measures into a larger insurgency. Traveling as both individuals and groups, impressive numbers of slaves endured tremendous hardships to return to their places of origin, or to establish new communities outside their masters' control. French colonial officials did little to actively assist those involved, but they also refused to consistently intervene to support their masters.[33] Many of the slaves who absconded had been enslaved relatively recently owing to constant warfare, and thus had not been fully integrated into local kinship structures. While the overall impact of this mass exodus should not be overstated (a majority of slaves still remained in bondage, with female slaves finding it particularly difficult to escape), it nonetheless presented a significant departure from the status quo. Similar patterns of collective flight, albeit on a smaller scale, have been documented in other parts of both Africa and the Americas.[34]

As we have already seen, slaves in Africa frequently remained within the social and economic orbit of their masters for decades after legal abolition. This widespread pattern reflected a combination of socialization, effective surveillance, and a paucity of attractive alternatives. It is clear, however, that colonial intrusions introduced new ingredients into established relationships, and thereby created qualified spaces within which slaves sought to renegotiate their established terms of service.[35] This usually found expression in a cumulative reconfiguration of work arrangements, such as the number of days slaves were required to work for their masters, or the overall share of their labors to which their masters were entitled. Other prominent issues were control over the family unit and the capacity to pursue external projects. Their masters were often reluctant to relax their authority, so they frequently responded by restricting access to, or imposing new rents for, resources such as land and shelter. These overlapping responses collectively brought about cumulative revisions in established forms of dominion and dependency. While these contests were sometimes characterized by forms of collective action,[36] they primarily involved a series of individual exchanges. The usual outcome was not radical transformation, but modest change.

Another key variable that had a profound influence on post-abolition practices was prevailing gender roles. In the colonial Caribbean, to take another more familiar example, legal abolition precipitated a major decline in female labor on plantations.[37] This withdrawal was emblematic of the more general influence of socially constructed understandings of appropriate male and female roles.[38] As a general rule, the options and opportunities available to female slaves were severely limited in comparison to their male counterparts. Thanks to dominant forms of patriarchy, female ex-slaves frequently found it difficult to secure viable employment opportunities or other means of support outside existing socioeconomic arrangements. This was a far-reaching problem. Women constituted a majority of slaves in many African societies, and even in places where they weren't a majority they were still a major presence. Whatever else it may have accomplished, the legal abolition of slavery did not have a major influence on models of patriarchy and dependency that left women in subservient, submissive, and vulnerable positions. This was particularly evident when it came to links between slavery, concubinage, and marriage.[39] Colonial authorities were reticent to interfere in local marriage practices in many jurisdictions.[40] Faced with recurring difficulties distinguishing between wives and slaves, they preferred to treat "domestic" issues as a private matter, rather than a public concern. This enabled masters in Africa and the Middle East to use the language of "marriage" to retain control of their female slaves.[41]

There were two sides to this enduring relationship between slavery and marriage. In some cases, declarations of marriage would be invoked to shield against anti-slavery. In other cases, the prevailing terms of married relationships were sufficiently heinous to invite close comparisons with slavery. From the early twentieth century onward, this second theme found expression in the concept of "servile marriage," which refers to unions where (young) women are forced into marriage and subsequently experience severe abuses. As we shall see in the next chapter, this would be one of four practices incorporated into the 1956 Convention covering institutions and practices similar to slavery. Like all abuses that now fall under the rubric of contemporary slavery, servile marriage can potentially include a range of practices of varying degrees of severity. While definitions vary, the "servile" moniker is usually taken to describe cases where marriage entails a "purely commercial transaction, in which a human being is the helpless victim, herself no more than a piece of property."[42]

Some of the more egregious abuses associated with servile marriage include the traditional right to sell wives, the inheritance of widows (and daughters), systematic rape, involuntary pawnage, and kidnapping for the purpose of "marriage."[43] This tends to overlap with "everyday" discrimination, such as severely limited rights to personal property, unequal legal protections, and physical and sexual abuse. Once women have children within these relationships, they frequently find it difficult to leave their abusers, because leaving can mean either giving up all contact, or attempting to depart with, their offspring. Whether certain forms of marriage deserve to be associated with slavery remains a contentious issue. Even if we set aside less clear-cut cases, the fact that at least some marriage practices can be plausibly compared with slavery provides both a powerful demonstration of ongoing links between issues of gender and anti-slavery, and an important illustration of the power of socially entrenched practices in the face of legal injunctions against slavery.[44]

This ambiguity surrounding the boundaries between slavery and marriage was emblematic of a larger historical pattern, which saw most slaves and ex-slaves gradually merge into other economic groupings or social categories following legal abolition. As we have seen, the most common response to legal abolition was for slaves to seek more favorable terms and conditions for the performance of the same sorts of roles they had previously occupied as slaves. This usually led to the gradual integration, both socially and economically, of ex-slaves and non-slaves who occupied similar positions. This meant that ex-slaves were progressively incorporated into broader occupational groupings, such as peasants, soldiers, laborers, domestics, and artisans, and broader social categories, based around prevailing notions of race, caste, ethnicity, or class. In most cases, ex-slaves were assimilated into the peasantry, the landless poor, or found work as manual laborers. While movement across occupational roles was generally more limited, it further accelerated the declining importance of slave status as a clear referent or primary marker of identity.

This general trajectory is captured by Rebecca Scott, who observes that

> the entire concept of postemancipation society necessarily expands beyond the counterpoint of former master and former slave to a world of employers and employees, patrons and clients, planters and small holders, in which these cross-cutting pairs do not strictly correspond to the older division of master and slave.[45]

This process was by no means universal. As we shall see, there are some communities where slave status and heritage continues to be socially significant. These cases feature prominently in Chapter 6, but it is important to recognize that they now represent the exception, not the rule. In most post-abolition settings the diffusion of former slaves into broader socioeconomic groupings created a new set of occupational categories and collective identities. This is especially an issue when it came to efforts to identify suitable replacements for roles that would otherwise have been performed by slaves.

"Suitable" Replacements

The legal abolition of slavery was based on a set of underlying standards, or benchmarks. These standards were essentially based on two interrelated legal and ethical claims: (1) that slavery was morally reprehensible; and (2) that it should be legally abolished and thereby brought to an end. These claims may appear to be fairly straightforward, but they ultimately offer limited guidance when it comes to a simple yet profoundly important question: how can we define and demarcate "slavery" in cases where slavery is no longer officially recognized? As we have already seen, efforts to resolve this issue have tended to be heavily influenced by political, ideological, and economic interests. Over the course of the nineteenth and twentieth centuries, policy-makers regularly invoked the language of "true," "real," or "proper" slavery in an effort to reconcile their official anti-slavery commitment with a variety of practices and regimes that frequently shared many features in common with historical slave systems.

We first encountered this general theme in the previous chapter, in relation to self-serving declarations by colonial authorities in Africa that slaves that remained with their masters were not really slaves, but more akin to servants, or serfs, since they were ostensibly free to leave if they so desired.[46] Taken to its logical conclusion, this formula effectively suggested that there can be no slaves once slavery has been abolished. Variations on this line of argument proved popular among officials in many post-abolition settings. Faced with requests for information from international organizations on the status of slavery, government officials have regularly responded by briefly citing anti-slavery laws.[47] Confronted with claims that slavery had continued to be a ongoing problem, government officials have regularly responded by citing relevant laws as evidence of their anti-slavery commitments. In order to interrogate these responses, we need to distinguish between practices that have been actively supported by the state, and practices that have been prohibited regularly, yet persist despite efforts at suppression. Most of the heinous abuses that occurred in the aftermath of legal abolition occurred because of—rather than in spite of—official policies.

Wherever slavery was legally abolished, former slave owners and policy-makers were faced with the challenge of securing "suitable" replacements for roles that might otherwise have been occupied by slaves. In this context, suitability can be understood in two quite different ways. On the one hand, previous legal and rhetorical commitments to anti-slavery require—at an absolute minimum—that a suitable replacement be someone who was not enslaved. On the other hand, suitability would be primarily determined, at least at a microeconomic level, by more narrow concerns revolving around strategic calculations concerning cost, reliability, and efficacy. If free labor had been (widely regarded as being) economically competitive, this may not have been a major problem. Once relevant policy-makers determined that free labor was not suited to their needs, it was almost inevitable that these two different understandings of suitability would come into conflict.

By invoking a minimalist understanding of slavery, or more precisely, a minimalist understanding of the types of practices that are sufficiently similar to slavery to be rendered illegitimate, political and economic elites in many corners of the globe ended up supporting a range of highly restrictive and coercive practices. Many issues could potentially be highlighted here, but there is one theme in particular that stands out: the global history of indentured migration during the nineteenth and early twentieth centuries. Indentured migration was a form of contract labor, which involved individuals who entered into legally binding contracts to work for a set number of years being transported great distances in order to bolster the labor market. While substantial numbers of indentured migrants crossed the Atlantic to labor in the Americas from the sixteenth century onward, the legal abolition of the transatlantic slave trade brought about a new phase in the history of indentured labor.

Unlike earlier centuries, when migrants were overwhelmingly European, the nineteenth century was defined by a rapid increase in non-European migrants. This increase can be directly attributed to the staggered closure of the transatlantic slave trade.[48] Once slavery was legally abolished, plantation economies in the Caribbean, Mauritius, and other regions turned to indentured migration as a way of ensuring continuing supplies of relatively cheap and reliable labor. The vast majority of laborers came from the Indian subcontinent, with Britain dominating the traffic in indentured migrants in much the same way as it had earlier dominated the slave trade. Other prominent slave traders, such as France and Portugal, also played important roles. Substantial numbers of indentured migrants were recruited from parts of Africa, China, Japan, and various Pacific Islands.[49] According to David Northrup, over two million people were implicated in this global traffic, with perhaps 800,000 of this overall total being transported to various colonies in the Caribbean basin, and an estimated 455,187 migrants being transported to the British West Indies.[50]

In this context, the concept of a suitable replacement not only refers to cases where it was necessary to find direct substitutes for roles previously occupied by slaves. It also extends to other cases where economic solutions had to be found because slavery was no longer regarded as a legitimate policy option. This dynamic incorporates regions that had no earlier involvement in transatlantic slavery, but might otherwise have turned to slavery in other circumstances. Nineteenth-century indentured migrants were not only found in places that had previously relied on slave labor, but were also employed on large plantations and other economic projects in Malaya, Peru, Fiji, Hawaii, and Australia. If slavery had not been legally abolished, it is entirely possible that "employers" in at least some of these countries would have preferred slavery over indenture. By delegitimizing an otherwise potentially attractive model, the Anti-Slavery Project inhibited the expansion of slavery into new arenas, and instead compelled various economic elites to turn to related alternatives.

Some of the most egregious examples of "indentured" migration oc-curred in Africa, where French and Portuguese merchants purchased slaves from mainland Africa, forced them to sign labor contracts obligating them to work for extended periods of time, and then shipped the now ostensibly free laborers to Caribbean colonies and other plantation economies such as the islands of São Tomé and Príncipe.[51] From an African perspective, there was no "great moral difference between the French buying slaves to make them free at a subsequent period, and the Spanish purchasing them to work them as slaves to the end of their lives."[52] When pressed by skeptical observ-ers that this was little more than disguised slave trading, government officials responded by citing the "voluntary" nature of the contracts, their (at least theoretically) finite nature, and the relatively favorable treatment that labor-ers ostensibly enjoyed on arrival. While these weak justifications were clearly far from convincing,[53] it would be overly simplistic to treat every branch of this global traffic as nothing more than a new form of slavery.[54]

When it comes to comparisons between slavery and indenture, we en-counter similarities and differences at the levels of both policy and practice. From a policy standpoint, indentured migrants were (at least theoretically) volunteers, were officially entitled to at least limited wages and health care, were only legally obligated to work for a predetermined period (typically for five or more years, with various provisions for renewal), and were usually entitled to return passage home. This can be contrasted with transatlantic slavery, which was usually characterized by coercive acquisition, perpetual servitude, and a lack of formal wages. When it comes to actual practices, the picture tends to be more complicated and ambiguous, since not all inden-tured laborers had the same types of experiences. When indentured migra-tion systems worked fairly well, they still resulted in arduous labor for limited rewards, but this was not necessarily an exceptional occurrence in an histori-cal period where highly exploitative labor was the norm. When indentured migration systems were poorly administered and abused, unscrupulous eco-nomic elites were able to re-create many of the worst features of historical slave systems.

Policies governing the global traffic in indentured laborers were open to abuse at various levels. One of the most significant elements was the extent to which those involved voluntarily entered into binding contracts without an adequate appreciation of the issues involved. Although direct physical coer-cion was relatively unusual (but by no means unheard of), there was usually a significant amount of deception inherent in the recruitment process, with accounts of working arrangements ranging from overly optimistic to highly misleading.[55] This introduces a recurring question: what level of distortion is sufficient to invalidate "voluntary" consent? While some of those who entered work contracts were coerced or deceived in ways that rendered their participation far from consensual, there is evidence that others exercised at least some degree of choice, albeit on the basis of imperfect or misleading information. In this context, a lack of attractive alternatives regularly proved to be a decisive issue. A majority of indentured migrants came from India, where poverty and caste discrimination could severely limit individual opportunities. In this environment, indentured migration potentially offered a means of escaping poverty, or an unsavory personal history, even if the conditions on offer were far from ideal.[56] The available evidence suggests that many people were prepared to take a chance, regardless of the potential downside, because they were not enamored with their other options. These twin themes of deception and a lack of attractive alternatives not only had a major influence on post-abolition practices, they continue to feature prominently in the present day.

These variable experiences extended to the treatment of indentured migrants once they reached their destination. In some cases—especially in the immediate aftermath of legal abolition—there were few tangible differences between slave labor and indentured labor, with migrants regularly taking on the same sorts of work regimes, physical spaces, and punishments that had previously characterized slavery.[57] Other institutionalized forms of abuse included penal sanctions, severe penalties for absences or "underperformance," and various mechanisms for forcibly extending or renewing work contracts.[58] Local political authorities were usually complicit in these abuses and routinely used their institutional and legal authority to favor established economic elites.[59] It is clear, however, that not all migrants' experiences echoed those of slaves. While the terms and conditions of their servitude were undoubtedly harsh, the work grueling and the wages low, there were usually at least some opportunities to accumulate resources and develop personal and social ties. Most migrants stayed on after their contracts had expired, with at least some individuals moving into other occupational roles. Others returned home. Some returned with accumulated earnings. Others returned with little more than when they originally left.[60] If we accept that only a portion of the millions of people involved in indentured migration should be characterized as (all but) "slaves," it is by no means clear where the line between slave and non-slave should be definitively drawn, or what proportion of "slaves" among the total number of indentured migrants would be sufficient to render the entire system illegitimate.

These considerations had a major influence on the political dynamics surrounding indentured migration. Although public criticism was by no means unusual, especially within Britain,[61] key policy-makers were reluctant to consider total prohibition, and instead primarily focused their efforts on reforming the system to prevent serious abuses.[62] In response to public outcry, the British government eventually prohibited foreign nationals, such as the French, from recruiting in their territories in India. This decision was fairly painless from an economic perspective, because it did not directly impact on the labor needs of British plantation economies. When it came to indentured labor schemes operated under British authority, both public and political debate chiefly concentrated on improving the administration of a legitimate and valuable institution, rather than on abolishing a wholly illegitimate practice. By adopting a qualified approach that focused on the improvement of existing institutions, many critics of indenture at least tacitly conceded that the overall system was (or could be made) legitimate. Unlike earlier campaigns against the slave trade, which centered around the definitive goal of legal abolition, the main focus was on finding an appropriate balance between sufficient safeguards and valid economic interests.

This more low-key political contest favored those with vested interests in the perpetuation and manipulation of the system, because both the extent of abuse and the level of reform required were open to differing interpretations. In a similar vein to debates over colonial forced labor, labor abuses would once again be characterized as aberrant or exceptional, rather than emblematic of indenture as a whole. By offering assurances that new reforms would improve matters—which in turn required time to ascertain whether changes had occurred—both planters and policy-makers were able to defend their economic interests for decades.[63] Despite being less efficient than slavery, indenture was nonetheless widely regarded as an attractive option when it came to labor costs, reliability, and economic productivity.[64] If it hadn't been effective, it wouldn't have continued for so long. Indentured migrants would also be used by Caribbean planters to alter the composition of the larger labor market, and thereby also suppress potential wage demands from ex-slaves.[65]

British support for indentured migration only came to an end in the early twentieth century, almost a hundred years after the legal abolition of slavery in the British Caribbean. In the final stages, the principal catalyst for abolition came from Indian nationalists. Unlike earlier British critics, these Indian nationalists forcefully advocated a complete end to indenture. Once the overall legitimacy of indenture was challenged, the strategic manipulation of the ambiguity surrounding reform proved to be far less effective, because the question was no longer what sorts of institutional safeguards were appropriate, but instead whether the entire system was irredeemably flawed.[66] In this new formulation, the basic problem with indenture was not unscrupulous agents, or a need for further safeguards, but the institutional structure as a whole. Once this stark diagnosis had been made, a simple political solution became available: the immediate abolition of the legal status of indenture.

This historical trajectory offers a larger point of departure for evaluating the political dynamics that characterized post-abolition societies. The main points at issue here are variation and ambiguity. If millions of ex-slaves and "suitable" replacements were collectively located on a multifaceted continuum comprised of factors such as consent, coercion, and working conditions, it is clear that there would be persons at many points on a diverse spectrum, ranging from cases where there were no obvious differences between service and slavery, to intermediate cases where there were clear parallels but differences of degree, to further cases that stretched the link with slavery to a breaking point. In some ways, this can be viewed as a positive development, since it suggests that at least some post-abolition experiences represented a departure from most heinous aspects of slavery. The main sticking point, however, is the political and analytical challenge of defining and demarcating the substantial number of people who would fall at the bottom end of this complex spectrum.

These variations had important political ramifications. Unlike the earlier campaigns against legal slavery, the problems at hand were no longer always particularly stark or readily solvable. Critics faced a recurring gulf between policy and practice, where legal frameworks that ostensibly regulated legitimate conduct were subverted or ignored in the pursuit of underlying economic interests. Finding conclusive evidence of abuses was not always easy, and apologists for the status quo were able to dilute criticism by pointing to laws prohibiting slavery, and procedural differences between slavery and other forms of service. When abuses came to light, government officials frequently found it difficult to acknowledge that there was a problem, or to take remedial action, because they had often been culpable in allowing abuses to take place in the first place.[67] Governments could also be reluctant to strongly criticize practices in other countries for fear of having their own misdeeds raised in turn. This made it difficult to mobilize political opposition, and when opposition did emerge it tended to chiefly focus on complex and uninspiring technical reforms.

It is important to emphasize that most forms of state-sponsored labor exploitation were not limited to ex-slaves or their descendants. They also implicated a broader cross-section of relevant populations based on more general factors such as race, ethnicity, or class. This was partially a reflection of the way in which most ex-slaves merged into other socioeconomic groupings, and partially a reflection of the fact that strategies such as forced labor, vagrancy, taxation as labor, and racial discrimination could not be specifically targeted at ex-slaves, but instead applied more broadly. This dynamic was particularly evident in the southern United States and the British Caribbean, where institutional constraints on African Americans as a whole became increasingly prominent in the aftermath of legal abolition.[68] Many of the people who found themselves in slave-like conditions as a result of attempts to develop "suitable" replacements were not ex-slaves, but were drawn from other social groupings.

This is not insignificant. In the case of (ex-)slaves and (former) masters, their prior status offers a clear point of departure from which to evaluate post-abolition developments. The search for replacements would be one step further removed, as it chiefly involved other socioeconomic categories, yet could nonetheless be traced to legal abolition. If we move further afield, we also encounter other forms of human bondage (such as serfdom or some forms of forced prostitution) that were not directly implicated in the historical processes surrounding legal abolition, yet nonetheless shared various features with slavery. As this historical distance increases, questions about whether the problems at hand can be legitimately equated with slavery become even harder to answer.

The main theme to emerge from the preceding analysis concerns the increasing political and conceptual difficulties associated with defining, identifying, and quantifying "slavery" in environments where slavery has no official standing. It remains an open question whether many of the practices and institutions identified above should be equated or otherwise associated with slavery. In most cases there were similarities and differences at the level of both policy and (to a lesser extent) practice, but the key question should not only be whether or not they were identical to slavery, but also whether they shared sufficient features with slavery to be rendered illegitimate as a result of prior commitments to the Anti-Slavery Project. By adopting a minimalist understanding of (anti-)slavery that centered around "true" or "real" slavery, political authorities in post-abolition societies consistently answered this question in the negative. This recurring theme remains in operation to this day.

Concluding Remarks

Most historical slave systems were heavily reliant on the sanction and support of political authorities. This ensured that slavery was relatively vulnerable to political challenge, because it allowed opposition to be organized around a simple, straightforward solution: legal abolition (of either slave trading or slavery itself). It was not always clear how this solution would be implemented, but there was usually little doubt about what ultimately needed to be done. With the passage of time, the politics of anti-slavery frequently boiled down to a basic question: was slavery legally sanctioned or legally prohibited? There is no doubt that this line of argument was politically effective, but it also ended up leaving the Anti-Slavery Project with relatively little momentum once abolition had actually taken place. In case after case, government officials disingenuously proclaimed that the legal abolition of slavery marked an end to their anti-slavery obligations, leaving a range of closely related practices and systemic problems unresolved. As this chapter makes clear, the legal abolition of slavery can be best understood as an important first step, rather than a decisive historical endpoint.

Historical responses to the legal abolition of slavery can be connected to contemporary problems and practices in a variety of different ways. This overall theme will be developed in subsequent chapters, so at this juncture it is sufficient to highlight a number of core themes. First, we have the long-term (micro-)economic appeal of coercive and involuntary labor techniques. Much like forced labor and indentured labor schemes, one of the prime attractions of contemporary forms of slavery stems from calculations that they offer greater profits (or lesser costs) than would be otherwise available using other methods. Second, we have the long-term contribution of various forms of social hierarchy and patriarchy. Much like former slaves and indentured migrants, most victims of contemporary slavery come from "inferior" social groups that leave them vulnerable to various forms of exploitation and abuse. In most countries where substantial concentrations of human bondage persist to this day, we also encounter deeply rooted forms of patriarchy and social hierarchy.

Third, we have the long-term contribution of various forms of negotiation and contestation in the face of tremendous obstacles. Much like slaves and ex-slaves, the more recent subjects of human bondage have continued to challenge their predicament using a variety of strategies. Fourth, we have the long-term contribution of government officials in sanctioning and supporting various forms of human bondage. Much like their nineteenth-century predecessors, contemporary governments have continued to play a central role in sanctioning and supporting human bondage. This starts with obvious cases such as forced labor for the state in places such as Eritrea, Myanmar, and North Korea, but also extends to less familiar issues such as exploitative migrant worker schemes in much of the developed and oil-producing world. Finally, we have the enduring long-term challenge of defining and demarcating "slavery" in settings that involve a variety of experiences along a complex continuum. Much like historical critics of indentured labor and colonial forced labor, modern activists often operate in an environment where it is not always easy to identify simple solutions to complex problems, or to develop strong coalitions to push for further reforms. Having somewhat belatedly recognized the historical limitations of legal abolition, more recent activists have gradually embraced a broader and deeper understanding of anti-slavery.

Chapter 5

Defining Slavery in All Its Forms

Slavery is traditionally defined using a combination of individual ownership, property rights, and extreme exploitation. These familiar themes not only have been reflected in various legal instruments, such as the 1926 Slavery Convention, they also have dominated popular impressions of slavery for centuries, serving as a series of cognitive benchmarks against which many different examples of servitude have tended to be conceptualized and evaluated. In the aftermath of the legal abolition of slavery, various government agents and human rights activists have consistently turned to these core themes of ownership and exploitation as part of evolving efforts to define and demarcate various forms of human bondage. At the heart of these efforts has been a simple yet fundamental question: what sorts of practices and institutions are sufficiently similar to historical slave systems that they can be legitimately classified as forms of slavery? This question has both analytical and political dimensions. From an analytical standpoint, we have the problem of determining what "counts" as slavery in various illicit and irregular settings, which tend to be defined by varying combinations of consent, coercion, compensation, and working conditions. From a political standpoint, we have the additional problems associated with a recurring tendency to invoke slavery as a rhetorical device in order to prioritize various political causes. Rhetorical allusions to slavery have a long pedigree, and include well-known categories such as "wage slavery" and "sex slavery" used by both labor groups and feminist pioneers during the nineteenth century. In more recent times, the boundaries between literal and rhetorical slavery have become increasingly blurred, further complicating efforts to determine where slavery begins and end.

This chapter examines various efforts to define and demarcate slavery over the course of the twentieth century. By focusing on changes over time, I aim to demonstrate that the recent emergence of the category of "contemporary forms of slavery" can be best understood as the latest phase in a cumulative response to the limitations of legal abolition. As we saw in the last chapter, the legal abolition of slavery usually resulted in a range of qualified yet still consequential improvements for slaves and ex-slaves, but it also left a variety of closely related problems and practices unresolved. While these problems had limited political resonance in the immediate aftermath of legal abolition, they have become increasingly prominent in recent times. This has gradually resulted in a broader and deeper understanding of anti-slavery. On the one hand, we have a broadening of the types of practices associated with slavery, culminating in the recent emergence of the category of contemporary forms of slavery. On the other hand, we have a deeper diagnosis of the types of measures that anti-slavery activism requires, culminating in a somewhat belated recognition that legal measures are necessary but not sufficient, and that concerted action is required when it comes to themes such as prevention, rehabilitation, amelioration, and larger socioeconomic reforms.

In order to develop this overall line of argument, I have divided the chapter into four main sections. In the first section, I explore how inherited images of transatlantic slavery have consistently dominated the way in which the more general category of slavery has been understood. In the second section, I examine pioneering efforts to legally define "slavery in all its forms" under the auspices of the League of Nations. These efforts would anticipate, but did not yet precipitate, a more expansive approach to slavery. In the third section, I explore the more recent activities of the United Nations, which have served to both legitimate and promote the broader model of contemporary forms of slavery in operation today. In the final section, I consider some of the primary features of this most recent phase in anti-slavery activism, paying particular attention to the popular yet problematic concept of "new" slavery. As we shall see, most of the problems that have recently been brought together under the rubric of contemporary forms of slavery primarily involve the extension and reconfiguration of enduring historical themes, rather than distinctively modern innovations.

Extreme Exploitation, Human Property, and Transatlantic Slavery

As we saw in earlier chapters, the pioneers of organized anti-slavery were able to frame slavery as a compelling problem that was both stark and solvable.

Unlike other problems such as war or poverty, transatlantic slavery displayed a number of distinctive characteristics that rendered it relatively vulnerable to political mobilization. From the late eighteenth century onward, the severe abuses that defined transatlantic slavery would be primarily attributed to a clear-cut, highly exploitative, and racially defined institution that could be legally abolished, and thereby ostensibly ended. The pioneers of organized anti-slavery generally had no problem identifying who the slaves were—or how they differed from non-slaves—because slavery was a clearly demarcated legal category with a venerable historical pedigree. Despite the fact that not all Africans in the Americas were slaves, the entrenched association between slavery and race further ensured that slavery was widely viewed as a discrete, readily identifiable category. This point of demarcation only became sharper with the uptake of anti-slavery propaganda, which presented slavery as an unconscionable evil that was outside "normal" (i.e., legitimate) practices and institutions, and thereby imbued the divide between slave and non-slave with a strong emotional and ideological resonance.

While there were many facets to the overall case against slavery, there would be two themes in particular that stood out: the *ownership of human beings* and *extreme dominion and exploitation*. These twin themes were fundamental to the Anti-Slavery Project from the outset, because they were at the heart of arguments about what set slavery apart from other practices and institutions. From an abolitionist standpoint, it was both the legal right to buy, sell, and own other human beings and the extreme brutality, mortality, exploitation, and debasement of transatlantic slavery that ultimately rendered slavery totally unacceptable. This was in contrast to the pro-slavery position, which (among other things) viewed slavery as natural, or normal, with slaves being collectively treated at least no worse than segments of the white working class. While there were strengths and weaknesses to both perspectives, the remarkable success of the Anti-Slavery Project over the course of the nineteenth century eventually resolved this contest in favor of the abolitionists.

These core themes of ownership and exploitation have long been closely associated with transatlantic slavery in general, and slavery in the colonial Caribbean and southern United States in particular. This is not especially surprising, since this was the historical milieu within which organized anti-slavery first emerged, but this connection also has broader ramifications because of the way in which the iconography of transatlantic slavery has dominated how the more general category of slavery has been understood.[1] A useful summary of this enduring theme is offered by Cooper, Holt, and Scott, who observe that:

> For North Americans, and perhaps others, the image of a sugar or cotton plantation in the early nineteenth century—with a labor force comprised of black slaves subject to arduous work routines and harsh discipline from white owners and overseers, living in "quarters" sharply demarcated from the housing of those not enslaved is so powerful that it tends to stand in for the very essence of slavery. These images make it hard to tell a more nuanced and complicated story, wider in space and deeper in time, about a set of practices that can still be usefully labelled slavery.[2]

This dominance is reflected in the vast quantity of printed material dealing with various aspects of transatlantic slavery, especially in the case of the United States, and the far smaller volume of work concerned with other historical slave systems.[3] This ethnocentric approach to slavery is strongest in the European world, but it also has broader social and political resonance in other parts of the globe, where many modern audiences are likely to be more familiar with transatlantic slavery than the history of slavery in their own societies.

This connection between transatlantic slavery and the twin themes of human property and extreme exploitation has had profound consequences for efforts to conceptualize and classify numerous practices and institutions. We have already encountered this dynamic in previous chapters in relation to repeated depictions of non-European slave systems as "mild" or "benign." Behind these descriptions was a self-serving assessment that the practices in question were less severe than inherited images of transatlantic slavery. Similar types of comparisons—either explicit or implicit—have tended to take place whenever observers have found it necessary to classify specific examples of enslavement and "slave-like" practices. Over the course of the twentieth century these inherited images of transatlantic slavery have been primarily invoked two quite different ways. In the first variant, we find a steady stream of government officials and other apologists seeking to sharply distinguish various activities from the horrors of transatlantic slavery. In the second variant, we find a growing number of human rights activists and other agents invoking comparisons with transatlantic slavery in order to legitimate the classification of specific practices as forms of slavery. While the first variant was dominant in the aftermath of legal abolition, the second variant has become more prominent with the passage of time. In order to better understand this historical trajectory, I turn to the activities of both the League of Nations and the United Nations, which have inaugurated a series of cumulative changes in the status of slavery under international law.

The League of Nations

The pioneering efforts of the League of Nations to engage with these issues offers a useful point of departure for evaluating linkages between historical practices and contemporary problems. Over the course of the 1920s and 1930s, the League tasked a series of expert committees with documenting and classifying slavery. Their outputs and deliberations provide a key source of information on efforts to define slavery during this period. The initial catalyst for this process was a successful resolution by Sir Arthur Steel-Maitland, a League delegate from New Zealand, to establish a committee to consider the best available methods of combating a "recrudescence of slavery in Africa."[4] This resolution paved the way for the establishment of the Temporary Slavery Commission, a small group of predominantly European experts charged with examining "slavery in all its forms." This commission was formed in 1924, after earlier requests by the League for information from governments on the prevalence of slavery proved to be unsatisfactory.[5] One of the most revealing features of the work of the committee was the way in which it dealt with the sensitive issue of defining slavery. Finding it difficult to settle on a single formula, the commission instead produced a list of various forms of bondage, including slavery, serfdom, debt bondage and forced labor.[6]

The language of "slavery in all its forms" anticipated, but did not yet precipitate, a profound transformation in the way in which the slavery would be conceptualized and discussed. On this front, the work of the commission can be best understood as an early attempt to deal with two increasingly salient questions: (1) on what basis should we differentiate between "classical" slavery and other forms of human bondage? And (2) if we accept that a range of practices and institutions can be legitimately associated or equated with slavery, what further remedial steps should be taken to address their problematic status? This later issue has proved to be particularly significant in the wake of legal abolition. Once topics such as servile marriage and forced labor became part of the anti-slavery equation, it also became necessary to formulate an additional set of solutions. Since there was never any question of ending marriage, and forced labor was held to be legitimate in certain cases, the main policy question became how to ensure adequate safeguards to prevent abuses. The overarching goal would no longer be total prohibition, but regulation and harm minimization.

The Temporary Slavery Commission haltingly paved the way for the 1926 Slavery Convention, which took the hugely important step of defining slavery as "the status or condition of a person over whom any or all of the powers attaching to the right of ownership are exercised," and bound parties both "to prevent and suppress the slave trade" and "To bring about, progressively and as soon as possible, the complete abolition of slavery in all its forms."[7] The exact nature of these forms was not clearly specified, leaving a significant window for governments to determine the scope of their obligations. In the negotiations that preceded the final Convention, the more expansive approach favored by the Temporary Commission was scaled back in favor of a more restrictive formula that "sought to ensure that only slavery as defined by Article 1(1) was included in the Convention and that other types of exploitation would be excluded."[8] At the heart of this strategy was a narrow reading of the practical applications of "powers attaching to the right of ownership."[9]

As we have already seen, the Convention specifically mentioned forced and compulsory labor, taking the qualified step of requiring parties to "prevent compulsory or forced labour from developing into conditions analogous to slavery."[10] This issue attracted the most interest from governments in the negotiations that preceded the Convention. By at least tacitly accepting that forced labor was legitimate in at least some cases, if only for "public purposes" or in "exceptional" circumstances, the Convention embraced a relatively cautious stance that did not directly antagonize colonial powers. Many states became party to the Convention in the years that followed,[11] but its overall impact appears to have been fairly limited. Despite repeated official assurances that slavery was both (obviously) abhorrent and (effectively) abolished, various forms of bondage continued on a global scale.

The 1926 Convention marked the culmination of a protracted period of political maneuvering, which saw various European powers attempt to frame (anti-)slavery in such a way that it did not significantly intrude on various practices occurring under colonial jurisdictions.[12] The 1926 definition of slavery did not put an end to these machinations, but instead introduced an important benchmark that would be incorporated into future deliberations over the boundaries between slave and non-slave. One of the main points at issue would be the ambiguity surrounding "any or all," when it comes to "powers attaching to the right of ownership." As we have seen, proprietary rights and claims have never been confined to classical slavery. If we take the term "any" at face value, it could potentially include a range of social categories, from well-paid professional athletes who are bound by contracts through which their services are bought and sold, to dependent relationships between husband and wife, or between guardians and minors.[13] A more judicious understanding of the 1926 definition could have potentially extended to the other types of practices identified by the Temporary Slavery Commission,[14] yet the Convention "was widely interpreted . . . as embracing only chattel slavery, and as inapplicable to analogous forms of servitude."[15]

In this environment, it was effectively left to relevant actors to determine whether specific practices involved no, any, or all the powers attaching to right of ownership. One prominent example of efforts to come to terms with these definitional dilemmas during this period comes from British anti-slavery activist Kathleen Simon. In her 1929 work *Slavery*, Simon maintained that the divide between slave and non-slave was "clear cut and sharp," and the 1926 definition had enshrined the simple, unambiguous fact that "a slave is property."[16] While her book chiefly focused on states where slavery then remained legal (such as Abyssinia), and states where slavery had been recently abolished (such as Nepal), it included a substantial section on other forms of servitude, where Simon bemoaned the use of "labour systems . . . which border upon crude slave-owning, many of them involving forms of oppression and cruelty hardly less terrible than those of actual slave-owning and slave-hunting."[17] These systems were described as peonage,[18] contract labor, forced labor, and pawnship, with particular mention being made to the severe exploitation of children.[19]

Simon had few doubts that other forms of human bondage routinely approximated chattel slavery when it came to cruelty and oppression, but she was not prepared to formally classify them as forms of slavery because they were not regarded as "out-and-out property-owning institution[s]."[20] This position was primarily based on the priority that anti-slavery activists and other actors continued to accord legal slavery in places such as Abyssinia and the Arabian peninsula. It is worth noting, however, that Simon's survey also highlighted a number of examples in Africa where legal abolition had proved ineffective, and slavery and slave-like practices persisted. The inclusion of these practices introduced an element of informal comparison that further complicated her efforts to distinguish between slavery and servitude. If some of the practices occurring under the banner of forced labor, or debt-bondage, closely resembled historical slavery systems, as Simon herself had concluded, it was not entirely clear why they should not be placed on the same footing as "slave-like" practices in the wake of legal abolition. As an activist, Simon had no obvious vested interest in favoring a narrow definition, but she nonetheless followed many of her contemporaries in seeking to uphold an increasingly slippery distinction between equivalence and similarity.

This conceptual ambiguity featured prominently in a series of Expert Committees appointed by the League to examine slavery in the 1930s. These committees were fairly low-key affairs with a small, exclusively European membership, limited mandate (forced labor was explicitly excluded), and no enforcement powers.[21] The first, the Committee of Experts, had been opposed by a number of governments, and ultimately required funding from anti-slavery groups to eventually go ahead.[22] In its report, the Committee advocated the formation of a more permanent group, which ultimately became the Advisory Committee of Experts. These committees held brief sessions every two (later one) years until the outbreak of the Second World War in 1939, producing a series of reports that offer valuable insights into efforts to define and demarcate slavery prior to decolonization. Three themes in particular proved to be significant here: (1) a heavy reliance on governments for information, which was frequently unreliable or not forthcoming; (2) repeated assurances that slavery was either dead or limited to residual pockets that were rapidly dying out, and which could not be considered "true" slavery; and (3) the increasing prominence—and problematic status—of various forms of human bondage.

Throughout the 1930s, the League primarily focused on territories where slavery remained legal, and on territories in which slavery had only recently been officially abolished. The main focus was again continental Africa. In the case of legal slavery, reports from this period include repetitive lists of the relatively small number of governments that sanctioned legal slavery, together with cautious entreaties to relevant officials to take further action against slavery. In territories where slavery had been officially abolished, the League was forced to heavily rely on government submissions, which routinely maintained that slavery was no longer a continuing problem within their jurisdictions. Some of these submissions took the form of blanket denials, but other colonial powers such as Britain and France adopted a more qualified stance, which saw officials cautiously declare that minor vestiges of slavery remained in some territories, but these acknowledgments tended to be accompanied with further claims that that any residual cases should be clearly differentiated from slavery "in the ordinary sense of that term." [23] A useful snapshot of this approach can be found in a League report from 1932, which (re)defined slavery in terms of

> certain kinds of social status in which men are not yet in enjoyment of full civil freedom, but which are in no sense inhuman, and which in certain ways (assistance to the sick and infirm) even present advantages. A social status of this kind cannot be equitably assimilated to slavery *in the usual sense of the term* without running the risk of giving the civilised world an incorrect and unfair impression of what may still remain of this ancient evil. Those kinds of social status have been abolished in law in the territories under the authority of the colonial Powers and are gradually disappearing. [24]

Government submissions repeatedly classified these relationships in terms of "serfdom" or as "domestic" or "voluntary" slavery. Those in bondage were said to be aware that they were free to leave, but were held to have maintained aspects of their previous relationships due to mutual bonds and favorable treatment. Since these residual cases were also reported to be in decline, there was a general consensus that they were not especially troublesome. In some submissions, the only outstanding issue that was reported in the aftermath of legal abolition was social discrimination. Since those involved ostensibly enjoyed "benign" treatment, their circumstances would be sharply distinguished from the horrors of transatlantic slavery.

This heavy reliance on official sources resulted in at least two fundamental limitations. First, many governments either failed to provide information on the status of slavery within their territories, or categorically denied that slavery remained a problem. This significantly narrowed the range of topics and territories on which the League was qualified to comment. Aside from some notable exceptions such as Liberia and Tibet, the absence of information on slavery was consistently equated with the absence of slavery itself, leaving the overall impression that slavery should not be considered an ongoing problem unless otherwise indicated. Second, the information that was available was partial and often misleading. [25] As the preceding quote makes clear, repeated declarations that slavery was effectively at an end often depended on slavery being narrowly defined, with a variety of conceptual gymnastics being employed to demarcate slavery in such a way that many otherwise troublesome cases were effectively excluded. This disingenuous distinction between "vestiges" of slavery (relatively benign) and "real" slavery (ancient evil) continued a longstanding pattern of government officials seeking to minimize the scope of their anti-slavery obligations.

As we saw in earlier chapters, the main problem was not that there had been no change, but that official statements typically made few allowances for territories where a substantial minority (and sometimes even an occasional majority) of slaves remained in bondage. From a modern vantage point, it is now clear that many of these "vestiges" were not inexorably disappearing, as optimistically reported, but were instead disappearing into international obscurity. It is important to emphasize, however, that this pattern is clearer in hindsight than it was at the time. We now know, for instance, that League reports on French West Africa were largely fabricated, and that slavery remained a problem throughout the 1930s and beyond, but this was not apparent to most leading experts at the time. Popular interest in slavery was limited. Legal slavery remained a major focal point, and there was a general tendency to take official statements (by Europeans) at face value. Once the absence of information on slavery was tacitly equated with the absence of slavery itself, the burden of proof would be placed on critics to offer compelling information that contradicted this default position. On the rare occasions when cases of enslavement and forced labor attracted sustained interest (such as labor scandals in Portuguese Africa, the Congo Free State, Liberia, Nazi Germany, and the Soviet Union and its satellites), they tended to be presented as anomalous events within a landscape that was otherwise free of such deviant activities.[26]

Despite their best efforts to firmly distinguish between slavery and other forms of human bondage, the slavery experts of the League of Nations regularly faced questions about whether specific practices and institutions should be classified as forms of slavery. While there was a clear consensus that slavery constituted a separate and distinct category, those involved often found it difficult to determine where the outer limits of this category should be established. The activities of the League were once again limited by available information, with many significant problem areas being only briefly touched on or even passed over entirely. Perhaps the most notable omissions here were peonage in Latin America and debt bondage in the Indian subcontinent. Both of these practices involved millions of laborers, but they were not (yet) a core component of the international anti-slavery agenda.

One problem area that received sustained consideration was the practice of Mui-Tsai in East Asia. Mui-Tsai involved the adoption or purchase of female children from poor families to work as domestic servants (or prostitutes). While Mui-Tsai was particularly prevalent in China, it was also practiced in Hong Kong, Singapore, and Malaya. British anti-slavery campaigners were particularly concerned with Mui-Tsai, and were firmly convinced that it was a form of slavery.[27] Others were not so sure. During this period, the Chinese government was involved in an ongoing war with Japan, which meant that it did not always have effective control over its territory. This made sustained action in China difficult. In jurisdictions under British authority, a series of well-publicized commissions on Mui-Tsai eventually resulted in the tightening of regulations governing the transfer of children.[28]

The relationship between Mui-Tsai and slavery was emblematic of a larger challenge, as Committee members found it necessary to expend considerable energies upholding their favored distinction between slavery and other forms of human bondage. Other practices that featured in their deliberations were serfdom, debt-bondage, marriage practices, and pawnship. Throughout this period, the contentious issue of forced labor was excluded from consideration for political reasons. In keeping with larger trends, the twin themes of property and treatment once again played a central role in attempts to classify various practices and institutions. On this front, the Committee generally followed Simon in seeking to establish procedural differences between slavery and other forms of bondage by invoking the legal criteria of "powers attaching to the right of ownership."[29] While the precise rationale for excluding other practices was not always fully articulated, there was nonetheless a general consensus that there were key differences, and that classical slavery should continue to be accorded pride of place. This position was reflected in government submissions. Official reports that slavery had come to an end in particular jurisdictions overwhelmingly focused on classical slavery. Other forms of bondage were invariably treated as separate and subordinate issues. In most submissions they were not mentioned at all. The more expansive approach favored by the Temporary Commission of 1924 remained a subordinate viewpoint.

The United Nations and Contemporary Forms of Slavery

The second half of the twentieth century was primarily defined by a gradual expansion of the boundaries of (anti-)slavery, both politically and legally.

This trend can be best understood as a cumulative response to the strengths and weaknesses of the historical events surrounding legal abolition. By the mid-twentieth century, the primary goal of the Anti-Slavery Project—the legal abolition of slavery—had finally been all but accomplished.[30] If legal slavery had remained a major global problem, there would have been less space on the political agenda for other practices and institutions. Prior to the Second World War, both activists and government officials had generally prioritized legal slavery and its immediate aftermath (outside periodic labor scandals), leaving most other forms of human bondage as secondary issues. Once legal slavery had been reduced to a handful of communities (most of whom abolished slavery in the 1950s and 1960s), related forms of human bondage came to be viewed in a new light, building on a somewhat belated recognition—in some quarters at least—of the historical limitations of the legal abolition of slavery.[31]

This new phase in the history of organized anti-slavery was inaugurated by the 1956 Supplementary Convention on the Abolition of Slavery, the Slave Trade and Institutions and Practices Similar to Slavery. This did not replace the 1926 Convention, which was officially taken over by the United Nations in 1953,[32] but was instead presented as an attempt to "augment" and "intensify" international efforts against slavery.[33] For our purposes, the key provisions of the 1956 Convention can be found in article one, which obligates parties to

> take all practicable and necessary legislative and other measures to bring about progressively and as soon as possible the complete abolition or abandonment of the following institutions and practices, where they still exist and *whether or not they are covered by the definition of slavery contained in article 1 of the Slavery Convention signed at Geneva on 25 September 1926.*[34]

Four distinct practices were identified here: debt-bondage, serfdom, servile marriage, and the transfer of persons under eighteen for the purpose of exploiting their labor.[35] The Convention did not explicitly classify these practices as types of slavery, referring instead to persons of "servile status," but this distinction has tended to be overlooked in subsequent discussions.[36]

In order to make sense of the 1956 Convention, it is necessary to distinguish between two broad approaches to the relationship between slavery and related forms of bondage: *strict equivalence* and *sufficient similarity*. Strict equivalence maintains that practices should only be equated with slavery in cases of close correspondence. This model does not deny that similarities can exist between slavery and other practices, but it nonetheless insists that similarity should not be confused with equivalency. This can be contrasted with sufficient similarity, which instead places other forms of bondage alongside slavery on the basis of "familial" resemblance. This model accepts that the practices involved may not be identical, but it nonetheless insists that they have sufficient features in common to be placed on the same legal and moral footing. The Supplementary Convention provided an authoritative endorsement of the underlying logic behind this more expansive approach.

The 1956 Convention not only incorporated practices such as debt-bondage and serfdom under the rubric of slavery, it also officially confirmed that slavery came in different forms, which could be accorded equal importance. From this vantage point, chattel slavery could be legitimately regarded as one of a series of problems, rather than an overarching priority. This shift in priorities is reflected in the increasing use of terms such as "traditional" and "classical" slavery. These sorts of qualifiers did not feature in anti-slavery circles during the nineteenth century, but they became more prominent over the course of the twentieth century as part of efforts to differentiate between various forms of slavery. The 1956 Convention did not bring an end to the strict equivalence approach, which continues to have ideological and sociological resonance to this day, but it nonetheless introduced a new legal and political framework that paved the way for the ascendance of sufficient similarity.

Much like the 1926 Convention, the 1956 Supplementary Convention emerged out of a period of protracted political maneuvering.[37] Slavery did not feature prominently on the agenda of the newly formed United Nations in the aftermath of the Second World War. It was largely thanks to the lobbying efforts of Charles Greenidge, secretary of the Anti-Slavery Society, that slavery was raised at all. Thanks to a personal lobbying campaign, Greenidge was able to eventually secure support for the formation of an Ad Hoc Committee on Slavery (1950–1951). This Committee was once again comprised of a small group of experts, but its composition was somewhat different than earlier incarnations, as it not only incorporated non-European voices, but also included Greenidge himself. The inclusion of a professional anti-slavery activist from a nongovernmental organization (NGO) was highly unusual and hugely significant, as Greenidge was able to use his position to set the terms of the debate that followed.[38] It is worth noting, however, that the Committee once again faced significant political opposition. Following the circulation of a questionnaire inquiring about the prevalence of a range of practices and institutions, the Peruvian government became alarmed about the prospect of an inquiry into peonage. After several failed attempts to alter the composition and mandate of the Committee, Peruvian diplomats eventually succeeded in halving the time allocated to the Committee, which significantly hampered its work. [39]

The most important recommendation to come out of the work of the UN Ad Hoc Committee concerned the creation of a supplementary convention dealing with the forms of human bondage identified above.[40] The ambiguity that continued to surround the 1926 definition of slavery was at the heart of this proposal. Faced with the recurring challenge of determining whether particular practices fell within the 1926 definition of slavery, the Committee presented the convention as a way of resolving this problem by establishing a further international instrument that explicitly defined analogous practices and institutions. The politically sensitive issue of forced labor was originally part of this mandate, but was later dispatched to another special committee, leading to the 1957 Abolition of Forced Labour Convention, which further restricted the terms under which forced labor could be legitimately practiced.[41] This exclusion of forced labor did little to ensure the smooth passage of the Convention. Building on categories and concepts developed by the Ad Hoc Committee, British diplomats circulated an initial draft in 1954, but it took two further years for the language of the Convention to be finalized. This process included an additional report on slavery by UN rapporteur Hans Engen in 1955, and a series of diplomatic exchanges that took place in the shadow of anti-colonial and Cold War politics.[42]

Another key proposal made by the Ad Hoc Committee revolved around the establishment of a permanent UN committee on slavery. This emerged as a high priority for anti-slavery groups and other human rights organizations, who were disappointed with the absence of formal mechanisms to monitor the 1926 and 1956 Conventions. This frustration was captured by anti-slavery activist Patrick Montgomery, when he observed in 1973 that "No single UN employee has a duty to inform himself about slavery, let alone do anything about it."[43] In the wake of decolonization, the political landscape of the United Nations proved to be an inhospitable environment for efforts to create a specialized committee (or even the appointment of a single slavery specialist). Following decades of protracted and often highly politicized debate, the Ad Hoc Committee proposal was finally realized with the formation of the UN Working Group on Slavery, which first met in August 1975.

Before we consider the recent activities of the Working Group, two further developments during this period need to be highlighted. The first revolves around a series of UN reports on slavery compiled by Dr. Mohammed Awad. Of particular importance here was a report from 1966, which was primarily based on official responses to another questionnaire.[44] This survey again yielded disappointing results, with most states simply citing relevant legal frameworks or declaring that there were no ongoing problems within their jurisdictions. The questionnaire was not only concerned with chattel slavery, but also sought information on the practices and institutions covered by the 1956 Convention. Despite the global nature of problems such as debt-bondage, very few states were prepared to acknowledge that any relevant practices and institutions could be found in their territories. This reluctance can be partly attributed to the fact that these practices had been formally linked to slavery. Officially admitting that debt-bondage or serfdom remained a problem could now be potentially construed as sanctioning slavery.

The second major development during this period was the establishment of a formal connection between slavery and the "slavery-like practices of apartheid and colonialism." This formula was first introduced in 1966 by W. E. Waldron-Ramsay, Tanzania's representative on the UN Economic and Social Council, during a debate over a proposal for the establishment of a permanent UN committee on slavery. With the support of similarly minded delegates, Waldron-Ramsay secured support for a motion that explicitly incorporated both apartheid and colonialism under the rubric of slavery. This not only helped to derail the proposed slavery committee for a number of years, it also had a profound influence on subsequent efforts to address slavery within the UN system.[45] After 1966, nearly all UN documents and deliberations concerned with slavery included reference to or discussion of the "slavery-like practices of apartheid and colonialism," later defined in terms of "forms of collective or group slavery that fundamentally oppress the human rights of several million people."[46] This expansion of the definition of slavery was primarily a political gesture, with slavery being invoked as a metaphor in order to underscore objections to the human rights abuses associated with apartheid and colonialism.[47] By incorporating collective forms of oppression under the rubric of slavery, Waldron-Ramsay not only extended the definition of slavery, he further complicated efforts to develop a coherent rationale for distinguishing between slave and non-slave. Instead of being focused on relationships between individuals, slavery now formally extended to collective experiences.

The UN Working Group on Slavery would extend the boundaries

of slavery even further. During its inaugural session in 1975, the Working Group officially endorsed an open-ended approach to slavery, which started with the premise that "The definitions in the existing relevant conventions did not . . . cover the concept of slavery under all its present aspects."[48] Despite a widespread belief that a "new and broader definition" was required, no final consensus was reached. Instead, the first meeting of the Working Group offered a series of reflections on what a new definition of slavery might look like. In one variant, slavery was conceived in terms of "any form of dealing with human beings leading to the forced exploitation of their labour."[49] In a second variant, slavery was framed in terms of "all institutions and practices which by restricting the freedom of the individual, are susceptible of causing severe hardship and serious deprivations of liberty."[50] This expansive approach to slavery was reflected in the range of topics taken up by the Working Group between 1975 and 2006. During this period, the problems that were considered ranged from more established issues such as debt-bondage and servile marriage, to a variety of problems that were only tangentially related to slavery, such as female genital mutilation, honor killings, and the illicit sale of organs. The contentious issue of forced labor, which had long been separated from slavery for political reasons, was belatedly incorporated into the remit of the group. Another key area that was identified was the exploitation of children, with a particular focus on the sale of children, child labor, prostitution, trafficking, and child pornography.[51]

The UN Working Group was organized in a similar manner to previous slavery committees, with a small group of experts from various parts of the world holding intensive public meetings annually in Geneva. The permanent nature of the group formally satisfied longstanding demands for a mechanism to monitor relevant issues, but its official mandate did not extend to either a permanent support staff or meaningful enforcement powers. This placed significant constraints on what the group could realistically be expected to accomplish.[52] Throughout its existence, the main role of the Working Group was to serve as a clearing house for information compiled by accredited NGOs. In the early 1990s, a voluntary trust fund was established to help the group hear from persons with first-hand information on particular abuses, but ensuring adequate financial support often proved to be difficult.[53] While a number of states contributed to deliberations on problems within their jurisdictions, most official submissions continued to downplay or disregard negative reports. In September 2007, the Working Group was supplanted by the introduction of the first UN Special Rapporteur on Contemporary Forms of Slavery, Its Causes and Consequences.[54]

The language of "contemporary forms of slavery" can be traced to a 1988 decision to rename the UN Working Group the Working Group on Contemporary Forms of Slavery. This name was held to be "more descriptive of its actual interests, namely exploitation of sex, debt-bondage, sale of children, apartheid."[55] Significantly, this list of "actual interests" did not include chattel slavery. While classical slavery did not disappear from the agenda entirely (continuing problems in Mauritania, Sudan, and Niger have all been considered by the United Nations in recent times), it was nonetheless overshadowed by other problem areas. This shift in priorities can be chiefly traced to the relative scale of the problems falling under the rubric of contemporary forms of slavery. By the late twentieth century, classical slavery was no longer a problem in more than a handful of jurisdictions, while related practices such as child labor and debt-bondage continued to afflict millions of people throughout the globe.

Another alternative title for the Working Group was the Working Group against Slavery, Apartheid, Gross Human Exploitation and Human Degradation.[56] This name was proposed in 1983, but not taken up. The descriptive terms included in this title offer a revealing insight into the underlying rationale behind the related concept of contemporary forms of slavery. It is important to note that this rationale marks a further departure from the 1956 Convention, which was primarily based on the close resemblance between classical slavery and other forms of bondage. As we saw earlier, these similarities were sufficient to raise questions during the 1920s and 1930s over whether these practices fit within the 1926 definition of slavery. The more recent activities of the United Nations have set aside this more demanding standard in favor of an open-ended approach that builds on the powerful images of suffering, cruelty, and debasement at the heart of the Anti-Slavery Project.

The main problem with this approach is that it can end up treating "slavery" as little more than shorthand for virtually any form of dominion and ill-treatment. Framed in these terms, slavery ceases to be an analytical category and instead primarily functions as an evocative concept, building on the iconography of human property, extreme exploitation, and transatlantic slavery. From a political standpoint, the "contemporary" appellation, or similar variants such as "new," "modern," or "twenty-first-century" slavery, can be best understood as an attempt to distinguish current events from "traditional" slavery, while harnessing the evocative imagery of slavery to prioritize cases of severe exploitation and abuse.[57] This approach is by no means entirely illegitimate, but it is also not without risk.

To further understand this issue, I turn to Ole Wæver's concept of "securitization." Building on speech-act theory, Wæver argues that the act of designating unconventional issues "security" problems, such as the environment or social integrity, involves an ethical claim that the issues at hand are urgent, unparalleled problems, and thus should be accorded the highest priority. When we describe a problem as a form of slavery, we similarly situate it within a specific historical and moral context. This not only entails an analytical claim that the issues at hand constitute slavery, it also invokes a preexisting ethical argument for uncompromising action to correct unconscionable evil. As a political strategy, this will hopefully imbue the issues at hand with a degree of urgency and priority. There is also, however, a potential downside: "When a problem is 'securitized,' the act tends to lead to specific ways of addressing it: Threat, defense and often state-centered solutions."[58] Invoking slavery can be a similarly polarizing move, narrowing space for ameliorative strategies. Framing child labor as child slavery suggests that it is not simply run-of-the-mill exploitation, but an abhorrent practice requiring immediate and uncompromising action. Actors and institutions with the capacity to bring about gradual improvements in specific areas may (or may not) be more receptive to a less combative approach. The potential downside of this strategy is captured in an earlier joint statement to the UN by various NGOs in 1972, which observes that "the emotive quality of the term 'slavery' and its associations have themselves contributed to the failure until now of all initiatives to eliminate slavery."[59]

A further consequence of the expansion of the boundaries of slavery has been growing confusion over whether recent treatments of slavery should be understood literally (actual slavery) or rhetorically (a loose metaphorical association). Throughout history, slavery has been repeatedly invoked as a rhetorical device for framing various cases of political tyranny and personal subjugation.[60] Familiar historical examples of this strategy include the concepts of "wage slavery" and "sex slavery" used by nineteenth-century labor groups and feminists. In both variants, activists primarily invoked the language of slavery as a rhetorical device to highlight the plight of marginalized groups.[61] When slavery was legal, the distinction between literal and rhetorical remained relatively clear-cut, but it has become increasingly ambiguous over time. In a political landscape where slavery now comes in many different forms, it can sometimes be difficult to clearly determine what is *not* slavery.

The New Slavery?

The political landscape of organized anti-slavery has changed dramatically in recent times. Three main themes can be identified here. The first theme revolves around the gradual expansion of the legal and political boundaries of slavery analyzed above. This process has been promoted and legitimated by the United Nations, which has played a decisive role in reshaping the way in which slavery has been conceptualized and discussed. The second theme revolves around a tremendous increase in levels of NGO activism over the last half-century.[62] As we saw in earlier chapters, the legal abolition of slavery was a predominantly "top-down" process that saw political elites responding to cumulative external pressures. More recent developments have been defined by a somewhat different pattern, with strong "bottom-up" pressures emerging as a consequence of the collective efforts of both local and international human rights organizations. As we shall see in later chapters, this has regularly involved local NGOs from the South taking the initiative (sometimes in combination with more established northern NGOs).[63] Not all these NGOs have been exclusively concerned with slavery, but the gradual emergence of the category of contemporary slavery has resulted in a substantial overlap between a variety of causes and constituencies. In some cases, NGOs have turned to the language of slavery as part of efforts to draw attention to preexisting political causes. In other cases, more "generalist" NGOs such as Amnesty International and Human Rights Watch have taken up forms of slavery as part of a broader portfolio. This has not only meant that many new voices have become part of anti-slavery conversations, it has also resulted in an unprecedented growth in the volume, quality, and dissemination of information on various abuses that had previously been largely unknown outside the countries involved.

The third and final theme to be discussed here revolves around a global sea change in the political fortunes of organized anti-slavery from the late 1990s onward. During the 1980s and early 1990s, contemporary slavery generally enjoyed a modest public and political profile. Despite previous increases in levels of NGO activism, neither government officials nor the general public demonstrated sustained interest in the problems at hand. This began to change in the mid-1990s, when increasing concerns about illegal migration following the end of the Cold War played a decisive role in sharply raising the political profile of human trafficking and forced prostitution. As interest in human trafficking increased, the profile of other forms of human bondage also greatly improved. By the early twenty-first century, contemporary slavery had rapidly and unexpectedly moved from being a marginal concern to a mainstream issue. During in the 1980s, few people were aware that slavery was an ongoing issue. Thanks to sustained (and often sensationalized) media coverage of human trafficking and other problems, public awareness of slavery has now reached a point where there are relatively few people who are not aware that slavery continues to be a global problem.

A similar story applies at a political and institutional level. Prior to the 1990s breakthrough, contemporary slavery rarely found a receptive audience among political elites. Over the last fifteen years, various forms of bondage have been regularly discussed at the highest levels. Over a hundred governments have recently drafted new anti-slavery (mostly anti-trafficking) laws. Some have also established specialized agencies and taskforces. New internal protocols have been established. Regional networks have been created. Numerous reports have been written.[64] Slavery has also been a prominent topic in a series of high-profile court cases, including a 2002 Appeals Decision (*Kunarac*) before the International Criminal Tribunal for the former Yugoslavia, a 2005 case (*Siliadin v. France*) before the European Court of Human Rights, a 2008 case before the Australian High Court (*Queen v. Tang*), a 2008 case before the Economic Community of West African States (*Hadijatou Mani v. Niger*), and a 2010 case (*Rantsev v. Cyprus and Russia*) before the European Court of Human Rights. These cases have revealed major differences of opinion over the definition of slavery. One ruling (*Kunarac*) speaks of "differences of degree" among forms of slavery, while another (*Siliadin*) saw a ruling that the victim was not held in slavery in "the proper sense."[65]

This most recent phase in the history of organized anti-slavery is considered in greater depth in subsequent chapters. At this point in proceedings, there is one topic in particular that requires further consideration: the popular yet problematic concept of "new slavery." Over the last decade, numerous officials, journalists, and activists have embraced the concept of new slavery—or the new slave trade—as part of broader attempts to diagnose and define the various practices falling under the rubric of contemporary forms of slavery.[66] As a popular frame of reference, the concept of new slavery has contributed to a widespread tendency to view historical practices and contemporary problems as independent fields of inquiry. This unhelpful separation has been predicated on two core assumptions/arguments. In the first variant, advocates of new slavery have encouraged a widespread tendency to approach current problems as a distinctively new phenomenon that can be primarily attributed to recent developments, such as economic globalization, technological innovation, Cold War collapse, and global demography. In the second variant, advocates of new slavery have encouraged a widespread tendency to view current problems in a qualitatively different light to the "traditional" (transatlantic) slavery of the past. Both of these formulations have helped to conceal the historical roots of many contemporary problems.

The most influential advocate of the concept of new slavery has been Kevin Bales, an American anti-slavery activist. In his seminal work, *Disposable People: New Slavery in the Global Economy* (1999), Bales introduced a series of claims and categories that have had a profound influence on more recent treatments of contemporary slavery. One of the main components of Bales's work was a stylized distinction between new and old slavery. According to Bales, old slavery was chiefly defined by legal ownership, high purchase costs, low profits, shortages of potential slaves, long-term relationships, slave maintenance, and ethnic difference. This was contrasted with new slavery, which was said to be chiefly defined by an avoidance of legal ownership, low purchase costs, high profits, the irrelevance of ethnic cleavages, and a global surplus of short-term, "disposable" slaves. Bales chiefly attributed the "rise of the new slavery" to two recent developments: a post-Second World War population explosion, and the adverse consequences of "rapid social and economic change."[67]

There are numerous problems with this overall framework. In his description of "old slavery," Bales uses historical experiences in the nineteenth-century United States to make a series of more general claims about the history of slavery as a whole. Many of the characteristics ascribed to "old" slavery do not align comfortably with experiences in other historical slave systems. If the relevant point of departure was not slavery in the United States, but was instead slave raiders in Africa, "purchase costs" could often take the form of dangers endured in order to capture victims. In territories where warfare was ubiquitous, there were rarely shortages of potential slaves.[68] Alternatively, we could instead look to slavery in Russia in the early modern era, where a portion of the local population was subjected to a distinctive form of self-enslavement on the basis of limited service contracts, thereby complicating Bales's emphasis on perpetual servitude and ethnic difference.[69] While focusing on the United States has various advantages, not least of which is familiarity, it can end up overlooking other essential aspects of the history of slavery and abolition.

Once slavery is divided into new and old, it is not difficult to take the further step of at least tacitly assuming that the study of the former does not require detailed analysis of the latter, since they come under different categories, have different characteristics, and are driven by different dynamics. Like most recent commentators, Bales has tended to confine his forays into the history of slavery and abolition to brief allusions to (selective aspects of) transatlantic slavery, while saying little about the history of legal abolition in other parts of the globe.[70] This not only exacerbates an unhelpful division between past and present, it also conveys an incomplete picture of *how* legal abolition came about (especially the uncomfortable role of European imperialism, which has rarely been acknowledged) and *how much* has actually been accomplished. According to Bales (among others), the second half of the twentieth century was characterized by the "rise" of the new slavery, yet the global prevalence of human bondage actually declined dramatically during this period. As we have seen, the historical zenith of slavery occurred in the nineteenth century, with tens of millions of slaves held in bondage across the Americas, Africa, the Middle East, and Asia. If we look more broadly, the historical zenith of human bondage arguably occurred in the first half of the twentieth century, reflecting a combination of communist gulags, ongoing slave systems, wartime labor abuses, and endemic forced labor practices under colonial rule. While some abusive practices have probably increased in certain circles in more recent times, the overall scale of human bondage has almost certainly declined in both relative and absolute terms.

According to Bales, there are three main forms of slavery in the world today: chattel slavery (a small proportion of slaves); debt bondage (the most common form); and contract slavery (the most rapidly growing and second largest).[71] While there is no doubt that recent developments, both macro and micro, have significantly impacted on the character and composition of various practices, this should not negate the basic point that the forms of slavery that Bales describes as "new" could be regularly found alongside "old" slavery for centuries. As we shall see in Chapter 7, debt-bondage was widespread in both the Indian subcontinent and Latin America in the nineteenth century. Similarly, the types of abuses that Bales groups under "contract slavery" share many features in common with the global market in indentured migrants during the same period. Even the very concept of new (or modern) slavery can itself be traced back at least as far as the early twentieth century.[72]

Once this broader history is taken into account, we can begin to rethink the underlying causes behind the various practices that fall under the rubric of contemporary slavery. As we have seen, Bales argues that the rise of new slavery can be primarily attributed to recent developments. While not entirely discounting the contribution of new additions, I believe that the historical events surrounding the legal abolition of slavery offers a better point of departure for understanding both the underlying causes and key characteristics of most ongoing problems. Many of the practices that have recently being described as new were practiced alongside classical slavery in the nineteenth and twentieth centuries, but the narrow terms on which legal abolition took place tended to leave them substantially intact. These practices tended to be overlooked in the immediate aftermath of legal abolition, but with the passage of time they have gradually come to be viewed in a different light.

Another key strand in Bales's work is the idea that all forms of slavery can be identified by reference to a common core that comprises three main elements: "the use of violence to control the slave, the resulting loss of free will, and the economic exploitation that normally precludes the slave receiving any recompense for their work."[73] By introducing this definition, he has sought to place an outer limit on the ever-expanding boundaries of contemporary forms of slavery. According to this line of argument, "Having just enough money to get by, receiving wages that barely keep you alive, may be called wage slavery, but it is not slavery. Sharecroppers have a hard life, but they are not slaves. Child labor is terrible, but it is not necessarily slavery."[74] Using his preferred definition, Bales has calculated that there are around 27 million slaves in the world today. For Bales, this figure is a conservative estimate based on documented cases of *real* slavery. To demonstrate how he reached this overall total, he published a table in 2002 that estimates slave numbers across 101 countries, together with a tentative assessment of human trafficking.[75]

Two countries in Bales's survey stand out. These are India and Pakistan, estimated to be home respectively to between 18 and 22 million and between 2.5 to 3.5 million slaves.[76] According to these two lower estimates, the two neighboring countries account for around 75 percent of the 27 million total enslaved population. The main issue here is bonded labor, which remains a significant problem in Nepal, Bangladesh, India, and Pakistan. As we shall see in Chapter 7, a substantial portion of these continuing problems in the subcontinent can be traced back to the failure of British colonizers to effectively abolish slavery in India in 1843. As this example demonstrates, most forms of contemporary slavery are not new. The main thing that is new is the way in which they have come to be conceptualized and discussed.

Concluding Remarks

In the nineteenth and early twentieth century, anti-slavery advocates prioritized one goal above all others: the legal abolition of slavery. Following many setbacks and false starts, this ambitious goal has now been finally accomplished, with every country in the world having legally abolished slavery. The main sticking point, however, is how we approach this achievement. If slavery has been legally prohibited, but its more heinous characteristics have continued under a range of other designations, or through various illicit activities, on what grounds can we conclude that slavery has truly come to an end? If enslavement remains a fundamental issue in the absence of legal recognition, on what grounds can we distinguish classical slavery from related forms of servitude? If various forms of human bondage remain widespread, what further steps in addition to legal abolition should be taken to address various problems? The full ramifications of these interrelated questions only became apparent over the course of the twentieth century, as political attention increasingly focused on a variety of practices and institutions that have come to be explicitly connected to the evocative images of transatlantic slavery popularized by the Anti-Slavery Project.

Under the auspices of both the League of Nations and the United Nations, the range of problems that have been formally equated or associated with slavery has expanded markedly, reflecting a transformation away from strict equivalence and toward sufficient similarity. Instead of functioning as an analytical category, slavery has been increasingly invoked as an evocative concept. By drawing on the political and moral opprobrium that slavery continues to evoke, this strategy offers an attractive way of prioritizing various issues. As we have seen, this strategy is not without complications. Questions about whether particular practices really constitute slavery come quickly and easily for audiences accustomed to thinking of slavery as a historical relic which belongs in the past, and can often be exacerbated by an indefinite amalgam of literal and rhetorical claims. It has become apparent, moreover, that it can not only be difficult to identify who the slaves might be, it can also be difficult to formulate a straightforward solution to their plight. The most obvious remedy—legal abolition—has already been adopted with mixed results, leading to a somewhat belated recognition that further measures are now required. There is no longer one readily identifiable solution, but many overlapping strategies, which tend to be geared toward harm minimization, regulation, and alleviation. Much like global challenges such as poverty and environmental degradation, recent efforts to address most forms of contemporary slavery have concentrated on cumulative reductions in their overall scale and severity. To further interrogate the historical roots of these contemporary problems, I will now go on to consider three central themes: classical slavery, debt-bondage, and human trafficking.

PART III

Contemporary Forms of Slavery

Chapter 6

"Classical" Slavery
and Descent-Based Discrimination

The recent history of the Anti-Slavery Project has been defined by a more expansive understanding of the breadth and depth of anti-slavery obligations. This has resulted in a landscape in which slavery is now widely held to come in a variety of different forms, which require a variety of overlapping solutions. "Classical" slavery occupies an anomalous position within this new political and legal landscape. In some settings, classical slavery appears as one of many forms of slavery. In others, it appears as a separate and exceptional category. While other forms of human bondage now enjoy much higher profiles, not everyone has embraced the shift from strict equivalence to sufficient similarity. While the overall numbers of people who fall within the rubric of classical slavery are now relatively small, their experiences of enslavement continue to be viewed in a different light because of their association with earlier slave systems. It does not necessarily follow, however, that recent examples of classical slavery can be easily equated with previous historical models. To the extent that traditional forms of slavery remain an ongoing issue, they now form only one part of a larger set of problems, such as descent-based discrimination and wartime abuses.

By the mid-twentieth century, classical slavery was much diminished but not entirely suppressed. This chapter focuses on a small number of cases where the historical categories of master and slave have continued to have a profound influence on contemporary life. In order to better understand both the political and analytical issues at stake, I have divided the chapter into three sections. In the first section, I present a partial snapshot of the sorts of information, or lack thereof, that was readily available on classical slavery at an international level during the 1960s and 1970s. In the second section, I focus more specifically on two countries—Mauritania and Niger—that have recently found it necessary to introduce legislation (re)abolishing slavery. As we shall see, this new legislation can be at least partially traced to moderate pressures generated by local anti-slavery activists. Despite recent progress on a number of fronts, it has become increasingly apparent that the problems involved are not confined to residual cases of slavery, but also extend to broader patterns of discrimination on the basis of slave descent. In the third and final section, I consider the recent history of wartime enslavement in Sudan. There are a number of recent conflicts in Africa that owe various debts to earlier historical slave systems, but the case of Sudan is of particular interest due to the way in which classical slavery has been invoked in order to prioritize a variety of severe human rights abuses. The best-known issue here has been the controversial practice of slave redemption, which has sharply divided human rights groups. As we shall see, the language of classical slavery continues to be an effective way of attracting international attention, but it remains hamstrung by a number of analytical and political shortcomings.

Anecdotes, Incidents, and Extrapolations

In 1948, British anti-slavery activist Charles Greenidge optimistically reported that "Except for Ethiopia, there are no other countries in Africa in which there is still any considerable amount of slavery." Greenidge accepted that some isolated remnants could be found elsewhere, but he believed that they were "rapidly dying a natural death."[1] Despite being one of the most informed anti-slavery activists of his day, Greenidge could only work with the information available to him at the time. While traditional forms of slavery continued to be a substantial problem in a number of parts of colonial Africa, information on these problems was not widely disseminated at an international level. Official declarations that slavery had effectively come to an end were usually taken at face value by outsiders. In a discursive environment where slavery was now (at least tacitly) assumed to no longer be an ongoing problem, the burden of proof fell on anti-slavery activists and other agents to produce compelling evidence that contradicted this default position.

This proved to be a difficult task. During the Cold War era, much of the evidence compiled by anti-slavery activists and international organizations regarding the persistence of slavery was heavily reliant on a fragmentary combination of anecdotes, incidents, and extrapolations. One illustration of the widespread use of anecdotal evidence comes from a 1957 article in the *Anti-Slavery Reporter*, which included testimonies from two former Mauritanian slaves that were taken as part of research conducted in southern Morocco (permission to enter Mauritania having been denied by the French).[2] These testimonies offered evidence of the persistence of cases of slavery, but they could not (be expected to) provide a clear picture of larger trends across French West Africa. One former slave, Abide El-Barka ben Mbark, reported that he had two sons who remained enslaved in Mauritania, and that the French were complicit in returning runways who attempted to escape to Morocco. A second slave, M'Barjarek ben Bilal, reported being detained by the French during an escape attempt, and being severely punished for attempting to leave: "my master made a hole in the lobe of my ear . . . he put a thong through this and led me with my hands tied behind my back walking beside him as he rode a camel . . . I wore nothing but rags when I was a slave."[3]

In their search for information on traditional forms of slavery, both anti-slavery activists and international organizations uncovered a number of isolated incidents. One example of this theme comes from a court case brought to light by an otherwise unsuccessful United Nations request to Interpol for information on slavery:

> On 3 May 1971, two Algerian nationals . . . were arrested and charged with "traffic in human beings and practices similar to slavery," acts specified in and punishable under article 189 of the Malian Criminal code. The first prisoner admitted that in 1968 he sold one of his slaves to another Algerian for 20 camels. The slave, a little ten-year-old girl, died of thirst in the desert while tending camels. The second prisoner admitted that he had sold a woman and her two children to another Algerian.[4]

A further example comes from Roger Sawyer, who reports the 1977 case of a Nicaraguan man who sought asylum in Britain, claiming to be an escaped slave. He testified that he was one of forty slaves, who had been branded to prevent escape.[5] Both incidents offer limited insight into broader patterns, as it is not clear whether they are individual cases or representative of larger trends. They are also fixed in time. Both sources are silent regarding subsequent developments. It is important, however, to not take this argument too far. For people who had firsthand experience of enslavement, or who were based in communities where slavery continued to be an ongoing issue, detailed information on slavery was clearly not in short supply. Properly understood, the main point at issue involved the dissemination of local knowledge to international audiences. In this respect, the perspective adopted here is that of an outsider looking in: receiving snapshots and reports that suggest that cases of enslavement continued, but finding it difficult to acquire an adequate picture of relevant practices.

In this environment, extrapolation becomes all but inevitable. Despite having limited information to work with, anti-slavery activists still wanted to provide some sense of both the overall numbers of people involved and their geographical distribution. This proved to be an empirically difficult and politically sensitive exercise. On this front, it was clear by at least the 1960s that traditional slavery no longer constituted the pervasive problem of the nineteenth and early twentieth centuries. By this stage, it was generally accepted that residual cases were chiefly concentrated in Saharan Africa and the Middle East, with scattered remnants in Asia, Latin America, and other parts of Africa. Speaking at the United Nations in 1967, Special Rapporteur Dr. Mohammed Awad offered a rough global estimate of two million slaves.[6] Another estimate from French academic Germaine Tillion in 1968 went as high as ten million slaves, but this was received with a degree of skepticism when it was initially published.[7] Tillion's research indicated that most slaves were found in the northern half of Africa. Specific reference was made to Algeria, Libya, Morocco, Mauritania, Senegal, Mali, and Niger. More recent estimates speak of hundreds of thousands of slaves, rather than millions. Sawyer cites a 1984 estimate of 250,000 slaves living in and around the African Sahel.[8] As we shall see below, more recent estimates have focused on specific countries.

One further illustration of the limited information available on slavery comes from a 1966 pamphlet published by the British based Anti-Slavery Society. Entitled *The Anti-Slavery Society: Its Task Today*, this pamphlet presents a dossier of recent evidence of slavery (or at least evidence of slavery that the society was prepared to make public). This material was organized into three categories: reliable information, reliable information more than five years old, and other reports. The first category includes scattered reports of slavery in places such as Yemen, Algeria, Cameroon, Lebanon, Mauritania, and Malaysia. It is worth noting, however, that these reports only deal with fairly small numbers of slaves. Outside the Arabian Peninsula, the largest estimate that was offered speaks of 20,000–40,000 slaves in Mauritania. This figure was based on the research trip discussed above, and was therefore somewhat dated by 1966. Many reports were based on stories that were only directly concerned with one or two cases of enslavement. Significantly, these cases were not confined to classical slavery, but also encompassed related practices. Similar themes populated the second and third categories, which covered further cases in places such as Colombia, Peru, Syria, Ethiopia, Sierra Leone, Nigeria, and the Philippines. These examples once again adhered to the same pattern of anecdotes and incidents.[9] The Society freely acknowledged the limitations of its material: "If we are asked if our reports represent a consistent pattern we readily admit that, with our limited resources . . . all that we are able to reveal is the tip of the ice-burg."[10] The fact that a longstanding and well-established anti-slavery organization could only present such limited material is emblematic of a larger shortage of reliable evidence.

In a political landscape characterized by limited information and international inertia, local political authorities were largely left to their own devices for much of the second half of the twentieth century. As we have seen, one of the most significant problem areas was Saharan Africa. According to historian Martin Klein, around 200,000 people still accepted some form of slavery in French West Africa at the conclusion of colonial rule in 1960.[11] This huge fiefdom covered most of the African Sahel and splintered into many independent states. It is not always easy to trace subsequent developments, but this does not mean there are no resources available here. On this front, a useful starting point comes from Jonathan Derrick, whose 1975 survey *Africa's Slaves Today* summarized much of what was known, or not known, about the dimensions of slavery in Africa during the 1960s and early 1970s.

Instead of presenting slavery as an overriding priority, Derrick's work instead started with a discussion of other serious problems in Africa, as he cautioned readers against thinking that "slaves are the only unfortunates in a 'system' in which others generally live well."[12] This measured approach avoided strident condemnation, and instead presented slavery as an intractable feature of traditional life that had proved resistant to legal resolution. Echoing other reports, Derrick observed that "It is above all in the Sahara Desert and its southern borderlands that traditional slavery, that is, where slaves are a separate and long-established part of society, still goes on."[13] This statement was supported by chapters devoted to the Moors of Mauritania, the nomadic Tuareg of the Sahara, and a more amorphous group of "Savanna slaves." Other parts of the continent were considered more briefly, with slavery being placed alongside serfdom, servile marriage, and forced labor for the state.

Based on the available evidence, Derrick concluded that "slavery in the Sahara is not like slavery in the Deep South."[14] In a harsh desert environment dominated by poverty, scarcity, and tradition, slavery represented a moderate evil, which saw relatively mild treatment offset by heinous controls over children and reproduction. Rather than focusing on legal solutions, Derrick favored social and economic development, envisaging an indirect end to slavery through an extended process of social transformation. It is not entirely clear, however, why legal intervention was given such limited support. When other parts of the continent were considered, the available evidence suggested that the legal abolition of slavery could be regarded as a qualified success. Accordingly, "The survival of some sort of slavery is no greater, perhaps less, than what one would expect in an area where slavery was a normal part of life for centuries, until two or three generations ago."[15] Derrick identified several countries where official intervention had proved effective. In Guinea, slavery was challenged by a revolutionary movement, eliciting government action. In Cameroon, the government facilitated the release of around 50,000 slaves in 1969. However, these appear to be the exception, rather than the rule. In the absence of sustained enforcement of anti-slavery laws, economic development was conceived as a viable long-term alternative.

Over the last three decades, there has been a marked improvement in both the quality and quantity of information on classical slavery and descent-based discrimination in Saharan Africa. This is partially attributable to the growth of local and international human rights organizations from the 1970s onward, and partially attributable to the parallel growth of a more sophisticated (and less sensationalist) academic literature that has recently generated a number of detailed anthropological studies of residual practices in various countries. This means that contemporary activists and institutional agents now have access to much greater material than their counterparts in the 1960s and 1970s. On this front, a useful starting point comes from a recent survey of the history of slavery in Saharan Africa from David Seddon.

Starting in the mid-nineteenth century, Seddon charts a complex process of long-term change, which began with the deterioration of transcontinental slaving networks in response to increasing European incursions in the second half of the nineteenth century. Colonial rule was established very gradually in the Saharan region, with many areas remaining outside effective control until at least the early twentieth century. Familiar compromises followed, resulting in a significant degree of informal sanction and support for established practices for many decades. This does not mean, however, that no major changes occurred. Over time, regional networks declined, slave markets closed, sources of fresh slaves decreased, and some existing slaves were able to seek out additional options and opportunities. In most cases, slavery remained a problem following decolonization. Some postcolonial states, such as Algeria, took direct action against slavery. Others states were less forthcoming:

> By the end of the 1970s all the countries of Africa north of the Sahara, as well as the newly declared Saharawi Arab Democratic republic [in Western Sahara], had effectively abolished slavery and related forms of institutional subservience. The southern Saharan states had not.[16]

This narrative draws on a variety of sources, integrating recent developments into a larger historical trajectory. Seddon makes clear that many changes have taken place, but he also identifies cases where anti-slavery remains an ongoing project, rather than a finished product.

Various factors are held responsible for the persistence of slavery. State weakness in the face of deep political and social cleavages is identified as a major issue in Mali, Niger, Chad, and Sudan. An elite commitment to traditional hierarchy is highlighted in Mauritania. These themes are considered in more depth below. At this juncture, it is worth noting that Seddon establishes a rough division between slavery, forms of slavery, and the heritage of slavery. This not only reflects the challenge of classifying many of the practices involved, it also points to situations where changes have occurred, yet a substantial socioeconomic legacy endures. This theme is most apparent where a master/slave axis persists, but operates on quite different terms. The most common example here concerns ex-slaves providing a portion of their crop, or performing unrewarded labor, for their former masters. Other related themes can be roughly grouped under the banner of social discrimination, comprising issues of social status, personal decorum, sexual mores, and religious standing.[17]

In some cases, discrimination occurs within a continuum that includes traditional slavery. Much more common, however, are settings where "slavery has disappeared as a structure, but still lives in a discourse that shapes the lives of those descended from both slaves and masters."[18] This tends to be manifested in social barriers to high office, public rituals, inheritance, and marriage practices. A good snapshot once again comes from Klein:

there are probably a couple of million people in West Africa who are referred to in their native languages as slaves. These people all descend from people who were slaves, who were captured or perhaps enslaved as a penalty for crime or a parent's debts . . . thus, many of their descendants are stigmatized as being different . . . status regulates social relationships, particularly marriage, and hierarchy is often indicated by kinship terminology, the descendant of the master being addressed as father and the descendant of former slaves being spoken to as if they were children.[19]

Klein concludes that there are now "very few people" who come anywhere near to historical definitions of slavery, but that there is nonetheless a much larger population who currently endure various disabilities and vulnerabilities on the basis of slave descent.[20] This general conclusion is supported by recent studies in places such as Mali, Niger, and Nigeria.[21]

These themes have often been grouped under the banner of "vestiges" of slavery. This operates at both a global level, where traditional forms of slavery have sometimes been reduced to a marginal international issue, and at a local level, where slavery has sometimes been reduced to a residual historical legacy. This language echoes earlier colonial rhetoric, and can therefore be invoked to legitimate political inaction, since the current status quo is tacitly assumed to be improving organically (locally), or the best we can realistically hope for (internationally). Several qualifications can be raised in response to this framework. For one thing, it is by no means clear that all of these "vestiges" are benign or inoffensive. It is also equally hazardous to assume that they will inexorably decline over time. In this environment, most problems remain at a local level, but some have gradually acquired a more prominent place on the international agenda.

The Further Abolition of Slavery

On November 9, 1981, the Islamic Republic of Mauritania issued a public ordinance that legally abolished slavery throughout the country. This followed in the wake of a largely symbolic pronouncement on June 5, 1980, which is widely held to have been a reluctant response to popular protests over the public sale of a female slave.[22] This reflected the path-breaking work of El Hor, an organization founded in 1978 by descendants of slaves, and which mounted a political campaign against slavery in the late 1970s.[23] This campaign was brutally suppressed and many of its leaders imprisoned, but it nonetheless aroused a sufficient furor for a short-lived military junta to take placatory steps.[24] As we have seen, the presence of slavery had not gone entirely unnoticed before 1980,[25] but the fact that further proclamations were issued would give "Mauritania a kind of notoriety by making it seem one of the last, if not the last country in the world where slavery was officially tolerated."[26] This stimulated the interest of journalists, activists, and officials, resulting in a steady stream of missions, reports, exposés, and hearings from the 1980s to the present.

Like most modern states in Africa, Mauritania is a European invention. It was once part of French West Africa, a sprawling colonial project built through conflict and compromise. French forces established their military preponderance in the late nineteenth and early twentieth centuries, but their authority remained fragile, especially among the nomadic peoples of the Sahara, who (when not in active revolt) were frequently left to their own devices. To placate their rebellious subjects, administrators favored a complicit approach, retaining slavery as an integral feature of life in Mauritania, despite the introduction of formal anti-slavery legislation from the 1900s onward. Some branches of the slave trade declined, some slaves acquired freedom (frequently through personal initiative),[27] but larger institutional and ideological structures remained mostly intact. Since independence, Mauritania has been repeatedly wracked by international turmoil, including a ruinous war in Western Sahara (1975–1978), a conflict with Senegal resulting in the forced repatriation of tens of thousands of people in 1989, and a period of international ostracism following an ill-judged alignment with Saddam Hussein in 1991.[28] A similar story can be told domestically, as a succession of mostly authoritarian rulers have reigned over one of the poorest countries in the world, while its people have endured drought, desertification, "Arabization," food riots, repeated coups, political repression, foreign intervention, and communal violence.

Life in Mauritania is dominated by enduring social cleavages. Alongside more parochial models of kin, caste, and tribe, the country can be loosely divided among "White" Moors (Beidane), "Black" Moors (Haratine), and "African" tribes. The former are the modern representatives of Arabic peoples from northern Africa, who established a preponderant position in the region over many centuries,[29] and continue to enjoy a dominant political and socioeconomic position. Within this complex social hierarchy, the superiority of

"White" Moors is chiefly based on the subjugation of their "Black" counter-parts, whose status remains bound up in slavery. Having been conquered, captured, and enslaved, these black Africans have taken on the linguistic and cultural mores of their masters. This heritage is typically rooted in the distant past, but can sometimes include more recent cases of enslavement.

There are also internal divisions between slaves and ex-slaves and their descendants. The former experience bondage at a personal level and have been further divided into "full" and "part" slaves, with the latter enjoying substantial levels of autonomy.[30] Slave descendants are defined by their slave heritage, and thus experience discrimination and social subordination, but no longer have extensive obligations to specific masters. They include persons whose ancestors were freed in previous centuries and individuals who enjoy considerable material prosperity. The term "Haratine" can be used in a limited sense to describe slaves and ex-slaves, or in a more expansive sense to describe all "Black" Moors. Standing outside this social order are a number of tribal groupings that are chiefly concentrated in the more fertile south. Having resisted Arab encroachment from the north, these tribes share an "African" perspective and—as with many colonial constructs—can often be found on both sides of the borders with Senegal and Mali. Most attention has focused on "Arab" slavery, but slaves have also been reported in other communities.[31] In all of these settings, a shared commitment to Islam provides much of the ideological glue holding slavery together.

The scale of slavery in Mauritania is a matter of ongoing dispute. In 1982, John Mercer referred to "a minimum of 100,000 total slaves, with a further 300,000 part-slaves and ex-slaves."[32] In a more recent survey, Kevin Bales provides an estimate for Mauritania of between 250,000 to 300,000 slaves.[33] Perhaps the most commonly cited figure has come from a 1994 report from the U.S. government, which put forward the (extremely tentative, upper estimate) figure of 90,000.[34] This figure proved somewhat controversial, because later reports presented a different picture by discarding concrete estimates and speaking instead of "vestiges" of slavery, which were expected to decline over time.[35] This stance has been endorsed by a number of other sources. It also echoes the general thrust of an earlier United Nations mission led by Mark Bossuyt, which reported in 1984 that "slavery as an institution protected by law has been genuinely abolished in Mauritania," and that "it is henceforth justified to speak of the elimination of the 'consequences of slavery.'"[36] While none of the estimates listed above are especially reliable, enough evidence of continuing problems has been generated in recent times to cast doubt on the notion of "genuine abolition."

In keeping with earlier precedents, human rights activists have continued to use individual testimonies to highlight the worst aspects of slavery. Take, for instance, this dramatic account of an escaped slave cited by the American Anti-Slavery Group in 2000:

> For Moussa, the horror of life was literally unspeakable. Born into slavery, he herded animals with his family for their master. Beatings were the norm for his father and brothers, and his sisters were frequently raped. His father's fingernails, he says, were once ripped out as punishment. As a young boy Moussa tried to escape; he was caught and his master's brother slashed his heel with a sword to prevent him from running again.[37]

Similar stories have featured prominently in reports for over two decades, chronicling torture, sexual abuse, dispossession, systematic exploitation, arduous work routines, official complicity, and the separation of families. Many of these stories concern women, reflecting (among other things) the gendered nature of recent practices. In some reports, slave trading and occasional kidnappings continue on a small scale, but they now offer very minor sources of slaves.[38] The vast majority of slaves acquire their status at birth, making the continued viability of the system dependent on the procreation of new generations.

In a frequently cited article in the *New York Times* in 1997, Elinor Burkett reported this lurid response from one slave on the question of rape: "they would come in the night when they needed to breed us. Is that what you mean by rape?"[39] Another human rights activist, Samuel Cotton, has also referenced forced breeding between slaves.[40] When female slaves escape, they can often be forced to leave their children behind. Claims of "marriage" have also been used strategically to retain control of their offspring. These reports are difficult to reconcile with the image presented in the UN report over a decade earlier, which held that "More often than not slavery in Mauritania took the form of servitude; as such it was contrary to human dignity, but was not attended by inhuman treatment."[41]

Faced with a seemingly endless stream of individual testimonies, it can be tempting to approach slavery in static terms, as if there had been little or no change from earlier historical periods. Given the enduring history of the issues involved, this temptation is understandable, yet still problematic. At a local level, a range of complex changes can be identified. These can be something of a mixed blessing, however. In a 1992 report, Anti-Slavery International concluded that: "Chattel slavery is probably decreasing, but it has not disappeared; rather, it has taken other forms. It is perhaps appropriate, therefore, to begin to describe some aspects of the Mauritanian situation in terms of modern forms of . . . slavery."[42] This involves a move away from classical slavery, narrowly conceived, to include related issues such as child labor, kidnappings, and domestic servitude, particularly in urban areas. This latter point has been taken up by Kevin Bales in his discussion of slavery in Nouakchott, the Mauritanian capital, where he argues the "movement of what was essentially an agricultural form of slavery into the city is transforming both city and slavery."[43] If slavery has been recently evolving (or even dissolving), what is it evolving into? What sorts of additional avenues are becoming available? What larger vulnerabilities and disabilities remain to be overcome? How do those involved negotiate their changing place within society?

In this context, I turn to the work of Urs Peter Ruf, which stresses the dynamic nature of slavery, servitude, and social hierarchy in Mauritania. Employing a sociological approach, Ruf presents a complex historical trajectory, where protagonists traverse an enduring tension between institutional form and actual condition. At a formal level, masters ostensibly exercise tremendous power and authority, but this can be tempered by a range of countervailing factors. Alongside the litany of individual horrors stories identified above, we find regular reports of slaves being well treated and establishing a variety of self-governing spaces. These can sometimes be not so much positive goods as lesser indignities, but they are nonetheless symptomatic of varying and changing patterns of behavior. For many slaves

> The game of ending slavery . . . is about successively cementing practiced condition into statutory definition. This is a paradoxical project as such, because the condition always symbolizes the individual's relationship to the slave estate even if this might be vanishing over time.[44]

For slave-holders in Mauritania, the recent dilution of their historical prerogatives has comparatively little to do with benevolent paternalism, but instead reflects a staggered response to various catalysts, including colonial policies, the crippling drought of the early 1970s, the disastrous war in Western Sahara, and more recent anti-slavery proclamations. The pace of urbanization and the growth of NGOs such as El Hor and SOS Esclaves have also produced (a vision of) qualified sanctuaries, giving further weight to the option of flight.[45] Over time, these influences appear have had a cumulative, but by no means uniform impact.

Faced with various challenges, many masters have found it necessary to let various prerogatives lapse in an attempt to retain at least some of their privileges in the face of cumulative acts of rebellion and resistance. With the opening up of additional options and opportunities, many slaves have secured varying degrees of autonomy. Instead of repudiating their bonds outright, both (ex-)masters and (ex-)slaves have tended to navigate within established structures and orientations. In this respect, slavery remains bound up in deeply internalized roles. Slave status does not represent an alien imposition, but is instead a social fact that reflects cultural and psychological horizons developed at a young age. This does not lead to cultural determinism, which can reduce slaves to self-regulating automatons, but to a more complex stance regarding the parameters of legitimate and appropriate conduct.

This usually takes the form of various rights and duties, where (ex-) slaves provide a portion of their crop, or make remittances out of a sense of obligation, or in terms of social deference, which links personal inferiority with social subordination. For Ruf, these can be loosely characterized as symptoms of "a mental state of slavery: arrogance on the part of the former masters . . . and subservience on the part of . . . slaves and manumitted slaves."[46] As we have seen, this extends far beyond classical slavery, narrowly conceived, to encompass broader patterns of descent-based discrimination. It is clear, moreover, that this ingrained dualism will remain at the heart of social and economic order long after classical slavery has faded away entirely. This underlying division has also been expressed in the language of caste discrimination, which offers another lens through which to approach Mauritanian society.[47] This standpoint is captured by Human Rights Watch in a 2001 report:

> Both the Arab and Afro-Mauritanian groups have long distinguished community members on the basis of caste, and both included a caste-like designation of "slave" within these systems. To this day a former "slave" distinction—particularly for the *Haratines*, Arabic speakers of Sub-Saharan African origin—still carries significant social implications. At best, members of higher and lower castes are discouraged from intermarrying. . . . At worst, however, there is a widespread sys-

tem of unpaid servitude required of communities whose members still self-identify as slaves.[48]

This frame of reference moves the focus away from terminological disputes over slavery, and instead highlights broader sociological cleavages and various gradations in status, dominion, and experience. One strength of this approach is that it situates (anti-)slavery within a larger complex that does not end with the eradication of classical slavery. This is not without political risk, however, as it skirts the "vestiges" framework that has been favored by the Mauritanian government. Framed as one of many problem areas, any remaining cases of classical slavery may get lost in the shuffle, or relegated to the worst examples of a larger trend that requires long-term change. It can also downplay the role of the government, by suggesting that both the source and solution to the problem can be found within social transformation, rather than official intervention.

On this front, the apparatus of the state has remained firmly in the hands of the "White" Moors. First, there are the forces of law and order, where police have regularly sided with disgruntled masters and sympathetic judges have repeatedly upheld many of their historical prerogatives. This is by no means a uniform, unproblematic characterization, since contrary practices have been reported,[49] but the sympathies of various government institutions appear to frequently rest with former masters. Of particular importance here is a willful blindness to systematic abuses committed in the defense of tradition. This theme is taken up in a report by Amnesty International in 2003, which concluded that "there are no known cases where anyone has been prosecuted for holding someone in slavery, or buying or selling such a person."[50] This permissive stance has obvious ramifications for the status of all forms of human bondage. It is clear, moreover, that state capture extends into larger political problems. On this front, Mauritania has been characterized as an "apartheid" state, based on a systemic pattern of forced expulsions, dispossession, political repression, human rights abuses, cultural discrimination, and institutionalized racism. In the eyes of its rulers, Mauritania will always be an Arab nation, leading to the systematic exclusion, if not denegation, of the non-Arab peoples that make up a substantial portion of the population.[51] The apartheid label invokes a totalizing image that sidesteps ongoing political contestation and the recent growth of civil society, but it does capture a central truth: ruling elites have embraced a vision of their country that has left little room for many of their compatriots.

On August 9, 2007, the Mauritanian Parliament unanimously passed a new bill making slavery a criminal offense punishable by up to ten years in prison. Significantly, this new legislation included provisions modeled on anti-Semitism laws in some European countries, prescribing a two-year prison term for the author of a cultural or artistic production that justifies or glorifies slavery. While this legislation is undoubtedly a welcome development, it remains to be seen whether it marks a decisive departure from the past. This uncertainty was recently compounded by a coup against Prime Minister Yahia Ould Ahmed El-Waqef in August 2008. This once again threw Mauritania into turmoil, and it remains to be seen whether anti-slavery efforts will continue in the face of renewed political instability. In 2009, the UN Special Rapporteur on Contemporary Forms of Slavery, Gulnara Shahinian, made a research trip to Mauritania. While commending the 2007 law, she went on to identify a: "vicious circle of slavery for men, women and children. The women . . . were the most vulnerable as they suffer triple discrimination firstly as women, secondly, as mothers and thirdly as slaves."[52] While traditional forms of slavery appear to have been reduced to a fairly small number of cases, there is every reason to expect that descent-based discrimination will remain a major problem for the foreseeable future.

During the 1980s and 1990s, Mauritania was regularly described as a unique exception: the only place in the world where "widespread, institutionalized slavery persisted into the late twentieth century."[53] This formula relied on a narrow approach that set classical slavery apart from other forms of human bondage. Even then, it still left a number of issues unresolved. In the late 1990s, a further connection was established between Sudan and Mauritania, but this tended to involve discussion of two "exceptions" rather than one.[54] The case of Sudan is discussed in more depth below. More recently, Mauritania has come to be regarded as the best documented example of practices that can be found in other parts of Africa. This most recent phase has once again been characterized by the partial elevation of local truisms to international issues. For locals, slavery and servitude have long been a fact of life, but their circumstances have only recently acquired a modest international audience.

Of particular importance here is the case of Niger, a landlocked, impoverished state that was once part of French West Africa. This is one of many parallels with Mauritania. On May 5, 2003, the government of Niger passed measures legally reabolishing slavery, following sustained campaigning by local activists. In this forum, I can only offer a brief sketch of this recent history. One prominent starting point comes from a 2004 report produced under the auspices of Anti-Slavery International and Association Timidria, a local anti-slavery group founded in 1991.[55] This report paints a familiar picture, starting with colonial duplicity, where large-scale slaving was suppressed, but slavery itself was regularly condoned under various euphemisms. When Niger became independent in 1960, its new constitution prohibited slavery and declared all humans equal, but a series of postcolonial governments—weakened by rebellion and political instability—continued to uphold colonial precedents supporting slave status in combination with traditional elites.

Much like in Mauritania, there were a variety of cumulative challenges to the status quo during both the colonial and postcolonial periods, but slavery and slave descent have nonetheless remained a major feature of social and political life in Niger. In the 2004 Timidria report, the problems involved are said to range from slavery "pure and simple," where slaves are characterized as beasts of burden, and "passive" slavery, where masters exercise claims over property and person, but are further removed from day-to-day activities, to associated problems relating to "concubines," social discrimination, and other forms of bondage. The report includes personal testimonials covering rape, sale, torture, murder, castration, breeding, abuse, separation, deprivation, and arduous work routines. A snapshot of slavery in Niger comes from research conducted through the International Labour Organization, which suggests "that slavery continues to exist as an institution that involves forced labor in the nomadic Tuareg, Toubou, and Arab Regions," while other parts of the country are again described in terms of "passive slavery," which ranges from "ordinary racism to discrimination, segregation, and in some cases perhaps serfdomlike situations."[56]

In 2002, Timidria conducted an extensive survey that provides a rough snapshot of contemporary problems, covering issues such as marriage, gender, education, treatment, and geographic dispersion. This was compiled into a database that includes names and locations of those in bondage. Based on 11,000 local respondents who volunteered information on slavery in their environs, the first draft of the survey generated the startling total of 870,363 slaves, comprising around 8 percent of the national population.[57] This figure was later supplemented with the much more modest total of 46,382 slaves, or 0.3 percent of the population, owing to problems with double counting. These highly variable figures can be further compared with "a rough estimate provided by human rights activist and Tuareg prince Moutstapha Kadi Oumani of 8,855 people held in slavery and slavery-like situations."[58]

The politics of slavery in Niger are extremely complex. In 2003, the British Broadcasting Corporation covered a ceremony where dozens of grateful slaves were formally issued certificates of freedom, but the ceremony was interrupted by police who seized equipment from journalists at the behest of the local governor.[59] In March 2005, the government aborted a similar event (which it had previously cosponsored),[60] where 7,000 slaves were to be formally granted their freedom. Afraid that the ceremony would draw unwanted attention, "[t]he authorities warned slave masters that any public declaration that they owned other people would leave them open to prosecution." This was followed by a number of arrests, including Ilguilas Weila, president of Timidria, who was charged with "propagating false information on slavery and attempting to raise funds illegally."[61] This arrest was reported to have provoked a 2,000 strong demonstration in the capital Niamey.[62]

Decades of official complicity in the continuation of slavery was highlighted by a high-profile court case in 2008, which saw the Community Court of Justice of the Economic Community of West African States (ECOWAS) determine that the government of Niger had failed to protect one of its citizens from slavery. The plaintiff in the case was Hadijatou Mani Koraou, who was born into slavery in 1984. At the age of 12, she was sold to a new owner for the sum of 240,000 Central African Francs (around U.S.$400). She subsequently endured years of systematic abuse and exploitation. Hadijatou's master, El Hadj Souleymane Naroua, had four wives and seven other "sadaka" (female slaves). In 2005, he decided to "liberate" Hadijatou to make her one of his wives. Having been issued with a formal liberation certificate, she subsequently refused to marry her master, triggering a series of legal proceedings that eventually ended up in the Supreme Court, the highest court in Niger. The court acknowledged Hadijatou's slave status, yet failed to condemn it as unlawful. The judiciary and police not only repeatedly failed to support her bid for freedom, they directly assisted her master. When Hadijatou later married another man, her former master had her successfully prosecuted for bigamy. She served two months of a six-month sentence for this "crime" before the ECOWAS regional court intervened. Rejecting government submissions that the case was a domestic matter, the court ruled in October 2008 that the government of Niger had failed to uphold its legal obligations, and should therefore pay 10,000,000 Central African Francs (around U.S.$20,000) in restitution, plus court costs.[63]

The long-term ramifications of this landmark ruling are still being processed, but the pattern of widespread official complicity that Hadijatou's case revealed strongly suggests that slavery remains firmly entrenched at cultural and institutional levels. Until relatively recently, most human rights groups and international organizations, "concentrated on Mauritania and Niger, and the subject . . . received relatively little attention in other Sahelian countries."[64] In 2005, the International Labour Organization somewhat belatedly embraced a more regional perspective, observing that: "It is principally in the Sahelian countries of West Africa, including Benin, Burkina Faso, Cameroon, Chad, Guinea, Mali, Mauritania and Niger, that some concern has been expressed about alleged ongoing slavery-like practices or discrimination against descendants of slaves."[65] This stance was not limited to slavery per se, but instead discussed a "spectrum of situations, from the highly exploitative to the relatively benign."[66] Framed in these terms, the move from legal abolition to effective emancipation constitutes an ongoing work in progress, which clearly extends far beyond a narrow focus on classical slavery. As we have seen, substantive practices rarely fit into neat categories, but instead regularly stretch both the analytical and political vocabulary of anti-slavery in a variety of ways. Analytically, the main issues are diversity and ambiguity. While the worst cases continue to attract the most attention, they represent the most extreme end of a complex continuum involving varying degrees of dominion and discrimination, and varying degrees of coercion and consent. Politically, the main challenge is coming to terms with these variations, and thus confronting a host of deeply rooted socioeconomic problems, while continuing to resist the official formula that no (true) slavery equals no (real) problem.

Wartime Enslavement

Many accounts of the historical origins of slavery begin with the enslavement of captives taken in wartime. This has tended to be expressed in the language of a bargain, with prisoners "consenting" to serve as slaves to avoid certain death. While this formula is not without merit, it captures only part of the issues involved. It is clear, for instance, that this one-sided bargain usually involved individuals deemed to be of both potential value and manageable risk, with more troublesome adult men often being slain. In some historical slave systems, enslavement was not simply an indirect consequence of warfare directed toward other ends, but also a major source of martial motivation, as internal and external demands for new slaves regularly proved to be a major catalyst for large-scale organized violence. This later theme would have a particularly grievous impact on the history of sub-Saharan Africa, where external demand for slaves was a major catalyst for many centuries of bloody combat and violent enslavement, which reached a historical zenith during the nineteenth century.[67]

While wartime enslavement markedly declined following colonial conquest, the various ingredients involved have continued to resonate in a number of parts of Africa. The main issue from an anti-slavery perspective has been the wartime practice of kidnapping women and children as part of organized raiding parties of varying sizes. This practice is most prominently associated with recent conflicts in Sudan and Uganda, but has been reported in other recent and ongoing sites of conflict, such as Sierra Leone, Liberia, and the Democratic Republic of Congo.[68] To further develop this theme, I will primarily focus on the history of civil war in Sudan, which took place between 1983 and 2005. This conflict is of particular interest due to the way in which the language of "classical," or "chattel" slavery was deployed in order to prioritize various wartime abuses. While these abuses do not mark an unbroken extension of earlier historical models, the history of slavery and abolition nonetheless continues to cast a long shadow over Sudan.

The nineteenth-century history of Sudan was chiefly defined by the rapacious advance of slavers from the north, acting at the behest of Muhammad Ali, Khedive of Egypt. This conquest was originally motivated by a desire for slave soldiers,[69] and it led to a protracted, multisided conflict involving (among others) Egyptian, Mahdist, and British military forces. Large numbers of southern Sudanese were enslaved during this period. While outright war ended under colonial rule, tensions between north and south continued to simmer, exacerbated by British colonial policies. On the eve of independence in 1956, Sudan erupted in civil war. The first phase of the conflict lasted nearly two decades, before a peace settlement secured a measure of political autonomy for southern Sudan. After a period of relative peace, the Sudanese government abrogated this settlement in 1983, provoking a return to the battlefield.[70] In 1998, it was calculated that this second civil war had killed over two million people and displaced over six million.[71] This conflict was defined by persistent, well-documented reports of wartime enslavement, which attracted a great deal of international attention. The havoc wreaked by these practices mainly fell on women and children, with female abductees enduring persistent sexual assault. A useful synopsis of the issues involved comes from the Report of the International Eminent Persons Group (2002):

Of particular concern is the pattern of abuses that occurs in conjunc-
tion with attacks by pro-government militias known as murahaleen
on SPLA-controlled areas near the boundary between northern and
southern Sudan. These are characterized by: capture through abduction (generally accompanied by violence); the forced transfer of victims to another community; subjection to forced labor for no pay;
denial of victims' freedom of movement and choice; and, frequently,
assaults on personal identity such as renaming, forced religious conversion, involuntary circumcision, prohibition on the use of native
languages and the denial of contacts with the victims' families and
communities of origin.[72]

The SPLA is the Sudan People's Liberation Army, which was the main military adversary of the government during the civil war. Despite official denials, most observers concluded that the militias conducting these raids were
aided and abetted by the Sudanese government as part of a broader military
strategy involving mass displacements and ethnic cleansing. The cultivation
of significant oil reserves in southern Sudan further complicated matters.[73]
Numerous atrocities were committed by opposition forces,[74] but allegations
of slave raiding were primarily directed against the Sudanese government
and its informal allies.

In the face of this broader history (together with the more recent genocidal conflict in Darfur), it should be clear that discussion of slavery cannot exist in isolation, but must be regarded as part of a much larger pattern
of human rights abuses. These can be dissected in various ways. From one
standpoint, slavery can be regarded as part of a larger pattern of servitude,
which also extends to debt-bondage, forced labor, work camps, human trafficking, "concubinage," and the exploitation of refugees.[75] In another, slave
raids can be regarded as but one example of wartime abuses that have been
inflicted on civilians by the Sudanese government for decades. These abuses
have regularly included extrajudicial killings, torture, displacement, dispossession, aerial bombings, scorched earth policies, mass murder, and forced
recruitment.[76] Similar themes have been reported in relation to the systematic abuse of children, where child slavery has been placed alongside child
labor, child soldiers, and the abuse of street children.[77] Widespread failures to
take action against slavery continues to be similarly bound up in a longstanding and pervasive culture of impunity.[78]

It is clear, moreover, that larger historical cleavages have been a major part of enduring tensions between north and south. On this front, the recent civil war can be best understood as but one phase in a protracted political struggle, which has been defined by the incomplete consolidation of two opposing (yet far from homogeneous) coalitions: an Arab north and a Christian/Animist south. These very rough categories do not reflect immutable divisions, but have emerged out of a contingent historical trajectory.[79] The history of slavery and abolition in Sudan is central to this story. Sudan is the largest country in Africa, bringing together a wide variety of linguistic, religious, and cultural groupings.[80] The citizens of Sudan can be divided along many different lines, yet the nexus between north and south has gradually emerged as a primary political axis. The origins of this divide can be traced to many centuries of mutual antagonism between northern Muslims and their southern neighbors. This mutual antagonism was not the only political fault line in the region (political elites within both north and south Sudan regularly fought among themselves), but it gradually gained additional depth and definition during the nineteenth century, which saw a succession of conquerors from the north preside over a massive expansion of slavery that peaked under the Madhist regime in the late nineteenth century (1885–1899).[81] Throughout this tumultuous period, the burden of enslavement fell heaviest on non-Muslims in the south.

The boundaries of modern Sudan were consolidated under the authority of an Anglo-Egyptian Condominium in the late nineteenth century. From the outset, the Condominium was a political artifice, with Britain exercising a dominant role.[82] Colonial rule gave further impetus to evolving geographic and political divisions.[83] This can be partially traced to armed resistance in parts of southern Sudan, which continued for decades after the establishment of colonial rule. Wealth, education, public works, and political life were concentrated elsewhere, leaving southern Sudan an undeveloped backwater. In the 1920s, the British espoused a policy of indirect rule, determining (among other things) that the three southern provinces would form a Closed District, which nonresidents required special permits to enter. This move was ostensibly designed "to stop Arab tribes from seizing slaves, cattle and grain from the south, and to end the alleged pressure to convert to Islam."[84] Instead, Christian missionaries were encouraged. The Closed Districts, which were only partially enforced, also applied to much of western Sudan. British influence was not limited to institutional mechanisms, but extended to cultural essentialism, where particular groups would come to be crudely defined in terms of dominant character traits. Northern peoples were linked together under an orientalist banner, as cultured yet indolent, while southern peoples were incorporated under an "African" or "Sudanese" placard, as energetic yet primitive. In the early decades of colonial rule, this was bound up in a complicit approach to slavery, where the British maintained that neither side of the (Arab) master/slave (African) relationship would function effectively without the other, and thus unofficially allowed substantial slave populations to remain in place.[85] A more proactive anti-slavery policy was adopted in the 1920s, but residual cases of slavery continued into the 1950s.[86]

If colonial rule gave depth and definition to divisions between north and south, the move toward independence brought these different perspectives into conflict.[87] Separate development was abandoned, northern agents took up key positions, and the reigns of power passed into Arab hands. This culminated in a "mutiny" in 1955, precipitating the first phase of the civil war. From a northern perspective, this was an unpardonable rebellion. From a southern perspective, it was legitimate resistance. Both perspectives form part of larger parochial narratives.[88] Whatever the merits of these stylized positions, decades of struggle have nourished general polarization. This has been further exacerbated by consistent political repression, which has seen a succession of authoritarian rulers stifle voices from all parts of the country. Religious radicalism has been a major part of this trajectory. The current regime came to power in a coup in June 1989, cementing the dominant position of Islamist forces.[89]

It is tempting to approach wartime enslavement as a symptom of conflict and lingering tradition. While there is some merit to this stance, it omits the crucial ideological and cultural dimensions of race and religion.[90] Writing in 2001, Jok Madut Jok observed that slavery was

> coded into the Baggara Arabic language, folklore, daily humor, and poetry. Southern Sudanese continue to be referred to as *abeed* (slaves) by North Sudanese . . . It is this long tradition of an ideology of dominance that Arab governments in Khartoum have always used to treat the South as a mere source of material resources, and its inhabitants as cheap laborers who can be useful only when they are stripped of their freedom. This long-standing racial/ethnic prejudice has partly prompted the current wave of slavery.[91]

Framed in these terms, racial/ethnic deficiencies not only rendered southerners legitimate candidates for enslavement, they could also be justified as a form of cultural redemption, where captives acquire a new name, language, or religion. However much wartime enslavement can be connected to strategic calculations and political and military ends, it has not taken place in an ideological vacuum. Recent acts of enslavement (and other grievous abuses) can ultimately be traced to underlying ideologies of human difference, which have once again been invoked to legitimate crimes against humanity.

Wartime enslavement in Sudan has attracted a great deal of international attention. The issues involved were first documented by two lecturers at the University of Khartoum in 1987, and they emerged as a focal point for journalists, international agencies, and NGOs in the 1990s.[92] More recently, there have been two best-selling autobiographies recounting personal experiences of enslavement.[93] There are many reasons for this sustained interest, ranging from the cataclysmic nature of human rights abuses in Sudan, of which slavery represents but a part, to larger political agendas concerning religion and Islamic fundamentalism. Media attention to slavery clearly helped to draw attention to larger problems that might otherwise have been overlooked. Another key factor in raising the profile of slavery in Sudan has been the controversial practice of slave redemption. This started with southern communities raising resources to ransom slaves, and was later taken up by international groups such as Christian Solidarity International (CSI).[94]

Since 1995, these international groups have paid millions of dollars—at around 50 U.S. dollars a head—to free tens of thousands of slaves. This attracted widespread coverage, helped to secure donations, and undoubtedly proved to be an effective way of raising global awareness of problems in Sudan. Redemption was sold as a straightforward and effective means of taking action in a situation where alternative solutions were hard to identify.[95] For critics, who included many human rights groups, redemption quickly became a case of good intentions gone awry, by creating incentives for further raids and opening the door for fraud and financial manipulation.[96] This led to many heated exchanges between competing voices, with advocates of redemption losing ground in recent times. It is by no means clear, moreover, just how many slaves have been taken. CSI has advanced the figure of 100,000 (or more), but others have presented far lower estimates of 10,000–20,000.[97] It is difficult to reconcile these various estimates, since the numbers of slaves that are said to have been freed through redemption far exceeds lower estimates of the total problem.[98] The most comprehensive source of available information is currently a database of over 10,000 names of people who had been abducted. This database was compiled by the Rift Valley Institute over eighteen months of fieldwork in an effort to establish a "baseline of fact."[99]

For over a decade, the Sudanese government wrapped itself in blanket denials and impugned the motives of its numerous critics. In May 1999, there was a small break in this longstanding pattern, as the Sudanese government finally responded to sustained international pressure by belatedly establishing the Committee for the Eradication of Abduction of Women and Children. This turned out to be a very qualified move forward. The Committee was able to identify some people who were enslaved, and to secure their release, but the pace of progress proved very slow.[100] Despite establishing the Committee, the Sudanese government continued to deny any official culpability, and instead blamed lingering traditions of communal raiding that had resulted in abductions and forced labor, but not slavery. Perpetrators escaped prosecution. Periodic raids continued.[101] Many of these vagaries can be traced to structural problems associated with wartime operations. It was extremely gratifying, therefore, when the government finally reached a peace settlement with southern forces. This officially came into force in January 2005, and contains commitments to southern autonomy, an end to Islamic law in the south, a revenue-sharing agreement on oil revenues, and the integration of the armed forces.[102] It also holds out the prospect of southern independence in a referendum in January 2011. Given past history, it is by no means clear that this settlement will hold, and several key issues are yet to be resolved, but it nonetheless signals a major political opportunity. While the peace negotiations ended wartime enslavement in southern Sudan, the return and rehabilitation of people who were enslaved remains an ongoing issue.[103] Despite sustained diplomatic pressure and over a decade of international media coverage, no one has ever been prosecuted for wartime enslavement.

In different circumstances, the peace settlement would nonetheless be cause for celebration, but it unhappily coincided with the advent of a further round of conflict in Darfur, which has resulted in as many as 300,000 deaths, and caused around "2.7 million people, mostly farmers and their families, to flee their homes to Internally Displaced Persons' (IDP) camps near big towns in Darfur, or across the border into neighbouring Chad."[104] It is not possible to do justice to this more recent conflict here, but a number of parallels can be briefly highlighted. The conflict in Darfur, which has similarly longstanding historical roots,[105] was triggered by military forays in early 2003 by two rebel groups demanding political autonomy. These incursions provoked a cataclysmic response from the Sudanese government, which once again turned to nomadic militias known as the Janjaweed: the "Arab" rivals of the "African" rebels. Both groups, who are again far from homogenous, share a common attachment to Islam, but this has not prevented the Sudanese government from engaging in a sustained campaign of genocide and ethnic cleansing.[106] This has been characterized by systematic attacks on civilians, numerous massacres, aerial bombardment, scorched-earth tactics, and forcible displacement.[107] This perilous situation has been compounded by the use of rape as a strategic weapon, and high levels of sexual violence more generally.[108] Although wartime enslavement has once again featured within this larger pattern of abuses, it has not received the same level of international attention as the earlier civil war.[109] Despite having been consistently raised at the highest levels, there is currently limited international resolve to address the conflict in Darfur. The Sudanese government, which denies official involvement, has talked about disarming the militias, but this is yet to be translated into meaningful action, and perpetrators continue to act with impunity. For many decades now, it has been clear that the political composition and geographic remit of the Sudanese state is the main source of the problem, rather than part of the solution.[110]

Concluding Remarks

Two overarching themes can be extracted from the preceding analysis of the recent history of Mauritania, Niger, and Sudan. The first theme revolves around the continuing ideological and political resonance of classical slavery as a singular category. While contemporary slavery can be found in many places, classical slavery has come to be confined to a small number of settings, ensuring that countries such as Mauritania have come to enjoy a very specific type of international notoriety. For ruling political elites (and at least some members of society), this notoriety not only poses a challenge to national honor,[111] it also provides a high-profile point of departure that has helped to draw attention to a broader set of problem and practices. This dynamic is particularly evident in the case of Sudan, where wartime enslavement represents only one component of a much larger cataclysm, but it has nonetheless proved to be a potent lodestone, helping to bring attention to the central role of the Sudanese government in extraordinary human rights abuses. As we have seen, local human rights activists in Mauritania and Niger have also been able to secure an international audience by invoking classical slavery.

This has also helped to bring about some recent institutional reforms, but in the absence of an ongoing "slavery" story this larger audience may fade away. Given both the past histories and relative poverty of the countries in question, it remains difficult to envisage anything other than a long-term struggle against a set of deeply rooted problems. The challenge now is to find ways of facilitating cumulative local reforms without falling into the trap of no true slavery equals no real problem.

This brings us to the second theme, which revolves around the limitations of classical slavery as both an analytical and political category. As we have seen, it can be extremely difficult to clearly separate classical slavery from both underlying social and ideological fault lines, such as enduring patterns of descent-based discrimination, and larger institutional failures, such as severe wartime abuses. Concentrating on the very worst examples of classical slavery has proved to be a good political (and journalistic) move, but it has also tended to complicate efforts to effectively diagnose complex variations in individual and collective behavior. As we have seen, most of the problems discussed above have more to do with culture and history than relevant legislation. In keeping with larger trends, ongoing contests over slavery and descent-based discrimination in places such as Mauritania and Niger invariably extend to questions of social membership, gender dynamics, political participation, and economic (mal)distribution. These complex problems are unlikely to be effectively addressed through the narrow lens of classical slavery, but instead require a broader vision that places slavery alongside a larger series of challenges. While descent-based discrimination may initially appear fairly innocuous in comparison to the worst cases of classical slavery, it quickly appears in a different light when placed alongside more familiar forms of severe discrimination involving racism and sexism. Whenever ideologies of human difference reduce certain categories of people to a subordinate and inferior status, systemic human rights abuses invariably follow. As we shall see in the next chapter, similar patterns of social discrimination have also been integral to bonded labor on the Indian subcontinent.

Chapter 7

Slaves to Debt

Bonded labor, or debt bondage, has long been identified as a form of servitude that shares many features in common with "classical" slavery. In its most basic form, bonded labor involves a "worker who renders service under conditions of bondage arising from economic considerations, notably indebtedness though a loan or advance." This usually involves an extended period of service, where "the worker (or dependents or heirs) is tied to a particular creditor for a specified or unspecified period until the loan is repaid."[1] Throughout history, debt and slavery have often been closely related.[2] In many historical slave systems, a failure to repay debts was a prominent route to legal enslavement.[3] It was also not uncommon for slavery and bonded labor to be practiced alongside each other. In a number of cases, foreign observers found it difficult to tell the two apart.[4] This enduring relationship became a politically sensitive issue following the emergence of organized anti-slavery. During the nineteenth and early twentieth centuries, bonded labor was regularly flagged as a problem area, yet this stance was often undercut by (politically motivated) assessments that it could represent a "step up" from slavery.[5] This general tendency to assign bonded labor an "intermediate" status between slavery and freedom gradually broke down over the course of the twentieth century, as part of the gradual shift from strict equivalence to sufficient similarity epitomized by the 1956 Supplementary Convention. By the late twentieth century, bonded labor had come to be widely regarded as a leading form of contemporary slavery.

This chapter examines the historical relationship between the legal abolition of slavery and the ongoing prevalence of bonded labor in the Indian subcontinent. This serves a number of purposes. As we saw earlier, the Indian subcontinent contains the greatest concentration of slaves in the world today. While individual estimates vary, this is the one location where both regional and country-specific estimates have been consistently expressed in millions, rather than in multiples of thousands.[6] By exploring the historical roots of this major contemporary problem, I not only aim to further deflate the problematic concept of "new" slavery, I also seek to develop a more nuanced diagnosis of the underlying causes behind modern problems. My primary argument is that more recent innovations and adaptations can be best understood as path-dependant responses to the limitations of British anti-slavery policies. To support this argument, I have divided this chapter into three sections. In the first section, I examine the history of slavery and bonded labor on the subcontinent. Instead of approaching slavery and bonded labor as exclusive categories, I explore how the boundaries between the two were gradually consolidated as a consequence of colonial legislation in 1843 and 1859.

The second section goes on to explore the more recent relationship between bonded labor and the law, paying particular attention to key legislative changes, the role of the courts, and the qualified achievement of recent rehabilitation schemes. Thanks to a combination of local activism and judicial intervention, there are now fairly comprehensive legal frameworks in place, but their enforcement continues to be undercut by official apathy and complicity. In the third and final section, I explore how bonded labor has gradually evolved in response to various structural dynamics, such as the growth of migrant labor, the expansion of non-agricultural sectors, and the emergence of bonds between relative strangers. As will become clear, however, that the continued prevalence of bonded labor reflects the more enduring contributions of poverty, inequality, caste discrimination, and economic advantage.

Slavery and Bonded Labor in the Indian Subcontinent

Like most forms of servitude, bonded labor was practiced in many parts of the globe for much of recorded history.[7] Of particular importance here is the widespread use of bonded labor in most parts of Asia. Until relatively recently, bonded labor was a significant (but by no means static) component of societies in Burma, China, Indonesia, Indo-China, the Indian subcontinent, Korea, and the Philippines.[8] During the eighteenth and nineteenth centuries, as much as half the population of central Thailand may have been bonded.[9]

Here, as elsewhere, debt was a prominent route to legal enslavement. In Cambodia, to take another example, people to whom excessive debts were owed was entitled to enslave the debtor for their own use, or to order the person's public sale.[10] During the same period, we also encounter widespread use of debt bondage in many parts of Latin America. The Spanish and Portuguese conquerors who constructed vast empires in the "New World" were not farmers but aristocrats and soldiers, and they viewed the indigenous peoples in the lands they conquered as a cheap and expendable source of labor. Their first impulse was to enslave Native Americans outright, but this strategy faltered in the face of high mortality and low work rates (thereby precipitating the trade in African slaves, with tragic consequences).

Over the course of the sixteenth and seventeenth centuries, large numbers of Portuguese and Spanish settlers complemented legal enslavement with other closely related forms of bondage, such as the *encomienda*, which saw hundreds of thousands of Native Americans forced to labor for Europeans under atrocious conditions (contributing to rapid population decline). Much like more recent forced labor schemes in colonial Africa, these abuses were justified using the language of benevolent paternalism, in which "backward" peoples were said to be in need of "tutelage." The most common template involved multiple generations of Native Americans being bound to specific plots of land, and thereby being compelled to furnish goods and services on highly exploitative terms. This basic arrangement is usually classified as a form of serfdom, but it was not uncommon for debt to be used as a further instrument of control. During the nineteenth century, bonded labor may have been the main method of securing labor in some regions.[11] Having accepted a loan or advance, desperate and vulnerable workers routinely found it impossible to repay their debts, thanks to poor wages and high prices, and thus lapsed into extended periods of bondage.[12]

In order to better understand these historical practices, we need take into account the contribution of both financial obligations and social dependency. The financial side of the equation is fairly straightforward. As a rule, bonded labor originated (when not inherited) with an ostensibly "voluntary" agreement, where a creditor offered financial assistance in exchange for a promise of service. Following this transaction, the person who incurred the debt was obliged to labor under unfavorable financial terms until the debt was discharged. In the worst cases, whole families were required to perform extraordinary endeavors, working twelve to fourteen hours a day, six or seven days a week, in return for a tenuous subsistence. Expressions of dissent would usually be met with physical violence. In many historical settings, this condition was hereditary, with children taking over their parents' obligations. In some cases, masters could sell those in bondage—through their debts—to third parties, inviting comparisons with slave trading. Not all forms of bonded labor meant a lifetime of servitude, but even more limited cases usually involved many years of arduous service for small rewards, with damaging ramifications for health, income, and future prospects.

It is important to emphasize, however, that many bonded labor systems also involved a substantial nonfinancial dimension. On this point, it is necessary to resist the temptation to project modern conceptions of debt backward through time. Instead of involving an exclusively financial transaction, many bonded labor systems involved elaborate social networks, where debt formed part of larger patterns of hierarchy and dependency.

This theme forms part of broader debates surrounding attitudes toward freedom and belonging. On this front, an influential point of departure comes from Orlando Patterson, who has provocatively argued that personal liberty should be regarded as a distinctively Western value, which non-Western peoples have historically equated with isolation, uncertainty, and vulnerability.[13] Patterson's argument has been challenged on a number of fronts,[14] but it nonetheless serves to underline a more general point: Western conceptions of slavery and freedom do not always fit comfortably alongside complex forms of social dependency found in many historical settings. From here, a further perspective comes from Gwyn Campbell, who has recently argued that the history of slavery in the Indian Ocean World becomes clearer:

> if Western notions of a division of society into free and slave, and of slaves as property, are replaced with a vision of society as a hierarchy of dependency in which "slaves" constituted one of a number of unfree groups from which menial labor was drawn to perform services both productive and nominally unproductive. It was a reciprocal system in which obligations implied servitude to an individual with superior status, to a kin group or the crown, in return for protection.[15]

Within this hierarchy of dependency, the chief goal was not "freedom," but the acquisition of a more favorable status within the prevailing social order. In the Indian subcontinent, this dynamic regularly involved multiple generations or future incarnations.[16]

This line of argument has far-reaching consequences when it comes to

European efforts to classify unfamiliar forms of human bondage. When British colonial officials sought to define and demarcate "slavery" in India, the categories and concepts that they clumsily imposed on local practices not only failed to adequately capture the lived experiences of those involved, they also introduced new legal and political benchmarks that would gradually remake established patterns of dependency. On this front, I turn to Gyan Prakesh's influential work on *Bonded Histories: Genealogies of Labor Servitude in Colonial India*. Focusing on *kamiās*, a class of agricultural laborers in the north eastern province of Bihar, Prakesh argues that colonial policies resulted in a new understanding of the foundations of bonded labor. When the British extended their authority in India over the course of the seventeenth and eighteenth centuries, they encountered a bewildering array of practices and institutions, which involved subtle variations—both de jure and de facto—in personal status. This was initially an issue for revenue collection, but came to be recast as an anti-slavery issue in the early nineteenth century.[17] Prakesh argues that colonial officials construed the "power of money" and "the right to freedom" as ontological facts, rather than exotic propositions, and thereby (re)conceptualized the condition of the kamiās in terms of a financial relationship that had compromised their status as hitherto "free" persons.[18]

British officials initially described the kamiās as slaves, but they were subsequently redefined as bonded laborers (or debt-serfs) following the legal abolition of slavery in 1843. This formula not only allowed the British to sidestep their anti-slavery commitments, it also encouraged *māliks* (or landlords) to reorganize their authority over their kamiās in order to take advantage of colonial institutions. Following the introduction of new labor regulations in 1859, Indian landlords gradually redefined the terms of their relationships with their kamiās by compelling them to sign new labor "contracts." This resulted in a gradual shift in the relative emphasis placed on land and labor, in which "land control replaced direct claims over people in determining the social relations of production. Whereas earlier, rights over land derived from relations between people, by the late nineteenth century, unequal control over land became the basis of social relations."[19] This gradual redefinition of the terms of bondage is said to have resulted in a stagnant yet market-oriented society, where relations between kamiās and māliks were increasingly articulated in contractual, financial terms, with low-caste peasants now also acting as māliks, and new groups becoming subject to debt bondage. For the British, the bonded labor of the kamiās represented an intermediate status between slavery and freedom, but it also usually involved a hereditary condition, and there appear to have been few attempts to settle debts. Having redefined bonded labor as a step up from slavery in the nineteenth century, India's colonial rulers later sought to end this form of bonded labor in the 1920s, but were disappointed (in the kamiãs) with a lack of results.[20]

This perspective is important on a number of levels. Most obviously, it offers a useful counterpoint to a modern tendency to approach classical slavery and bonded-labor as clearly demarcated categories. In the Indian subcontinent, British colonial policies played a central role in a gradual reconfiguration in the parameters of bondage, resulting in an ethnocentric separation between "slavery" and "bonded labor" that was clumsily imposed on local practices. Instead of being exclusive categories, the first of which (slavery) was legally abolished, while the second (bonded labor) continued to this day, we are instead left a dynamic picture in which modern forms of bonded labor can be at least partially traced to complex adjustments to colonial policies surrounding the legal abolition of slavery. Equally relevant here is the emphasis on the nonfinancial dimensions of bonded labor. In most recent treatments of bonded labor, debt serves as the key focal point around which other aspects of a servile relationship are built. The preceding analysis opens up a countervailing perspective, in which economic relations can be at least partially construed as evolving symptoms of larger forms of social hierarchy and dependency.[21] More recent bonds may no longer be constructed on the same terms,[22] but this does not preclude a more general caution about reducing all forms of bonded labor to atomistic, "voluntary" arrangements between creditor and debtor.

In order to further develop this line of argument, we need to look more closely at the historical events surrounding the legal abolition of slavery in colonial India. When the British Parliament passed legislation abolishing slavery in 1833, British territories in India were not affected because they fell under the jurisdiction of the East India Company. When British abolitionists somewhat belatedly took up this omission, they were surprised to learn there may have been as many as sixteen million slaves in India. This figure "was 20 times the number freed in Britain's colonies by the 1833 Emancipation Act and some four times greater than the entire slave population of the New World."[23] This was still not an especially large proportion of the overall population, but it nonetheless constituted a tremendous challenge for colonial agents numbering in the tens of thousands. As we have already seen, slavery in India involved a highly variegated set of practices that did not conform to European expectations of slavery.[24] Despite a longstanding international traffic in slaves spanning Africa, the Middle East, and East Asia,[25] the vast majority of slaves came from within the subcontinent.[26]

In this environment, the primary marker of social identity was not race, but caste. In its most basic form, the caste system involved (and continues to involve) the organization of Indian society around a series of hereditary social groups who were assigned different levels of social status based on assessments of their relative purity.[27] While most slaves were assigned to "lower" castes, a minority came from "intermediate" castes. Instead of being concentrated in market-oriented, capitalist ventures, slaves in India were compelled to serve in a wide range of capacities. While some forms of slavery involved agricultural production,[28] it was not uncommon for slaves to also fill various niches in privileged households. The most common example is that of the domestic servant, but slaves also regularly functioned as retainers, bodyguards, concubines, and administrators (including eunuchs). Since these duties often required slaves to work in close proximity to their masters, they could not be performed by the "polluting" presence of lower castes. In keeping with larger trends, colonial officials repeatedly described slavery in India as "mild" or "benign."[29] This was by no means true in the vast majority of cases, but it was nonetheless possible to point to a minority of slaves who occupied comparatively privileged positions.[30]

Some historians have argued that the British introduced a steady stream of anti-slavery measures in the late eighteenth and early nineteenth centuries, culminating in legal abolition in 1843.[31] According to Indrani Chatterjee, this linear trajectory is deceptive, because the measures in question were limited to targeted moves to restrict slaving by European competitors, leaving British and Indian rights unaffected.[32] When events in Britain placed India on the anti-slavery agenda, colonial officials predictably opted for delay and dilution, but they were unable to throw back the anti-slavery tide entirely.[33] The eventual result was Act V of 1843, which forbade courts from recognizing slavery, banned officers from selling persons for nonpayment of taxes, and formally prohibited judicial discrimination against slaves. The Act was presented as a robust step to end slavery, alarming some sections of the Indian population.[34] In practice, it quickly proved to be impotent in both design and implementation.[35] Chatterjee has identified many cases where courts continued to uphold slave status throughout the nineteenth century, along with multiple reports of officials returning runaway slaves.[36] In 1860/61, the Indian Penal Code introduced stronger anti-slavery provisions, making trading and holding slaves a criminal offence, punishable by up to ten years incarceration. This legislation once again proved to be largely ineffectual.[37]

The main catalyst for reform came not from anti-slavery legislation, but from larger economic, legal, and institutional changes that took place under colonial rule. As the colonial economy expanded, demand for cheap migrant labor increased markedly. Large numbers of Indians were able to build new lives by working as laborers on railways and public works (or even serving in the armed forces). During the same period, millions of Indians escaped problems at home by turning to indentured migration.[38] As we have seen, this frequently meant exchanging one objectionable situation for another. A comparable story can be told on the subcontinent. Traditional forms of bondage in India were frequently extremely arduous and unpleasant, but the newer innovations that followed in the wake of colonial conquest could involve equally high levels of exploitation and abuse.[39] Faced with few attractive opportunities, multiple generations remained subject to various forms of bondage.

Once slavery had been legally abolished, British and Indian elites gradually found it necessary to organize their activities around new principles.[40] In this legal environment (the language of) debt bondage represented a particularly attractive alternative.[41] One snapshot of this cumulative process of redefinition comes from Jacques Pouchepadass, who observes that:

> In the new legal order, it was the outwardly contractual credit relationship that was singled out as the original foundation and legal justification of labour attachment. This recasting of the relations between master and dependent as a single-interest economic relationship was not without traditional precedents. . . . However that may be, the modern liberal notions of property, equity and contract embodied in British colonial law were soon understood and assimilated by the dominant strata of Indian rural society. A person who formerly would have been called a slave was now a man or woman who had mortgaged his/her labour in return for a loan. Such a transaction was recognized by law, and the master/creditor, in the event of breach of contract on the part of the debtor, was entitled to refer to the Workman's Breach of Contract Act of 1859.[42]

While bonded labor was not in itself a new phenomenon, it gradually acquired new dimensions in response to various colonial institutional and economic pressures. The noncommercial functions that more privileged slaves had historically performed slowly faded from view, but bonded labor consolidated a major economic presence in many settings.

This was by no means a uniform process. Despite the centralizing impulses of India's British overlords, there remained considerable variations between regions, reflecting differences in both local convention and colonial penetration. In north east India, slaving remained a frontier issue decades after legal abolition, involving India, Nepal, Bhutan, and Burma.[43] In Arunachal Pradesh, tribal communities continued to practice slavery throughout the colonial period. Following independence, the Indian government introduced a cautious emancipation program. Thousands of slaves were gradually freed over many decades, with compensation being paid to their former masters.[44] It is also worth noting that some key pieces of legislation, such as the 1920 law regulating bonded labor, were confined to specific regions.[45] Further complicating matters was the fact that two-fifths of British India was formally governed by semi-independent princes allied to Britain. This not only raised jurisdictional issues, but also resulted in different structures, prerogatives, and capacities. Some princes embarked on successful modernization programs. Some were otherwise inclined, or lacked the requisite capabilities.[46] The British government was sufficiently concerned about this situation to exclude these states from the 1926 Slavery Convention.[47] In (what would become) Pakistan, relatively small numbers of child slaves continued to be traded to the Arabian peninsula during the mid-twentieth century.[48] In this context, many historical issues still need to be fully explored, but an overarching trajectory can nonetheless be identified. In the century that followed the legal abolition of slavery, bonded labor secured an integral position in the socioeconomic life of the Indian subcontinent. Following the partition of British territories into the states of India and Pakistan in 1947, newly independent rulers in both countries continued to uphold earlier colonial precedents.

Bonded Labor and the Law

The recent history of bonded labor in the Indian subcontinent has been primarily defined by a combination of institutional apathy and official complicity. An excellent illustration of this enduring dynamic is the length of time that passed before comprehensive legislation prohibiting debt bondage was introduced. As we saw in Chapter 5, bonded labor was one of four practices specifically covered by the 1956 Supplementary Convention on practices similar to slavery. This was not the first time that bonded labor was identified as a serious problem, but the Convention took the key step of introducing obligations under international law on terms which formally equated debt bondage with slavery. Many states quickly adopted the Convention, including India (1956/1960), Pakistan (1956/1958), and Nepal (1963).[49] Like many international instruments, the Convention calls for progressive action rather than an immediate abolition, but it still requires parties to take "all practicable and necessary legislative and other measures . . . as soon as possible."[50] Having formally ratified the Convention in 1960, it took sixteen years for the Indian government to approve the Bonded Labour System (Abolition) Act of 1976 (which passed under the authoritarian rule of Indira Ghandi during the "Emergency"). Decades later, Pakistani officials was compelled to act by the Supreme Court of Pakistan, and thus passed a largely symbolic act in 1992. This was finally given force by the introduction of the Bonded Labour System (Abolition) Rules of July 1995. In 2000, the Nepalese government belatedly introduced the Kamaiya Labour (Prohibition) Act. This law emerged thirty-seven years after Nepal ratified the 1956 Convention.[51]

These belated legislative measures have not been driven by external pressures, a pattern typical of the abolition of the legal abolition of slavery, but have instead been chiefly defined by political agitation within the states in question. In India, early contributions came from the Bonded Labour Liberation Front, Volunteers for Social Justice, the South Asia Coalition against Child Servitude, and the Gandhi Peace Foundation. The cause of bonded labor has been taken up in Pakistan by groups such as the Human Rights Commission of Pakistan, the Pakistan Institute of Labour, Education and Research, and the Bonded Labour Liberation Front of Pakistan. In Nepal, important contributions have come from Backward Society Education and the Informal Sector Service Centre. The importance of local activism is illustrated by variations in the timing of key legislation, as the relative "lateness" of Nepal can be largely traced to the fact that NGOs and local opposition emerged only fairly recently. These groups have been further bolstered by contributions from international groups such as the International Labour Organization and Human Rights Watch, and by judicial rulings in India and Pakistan. One of the main strategies that has been employed by campaigners has been public litigation. Faced with official indifference, human rights activists have repeatedly turned to the judiciary for redress, securing a number of important breakthroughs.

In a watershed case in 1988, *Darshan Masih and others v. the State*, the Pakistan Supreme Court ruled that bonded labor was inconsistent with fundamental rights guaranteed by the constitution, thereby forcing the introduction of new legislation.[52] This forms part of a larger pattern, which has seen courts in both India and Pakistan periodically instigate official investigations, issue targeted release orders, and otherwise compel state officials to take various remedial actions. The Indian Supreme Court may be "the world's most powerful court," owing to the introduction of public (or social) interest litigation, which has seen the Court treat newspaper articles, postcards, letters and other materials from civic-minded third parties as writ petitions. From this novel starting point, the activist Court has issued a steady stream of expansive, often highly detailed directives, covering issues such as prison reform, health care, education, privacy, sexual harassment, and prostitution.[53] From 1981 onward, there have been a series of cases dealing with various aspects of bonded labor.

In cases brought to the court, abuses committed by private parties have frequently been overshadowed by official failings at a state or federal level. The activities of the court have not been confined to legal rulings, but have extended to requests for information, repeated calls to comply with the terms of the 1976 Act, the appointment of specific officials responsible for investigating and correcting individual problem areas, and detailed directives regarding rehabilitation. Faced with official intransigence, the Court has often found it necessary to revisit particular cases multiple times.[54] Despite focusing on specific sites involving relatively small numbers of bonded laborers, these activities have presented a recurring challenge to official indifference and complicity. In 1997, the court established a relationship with the National Human Rights Commission, which saw the Commission tasked with monitoring bonded labor. This partnership allows for more sustained, systematic investigations, enabling the court to draw on the resources of a small group of Special Rapporteurs and various working groups.[55] The high profile Human Rights Commission was launched by the Protection of Human Rights Act of 1993 and enjoys a wide range of civil powers, but it does not have the ability to bring criminal prosecutions. Instead, it seeks to pressure and persuade officials to take action through a combination of public shaming, investigative reporting, and awareness campaigns.[56] In this respect, it suffers from a similar constraint to the Indian Supreme Court. Regardless of how much evidence the Human Rights Commission compiles, it remains dependent on other agencies to enforce the law.

For most of the twentieth century, there were no national laws specifically prohibiting debt bondage. There may have been laws that touched on aspects of the problems involved, but they were usually weak or piecemeal in nature.[57] This began to change in the 1970s, and there are now comprehensive legal regimes in place throughout the Indian subcontinent. Some loopholes persist, particularly when it comes to child labor,[58] but the key issue is no longer comprehensive legislation, but effective enforcement. The Indian Bonded Labour System (Abolition) Act of 1976 has been described as "one of the finest pieces of legislation on the statute book,"[59] but this means little if government officials do not take their obligations seriously. From a legal standpoint, the 1976 Act is both clear and comprehensive. Bonded labor is defined as a system of forced or partly forced labor, where a debtor enters (or is presumed to have entered) into an agreement (oral or written) with a creditor, where an "advance" compels the debtor (or any family members) to labor for either a specified or unspecified period. This forms part of an expansive approach, which specifically prohibits customary or social obligations, obligations based on parental succession, or from birth in a particular caste or community, and acts that forfeit freedom of employment, movement, property, or labor products.[60] Practices that display "any or all" of these features come under the ambit of bonded labor systems, and are thereby legally covered under the terms of the Act. By way of further clarification, the Act also states that

> The existence of an agreement between the debtor and creditor is ordinarily presumed, under the social custom, in relation to the following forms of forced labour, namely: Adiyamar, Baramasia, Basahya, Bethu, Bhagela, Cherumar, Garru-Galu, Hali, Hari, Harwai, Holya, Jana, Jeetha, Kamiya, Khundit-Mundit, Kuthia, Lakhari, Munjhi, Mat, Munish system, Nit-Majoor, Paleru, Padiyal, Pannayilal, Sugri, Sanji, Sanjawat, Sewak, Sewakia, Seri, Vetti.[61]

This scheme has been expanded further by the Supreme Court, where forced labor is also said to include "force arising from compulsion of economic circumstances" leading to payments at less than the minimum wage.[62] This addition has been somewhat controversial, but it does not detract from the more general point: comprehensive legal criteria have been established.

Under the terms of the 1976 Act, chief responsibility for enforcement lies with district magistrates and their designated subordinates, but many magistrates have been reluctant to report bonded labor, because "admitting that bonded labor exists in their district may be taken as evidence of their own failure to address it."[63] For decades, officials have been claiming that bonded labor is no longer a problem within their jurisdictions.[64] These claims frequently lack credibility, but they continue to be made in the face of contradictory evidence because they do not require any further action. Rather than seeking out those in bondage, many officials have placed the onus on affected parties to express their grievances. This is not realistic. Surveys have repeatedly demonstrated that many bonded laborers have little or no knowledge of relevant laws,[65] and even if they are aware of their legal rights, there is no guarantee that any compliant will be taken seriously. One of the main sticking points has been the status of outstanding debts. On this front, the 1976 Act is unambiguous: all debts associated with bonded labor should be immediately extinguished without compensation, but officials have routinely ignored the law by endorsing debts as legitimate contracts. This may sometimes result from genuine confusion, but there is evidence to suggest various forms of corruption and complicity at work. Researchers have documented numerous cases where police officers have tracked down runaways and returned them to their masters.

Another key feature of the 1976 Act is the establishment of Vigilance Committees in each district and subdivision. These committees are designed to ensure that the Act is being properly implemented and are formally tasked with liaising with district magistrates, identifying bonded laborers, cataloguing abuses, and assisting with rehabilitation.[66] This innovative model has also been formally adopted in Pakistan, but has not achieved the progress that might have been expected. Many years after the passage of enabling legislation, there remained places in both countries that did not have vigilance committees. When committees have been established, often at the behest of activists, they have tended to be dominated by local landlords and other elites. It is not surprising, therefore, that most vigilance committees have long been moribund and have thus failed to provide much in the way of either oversight or accountability.[67] This is but one symptom of a larger trend. When junior officials fail to enforce the law, they do not expect to be reprimanded by their superiors. When regional administrators neglect their statutory obligations, or the rulings of the courts, they do not expect to be penalized by the central government. In this environment, we should not be surprised when only a handful of individuals are prosecuted, let alone convicted or imprisoned, for employing debt bondage.[68] In India the penalty for bonded labor is up to three years imprisonment, and a fine of up to Rs.2000 (around 44 USD),[69] but in the vast majority of cases the best available outcome is limited to securing the release of those who are bonded.

This brings us to the critical issue of release and rehabilitation. Of the millions of people caught in debt bondage, only a fraction have ever experienced (judicial) release, let alone rehabilitation. This does not make the issue of rehabilitation any less important, but it does provide further confirmation of how much remains to be done. At this juncture, it is necessary to make a further distinction between direct and indirect approaches to combating bonded labor. The latter are primarily concerned with cumulative structural change, involving issues such as education, poverty, land reform, financial services, and economic development. If all goes to plan, a larger transformation in the prevailing social order indirectly precipitates a steady decline in the prevalence of bonded labor.[70] This nonconfrontational approach is hard to evaluate on a macro level. There have been some signs that bonded labor has receded in some sectors and regions, particularly in agricultural production, but it is not entirely clear whether this trajectory has been offset by expansion elsewhere.[71] Attempts to identify overarching trends are further complicated by the fact that estimates of specific regions and industries can range from many millions to tens of thousands.[72] The main problem with indirect models is that they offer limited assistance to those who are currently bonded. In this context, release and rehabilitation offers a more immediate solution. Here, as elsewhere, there is an institutional framework in place, yet there remain numerous obstacles when it comes to implementation. This not only applies to the limited scope of existing programs, but also extends to internal problems within established schemes. In many respects, this brings us back full circle to the structural issues identified above.

It has long been recognized that a lack of viable alternatives is a key component of bonded labor. When there are few other sources of work, credit, or sustenance, bondage can come to be construed as a relatively secure, if otherwise unattractive livelihood. When people enter into debt bondage, they usually do so because there are few obvious alternatives. They may even reconcile themselves to their situation as a way of securing some form of employment or avoiding exposure.[73] If they are fortunate enough to be released, either through their own efforts or through third-party intervention, they may find it difficult to avoid slipping back into bondage unless alternative avenues become available. At this point, rehabilitation is essential. Since 1976, the Indian government has made significant resources available for rehabilitation schemes. At first glance, the numbers involved are fairly impressive. In 2001, a cumulative total of 280,411 bonded laborers had been reported as having been rehabilitated.[74] This is clearly a substantial figure, but it pales in comparison to a 2003 estimate from Human Rights Watch that there could be as many as sixty-five million people trapped in debt bondage in India.[75] When bonded laborers are officially identified, they are entitled to resources administered through a centrally sponsored scheme. This starts with a subsistence grant and may also include land allotments, the provision of animals, or tools and training, along with preferential treatment in development programs.[76]

The outcomes of these schemes have been mixed, reflecting both regional differences and individual circumstances.[77] At a national level, it seems that the Indian government has made far more progress than its Pakistani counterpart.[78] Some promising results have been achieved,[79] but a number of serious problems can also be identified. One of the main issues is the length of time between identification and rehabilitation, which can often be measured in months, if not years, leaving vulnerable individuals without assets and income for extended periods. Some end up receiving no support at all, either because they are "not available for rehabilitation," an official euphemism that conceals a variety of sins, or because their release was not formally certified. When support does come, the mix of provisions can sometimes be heavy-handed or inappropriate. These failings can be largely traced to overly bureaucratic procedures and official ineptitude, but alongside administrative issues we find reports of corruption and fraud, involving both funding and falsified figures.[80] It is also not uncommon for allocated funds to go unused.[81] Despite these deficiencies, there are many cases where rehabilitation programs appear to have made a substantial difference. This is partially a matter of securing greater autonomy, particularly when it comes to physical movement and (modest) bargaining power, and partially a matter of acquiring basic assets such as land, training, and education. Neither axis should be confused with radical change. The provisions available for rehabilitation are fairly modest, and the psychological scars left by servitude can be severe, but the existence of such schemes nonetheless represents an advance on the "sink or swim" approach typical of the legal abolition of slavery.

An Evolving Problem

As we saw in the last chapter, information on "classical" slavery has sometimes proved hard to come by and has often been limited to isolated anecdotes and incidents. This is much less of an issue as far as bonded labor is concerned, especially in places like India, because an extensive body of research has been conducted over many decades. This has involved both national studies and more focused inquiries into specific industries, activities, and locations.[82] This research often conveys a discouraging, highly repetitive picture, with recent works making similar points to earlier studies, and personal stories from various eras displaying many common traits.[83] It has long been recognized that bonded labor can be connected to a lack of resources, endemic poverty, official complicity, and discrimination, yet an awareness of these ingredients has not necessarily translated into effective remedial action.

The archetypal image of bonded labor throughout the Indian subcontinent is that of a downtrodden peasant farmer, who is perpetually beholden to a local landowner with no real hope (or expectation) of release. In return for a basic subsistence, entire families undertake remarkable exertions year after year, with children taking up their parents' obligations when they are unable to continue. These intergenerational ties can sometimes still be linked to "feudal" traditions and customary obligations, with debt serving as a focal point for patron-client relations that have provoked comparisons with medieval serfdom. This form of bonded labor can still be found in rural areas in some parts of the subcontinent, but it has been increasingly overshadowed by more recent innovations.[84] While bonded labor continues to feature prominently in agricultural production, family ties and customary obligations have been gradually displaced by more limited fiscal attachments of comparatively recent origin. Many cases of bonded labor now involve relative strangers, with specialized intermediaries such as recruiters and overseers often standing between "worker" and "employer." This can be chiefly attributed to cumulative changes in agricultural production, reflecting commercial pressures, capitalist ventures, decline in self-employment, the "Green Revolution," and the increasingly casual organization of the labor market.[85] According to Ravi Srivastava, the recent history of bonded labor has often been characterized by a "U"-shaped relationship. While intergenerational forms of bondage have declined in the face of various structural changes, increasing numbers of individuals have incurred debts of more recent origin.[86] The main driving force behind this pattern has been internal migration. According to one recent estimate, migrant workers now comprise around 40 percent of all agricultural laborers.[87] Following in the footsteps of colonial agents, recent labor recruiters have established complex migration networks, where poverty-stricken workers from depressed regions migrate in pursuit of a better life, borrow funds in order to support relocation, and find themselves bound to an "employer" for many years, if not decades.

Like other states on the subcontinent, agriculture continues to be the single largest contributor to India's gross domestic product, as well as the largest sector for employment.[88] It is also the area where bonded labor is especially prevalent. This is not particularly surprising. All the recognized ingredients for bonded labor are present: enduring historical precedents, landlessness, unemployment (or underemployment), individualized bargaining and endemic poverty, illiteracy, and social discrimination. Population growth in rural areas has helped dampen wage pressures in many regions, sustaining a labor surplus landowners have been happy to exploit for their own ends. This does not, however, mark the end of the equation. "Beyond the agricultural sector, significant bonded labour incidence has been detected in industries including mining, brick making, fish processing, gem cutting, carpet weaving, and such hazardous industries as tanneries and fireworks production."[89]

Most industries tended to be primarily geared toward domestic consumption, rather than international trade, but there are some sectors such as carpet weaving or fish processing that have substantial links with foreign markets. Another prominent theme has been the use of debt bondage in prostitution and human trafficking, where families have been known to sell their daughters, or "wives," into sexual servitude.[90] The existence of bonded labor in nonagricultural sectors has received greater attention in recent times. In some settings, such as debt bondage in domestic servitude, there continues to be relatively little information available.[91] Common to all these activities is a demand for hard physical labor over long hours. The widespread use of debt bondage in these diverse settings suggests that something more than tradition is involved; that bonded labor may enjoy, or at least be perceived to enjoy, a competitive advantage over free labor.

Poverty is an endemic feature of life throughout the Indian subcontinent. Employers are well placed to take advantage of millions of vulnerable workers, leading to "voluntary" arrangements on highly exploitative terms. In this environment, it has been suggested that "there is only a very small difference between the living conditions of free agricultural labour and those of bonded labour."[92] Instead of representing a positive good, many examples of free labor can be regarded as lesser evils, and even this modest claim may overstate their virtues. If free labor consistently permits severe forms of labor exploitation, why would employers continue to illegally employ bonded labor? Many answers can be offered here, but one theme in particular deserves to be highlighted: the fact that those in bondage find it extremely difficult to pursue other opportunities until their debts are redeemed. Of course, those in bondage can (and do) flee, following a path common to slaves throughout history, but this typically means risking violent retribution, either individual or collective, and the indefinite life of a fugitive. Free laborers can undoubtedly find it difficult to move on, or to even threaten to move on, but their bonded counterparts usually face greater constraints.

This simple yet fundamental point provides a key insight into the ongoing appeal of bonded labor. By trapping vulnerable laborers in prolonged debt, "employers" not only secure a long-term supply of extremely cheap labor, they also deny workers one of their only bargaining chips: the ability—however slight—to pursue other means of employment. This has profound implications for labor relations more generally, starting with the issue of wages. In certain cases, those in bondage receive no wages at all, but in-kind payments of basic food and provisions. The most common model, however, involves bonded laborers receiving at least some wages, but at a lower rate than their free counterparts. While formal differences in wage rates may not always be that great, bonded laborers may only receive part payment, or be required to make contributions against their debts, thereby further reducing their income. These parlous returns are further compounded by fraudulent accounting, where illiterate workers have no way of keeping track of their debt, and thus consistently end up paying many times what they should. Unable to leave and unable to renegotiate, the typical bonded laborer must accept the highly unfavorable terms offered by their master.

In Chapter 4, I briefly discussed the role of indentured migration in undercutting the bargaining position of unattached workers by dividing the workforce and depressing wage demands. A similar dynamic has been identified when it comes to the relationship between free and bonded labor, with the limited bargaining power of poverty-stricken free laborers being further undercut by the widespread availability of their more restricted bonded counterparts. Working conditions can also be further undermined by other complementary strategies. This can be as simple as using piece rates, where workers are paid per unit rather than per hour. This popular model can be found in many industries, from cigarettes and bricks to quarries and crops. To secure a basic subsistence, workers engage in intense exertions over long hours, receiving a pittance for voluminous production. Piece rates also shift expenses associated with spoiled goods onto workers. This vulnerability also extends to bonded peasants (among others), who tend to bear all the risk if their crops fail.

Another way "employers" secure labor involves the family unit. In some cases, relations between creditor and debtor operate on an individual level. In others, the head of the household acquires a debt and an entire family is called on to meet its attendant obligations. Not all debts are incurred to ensure survival. Some loans are incurred to support social rituals such as weddings (or funerals), sustaining a complex relationship between economic destitution and social expectations in which new couples incur extensive obligations at the point where they formally begin married life. From a family perspective, bondage can involve either a formal arrangement in which husband and wife have assigned roles, or an informal arrangement whereby family members share collective burdens.[93] Both of these variants can be found among other segments of the working poor, creating a substantial overlap between the various mechanisms that are used by "employers" to extract the most out of their "workers." Unsurprisingly, relevant labor laws involving wages and hazardous conditions tend to be routinely violated. In this environment, it can frequently be difficult to draw a clear line between outright slavery and the simply unsavory.

Given the tremendous scale of the problems involved, it is not overly surprising that a major portion of recent political activity concerned with bonded labor has concentrated on children. This orientation marks the convergence of high profile campaigns against child labor and more modest campaigns against bonded labor. When children are sold, indebted, or put to work, they rarely have a choice in the matter. This tends to simplify the complex issue of consent. It is clear, moreover, that child bondage can have lifelong consequences when it comes to physiological and educational development, leaving mature adults with poor health and poor prospects. These distinctive characteristics feed into the political dynamics surrounding bonded children, sustaining a level of interest that sets them apart from their adult counterparts. Children usually end up in bondage in one of two main ways. The first method involves collective responsibilities, where children are called on to help fulfill their parents' obligations, but are not bonded individually. This can mean stepping into the breach when senior family members are unable or unwilling to work. This dynamic is not limited to sons inheriting their father's obligations, but can involve debts being passed between siblings. For poor families, children can be both a resource and a burden, and are expected to make contributions to communal welfare. The second method involves an individual arrangement, whereby parents or guardians receive an advance against the labors of their progeny. This usually involves children working for relative strangers.

Both of these models are predominantly concentrated in agricultural settings, but substantial numbers of bonded children can be found in other informal sectors:

> Industries with significant child bondage include silk, beedi (hand-rolled cigarettes), silver jewelry, synthetic gemstones, leather products (including footwear and sporting goods), handwoven wool carpets, and precious gemstones and diamonds. Services where bonded child labor is prevalent include prostitution, hotel, truck stop and tea shop services, and domestic servitude.[94]

This pattern can be found throughout the Indian subcontinent, which has long been recognized as having the greatest number of working children in the world.[95] Bonded children not only fall under the ambit of laws prohibiting debt bondage, they are also subject to regimes governing child labor. This has consistently resulted in a selective attitude toward the law, in which prohibitions on bonded labor have been discounted in favor of weaker laws regulating child labor.[96] Even then, enforcement remains weak, thanks to official indifference, legal loopholes, and prosecutorial dilemmas.[97] Child bondage has been most commonly justified in terms of "training," or the need for "nimble fingers," but these weak formulas usually conceal more narrow economic interests in securing cheap and docile labor.

The use of bonded children in export industries, such as carpets and sporting goods, has recently received a great deal of international media attention. In this context, bonded child labor becomes part of larger critiques of global capitalism, where rapacious multinational companies are said to have made tremendous profits by depressing local wages to the point where child labor becomes all but unavoidable.[98] Somewhat paradoxically, this international connection has created additional scope for political action, as consumer boycotts, ethical alternatives, and public shaming have brought modest pressure on multinationals to improve the situation.[99] It is worth noting, however, that these political openings apply only to selected industries.[100] In most cases, contests over bonded labor continue to take place at a national (or local) level within industries that are geared toward domestic markets.

For the desperate and vulnerable, bonded labor frequently represents a survival strategy, which offers a means for forestalling starvation and exposure. While there is no doubt that poverty and a lack of viable alternatives have always been an essential component of bonded labor, it is important not to detach poverty from other sociological considerations. It is not uncommon for landowners to portray their activities in paternalistic terms, in which a benevolent proprietor offers sanctuary in exchange for service. This language is often accompanied with derogatory characterizations that echo historical depictions of slave populations, where those in bondage are depicted as lazy, dirty, simple, or brutish. This combination of poverty and paternalism not only sidesteps the economic returns that accrue to "benevolent" proprietors, but avoids the broader relationship between poverty, social hierarchy, resource concentration, and enduring patterns of caste-based discrimination.

The vast majority of bonded laborers in India are Dalits, or "untouchables," who occupy the bottom rung of a complex social hierarchy. Caste plays a key role throughout the subcontinent, albeit with variations in the groups found at the bottom of the social ladder. Despite being legally prohibited, caste discrimination continues to be a pervasive problem, encompassing education, employment, funding, marriage, communal violence, place of residence, and even physical contact.[101] Caste continues to be bound up in bonded labor in a variety of ways. This starts at birth, as persons of lower caste are more likely to have parents who are bonded and are therefore more likely to inherit debts. Those who escape this fate (the majority) are still likely to have fewer resources, prospects, and assets, and are therefore prone to falling into bondage later in life. Caste discrimination not only helps to explain why so many Dalits are bonded, it also helps explain official failures to make proactive efforts to address their plight. Socially conditioned to accept their station, lower castes can often expect widespread indifference, if not active hostility, when they seek to challenge the status quo. In this context, the politics of caste continues to be bound up in various acts of violence.[102]

In this complex environment, there will always be a substantial overlap between different perspectives and political projects. This is often a question of emphasis rather than qualitative difference, marking a convergence of viewpoints that focus on caste, child labor, migration, poverty, slavery, and even broader themes such as rural development and microfinance. The 1956 Convention ensures that bonded labor is now widely recognized as a form of slavery, but different contributors have approached this relationship in different ways. On many occasions, slavery has been invoked in evocative, rather than analytical terms, with personal testimonies of outrageous exploitation being used to establish a self-evident equivalence. Other accounts steer clear of slavery entirely, favoring less combative language. Both variants often end up condensing, or otherwise passing over, the historical relationship between legal slavery and bonded labor, and the way in which the parameters of bond-age have evolved in response to legal abolition. Official shortcomings do not begin with a failure to enforce the 1976 Act, or other similar instruments, or even with the many decades that passed before governments began to meet their international obligations, but with the systematic failures associated with the legal abolition of slavery itself. By defining slavery in narrow legal-istic terms, administrators could avoid "disruption," while tacitly condoning and encouraging bonded labor as a viable institution. Once established, this formula may well have continued indefinitely, but for the emergence of local activism. The task now is to bridge the gap between legal abolition and effec-tive emancipation. As we have seen, this goes well beyond legal solutions to incorporate issues such as caste discrimination, land concentration, educa-tion, and rehabilitation. Thanks to decades of struggle, the requisite frame-works appear to be in place, but implementation continues to be a pervasive problem.

Concluding Remarks

The overall scale of bonded labor in the Indian subcontinent cannot be ex-plained by reference to poverty alone. There are other parts of the globe, such as sub-Saharan Africa, which also endure extreme poverty, but they do not necessarily have the same levels of contemporary forms of slavery. In order to understand why bonded labor remains such a substantial issue on the Indian subcontinent, we need to take into account at least two additional factors: the continuing consequences of the historical limitations of the legal abolition of slavery, and the continuing consequences of enduring patterns of social hierarchy and caste discrimination. The former has provided a crucial foun-dation on which more recent innovations have gradually been built, while the latter has provided the ideological and institutional glue that tends to be required in order to keep relatively large numbers of people in a servile or socially marginal condition. Much like historical slave owners, upper-caste Indians regard personal deference and elevated social recognition as their rightful due, since this represents the "natural" order of things, while infe-riority and dependency continue to be viewed as the "natural" role of lower castes. Thanks in large part to the pervasive role of caste in India, Pakistan, and Nepal, government institutions do not function as they should.

As we have seen, the main challenge to this enduring complex has not come from above, at an international level, but from below, reflecting various forms of internal agitation. Having ignored the 1956 Convention for decades, governments have been reluctantly forced into action by domestic activism.[103] The legal breakthroughs that followed represent a crucial first step, but familiar problems of enforcement are yet to be resolved. It should be clear, however, that enforcement is only one aspect of a much larger equation. For millions of people on the subcontinent, the struggle against bonded labor is closely connected to caste, gender, demography, land reform, and social roles. This inevitably impinges on politically sensitive terrain, which is no longer specifically (or even primarily) concerned with slavery, but with the composition of society as a whole. Improving access to land, alleviating poverty, and ending caste discrimination would collectively have a major impact on the prevalence of bonded labor, but this necessarily involves a far-reaching, cumulative challenge to the status quo. Taking effective action against bonded labor on the subcontinent would greatly reduce the overall prevalence of contemporary slavery, but it cannot be expected to bring bonded labor entirely to an end. As we shall see in the next chapter, debt has also proved to be a popular instrument of control when it comes to human trafficking.

Chapter 8

Trafficked into Slavery

In the aftermath of the Cold War, the Anti-Slavery Project has been dominated by the issue of human trafficking. The main topic of conversation in this ongoing phase in the evolution of organized anti-slavery has been "sexual slavery," or forced prostitution. This is a topic that inevitably impinges on broader preoccupations with sex, gender, and the status of prostitution more generally. In this respect, human trafficking is not so much a singular issue as a powerful lodestone for a range of interests, orientations, and agendas. This dynamic not limited to sexual exploitation, but extends to immigration, people smuggling, organized crime, migrant labor, tourism, social cohesion, citizenship, and, perhaps most importantly, structural inequalities. While recent interest in trafficking has tended to concentrate on forced prostitution, there has been a growing—albeit still fairly modest—recognition of trafficking for other purposes, opening the door to an expansive approach that incorporates many different forms of human bondage. When this formula is taken to its logical conclusion, trafficking effectively ceases to be one dimension of an overarching struggle against many forms of slavery and instead becomes synonymous with the Anti-Slavery Project in its entirety. This raises both analytical and political questions. While recent interest in trafficking has helped to raise the profile of all forms of contemporary slavery, the trafficking template comes with a number of limitations and preoccupations that can also complicate efforts to effectively come to terms with the full spectrum of global issues. On the one hand, we have the use of transit, or transfer, as an organizing device, which has tended to prioritize international migration. On the other hand, we have an enduring nexus between trafficking and other agendas, covering issues such as prostitution, patriarchy, and border protection.

During the long struggle against legal slavery, slave trading was consistently singled out as a unique and exceptional evil. Slavers forcibly separated people from family and friends to face long and uncertain journeys followed by purchase by total strangers in a highly degrading fashion. Some forms of trafficking follow a comparable pattern, with unfortunates being candidly bought and sold. It is here that the links between trading and trafficking are most apparent, but such cases represent only a small minority of the diverse experiences involved. Unlike slave trading, trafficking tends to be chiefly defined by what happens *after* migrants reach their eventual destination. The pursuit of a better life can lead migrants down many paths of varying degrees of legality. If they manage to circumvent increasingly restrictive immigration controls, they can end up being treated as a menace to social order. If they manage to circumvent immigrations controls, but then end up trapped in bondage, they can instead end up as (qualified) objects of sympathy. There is not one path for migrants and one path for trafficking victims, but many overlapping paths with many overlapping destinations. Unlike slave trading, many of the people involved migrate voluntarily, albeit on the basis of imperfect or fraudulent information. This raises the difficult issue of consent, and the extent to which unsavory outcomes can be linked to individual choices. In cases of severe abuse, consent should be inconsequential, but this is not always how it works in practice. In many settings, there continues to be an inordinate focus on "innocent" victims, reflecting the enduring legacy of earlier "white slavery" campaigns. In order to understand the historical roots of contemporary problems, we need to investigate a range of issues and associations that have rarely featured in recent discussions of trafficking.

The "White Slavery" Dilemma

Human trafficking has tended to be approached as a distinctively modern problem, which can be primarily traced to increasing inequalities, post-Cold War dislocations, demographic strain, the rise of informal labor markets and neoliberal economics, and growing migratory pressures in an era of selectively tightening immigration controls. This diagnosis undoubtedly captures some of the key issues involved, but it can also end up expunging a much larger story, in which modern problems represent the latest phase in enduring campaigns against trafficking and forced prostitution. These campaigns fall under the rubric of the "white slave trade." As a rule, white slavery receives limited consideration in current debates. This may simply be a question of priorities, with current concerns leaving little scope for a detailed consideration of past events, but alongside this general point there is the more specific matter of the racist, sensationalist, and now quaintly archaic language that typically characterized white slavery discourse. In light of these troubling characteristics, it can be tempting to dismiss white slavery as a period of foolishness that was responsible for some outdated treaties, but was otherwise lacking in merit or achievement. This is problematic. First, there is the sheer scale of white slavery activity, which resulted in extended, high-profile political campaigns, hundreds of dedicated societies in many countries, a voluminous literature that may have reached a billion pages, and an extensive institutional architecture.[1] This was not a short-lived, unimportant excursion, but a major political exercise. Second, many of the problems, practices, and propositions that defined earlier contests over white slavery have left a complex legacy. Finally, white slavery, like anti-slavery more generally, did not function as an isolated issue, but was also embedded within larger agendas.

The concept of white slavery offers an archetypal example of the recurring challenge of separating literal and rhetorical claims. White slavery appears to have initially been a variant on "wage" slavery and can be found describing working children in the 1830s, before being taken up in the 1870s as part of campaigns against state regulation of prostitution. [2] In Britain, the main focal point was the Contagious Diseases Acts (1864/1866/1869), which introduced regulated prostitution in selected garrison and seaport towns. Especially controversial were provisions for compulsory health inspections, which were denounced as humiliating, hypocritical, ineffectual, and arbitrary, with police suspicion being sufficient to compel examination. Opposition to these acts came from a broad cross-section of society, and developed under the able leadership of Josephine Butler, who repeatedly denounced state regulation of prostitution as white slavery.[3] In this formative period, the language of "slavery" was chiefly used as *rhetorical* device, which sought to establish a metaphorical connection between the collective status of prostitutes and the plight of chattel slaves. [4]

As the campaign evolved, a second understanding of white slavery gradually emerged, revolving around the procurement of "innocents" for the purposes of forced prostitution. In this variant, white slavery would be understood in more narrow terms, with the status of specific individuals being characterized as the *literal* equivalent of legal slavery. Over time, this second understanding would come to dominate discussion of white slavery, but the earlier variant never faded away entirely, sustaining an environment where it was not always clear whether the term referred to all forms of prostitution, albeit to varying degrees, or only those subject to particularly heinous abuses. On this front, the white slavery literature of the period is plagued by ambiguity, inconsistency, and a lack of clear definition.[5] This ambiguity should come as no surprise. The main focal point of the campaign was not "classical" slavery, but prostitution, and its historical lineage owes more to centuries of anti-vice campaigning than organized anti-slavery. In Britain, anti-vice operations date back to the 1690s and the emergence of societies for the reformation of manners, which set in motion a series of heavy-handed, intrusive, and only sporadically effective programs of social reform.[6]

When it comes to the politics of white slavery, two main axes can be identified, with particular themes being called on to advance a larger agenda. First, there is the specific issue of forced prostitution, which would in turn inform attitudes toward *all* forms of prostitution (or even social order as a whole). This started as a public policy issue. Many instruments available to combat the problem, such as raising the age of consent, restrictions on movement, or criminalizing commercial sex, would necessarily apply to all (potential) prostitutes, not only those in sexual servitude. In fact, this was a major part of the appeal of white slavery. By focusing on (and periodically fabricating)[7] stories of egregious abuses, campaigners fashioned a wedge that could be used to advance their preferred approach to prostitution as a whole.[8] Ironically, this frequently led to prostitutes suffering at the hands of public officials.[9] Second, there is a more general nexus between prostitution, sexuality, and gender roles. On this point, opinion was divided. More progressive voices linked prostitution to male hypocrisy and institutionalized discrimination, but this perspective was ultimately drowned out by conservative defenders of "traditional" mores and female purity. Religious groups were especially prominent here, continuing a pattern from earlier anti-vice campaigns.

The overall thrust of this relationship was a form of overwrought paternalism, where respectable, patriarchal families were charged with protecting their vulnerable daughters from the rampant evils of a modern market society.[10] Instead of dealing with autonomous adult women, campaigners focused on "innocent" girls, feeding a reactionary assault against all forms of nonmarital, nonreproductive sexuality.[11] This sort of protection tended to be a double-edged sword.[12] For prostitutes who were not unambiguous victims, and instead came to their vocation through some form of personal, if often highly circumscribed "choice," the penalties for falling from grace could be severe. Having transgressed the line between innocent and harlot, these women could expect to be defined as corruptors of moral values, or symptoms of a larger social malaise. By making "innocents" a focal point, many campaigners at least tacitly endorsed an informal distinction between deserved and undeserved hardships.

It is not always clear where chattel slavery fits into this equation. At first glance, there are obvious links. [13] In Britain, the "new abolitionists" consciously emulated both the rhetoric and tactics of earlier anti-slavery campaigns, forging a popular coalition with evangelical groups once again playing a leading role. Once we delve deeper, however, some curious discrepancies emerge. To start with, much of the white slavery literature only makes (at best) fleeting references to chattel slavery. On the rare occasions when slavery was mentioned, it was usually in the context of assertions that white slavery was worse than the black slavery of the past.[14] Interest in white slavery ebbed and flowed, but the peak period occurred between 1870 and 1914. During this timeframe, European powers were cautiously grappling with slave populations places such as Africa and India, but most of the white slavery literature from this period has next to nothing to say about this global trajectory. While some individuals were actively engaged in both topics, they tended to be the exception, not the rule. Throughout the late nineteenth and early twentieth centuries, white slavery and anti-slavery were organized around separate conversations, separate literatures, and distinctive political dynamics. There were some moves toward convergence following the Great War, as practices such as Mui-Tsai became a more prominent part of the anti-slavery agenda, but full integration only occurred in the final stages of the twentieth century.

If chattel slavery does not figure prominently in white slavery what was the source of its appeal? While there is no one answer to this question, a number of related factors can be identified. First, there is the voyeuristic sensationalism that defined much of the literature from this period. Take, for example, this lurid passage by Ernest A. Bell (1910), where:

> murderous traffickers drink the heart's blood of weeping mothers while they eat the flesh of their daughters, by living and fattening themselves on the destruction of the girls. Disease and debauch quickly blast the beauty of these lovely victims. Many of them are dead

in two or three years. Cannibals seem almost merciful in comparison with the white slavers, who murder the girls by inches.[15]

In light of such material, it should not be surprising that white slavery can be viewed as a literary genre, which included magazine articles, novels, plays, and even popular movies. By bringing "together absolute innocence and unspeakable evil in the mysterious setting of the big city, white slavery literature has ties to the detective story and descends from the genre known as 'mysteries and miseries of the city' as well as from the captivity narrative."[16] The issues involved may well have been serious, if decidedly exaggerated, but the popular appeal of white slavery can be at least partially traced to a subtext of sexual voyeurism.

This goes some way to explaining a cultural phenomenon, but it does not really get the heart of its political dimensions. On this front, it is necessary to explore the role of white slavery in advancing or expressing various political projects. This is not simply a matter of gender roles and patriarchal protection, but also extends to underlying themes of nationality, race, and respectability. From this standpoint, a useful point of departure is provided by Jacqueline Berman, who contends that women's "symbolic position as guardians of the nation and protectors of morality . . . renders women's bodies . . . sites of increased surveillance through which the 'sanctity' of community can be preserved and (state) authority re-established."[17] Understood in these terms, white slavery can be viewed as a form of collective dishonor, where abuses inflicted on innocent girls were construed as an affront to cherished ideals of feminine virtue, and thereby undercut the moral health of society as a whole. For communities confronted by social upheaval, unprecedented migration, and rapid urbanization, white slavery represented both a response to a general sense of disorder and dislocation, and a rallying point for defenders of stylized traditional values. These themes are evident in the types of "dangers" identified by campaigners; big cities, dance halls, theaters, unaccompanied travel, urban isolation, and (excessive) material desires. Since the pace of modern life was leading girls astray, paternal intervention by state and society was required.

This leads us to a complex partnership between racism, respectability, and nationalism. These are difficult, expansive issues, and only a brief sketch can be offered here, starting with the concept of "respectability," which was integral to prevailing understandings of manners, morals and "proper" sexuality. This began as a bourgeois, middle-class concept but was also later embraced by a larger cross-section of society. In moving beyond its middle-class roots, respectability worked in partnership with nationalism, which "absorbed and sanctioned middle-class manners and morals and played a crucial part in spreading respectability to all classes of the population, however much those classes hated and despised each other."[18] In both the middle-class and nationalist variants, female virtue (and maternal fervor)[19] occupied a prime position. This is fairly straightforward when it comes to respectability, which is bound up in the aforementioned theme of patriarchal protection, but requires further elaboration in the case of nationalism, where migration moves to center stage.

White slavery was both a national and international issue, yet movements across borders always aroused particular concern. This was again partially a matter of public policy, as governments sought to pool resources, toughen sanctions, and coordinate policing. This is reflected in the development of a series of largely ineffectual international agreements (1904, 1910, 1921, 1933), designed to combat "the procuring of women or girls for immoral purposes abroad."[20] Another prominent feature of this period was the development of travelers' aid networks, where countless agents monitored ports and railway stations across the globe in an effort to prevent recruiters and to shield unaccompanied female migrants. However much white slavery occasioned universal censure, there was nonetheless a widespread tendency to focus on abuses inflicted on female compatriots by foreign interlopers.[21] One perspective on this theme comes from Donna Guy:

> For many Europeans it was inconceivable that their female compatriots would willingly submit to foreign, racially varied men. In one way or another these women must have been trapped or victimized. So European women in foreign bordellos were construed as "white slaves" rather than common prostitutes, and the campaign to rescue them became a glorious battle pitting civilization at home against barbarism abroad.[22]

This statement involves a series of overlapping claims. First, there is an assertion of superior virtue. Second, there is the idea that an unwitting "fall" at the hands of uncouth foreigners represents an affront to national dignity and, finally, there is the further claim that the only way collective honor can be reaffirmed is by taking remedial action.[23] This formula is equally applicable when it comes to race. Despite later misgivings over the overt racism of *white* slavery, and an occasional addendum stating that victims came from all races, there was always a clear racial hierarchy at work. This was not simply a matter of priorities, but extended to deeper concerns over white slaves being ravished by racial inferiors, and thereby dishonoring their communities.[24]

What should we make of this cultural and political phenomenon? Unsurprisingly, most recent commentators have concluded that white slavery ultimately reveals far more about larger social dynamics than substantive practices, and that the scale of the problem was greatly exaggerated, with only a fraction of cases fitting the dominant narrative. [25] From this starting point, two further themes can be identified, each representing different sides of a fundamental dilemma. In the first variant, white slavery was simply not credible and therefore has little bearing on contemporary problems. This can mean passing over historical links between white slavery and human trafficking out of fear that its dubious character will tarnish current campaigns. Unfortunately, this can also leave us with historical silence. In the second variant, white slavery remains highly dubious, but this does not necessarily mean that there were no substantive problems, only that the activists of the time dramatically distorted the issues involved.[26] Consequently, "Moral panic about trafficking does not mean that women were not forced into prostitution."[27] This argument is eminently plausible, but is not always easy to verify, since relevant materials remain compromised by the more egregious aspects of white slavery.[28] This perspective opens the door to a more nuanced perspective, but it will always be partially constrained by historical sources.

In this context, the archetypal example of an innocent white girl being led astray appears especially pernicious. The problem is not that there were only a handful of cases of sexual servitude, but that cases of sexual servitude rarely conformed to this unrealistic template. To start with, perhaps "99 percent of traffic victims were in fact women of color—broadly defined by contemporaries to include Jews—distributed throughout the world but concentrated in colonial areas." [29] This included Chinese prostitutes in California, Jewish prostitutes in Europe, and a multinational traffic across Asia and the Middle East.[30] During the 1920s and 1930s, a number of reports on the "traffic in women and children," were produced under the auspices of the League of Nations, documenting a relatively modest international traffic involving prostitutes of many nationalities. These reports make clear that prostitution covered a range of experiences and varying degrees of coercion and consent, but there also appears to have been no shortage of cases at the bottom end of the spectrum. [31]

Some cases documented by the League invite comparisons with contemporary reports. In one example from Singapore (1932), prostitution is reported to involve "Chinese girls of 6 to 8 years, bought or received in pledge from poor people in China or sometimes kidnapped, [being] brought into the colony after having been coached to answer the questions of the protectorate."[32] On this front, it is worth keeping in mind that both slave trading and indentured migration continued well into the twentieth century, and that analogous practices such as debt-bondage, pawnage, servile marriage, and forced labor were similarly widespread. If we move away from the limited hyperbole of white slavery, and toward a modern conception of trafficking (or anti-slavery), it is clear that there was a great deal going on beneath this parochial radar. This situation was not easily rectified, however. Popular interest in white slavery underwent a dramatic decline in the interwar years. Sporadic reports continued well into the second half of the century,[33] along with periodic scares,[34] but their political traction was limited. This does not, however, mark the end of the matter. As we shall see, white slavery leaves a complex legacy, especially when it comes to political priorities (transit, prostitution, and migration) and behavioral models (the innocent victim).

The Evolution of Human Trafficking Under International Law

Trafficking has always been a difficult concept to pin down, since not everyone uses the concept in the same way.[35] There is general agreement that it denotes a subcategory of migration, but it is not always clear where trafficking ends, and people-smuggling, asylum-seeking, or economic migration begins. Definitions are never easy, but trafficking can be especially troublesome because its defining features are often determined by what happens after migrants reach their destination, rather than a set of distinctive experiences in transit. It is not unusual for victims of trafficking to initiate contact and to take proactive steps to reach their destination, including deceiving or circumventing relevant immigration controls, only to find themselves subject to bondage at the end of their journey. Further complicating matters, individuals subjected to human trafficking do not always see themselves as powerless victims, but as autonomous agents.[36] In the following remarks, I explore a number of key features of modern conceptions of human trafficking, starting with the evolving status of trafficking under international law, the dimensions of a global problem, and major tactics and techniques. Having examined some of the core characteristics of the problems involved, I then turn to underlying associations with larger structures and political agendas. It is in this context that the ongoing legacies of previous white slavery campaigns are especially apparent, raising difficult questions about the larger ramifications of trafficking policies, and the associated wisdom of extending a trafficking lens to organized anti-slavery as a whole.

Until December 2000, there was no definitive definition of trafficking under international law. This does not mean, however, that international law had little to say on the matter prior to this date. One starting point is the 1949 Convention for the Suppression of the Traffic in Persons and of the Exploitation of the Prostitution of Others, which moved to consolidate earlier instruments concerned with white slavery and traffic in persons. Like most human rights treaties, the Convention has weak enforcement and monitoring provisions, but it nonetheless introduced and reaffirmed some important ingredients, and was long a major port of call for discussion of sexual servitude. Building on earlier precedents, parties

> agree to punish any person who, to gratify the passions of another: (1) Procures, entices or leads away, for purposes of prostitution, another person, even with the consent of that person; (2) Exploits the prostitution of another person, even with the consent of that person.

The main focal point here was not trafficking, which was left undefined, but prostitution and pimping.[37] The Convention is not confined to international migration, but incorporates domestic activities. By rendering consent irrelevant, it (re)affirmed the idea that a person (a gender-neutral first) cannot legitimately consent to abuses inflicted on them.

Compared with more recent innovations, the scope of the Convention is decidedly limited. Other forms of forced labor and sexual exploitation were *not* covered, but found various homes in other international instruments, including the 1956 Supplementary Convention, where two of four analogous practices—servile marriage and the transfer of children for the purposes of exploitation—clearly anticipate modern conceptions of trafficking. This is representative of a larger trend. Over the years, many agreements raised the problems associated with trafficking without endorsing an overarching definition.[38] This pattern extended to domestic legislation. In recent times, many countries have introduced legislation to make trafficking a specific criminal offense,[39] thereby filling a void where grievous abuses were indirectly covered by a range of legal instruments, from laws prohibiting slavery, forced labor, or pimping, to injunctions against rape, assault, and kidnapping.[40] This shift is particularly important, since criminal penalties available using the indirect approach often tended to be fairly lenient.[41] Of course, even this modest outcome requires a successful prosecution, which can be a rare event in many jurisdictions.

This brings us to the United Nations Protocol to Prevent, Suppress and Punish Trafficking in Persons Especially Women and Children (Trafficking Protocol).[42] Breaking with the earlier focus on prostitution, the Protocol embraces a more expansive approach:

> Trafficking in persons shall mean the recruitment, transportation, transfer, harbouring or receipt of persons, by means of the threat or use of force or other forms of coercion, of abduction, of fraud, of deception, of the abuse of power or of a position of vulnerability or of the giving or receiving of payments or benefits to achieve the consent of a person having control over another person, for the purpose of exploitation. Exploitation shall include, at a minimum, the exploitation of the prostitution of others or other forms of sexual exploitation, forced labour or services, slavery or practices similar to slavery, servitude or the removal of organs."[43]

This multi-barreled definition is indicative of the complexities and ambiguities that now surround trafficking. This is particularly evident when it comes to the sizable number of qualifying conditions, which can be broken down into transit (recruitment, transportation, transfer, etc.), technique (force, coercion, abduction, etc.), and terms of exploitation (sexual exploitation, forced labor, slavery, etc.). To constitute trafficking, only one condition from each of these categories is required, with the burden falling on states to identify those subject to trafficking (and, more problematically, to distinguish them from smuggled migrants).[44] Following precedent, the Protocol goes on to state that consent is "irrelevant" in such circumstances. As we shall see, this formula potentially encompasses both an extraordinary range of permutations, and an extraordinary range of problem areas.

This definition is now widely acknowledged as an authoritative benchmark, but the Trafficking Protocol remains subject to a number of limitations and preoccupations. Significantly, the Protocol was established as one of three supplementary treaties to the 2000 Convention Against Transnational Organized Crime. The other two Protocols deal with the Smuggling of Migrants by Land, Sea and Air, and the Illicit Manufacturing of and Trafficking in Firearms. This nexus is important on a number of levels, beginning with the institutional framework itself, which requires states to sign up to the "parent" Convention before they can sign up to any of the Protocols. As its name suggests, this lengthy Convention is designed to strengthen cooperation against organized crime, and it contains a series of provisions criminalizing "safe havens," money laundering, corruption, and other such matters. Importantly, these provisions only apply to "serious crimes" with a transnational dimension, involving an organized criminal element (a structured group of three or more persons).[45]

These conditions extend to the supplementary Protocols. Under the 2000 definition, it does not matter if people cross borders legally or illegally, but if both traffickers and trafficked operate within the boundaries of a single state, they are not formally covered by the Protocol. This tells us something about the overarching concerns animating these recent instruments. Most obviously, there is the focus on organized crime, rather than human rights. This may help to facilitate greater engagement among states, but it can also reinforce a "securitized" view of trafficking, smuggling, and border protection. This is captured by Anne Gallagher, who observes that "While human rights concerns may have provided some impetus (or cover) for collective action, it is the sovereignty/security issues surrounding trafficking and migrant smuggling which are the true driving force behind such efforts."[46]

A Global Snapshot

Interest in human trafficking has grown almost exponentially in recent times. When Kathleen Barry wrote her pioneering study *Female Slavery* in the 1970s, she found that little information on the subject was readily available.[47] A 1983 bibliography on trafficking contains around a hundred sources.[48] A similar exercise today would incorporate tens of thousands of sources. It does not automatically follow, however, that this recent explosion of interest can be primarily attributed to a recent explosion in human trafficking. While human trafficking was on the political backburner for much of the twentieth century, there are still sufficient materials available to suggest a persistent global problem. With the rapid growth of human rights organizations and other relevant actors from the 1970s onward, a variety of preexisting problems have received much greater attention. It is clear, moreover, that the language of trafficking is now being used to describe practices that might have previously fallen under other designations. In this environment, interest in human trafficking can be at least partially explained by an increasing awareness of a variety of problems that had previously not been part of a common international language. However, there are some indications that recent events, such as the rise of informal labor markets and increasing inequalities, have contributed to a growing problem in some parts of the globe. Despite reports indicating that trafficking has become more prominent in some circles, our capacity to evaluate global trends remains hamstrung by a lack of solid data.[49] When several case-specific estimates of the current scale of sex trafficking were subjected to scrutiny, they were found to have greatly overstated the scale of the issues involved.[50]

This qualified stance may not be particularly satisfying, but it guards against a tendency to (over)dramatize the issues at hand.[51] Most recent accounts of trafficking start with the premise that trafficking has been rapidly increasing, but there have also been a growing number of more skeptical voices, who maintain that "there can be no trustworthy numbers, so the published statistics are mostly fantasies."[52] Like white slavery, trafficking in persons has larger implications for policies toward migrants and prostitutes more generally, so its qualitative dimensions are inevitably fraught with political implications. This is particularly evident when it comes to sex work, where it is not uncommon for reports to conflate trafficking and prostitution, leading to a distorted picture of the overall problem.[53] This complicates an already difficult situation. Trafficked persons come from numerous countries, speak many languages, and have a wide range of geographically dispersed experiences, which they are often reluctant to share. Research tends to focus on cases that come to light through official channels, or support networks, which can result in sampling issues and selection bias. Recent scholarship has made some progress in grappling with these issues, but serious obstacles remain, particularly when it comes to extrapolating larger trends from relatively small samples.[54] It is not unusual for estimates of trafficking to be in the hundreds of thousands, or millions, but such figures remain subject to the vagaries of the subject. In many cases, it is not clear what definition or methodology has been used.

Despite these limitations, it is possible to cautiously discern some over-arching characteristics. There is now no doubt, for instance, that the issues involved are global in scope. For the most part, the main focus has been on movements between countries, rather than within countries. This is conventionally divided into places of origin, destination, and transit, but many countries fall into multiple categories. This is illustrated by a 2005 report on trafficking in Central Asia, where the political and economic dislocations that have followed Soviet collapse have meant increases in migration, including trafficking in persons. This encompasses both sexual exploitation and forced labor for nonsexual purposes. The former includes trafficking into brothels in countries as diverse as South Korea, Israel, Thailand, Russia, and the United Arab Emirates.[55] "In the main, women leave on tourist visas, with the promise of jobs as nannies or domestic workers or in the hotel, catering, and entertainment sectors. A minority, as in other contexts, know that they will engage in prostitution."[56] In this environment, countries can be both origin and transit points, with Uzbeks and Tajiks using Kyrgyzstan as a transit country because of the ease of acquiring passports, or traffickers channeling women through the international airport at Almaty in Kazakhstan.[57] Central Asian countries can also be destination points for sexual exploitation, but this can be overshadowed by other forms of labor migration, particularly into Kazakhstan, which forms part of a growing intraregional market in irregular migrant labor. The numbers of people involved in this far-reaching transnational complex easily outstrip those involved in prostitution, but experiences range from trafficking/forced labor, to "every-day" exploitation and even relatively favorable circumstances, where migrants can earn more than is readily available at home. As a general rule, trafficking encompasses only a very small percentage of overall migration, yet some categories of migrants tend to be more problematic than others.[58]

Similar stories can be told in other parts of the globe. In a 2003 report covering 53 (of 54) countries in Africa, UNICEF concluded that nearly all parts of the continent have served, at one time or another, as origin, transit, and destination points.[59] This does not mean, of course, that all countries are equally occupied or involved in the same way. One major focal point has been child trafficking in West Africa, which has attracted considerable international interest, including widely disseminated reports on the horrors of "slave boats."[60] A long list of countries have been implicated here, including Mali, Côte d'Ivoire, Benin, Gabon, Ghana, Togo, Nigeria, Niger, and

Burkina Faso, with routes being influenced by the distribution of wealth within the region.[61] This typically results in girls being acquired for domestic work or market labor, and boys for agricultural labor, but can extend to other forms of exploitation, such as prostitution.[62] Some child trafficking networks can involve an extension/distortion of a traditional practice of placing children with wealthier kinfolk. This has provoked activity on a number of fronts, including wide-ranging legal reforms, various international agreements and codes of conduct, the introduction of "vigilance committees" and other monitoring efforts, educational and vocational programs, and the politicization of "slave chocolate."[63] Revealingly, this can be approached as either a trafficking issue or a child labor issue, marking a convergence of overlapping perspectives. It is clear, moreover, the trafficking in West Africa comprises local, regional, and transcontinental elements, with more localized practices persisting alongside trafficking into Europe, the Middle East, and elsewhere.[64]

Another similar, albeit less topical, example comes from the Indian subcontinent, where trafficking within specific countries occurs alongside larger international networks, the most well known arguably being the traffic between India and Nepal, but also reaching much farther afield.[65] It appears, however, that internal movements greatly outweigh international transfers. Take India, for instance, where one survey has calculated that

> Trafficking from neighbouring countries accounts for only 10 per cent of the coerced migration, with approximately 2.17 per cent from Bangladesh and 2.6 per cent from Nepal. The share of interstate [i.e., internal] trafficking is estimated to be around 89 per cent.[66]

This is by no means true in all cases, but is nonetheless worth keeping in mind when it comes to the link between trafficking, border protection, and the confines of the 2000 Protocol.

The Indian subcontinent provides a further illustration of the type of activities that are now commonly associated with trafficking. This starts with the most topical issue of forced prostitution, which can be broken into one-step and two-step strategies, with the former referring to the targeting of non-prostitutes, and the latter involving the recruitment of established sex workers, who then find themselves in bondage.[67] This is only the beginning, however, as trafficking is also held to involve domestic service, agricultural labor, construction and factory work, drug peddling, organ trading, forced marriage, begging syndicates, adoption rackets, and camel racing.[68] Within this broader frame of reference, nearly every form of contemporary slavery can be subsumed under a trafficking template.

Tactics, Techniques, and Vulnerability

Victims of human trafficking can end up in bondage in various ways, both overt and subtle. The clearest example of the former is kidnapping, with victims being forcibly captured and forced into servitude. This is comparatively rare, but is still far from unheard of in some parts of the world. Another more common variation involves families selling their kin to third parties. In such circumstances, those involved are often deceived about the specific terms of service, but they will nonetheless have a general impression of what is involved, securing modest financial rewards out of a variety of motives. The frequency of such transactions, which often involve children, serves as a powerful testament to poverty, insecurity, and desperation. Tragically, these exchanges can be instrumental in ensuring compliance, as victims are afraid that their kin will have to return the money if they fail to perform. Alongside these methods, we find more subtle devices, based around fraud and deceit. Trickery can take the form of informal, ad hoc approaches, or more elaborate strategies, using employment agencies and job advertisements. In both variants, those involved take up a favorable offer of employment, training, or education, only to face subsequent indignities.[69]

A key starting point here is physical violence and constraint, which sits at the heart of all forms of human bondage. Violence is typically used for "seasoning" in the early stages of bondage and as a strategic platform for discipline and retribution. Not all violence will be calculated, but may also reflect sadistic urges. This is not an isolated issue. The prospect of (further) violence provides the backdrop against which all other techniques are employed. Another key theme is isolation. This encompasses physical distance from place of origin, language barriers, exclusion from wider society, and the absence of larger support networks. This potent amalgam of geographic distance and social marginalization not only makes escape difficult, but can lead victims to endure their current situation, however unpleasant, out of dread of uncertain hardships on departure. Another familiar theme is debt, as costs incurred in transit, or payments to various parties, are used to ensure compliance. As we saw in the previous chapter, one of the strengths of this strategy is that it establishes a target to work toward, leading to active endeavors to achieve redemption. This is obviously by no means easy, thanks to low wages, excessive "deductions," and accounting tricks, yet it is not unheard of for people to secure their autonomy after enduring extended hardships.[70]

Like other forms of migration, trafficking is often discussed in terms of push-and-pull factors, with the former referring to the deprived circumstances that impel migrants to seek prospects elsewhere, and the latter referring to the relative attractions, real or perceived, of life in other parts of the globe. The most obvious push factor is widespread poverty, which encompasses both long-term miseries and more immediate cataclysms, such as a loss of livelihood. In this context, it is easy to treat poverty as a constant, unavoidable fact of life, but this neatly sidesteps its relationship to state and society. This goes well beyond failures to help those afflicted and extends to policies and practices that negatively affect the most vulnerable. Many culprits have been identified here, with neoliberal economic policies and ideologies proving to be especially prominent. Framed in these terms, poverty becomes an inherently political exercise, rather than a natural feature of human existence. Of particular relevance is the "feminization of poverty," where women are said to bear a disproportionate and growing share of global penury. This complex, contested concept can be linked to trafficking in a number of ways, where it is primarily applicable to the global south. Gender discrimination is a long-standing, endemic problem. The feminization of poverty encompasses a further exacerbation of this already bad situation along multiple axes, including the adverse affects of structural adjustment programs, increasing numbers of female-headed households, the growth of the informal labor markets, and the rise of (solitary) female migration.[71] Faced with increasing burdens and diminishing support, large numbers of poor women increasingly operate within inhospitable labor markets and are thus held to be particularly susceptible to various forms of exploitation.

These techniques are common to all forms of trafficking, but when it comes to international migration a new round of dangers and disabilities emerge. In this context, a useful point of departure is provided by Alison Brysk, who observes that "the violations and vulnerabilities of migrant rights . . . can be understood as extensions of a cultural logic in which even human rights are framed as entitlements exclusive to citizens."[72] This represents a practical manifestation of an enduring divide between human and citizen, where ethical obligations and institutional entitlements end up being reserved for compatriots, and outsiders are collectively consigned to a subordinate status.[73] Traffickers (among others) have proved to be adept at exploiting this divide, starting with the migration process itself. Migration has long been a divisive issue, which routinely places economic interests in securing relatively cheap, abundant labor in conflict with more parochial concerns about social integrity. This tension can be decided in various ways, with transatlantic slavery representing a particularly tragic example of a decisive victory for economic interests. It is still not unheard of for governments to promote certain types of large-scale migration, but the general trend in recent times has been toward a selective constriction of legal avenues, coinciding with a concurrent growth in illegal movements and the further politicization of asylum. Efforts to restrict movement will always be an uphill struggle as long as migration remains an attractive or unavoidable strategy. What government actions can do, however, is exacerbate its inherent hazards, as restrictions on movement funnel migrants into more dubious and expensive channels,[74] which tend to be dominated by profit seekers of various stripes. [75]

The politics of exclusion not only encourages outsiders to turn to traffickers, smugglers, and other migration agents, it also conditions their behavior on arrival, where they are consistently excluded from a wide range of protections and entitlements. This is fairly straightforward when it comes to illegal migrants, who have obvious reasons to fear the agents of the state, but can extend to legal migrants, who are frequently ineligible for various forms of institutional support. In some cases, legal residency will be contingent on employment, making it difficult or dangerous to leave an otherwise unpleasant situation. Take Saudi Arabia, for example, where an estimated 8.8 million expatriates coexist alongside an indigenous population of around eighteen million. This figure comprises workers from many parts of the globe, including India, the Philippines, and Indonesia.[76] Under Saudi law, foreign workers operate under contracts that must be guaranteed by a sponsor. In this institutional environment, "Migrants who fled abusive employers and thus lost their legal status have been arrested and summarily deported without the opportunity to press claims through the government's labor grievance process."[77] This is in turn symptomatic of larger patterns of vulnerability based on citizenship. While citizens of wealthy industrial countries are occasionally subject to human trafficking and enslavement, these cases represent the exception, not the rule. Citizens of poorer countries tend to be much more vulnerable.

Another recurrent theme that is common to all forms of trafficking is the confiscation of passports and other documents, making it difficult for victims to establish a legal personality. This is in keeping with the legal ambiguity that surrounds informal labor markets, which sustain amorphous niches where trafficking and other human rights abuses can flourish. Informal labor markets are defined by "instability of employment, an avoidance of most labor laws, and a tendency to remain outside normal capitalist rules of contract, licensing and taxation."[78] They are especially prevalent in the South, but have also become more prominent in many industrialized countries, leading to talk of the "Brazilianization" of the North.[79] Informal labor markets provide fertile ground for many forms of exploitation, as employers are able to ignore various labor laws, resulting in extended working hours, marginal wages, and unchecked authority. In this context, a spectrum of experiences can once again be identified, so it is often by no means clear where trafficking begins or ends.

Like most forms of contemporary slavery, human trafficking tends to apply to a subset of experiences at the bottom end of a larger spectrum comprising factors such as coercion, working conditions, and compensation. One way of distinguishing between human trafficking and other forms of exploitation is to focus on penalties for exit. There are currently tens of millions of workers throughout the globe who toil for marginal wages under poor working conditions. The majority of these workers have at least some capacity to leave their current job and pursue other opportunities. When they do leave, their employer looks for new recruits. In cases of contemporary slavery, individuals (or their families) usually face severe punishments for trying to leave, and are unable to quit. If they do manage to escape, their masters often expend considerable energies tracking them down.

In this environment, it is reasonable to assume that intervention by (uncorrupted) government agents would be welcomed, but initial relief will often quickly give way to justified fears over arrest and deportation. In recent times, a number of countries have introduced measures designed to support trafficking victims, which can include support networks, state assistance, and visa provisions.[80] Unfortunately, these qualified provisions are applicable only in certain states, so it is not uncommon for victims of trafficking to end up in channels designed for criminals or illegal migrants. This harsh fate is far from anomalous, but represents a logical extension of an enduring institutional divide between human and citizen.

Politics, Prostitution, and Border Protection

In this complex and often uncertain environment, the "innocent victim" model holds obvious attractions. In keeping with historical precedent, popular reports often lead with stories of naive girls (autonomous women are again largely absent) who are sold into sexual servitude, where they endure a range of horrific abuses.[81] This undoubtedly makes for a compelling narrative, with polarized protagonists, clear parallels with slavery (buying, selling, severe exploitation), and an undeniable case for immediate salvation. This model not only elevates trafficking to an urgent, unambiguous problem, it can also form the basis for larger claims about trafficking as a whole, as a distinctive set of experiences are again held to epitomize, or to stand in for, the experiences of trafficked persons more generally. This is problematic on at least two levels. First, it confirms the popular belief that the trafficking is confined to sexual servitude involving women and children, leaving little space for trafficking for other purposes, or involving adult males. This focus was evident in early drafts of the trafficking protocol, which explicitly confined its application to women and children.[82] Second, it can sustain a misleading image of trafficking, which poses problems for victims that fall short of this unworldly standard. Many trafficking cases involve proactive migrants, who may have some knowledge of the circumstances that await them, and will routinely make various compromises to make the best out of a bad situation. They may not be "innocent victims," but this should not be allowed to detract from their plight.[83]

This situation has been complicated by fractious debates over the nature and status of prostitution. The main dispute is not between states, although states are certainly involved, but between different coalitions of feminists and NGOs. These are by no means homogenous, but can be loosely grouped around an ongoing schism between radical feminists, who view all forms of prostitution as an abuse of human rights that should be prohibited, and sex radicals, who combine a nonconformist approach to sexuality with more pragmatic concerns about improving the rights and reputation of sex workers.[84] This rift was evident in negotiations over the Trafficking Protocol, with one coalition striving to link trafficking with all forms of prostitution, and the other seeking to ensure that trafficking would not be invoked to obstruct or otherwise penalize consensual sex work.[85] In both perspectives, trafficking represents one component of a broader political agenda, which in turn colors the way in which the issue is portrayed. For radical feminists, prostitution is emblematic of patriarchal violence and subordination, and can thus be placed alongside rape, sexual harassment, the sexual abuse of children, and pornography. Framed in these terms, "voluntary" prostitution is untenable; all forms of prostitution inevitably involve subjugation and abuse. Once the lines between forced and voluntary are blurred, radical feminists can use cases at the bottom end of the spectrum to challenge prostitution in general.[86]

Sex radicals accept that trafficking and forced prostitution can be a (modest) problem, but they have also devoted considerable energies to preventing these emotionally charged issues from undercutting nascent moves toward the normalization of sex work. This project starts with a challenge to social stigmas and extends to collective action, empowerment, improved rights and protections, and a meaningful political voice. This involves a multifaceted critique of deviance and discrimination. One line of argument is specific to trafficking, and can be expressed in the following statement from Marjolein van der Veen:

> the stigmatization and criminalization of prostitution may actually render (and, I would argue, has rendered) sex workers more vulnerable and more dependent on slave owners, agents or traffickers while denying them the legal or political rights that might assist them in escaping from a slave arrangement.[87]

This argument builds on the idea that criminalization forces prostitutes into the informal economy, leading to exploitative relationships with few safeguards.[88] If prostitution was legal, taxable, and subject to relevant labor laws, then perhaps some of these abuses could potentially be avoided, or at least mitigated. This stance is strongly opposed by radical feminists, who contend that legalization ultimately "makes more prostituted women available to more men," while further commodifying gender relations.[89] Their favored approach is instead the "Swedish Model," which is based on legislation introduced in Sweden in 1999 that decriminalizes women involved in prostitution, yet retains various legal sanctions against those who seek to purchase sex.[90] One of the main problems with sex radicalism is that it can overemphasize the scope for autonomous action, giving lesser consideration to the many structural factors that can constrain individual "choices." This is a common trait among approaches that stress individual agency. The obverse is true of radical feminists, who espouse a highly structural, deterministic approach, which tends to reduce women to victims and objects of patriarchical dominance, leaving relatively little scope for personal autonomy. This is a common trait among structural approaches.

Debates over prostitution feed into another key axis; the nexus surrounding trafficking, migration, and border protection. In keeping with earlier

white slavery campaigns, efforts to curb trafficking have consistently translated into efforts to restrict movement. This is a universal issue, but it is especially applicable to women. On this topic, a powerful indictment is leveled by
Ratna Kapur, who contends that:

> anti-trafficking initiatives reproduce assumptions about women as
> passive, incapable of decision-making, and in need of protection.
> They . . . are frequently used merely as a facade to deter the entry of
> certain categories of migrants or to clean up establishments within
> the sex industry. The anti-trafficking framework has not succeeded in
> detaching itself from these hidden agendas, and consequently it has
> proven to do little good for the trafficked person and great harm to
> migrants and women in the sex industry. [91]

This forms part of a growing critique. [92] The key problem is not trafficking per
se, which at least most critics acknowledge (albeit mostly in passing) as a legitimate (albeit mostly exaggerated) concern, but the projects that trafficking
has been repeatedly invoked to support, including "illegal migration, fighting
prostitution, and even combating terrorism." [93]

In this context, preventing trafficking can quickly come to mean fortifying
national borders and deterring or restricting migrants, which is a course of action already popular with large anti-immigrant constituencies in many countries. This is problematic on multiple levels. First, there is a simple question of
efficacy. Borders are irrelevant when it comes to trafficking within states, which
can be a major issue in many parts of the globe, but this point often gets lost in
the shuffle as states concentrate their energies on international borders. Moreover, it is not always clear that toughening controls will have the desired effect,
as migrants turn to ever more dangerous means of circumventing restrictions
on legal movement. Second, the idea of simply "staying at home"—the underlying message of many anti-trafficking (and anti-immigration) initiatives—is
by no means a neutral or easy exercise. Migration may be dangerous, but it
can also be rewarding. Migrants can not only secure individual rewards, both
personal and financial, they can also make a decisive contribution to the well-
being of their relatives and communities, as the extensive literature on remittances will attest. If migration can offer improvement, "staying at home" can
alternatively be unrewarding or even unsustainable. When "home" means poverty, insecurity, conformity, or conflict, leaving becomes an entirely reasonable
decision, despite the attendant risks.

At this juncture, it is important to emphasize that traffickers and their associates are not the only villains in this story. If poverty is a major cause behind trafficking, as many accounts rightly suggest, we need to look to the reasons why people remain poor. If the gap between rich and poor is vast and growing, and thereby encouraging migration to richer areas, we need to understand and redress this underlying imbalance, rather than patching over its undesirable symptoms. If there is a widespread demand for the goods and services produced by victims of human trafficking and contemporary slavery, we need to look at where that demand comes from, and who benefits, rather than narrowly focusing on one link in a complex chain. In a recent article, Nandita Sharma has gone as far as suggesting that anti-trafficking campaigns form part of a system of global apartheid, which not only unjustly criminalizes migration, but also passes over northern complicity in the structural inequalities that foster migration in the first place. In this perspective, many migrants can be regarded as

> victims of the daily, banal operation of global capitalist labor markets that are governed by nation-states. They are victimized by border control practices and the ideologies of racism, sexism, and nationalism that render *unspectacular* their everyday experience of oppression and exploitation. [94]

This viewpoint can be somewhat totalizing, because it merges "every-day" exploitation and the extreme abuses commonly associated with trafficking and contemporary slavery. This is an entirely legitimate approach, but it may not be the most effective political strategy.

The last decade has been defined by rapid growth in the profile of human trafficking, together with attendant improvements in efforts to combat the problems involved. The crucial issue, however, revolves around the nexus between trafficking and other political projects, and the extent to which these projects have ended up doing more harm than good. In many ways, this represents a throwback to white slavery, where a subset of experiences would shape institutional and ideological responses to (potential) prostitutes more generally. Since efforts to combat trafficking inevitably merge into policies that apply to migrants, prostitutes, and workers, it is necessary to evaluate these policies as a whole, rather than perpetuating a misleading focus on "innocents." From here, we can end up being faced with a difficult balancing act between clarity and complexity. The "innocent" victim offers the former, providing a compelling platform for political advocacy, yet this can mean either sidestepping larger structural forces or, more problematically, invoking stylized personal tragedies to support various contentious goals. More nuanced perspectives can offer a much better diagnosis of the larger issues and associations at work, but they may lack the emotional and political weight of a simplified, unambiguous struggle between good and evil. As we expand our moral and political horizons, the crucial issues are no longer limited to human trafficking per se, but extend to the more general organization and composition of political, social, and economic life.

Concluding Remarks

In June 2010, the United States of America published its tenth Trafficking in Persons Report. Like its predecessors, this most recent report presents a fairly comprehensive survey of both global problems and recent innovations.[95] One of the most revealing features of these annual reports (leaving aside a very complicated political back-story)[96] is the sheer variety of the problems that have come to be discussed under the banner of human trafficking. During the late nineteenth century and early twentieth centuries, there was little or no overlap between white slavery and organized anti-slavery. The legal and political integration of these separate historical campaigns under the banner of human trafficking has been the single most important development that has taken place in the recent history of the Anti-Slavery Project. Every time a Trafficking in Persons Report is published, a diverse array of issues are documented and discussed, ranging from "classical" slavery in Niger and "abductions" in Sudan or Uganda, to bonded labor in the Indian subcontinent. Alongside familiar themes of sexual exploitation, we find repeated discussion of agricultural labor, begging, child soldiers, construction, domestic servitude, marriage, mining, plantations, porterage, and vending. Once we move beyond a narrow focus on sexual servitude, human trafficking ends up as another way of organizing and describing all forms of contemporary slavery.

This has mixed consequences. On the one hand, it is clear that trafficking has played a crucial role in the development of a common political and legal language, and has thereby brought together previously isolated topics into a genuinely global conversation. While sexual servitude continues to attract the most interest, the more expansive version of trafficking found in the 2000 Protocol has also undoubtedly helped draw attention to a range of issues that might otherwise have struggled to attract an international audience. On the other hand, there is the more problematic nexus between trafficking and other political agendas. Despite recent innovations, trafficking continues to be primarily associated with sexual servitude, and the polarized nature of recent debates over prostitution has tended to complicate efforts to give appropriate billing to nonsexual problems. A similar story applies in relation to border protection and immigration, where an inordinate focus on international movements has overshadowed internal movements (or even no movement at all). Even more fundamental is the concept of trafficking itself, which uses transfer, or transit, as an organizing device. As we have seen, *how* someone comes to a particular end is often far less important than the end itself. The language of buying and selling establishes powerful links with slave trading, but few cases tend to be this clear-cut. From this standpoint, it is by no means clear that trafficking constitutes the most effective frame of reference, given both its historical and political baggage and underlying emphasis on point of transfer. While other concepts such as forced labor and sexual servitude may offer greater analytical clarity,[97] the scale of recent public and political investment in the category of trafficking means that it is likely to play a major role in discussion of contemporary slavery for the foreseeable future.

Contemporary Slavery
in the Shadow of History

> No one shall be held in slavery or servitude; slavery and the slave
> trade shall be prohibited in all their forms.
> > —Universal Declaration of Human Rights, Article Four

The past two and a half centuries have witnessed a remarkable transformation in attitudes toward slavery. What was once a natural feature of human existence has instead come to be regarded as an unconscionable crime against humanity. This book has sought to understand the primary causes and consequences of this far-reaching global transformation. My overall argument can be divided into two main strands. The first strand focuses on the underlying causes that eventually led to the legal abolition of slavery throughout the globe. On this front, I have demonstrated that the remarkable achievements of the Anti-Slavery Project can be best understood in terms of three central themes. First, we have the construction of slavery as a stark and solvable problem, which facilitated political mobilization around a clearly defined policy (rather than political) agenda. Second, we have the construction of slavery as a bounded category, which ensured that slavery was framed as a unique and exceptional evil, allowing other forms of suffering and maltreatment to be tacitly excluded and sometimes indirectly legitimated. Finally, we have the construction of slavery as a symbolic yet nonetheless politically significant test of collective honor and identity, which resulted in cumulative international pressures to legally abolish slavery in the absence of popular support for anti-slavery. While both economic and strategic considerations played a major role both pre- and post-abolition, they most commonly involved various efforts to minimize costs, rather than maximize gains. As we have seen, the success of anti-slavery was also bound up in the expansion of European international society. While popular mobilization played a key role in placing anti-slavery on the political agenda, it was European imperialism that translated this agenda into a global phenomenon. In this context, legal abolition was invariably associated with various problems and complications.

This brings us to the second strand of my overall argument, which focuses on the historical limitations of the legal abolition of slavery. On this front, I have demonstrated that the recent emergence of the category of contemporary forms of slavery can best be understood as the latest phase in an evolving response to the limitations of legal abolition. This has found expression in a broader and deeper understanding of anti-slavery obligations, resulting in a landscape in which slavery is now widely held to come in a variety of different forms, which require a variety of overlapping solutions. From this vantage point, the legal abolition of slavery represents as a qualified first step, rather than a historical endpoint. The substantive limitations of the legal abolition of slavery were not widely recognized at the time, but they have become increasingly salient over the last half century. Despite the popularity of "new" slavery, most forms of contemporary slavery have tended to involve an extension of enduring historical themes, rather than distinctively modern innovations. In stark contrast to the legal abolition of slavery—which frequently came about as a consequence of external pressures—this most recent phase in the ongoing evolution of the Anti-Slavery Project has instead been characterized by the sustained growth of domestic activism. From the 1970s onward, this more expansive approach to defining slavery has intersected with increasing levels of human rights activism more broadly, culminating in an unexpected breakthrough in the late 1990s that resulted in the emergence of human trafficking and contemporary slavery as mainstream issues, rather than marginal concerns.

In this concluding chapter, I draw on these interlocking arguments in order to develop a series of broader reflections about the complex relationship between anti-slavery, political activism, and human rights. To this end, I have divided this chapter into two main sections. In the first section, I reflect on the extent to which the history of organized anti-slavery can be regarded as a historical prototype for contemporary political activism. Modern human rights activists and other commentators have regularly looked to the early history of anti-slavery in Britain and the United States for inspiration and instruction. Once the larger relationship between anti-slavery and imperialism becomes part of the equation, a somewhat different series of historical "lessons" come into focus. In the second section, I go on to reflect on the extent to which the history of organized anti-slavery can offer a useful platform from which to understand and eradicate current forms of human bondage. By highlighting a number of underlying linkages between past and present, I aim to shed further light on recent efforts to combat contemporary slavery.

Organized Anti-Slavery as a Historical Prototype

Within the recent literature on contemporary slavery, the history of organized anti-slavery has been primarily conceptualized in terms of a historical inspiration and a strategic framework.[1] As a historical inspiration, organized anti-slavery has been chiefly approached as an enduring source of ethical and political motivation. This starts with the personal virtues associated with leading abolitionist figures such as William Wilberforce and Harriet Tubman, whose commitment to their cause has not only been identified as a compelling personal example for modern individuals, but also extends to the achievements of organized anti-slavery as a whole. By successfully agitating for the abolition of slavery in the face of tremendous political and economic obstacles, these anti-slavery pioneers are said to have illustrated that fundamental changes are both possible and desirable. If an enduring institution such as slavery can be abolished, then perhaps other radical goals, such as an end to international war, could also be more realistic than has commonly been assumed?[2] As a strategic framework, organized anti-slavery has been chiefly approached from an organizational perspective, with pride of place going to the tactics and techniques used by activists in Britain and the United States, such as petitions, publications, organizational networks, boycotts, legal proceedings, public meetings, artistic icons, and Parliamentary maneuvers. From this vantage point, organized anti-slavery has tended to be viewed as a historical prototype that not only occupies a foundational position as the first in a series of related humanitarian projects, but also continues to offer important insights for modern human rights activism.[3]

While the early history of organized anti-slavery undoubtedly offers many important insights into both historical practices and contemporary problems, various difficulties arise when the history of transatlantic slavery is allowed to almost entirely overshadow the history of legal abolition in other parts of the globe. By focusing on selected aspects of transatlantic slavery, most recent efforts to generate historical lessons from organized anti-slavery have ignored the crucial historical relationship between the legal abolition of slavery and European imperialism (and, more generally, the history of slavery and abolition outside the Americas). Once this relationship becomes part of the conversation, the history of anti-slavery becomes a story of caution and complication, as well as instruction and inspiration. While anti-slavery pioneers undoubtedly played a decisive role in the fight against slavery in places such as Britain and the United States, developments in other parts of the world reveal a much less salutary picture. It is possible to argue that European colonial conquests would have been even more brutal if anti-slavery had not been part of the equation, but this is an argument that rests on the role of anti-slavery in mitigating harm, rather than promoting human welfare. While the legal abolition of slavery may well have been a positive development—at least in the long-term—it frequently came about through processes that at best left a great deal to be desired, and at worst heralded the acceleration of other human rights abuses. Once European imperialism is included in the balance sheet, anti-slavery may no longer serve as a source of historical inspiration. If the end of international war came about through unprovoked wars of global conquest, would it still represent a laudable achievement?

The tactics and techniques employed by the early pioneers of anti-slavery are also less straightforward than they might first appear. As we saw in Chapter 1, British anti-slavery activists called on a variety of strategies in order to mobilize popular support. The initial transition from philosophical reflection to political struggle and legislative action would not have taken place without various audiences determining that the legal abolition of slavery was not simply desirable, but also feasible. As we have seen, the key breakthrough of 1787–1788—which unexpectedly placed anti-slavery firmly on the Parliamentary agenda in Britain—was primarily driven by mass petitions and other forms of popular mobilization. It does not automatically follow, however, that this historical trajectory offers substantially new insights for contemporary political activism. All the tactics and techniques used by abolitionists are already very familiar to modern human rights advocates. Over hundreds of years, numerous political activists have added further improvements and refinements to these historical templates, ensuring that modern campaigns are now far more sophisticated than their historical counterparts. If we delve deeper, however, a more substantive problem arises. If anti-slavery ideas had not enjoyed a significant level of popular support, all the techniques used by the early abolitionists would have ultimately fallen on deaf ears.

This brings us to the mutually reinforcing relationship between political mobilization and popular support. Without effective avenues for political mobilization, popular antipathy toward slavery would not have found sufficient political expression. Without popular antipathy toward slavery, the strategies used by anti-slavery activists would have proven ineffective. In order to evaluate the value of anti-slavery as a historical prototype, we also need to reflect on the underlying motivations behind anti-slavery advocacy. As we have seen, this is not an easy question to resolve. In many histories of human rights, the origin and subsequent evolution of anti-slavery appears as one of a series of Enlightenment projects based around an early commitment to human equality.[4] In the case of Britain, this has traditionally involved placing anti-slavery alongside other parallel political campaigns, such as Catholic emancipation, Parliamentary reform, and the expansion of voting rights.

When the focus shifts to incorporate more recent human rights campaigns, the early history of anti-slavery regularly features as the first in a larger series of political campaigns seeking a gradual end to racial discrimination. The two most common reference points here have tended to be the legal abolition of slavery in the United States in the 1860s, and the more recent civil rights campaign that reached its historical peak in the early 1960s. I have no doubt that there are some significant connections between these landmark events, but it is equally important not to lightly pass over the hundred years that separate these two periods. During this intervening century, the European world embraced pseudo-scientific theories of human difference, such as Social Darwinism, and forcibly established colonies throughout the globe via wars of conquest. Even if we accept—if only for the sake of argument—that the pioneers of anti-slavery where chiefly motivated by a commitment to racial equality, it is hard to see how this commitment continued into the late nineteenth century, yet European political elites nonetheless continued their official advocacy of legal abolition.

In order to better understand this global historical trajectory, I have sought to distinguish between two different (yet not entirely separate) approaches to the underlying motivations behind anti-slavery advocacy. The first approach revolves around the familiar idea that anti-slavery activism was driven by a proto-egalitarian commitment to human and racial equality. While this approach was by no means inconsequential or irrelevant, I do not believe that it was the primary driving force behind the legal abolition of slavery. There were undoubtedly some early abolitionists who were committed to racial and human equality, particularly among activists in the United States, but they represented a small minority. The European world of the nineteenth and early twentieth centuries was deeply hierarchical, reflecting entrenched cleavages based on sex, class, race, religion, and "civilization." The Anti-Slavery Project was chiefly based on a well-constructed claim for better treatment of a depressed category of persons. This did not necessarily entail a commitment to human equality, but instead revolved around a qualified commitment to sufficient commonality.

This brings us to my preferred explanation of the underlying motivations behind anti-slavery advocacy, which is chiefly concerned with what slavery came to signify—or otherwise symbolize—about the distinctive virtues (or vices) of particular communities. This approach connects anti-slavery to ideologies of benevolent paternalism, in which peoples who considered themselves to be blessed with "superior" sensibilities and opportunities were held to be duty-bound to assist "lesser" peoples. In order to properly evaluate the value of organized anti-slavery as a historical prototype, we need to resist the temptation to project contemporary categories backward through time, and instead concentrate on the role of collective honor and identity in bringing about the legal abolition of slavery. This overall line of argument has important ramifications for any lessons that might be generated from the history of anti-slavery. If this focus on the relationship between collective identity and anti-slavery is substantially correct, it is likely that there will be other occasions when well-crafted appeals to national honor and religious identity will have much greater resonance than appeals to common humanity. This is not necessarily the most satisfying conclusion, but the history of anti-slavery nonetheless points in this general direction.

It is important to emphasize, however, that historical slave systems also displayed a number of characteristics that rendered them relatively vulnerable to political challenge. As a legal institution, slavery presented a compelling political target. It was not only sanctioned by the state, but also required proactive support from public officials to uphold the elaborate structures that regulated the trading and holding of slaves. In this environment, every degraded life, broken family, personal torment, and unnecessary death could be primarily traced to the institutional order that allowed these activities to take place. From here, legal abolition was widely held to offer a simple, singular solution for alleviating these grievous abuses. It was not always clear how this solution would be realized, but there was little doubt about what ultimately needed to be done. While this was undoubtedly an effective formula, it now provides limited guidance when it comes to contemporary issues, where there is no longer one clear, readily identifiable solution, but many overlapping strategies.

Most modern human rights problems—such as poverty, wartime abuses, indigenous rights, torture, support for the disabled, reproductive rights, and freedom of movement—tend to have very different political profiles to historical slave systems. In their seminal analysis of the strategies used by transnational advocacy networks, Margaret Keck and Kathryn Sikkink argue that some issues and activities have proved more amenable to political mobilization than others. Two types of issues are held to have particular resonance here:

> (1) issues involving bodily harm to vulnerable individuals, especially when there is a short and clear causal chain (or story) assigning responsibility; and (2) issues involving legal equality of opportunity. The first respond to a normative logic, and the second to a juridical and institutional one.[5]

These two general criteria help to capture some of the distinctive political dynamics that surrounded the legal abolition of slavery. Most modern problems are less amenable to political mobilization, which can make it difficult to replicate the success of anti-slavery in other modern settings. It is worth noting, however, that these characteristics mostly apply to legal slavery. Concentrating on the specific solution of legal abolition clearly proved to be a politically effective strategy, but it left the Anti-Slavery Project with relatively limited political momentum once abolition had taken place. In this context, we need to take into account both the strengths and weaknesses of legal abolition as an institutional solution.

Contemporary Slavery in the Shadow of History

The legal abolition of slavery can be best understood as an imperfect change in official status, which left a variety of practices and problems unresolved. In the vast majority of cases, the initial impetus for institutional change was driven by international pressures, as wavering political elites sought to balance external pressures for abolition with local constituencies who remained invested in established slave systems. Popular support for anti-slavery was often limited or nonexistent prior to the legal abolition of slavery (at least among non-slaves). In this environment, legal abolition usually involved a partial reconfiguration of previous political, social, and economic cleavages, with ex-slave-owners and their sympathizers seeking to defend their earlier ideological and economic prerogatives, and ex-slaves (often cautiously) seeking out new options and opportunities. These complex cleavages were further complicated by various forms of state intervention, as officials regularly sought to reconcile their anti-slavery obligations with more parochial economic and political interests.

Three main themes can be identified when it comes to post-abolition shortcomings. First, we have the persistence of slavery and slave-like practices in many jurisdictions long after slavery had ostensibly been abolished. As we have seen, the legal abolition of slavery did not always involve a definitive change in status according to a clear timetable, but regularly took the form of a "slow death," which often involved substantial numbers of slaves remaining in place decades after legal abolition. Second, we have the growth of closely related forms of human bondage, most notably forced, bonded, and indentured labor, in many settings following legal abolition. In this variant, the expansion of other abusive labor practices can be primarily traced to strategic responses to legal abolition. Finally, we have the parallel continuation of closely related forms of human bondage. This variant brings together practices that share many features in common with historical slave systems, such as servile marriage and forced prostitution, but that are not always directly connected to the specific events surrounding legal abolition. The main issue here is similarity, rather than causality.

The more recent history of the Anti-Slavery Project has been chiefly defined by a cumulative recognition of the historical limitations of the legal abolition of slavery. This has not only involved a broadening of anti-slavery obligations, but has also seen a deepening of anti-slavery commitments, building on a somewhat belated recognition that legal measures can go only so far in the absence of a larger series of reforms.[6] In this context, the growth of global civil society and domestic activism has been especially prominent. The legal abolition of slavery was a primarily a top-down, externally driven event, with international agents and political elites operating in the face of internal resistance. While (ex-)slave agency played a vital role in the aftermath of legal abolition, the primary impetus behind the initial decision to abolish usually came from above. More recent campaigns against contemporary slavery have inverted this earlier historical pattern, with the primary impetus for change instead coming from below. On this front, we encounter a larger pattern of convergence, which has seen a more expansive approach to anti-slavery combine with activism in related arenas, such as human rights, wartime abuses, child labor, state crime, sexual exploitation, and development. This has translated into a multifaceted agenda, which not only covers many different issues, but also pursues remedies on many different fronts, covering themes such as prevention, regulation, rehabilitation, amelioration, further legal reform, and social justice.

In this evolving political environment, the number of practices and institutions that have been formally equated with slavery has steadily increased, making it difficult to identify a coherent rationale linking them together. Is slavery now an analytical category, or an evocative concept? Is slavery now being invoked literally, rhetorically, or some indefinite combination of the two? Once slavery is held to come in any number of forms, it is not always easy to determine a point at which slavery begins and ends. In some contexts, slavery has been reduced to little more than shorthand for all forms of suffering and exploitation. This is particularly an issue when it comes to the range of issues that have recently been associated with slavery by the United Nations, such as genital mutilation, incest, honor killings, and the sale of organs. This agenda not only involves a more expansive approach to slavery, but also reflects ongoing efforts to repackage various causes as forms of slavery. From this standpoint, the concept of contemporary slavery can be viewed as an attempt to distinguish current problems from legal slavery, while retaining the evocative imagery of slavery to prioritize cases of acute exploitation and abuse. While this may well be a good political strategy, it at least tacitly suggests that current problems can be sharply separated from historical slave systems. Outside of occasional cursory references, the history of slavery and abolition has rarely featured in recent treatments of contemporary slavery.

Instead of being driven by distinctively modern developments, most forms of contemporary slavery have complex historical roots, but these connections and associations have tended to be obscured by a widespread assumption that the history of slavery and abolition came to an end in the late nineteenth century, and therefore has no direct bearing on more recent problems. This has resulted in an incomplete diagnosis of the sources of—and solutions to—a variety of contemporary problems. As we have seen, the main point at issue here has been an informal separation between past and present, or "new" and "old." Most works on contemporary slavery have attributed the "rise" of contemporary slavery to recent innovations, such as economic globalization, technological change, Cold War collapse, and demographic trends. While there is no doubt that recent developments—both macro and micro—have made important contributions, there are also longer-term issues at work here.

In order to understand why contemporary slavery remains especially problematic in some parts of the globe—such as India, Mauritania, or Sudan—we need to take into account at least two enduring historical legacies. First, we have the continuing consequences of the substantive limitations of the legal abolition of slavery. Second, we have the continuing consequences of enduring ideologies of human difference and social discrimination. As we have seen, the former has provided a historical foundation on which recent practices have persisted or developed, while the latter continues to provide an ideological rationale for keeping relatively large numbers of people in a servile or socially marginal condition. I am not suggesting here that historical practices are fixed or immutable, but instead making the more qualified claim that contemporary practices and problems represent the most recent manifestation of a long-term process of transformation and adaptation. While poverty makes an important contribution to contemporary slavery, it is also necessary to take into account other institutional and ideological factors in order to explain why contemporary slavery is concentrated in some countries and not in others. Most victims of contemporary slavery come from "inferior" social groups that leave them vulnerable to various forms of exploitation. By giving pride of place to recent developments, much of the literature on contemporary forms of slavery has failed to sufficiently engage with these enduring historical legacies.

By fostering an artificial division between old and new, contemporary campaigners have neglected some useful analytical and political resources. Charges of slavery are unlikely to be political compelling—or at least not as compelling as they could be—when they rest on a limited historical foundation. As we have seen, the most common reference point for discussion of slavery has long been the slave systems of the Americas, which have consistently served as an unofficial yardstick against which other forms of bondage have tended to be evaluated. In the case of contemporary slavery, this process of comparison has often involved using the iconography of nineteenth-century slave plantations as a benchmark from which to classify a variety of contemporary practices.[7] This process of comparison between past and present has rarely featured other historical slave systems. To credibly determine what "counts" as contemporary slavery, we need to take into account the diverse forms that slavery has taken in other historical settings. This is particularly significant when it comes to understanding the relationship between slavery, bonded labor, wartime enslavement, and servile marriage. These overlapping categories were central to various historical slave systems outside the Americas, yet these connections and associations have been notably absent from discussions of recent events. In order to determine where contemporary slavery begins and ends, we need a historical canvas that places slavery in Asia, Africa, the Middle East, and India alongside more familiar images of plantations in the Americas. By jumping between the nineteenth-century Americas and the present day, modern human rights activists have overlooked a variety of associations and connections that could strengthen their case for using the language of slavery to describe many current practices.

Another key theme that needs to be highlighted here revolves around the continuing contribution of various governments in sanctioning and supporting various forms of human bondage. As we have seen, many of the worst human rights abuses that occurred in the aftermath of the legal abolition of slavery occurred because of—rather than in spite of—official policies. This pattern has continued to this day. This is not simply an issue that applies to forced labor systems in places such as Eritrea and North Korea, but extends to less familiar issues such as exploitative migrant worker schemes in much of the developed and oil-producing world. While citizens of wealthy industrial countries are occasionally enslaved, these cases represent the exception, not the rule. Citizens of poorer countries tend to be much more vulnerable, and thus constitute the vast majority of slaves in the world today. This dynamic is not confined to their countries of origin, where vulnerable individuals can be trapped in bondage thanks to poverty, social discrimination, and desperation, but also extends to citizens from poorer countries who attempt to migrate to richer parts of the world.

Despite repeated expressions of support to anti-slavery causes, governments throughout the globe continue to embrace policies that leave migrants vulnerable to various forms of exploitation and abuse. Most of these situations do not amount to contemporary slavery, but cases that fall short of this standard can still leave a great deal to be desired. While there is no question that migration can be rewarding, in far too many cases the search for a better life remains defined by limited protections and vulnerability. This pattern applies to both undocumented migrants and migrants who legally reside in another country, yet are restricted by conditions of entry that leave them vulnerable to abuse. By adopting specific types of immigration policies and migrant worker schemes, wealthy governments have helped to facilitate a range of systematic abuses. While the terms of specific schemes vary, the core principles are much the same as earlier indentured labor schemes. In keeping with historical precedents, one of the main attractions of these policies continues to be the prospect of greater profits (or lesser costs) than might be available using other means.

Contemporary forms of slavery tend be found alongside poverty, inequality, political complicity, and social discrimination. In order to effectively combat contemporary slavery, it is necessary to address these larger socioeconomic problems. This invariably means confronting a number of complex and politically contentious issues. In countries such as India and Pakistan, combating slavery means combating the centuries-old caste system at the heart of the prevailing social order. In richer countries, combating slavery means confronting the privileges associated with citizenship, and the widespread exploitation and vulnerability of migrant workers. In countries such as Sudan and Myanmar, challenging slavery means recognizing the complicity of political regimes that continue to enslave their own citizens. In all these examples, ending slavery is likely to be a cumulative, long-term process. Much like global poverty and environmental degradation, ongoing efforts to address contemporary slavery are now geared toward cumulative reductions in their overall scale and severity, rather than a single decisive solution. Framed in these terms, anti-slavery does not exist as an isolated issue, but instead becomes part of larger challenges such as racism and discrimination, poverty and inequality, human rights and development, migration and citizenship, and ethical trading and corporate responsibility. This frequently impinges on sensitive terrain, where the issues involved are no longer specifically (or even primarily) concerned with anti-slavery, but instead extend to the overall composition of social and economic life. It is one thing to agree that slavery should be brought to an end, and another to come to agreement over how these larger challenges should be addressed.

Introduction: The Anti-Slavery Project

Epigraphs: Jonathon Derrick, *Africa's Slaves Today* (New York: Schocken, 1975), 14–15; Henry W. Nevinson, *A Modern Slavery* (London: Harper & Brothers, 1906), 12; Friedrich Nietzsche, *On the Genealogy of Morals and Ecce Homo* (New York: Vintage, 1989), 80.

1. Peter Landesman, "The Girls Next Door," *New York Times Magazine*, January 25, 2004, 32.

2. Ibid., 33, 36, 37.

3. Jack Shafer, "Sex Slaves of West 43rd Street: The *New York Times Magazine* Gets Carried Away in Its Investigation," *Slate.com*, January 26, 2004, http://www.slate.com/id/2094414/.

4. Jack Shafer, "Doubting Landesman: I'm Not the Only One Questioning the *Times Magazine*'s Sex-Slave Story," *Slate.com*, January 27, 2004, http://www.slate.com/id/2094502/.

5. Cathy Young, "Was Story About Sexual Trafficking Exaggerated?" *Boston Globe*, February 9, 2004, http://www.boston.com/news/globe/editorial_opinion/oped/articles/2004/02/09/was_story_about_sexual_trafficking_exaggerated/.

6. Eartha Melzer, "Trafficking in Politics: Bush's Strong Rhetoric on Sex Slavery Masks Policy Failures," *In These Times*, March 14, 2005, http://www.religiousconsultation.org/News_Tracker/trafficking _in_politics.htm; Jack Shafer, "Enslaved by His Sources: Reading Peter Landesman's Sex-Slave Story One More Time," *Slate.com*, February 3, 2004, http://www.slate.com/id/2094896/.

7. Debbie Nathan, "Oversexed," *The Nation*, August 29–September 5, 2005, 27–30; "Sex and the Single Reporter," *The Nation*, October 3, 2005, 2–3.

8. Daniel Okrent, "The Public Editor; What Do You Know, and How Do You Know It?" *New York Times*, February 29, 2004, 63, http://query.nytimes.com/gst/fullpage.htm l?res=9E0DE1D71F3CF93AA15751C0A9629C8.

9. Kevin Bales, *Ending Slavery: How We Free Today's Slaves* (Berkeley: University of California Press, 2007), 118–26; Binka Le Breton, *Trapped: Modern-Day Slavery in the*

Brazilian Amazon (London: Kumarian Press, 2003); Leonardo Sakamoto, "Slave Labor in Brazil," in Beate Andreas and Patrick Belser, eds., *Forced Labour: Coercion and Exploitation in the Private Economy* (Boulder, Colo.: Lynne Reinner, 2009), 15–33.

10. Annette Weber, Jemera Rone, and Joseph Saunders, *Abducted and Abused: Renewed Conflict in Northern Uganda* (New York: Human Rights Watch/Africa, 2003), http://www.hrw.org/reports/2003/uganda0703/uganda0703.pdf; Randall Fegley, "Bound to Violence: Uganda's Child Soldiers as Slaves," in Jay Spaulding and Stephanie Beswick, eds., *African Systems of Slavery* (Trenton, N.J.: Africa World Press, 2010), 203–28.

11. David Hawk, *The Hidden Gulag: Exposing North Korea's Prison Camps, Prisoners' Testimonies and Satellite Photographs* (Washington, D.C.: U.S. Committee for Human Rights in North Korea, 2003).

12. Bridget Anderson, *Britain's Secret Slaves: An Investigation into the Plight of Overseas Domestic Workers* (London: Anti-Slavery International, 1993), and "Migrant Domestic Workers and Slavery," in Christien van den Anker, ed., *The Political Economy of the New Slavery* (Hampshire: Palgrave, 2004); Judith Sunderland and Nisha Varia, *Swept Under the Rug: Abuses Against Domestic Workers Around the World* (New York: Human Rights Watch, 2006).

13. See Joseph C. Miller, *Slavery and Slaving in World History: A Bibliography*, vol. 1, *1900–1991*, vol. 2, *1992–1996* (New York: M.E. Sharpe, 1999). In the early 1980s Igor Kopytoff concluded that "historical effort has been concentrated out of all reasonable proportion on Afro-American slavery and the Atlantic slave trade." Despite some recent improvements, this remains true today. Igor Kopytoff, "Slavery," *Annual Review of Anthropology* 11 (1982): 225.

14. See, for example, David Brion Davis, *Slavery and Human Progress* (Oxford: Oxford University Press, 1984), 317–20; Robert William Fogel, *Without Consent or Contract: The Rise and Fall of American Slavery* (New York: Norton, 1989), 17. This is also reflected in popular textbooks on slavery. See Stanley Engerman, Seymour Drescher, and Robert Paquette, eds., *Slavery* (Oxford: Oxford University Press, 2001), where only one of 186 entries is concerned with contemporary slavery, and Gad Heuman and James Walvin, *The Slavery Reader* (London: Routledge, 2003), where modern slavery is entirely absent.

15. See Joel Quirk, "Uncomfortable Silences: Contemporary Slavery and the 'Lessons' of History," in Alison Brysk and Austin Choi-Fitzpatrick, eds., *Human Trafficking and Human Rights: Rethinking Contemporary Slavery* (Philadelphia: University of Pennsylvania Press, forthcoming).

16. This distinction is developed further in Joel Quirk, "Ending Slavery in All Its Forms: Legal Abolition and Effective Emancipation in Historical Perspective," *International Journal of Human Rights* 13, 4 (2009): 529–54.

17. Ken Booth, "Three Tyrannies," in Nicholas Wheeler and Tim Dunne, eds., *Human Rights in Global Politics* (Cambridge: Cambridge University Press, 1999), 43. See also Richard Wyn Jones, *Security, Strategy, and Critical Theory* (Boulder, Colo.: Lynne Rienner, 1999), 76–78.

18. Orlando Patterson, "Slavery," *Annual Review of Anthropology* 3 (1977): 430.

19. Kopytoff, "Slavery," 219–21; Igor Kopytoff and Suzanne Miers, "African 'Slavery' as an Institution of Marginality," in Suzanne Miers and Igor Kopytoff, eds., *Slavery in Africa: Historical and Anthropological Perspectives* (Madison: University of Wisconsin Press, 1977); Orlando Patterson, *Slavery and Social Death: A Comparative Study* (Cambridge, Mass.: Harvard University Press, 1982), 21–27. These models do not have to be discrete alternatives. See Martin A. Klein, *Slavery and Colonial Rule in French West Africa* (Cambridge: Cambridge University Press, 1998), 14–15.

20. Patterson, "Slavery," 430–31.

21. Patterson, *Slavery and Social Death*, 13, emphasis original.

22. Ibid., 21–27.

23. Ibid., 1–101.

24. Claude Meillassoux, *The Anthropology of Slavery: The Womb of Iron and Gold* (London: Athlon, 1991), chap. 5.

25. *Contemporary Forms of Slavery*, Fact Sheet 14 (Geneva: United Nations Press, 1991), 1.

26. Peter Landesman's article is a representative example here, as slave status is treated as a self-evident property, which follows automatically from the severe abuses involved.

27. Christien van den Anker, "Introduction: Combating Contemporary Slavery," in van den Anker, ed., *Political Economy of the New Slavery*, 1.

28. *Stopping Forced Labour, Global Report Under the Follow-Up to the ILO Declaration on Fundamental Principles and Rights at Work*, International Labour Conference, 89th Session, 2001, 10, http://www.ilo.org/dyn/declaris/DECLARATIONWEB.DOWNLOAD_BLOB?Var_DocumentID=1578.

29. This approach is by no means new, but its political significance has increased immeasurably in recent times. For an early example of this theme see Patrick Brantlinger, *Dark Vanishings: Discourses on the Extinction of Primitive Races, 1800–1930* (Ithaca, N.Y.: Cornell University Press, 2003), 73–99.

30. It is also clear, however, that southern autonomy could have potentially created a countervailing force, creating various international complications. See Fogel, *Without Consent or Contract*, 411–17.

31. Kevin Bales, *Disposable People: New Slavery in the Global Economy* (Berkeley: University of California Press, 1999), 9.

32. *Human Development Report 2007/2008: Fighting Climate Change: Human Solidarity in a Divided World* (New York: UNDP, 2008), 25, http://hdr.undp.org/en/media/HDR_20072008_EN_Complete.pdf.

33. Bales, *Disposable People*, 8–9; van den Anker, *Introduction*, 18.

34. For a rough snapshot of the quantitative dimensions of slavery as a global phenomenon, see Joel Quirk, *Unfinished Business: A Comparative Survey of Historical and Contemporary Slavery* (Paris: UNESCO, 2009). Once slave systems outside the Americas are taken into account, it is by no means obvious that what is happening today is of a

greater order of magnitude than the legal slavery of the nineteenth century. If we also factor in other forms of human bondage that many modern commentators now regard as forms of slavery, it quickly becomes clear that "slavery" is much smaller today than in the past.

35. The two most popular estimates of the scale of contemporary slavery are 27 million (Bales) and 12.3 million (ILO). Both figures rest on a limited methodological foundation, but they nonetheless offer a rough snapshot. As far as I know, there are no global estimates available for earlier historical periods, but a number of country/region specific estimates strongly suggest that the global scale of human bondage has diminished in both relative and absolute terms. For the first half of the twentieth century, the two most significant cases are Nazi Germany and the Soviet Union. During the Second World War, an estimated 12 million people were subject to Nazi forced labor. Between 1929 and 1953, labor camps in the Soviet Union housed an estimated 18 million people, and when other forms of forced labor are included the total increases to 28.7 million. These are overall totals (not all those involved were subject to forced labor at the same time), but they nonetheless provide a sense of the magnitude of the systemic abuses involved. While figures for other parts of the world are not readily available, it is clear that these cases are only part of a larger total. It is also necessary to take into account an unknown—but clearly substantial—number of victims who were subjected to communist gulags outside the Soviet Union, various forms of forced labor under colonial rule, bonded labor in the Indian subcontinent and elsewhere, and residual slave systems in Africa and the Middle East (an estimated 500,000 people were still in legal slavery in the Arabian peninsula in the 1950s). According to both Bales and the ILO, the largest concentration of human bondage today is in the Indian subcontinent, but this is not a new phenomenon. Large numbers of bonded laborers could be found in the subcontinent during the first half of the twentieth century as well. To demonstrate that the overall prevalence of human bondage has increased in absolute terms, it would be necessary to identify a level of growth in other parts of the world (outside the subcontinent) of sufficient magnitude to offset widespread use of forced labor by governments in most of the globe during the first half of the twentieth century. The above estimates are drawn from Quirk, *Unfinished Business*, 45–47, 97–98.

Chapter 1. A Short History of British Anti-Slavery

1. Two treatments of this backward reading of history come from Moses Finley, *Ancient Slavery and Modern Ideology* (London: Chatto & Windus, 1980), 12–16, and David Brion Davis, *Slavery and Human Progress* (Oxford: Oxford University Press, 1984), 24–27.

2. This discussion focuses on Britain rather than England, and thus sidesteps various social cleavages. British identity is understood here as a frame of reference dominated by English history and society, but which nonetheless offered qualified scope for broader identification. For alternative readings, see Douglas Hamilton, *Scotland, the Caribbean and the Atlantic World, 1750-1820* (Manchester: Manchester University Press,

2005); Iain Whyte, *Scotland and the Abolition of Black Slavery* (Edinburgh: Edinburgh University Press, 2006); and Nini Rodgers, *Ireland, Slavery and Anti-Slavery: 1612–1865* (Houndsmills: Palgrave, 2007).

3. Martin A. Klein, "Introduction: Modern European Expansion and Traditional Servitude in Africa and Asia," in Martin A. Klein, ed., *Breaking the Chains: Slavery Bondage and Emancipation in Modern Africa and Asia* (Madison: University of Wisconsin Press, 1993), 14–15.

4. See, for example, William Gervase Clarence-Smith, *Islam and the Abolition of Slavery* (Oxford: Oxford University Press, 2006), 22–48; Claude Meillassoux, *The Anthropology of Slavery: The Womb of Iron and Gold* (London: Athlone, 1991) 73–75.

5. Orlando Patterson, *Slavery and Social Death* (Cambridge, Mass.: Harvard University Press, 1982), 43, 126.

6. David Eltis, *The Rise of African Slavery in the Americas* (Cambridge: Cambridge University Press, 2000), xiii.

7. See Robert Davis, *Christian Slaves, Muslim Masters: White Slavery in the Mediterranean, the Barbary Coast, and Italy, 1500–1800* (Houndsmills: Palgrave, 2004).

8. Klein, "Introduction," 14.

9. See David Brion Davis, *The Problem of Slavery in Western Culture* (Ithaca, N.Y.: Cornell University Press, 1966), 29–121; William Phillips, *Slavery from Roman Times to the Early Transatlantic Trade* (Minneapolis: University of Minnesota Press, 1985); and "Continuity and Change in Western Slavery: Ancient to Modern Times," in Michael Bush, ed., *Serfdom and Slavery: Studies in Legal Bondage* (New York: Longman, 1996), 78–81.

10. In some early twentieth-century histories the terms negro and slave are used as synonyms. See Frank Klingburg, *The Anti-Slavery Movement in England: A Study in English Humanitarianism* (New Haven, Conn.: Yale University Press, 1926). A more nuanced perspective comes from David W. Cohen and Jack Greene, eds., *Neither Slave Nor Free: The Freedmen of African Descent in the Slave Societies of the New World* (Baltimore: Johns Hopkins University Press, 1972).

11. See, for example, Benedetta Rossi, "Introduction: Rethinking Slavery in West Africa," in Benedetta Rossi, ed., *Reconfiguring Slavery: West African Trajectories* (Liverpool: Liverpool University Press, 2009), 1–8; Dharma Kumar, "Colonialism, Bondage and Caste in British India," in Klein, ed., *Breaking the Chains*, 112–17.

12. David Eltis, "Slavery and Freedom in the Early Modern World," in Stanley L. Engerman, ed., *Terms of Labor: Slavery, Serfdom, and Free Labor* (Stanford, Calif.: Stanford University Press, 1999), 26. See also Eltis, *The Rise of African Slavery*, 116–17.

13. Ehud Toledano, "Ottoman Concepts of Slavery in the Period of Reform, 1830–1880," in Klein, ed., *Breaking the Chains*, 56–58. See also Y. Hakan Erdem, *Slavery in the Ottoman Empire and Its Demise,1800–1909* (London: Macmillan, 1996), 6–17, 43–66, and Ehud Toledano, *As if Silent and Absent: Bonds of Enslavement in the Islamic Middle East* (New Haven, Conn.: Yale University Press, 2007) 13–23.

14. Igor Kopytoff, "Slavery," *Annual Review of Anthropology* 11 (1982): 224. See

also Richard Hellie, *Slavery in Russia 1450-1725* (Chicago: University of Chicago Press, 1982), 15-21.

15. Gwyn Campbell, "Introduction: Slavery and Other Forms of Unfree Labour in the Indian Ocean World," in Gwyn Campbell, ed., *The Structure of Slavery in Indian Africa and Asia* (London: Frank Cass, 2004), xi, xx-xxvi.

16. Anthony Reid, "Introduction: Slavery and Bondage in Southeast Asian History," in Anthony Reid, ed., *Slavery, Bondage and Dependency in Southeast Asia* (St. Lucia: University of Queensland Press, 1983), 18-21.

17. Patterson, *Slavery and Social Death*, 49-51.

18. Howard Temperley, "The Delegalization of Slavery in British India," in Howard Temperley, ed., *After Slavery: Emancipation and Its Discontents* (London: Frank Cass, 2000), 179.

19. Davis, *Slavery and Human Progress*, 159.

20. Orlando Patterson, *Freedom* (United States: Basic Books, 1991), x.

21. Ibid. 33-43. See also David Kelly, "Freedom: A Eurasian Mosaic," in David Kelly and Anthony Reid, eds., *Asian Freedoms: The Idea of Freedom in East and Southeast Asia* (Cambridge: Cambridge University Press, 1998), 8-11; Igor Kopytoff and Suzanne Miers, "African 'Slavery' as an Institution of Marginality," in Suzanne Miers and Igor Kopytoff, eds., *Slavery in Africa: Historical and Anthropological Perspectives* (Madison: University of Wisconsin Press, 1977), 14-18.

22. Patterson, *Freedom*, x, 20, 22-23, and *Slavery and Social Death*, 27-28. See also Reid, "Introduction: Slavery and Bondage in Southeast Asian History," 21.

23. Eltis, *The Rise of African Slavery*, 21-22; Robert Steinfield, *The Invention of Free Labor: The Employment Relation in English and American Law and Culture* (Chapel Hill: University of North Carolina Press, 1991), 96-104.

24. This figure is taken from the latest version of the transatlantic slave trade database. When the database was first published in 1999, overall exports from Africa were estimated at around 11.8 million slaves. The new version was made available at http://www.slavevoyages.org in late 2008. See also David Eltis and David Richardson, *Extending the Frontiers: Essays on the New Transatlantic Slave Trade Database* (New Haven, Conn.: Yale University Press, 2008); Joel Quirk, *Unfinished Business: A Comparative Survey of Historical and Contemporary Slavery* (Paris: UNESCO, 2009), 35-40.

25. See Robert William Fogel and Stanley Engerman, *Time on the Cross: The Economics of Negro Slavery* (Boston: Little, Brown, 1974), 16; Sidney Mintz, *Sweetness and Power: Place of Sugar in Modern History* (London: Penguin, 1986).

26. Herbert S. Klein, *The Atlantic Slave Trade* (Cambridge: Cambridge University Press, 1999), 86-89; Patrick Manning, *Slavery and African Life: Occidental, Oriental, and African Slave Trades* (Cambridge: Cambridge University Press, 1990), 22, 100-102.

27. This chapter is primarily concerned with the history of anti-slavery, rather than the history of slavery. For further analysis of transatlantic slavery, see David Brion Davis, *Inhuman Bondage: The Rise and Fall of Slavery in the New World* (Oxford: Oxford University Press, 2006), 77-140; Joel Quirk and David Richardson, "Anti-Slavery, European

Identity and International Society: A Macro-Historical Perspective," *Journal of Modern European History* 7, 1 (2009): 71–77; John Thornton, *Africa and Africans in the Making of the Modern World, 1400–1800* (Cambridge: Cambridge University Press, 1998), 72–151; and Robert William Fogel, *Without Consent or Contract: The Rise and Fall of American Slavery* (New York: Norton, 1989), 17–40.

28. Taken from http://www.slavevoyages.org/, accessed October 22, 2009.

29. Seymour Drescher, "Free Labor vs. Slave Labor: The British and Caribbean Cases," in Stanley Engerman, ed., *Terms of Labor: Slavery, Serfdom, and Free Labor* (Stanford, Calif.: Stanford University Press, 1999), 51.

30. David Brion Davis, *The Problem of Slavery in the Age of Revolution, 1770–1823* (Ithaca, N.Y.: Cornell University Press, 1975), 84–89, 104–7, 119–37, 152–59, 164–212; Ira Berlin, *Many Thousands Gone: The First Two Centuries of Slavery in North America* (Cambridge, Mass.: Harvard University Press,1998), 219–55.

31. Robin Blackburn, *The Overthrow of Colonial Slavery, 1776–1848* (London: Verso, 1988), 215–64; Davis, *The Problem of Slavery in the Age of Revolution*, 94–99, 107–12, 137–48, 150–51; Laurent Dubois, *A Colony of Citizens, Revolution and Slave Emancipation in the French Caribbean, 1787–1804* (Chapel Hill: University of North Carolina Press, 2004).

32. Svend E. Green-Pedersen, "Slave Demography in the Danish West Indies and the Abolition of the Slave Trade," in David Eltis and James Walvin, eds., *The Abolition of the Atlantic Slave Trade: Origins and Effects in Europe, Africa and the Americas* (Madison: University of Wisconsin Press, 1981).

33. Blackburn, *The Overthrow of Colonial Slavery*, 9, 331–79; Davis, *The Problem of Slavery in the Age of Revolution*, 65–72, 90–92; Herbert S. Klein, *African Slavery in Latin America and the Caribbean* (Oxford: Oxford University Press, 1986), 250–53.

34. For a more comparative approach, see Quirk, *Unfinished Business*, 73–91; Seymour Drescher, "The Long Goodbye: Dutch Capitalism and Anti-Slavery in Comparative Perspective," *American Historical Review* 99, 1 (1994): 44, and "Brazilian Abolition in Comparative Perspective," *Hispanic American Historical Review* 68, 3 (1988): 429.

35. David Eltis, *Economic Growth and the Ending of the Transatlantic Slave Trade* (Oxford: Oxford University Press, 1987), 5, 11, 15, 18, 40.

36. Roger Anstey, *The Atlantic Slave Trade and British Abolition* (London: Macmillan, 1975), 3.

37. Howard Temperley, "The Ideology of Anti-Slavery," in Eltis and Walvin, eds., *The Abolition of the Atlantic Slave Trade*, 29–30; Seymour Drescher, *Capitalism and Anti-Slavery, British Mobilization in Comparative Perspective* (Oxford: Oxford University Press, 1986), 28–29.

38. Duncan Rice, *The Rise and Fall of Black Slavery* (London: Macmillan, 1975), 161.

39. Anstey, *The Atlantic Slave Trade and British Abolition*, 95.

40. Paul Thomas, "Changing Attitudes in an Expanding Empire: The Anti-Slavery Movement, 1760–1783," *Slavery and Abolition* 5, 1 (1984): 54.

41. Davis, *The Problem of Slavery in Western Culture*, 394–96, 402–10; Rice, *The Rise*

260 Notes to Pages 31–34

and Fall of Black Slavery, 167–80; James Walvin, *England, Slaves and Freedom, 1776–1838* (London: Macmillan, 1986), 98–100.

42. Rice, *The Rise and Fall of Black Slavery*, 163–76; Whyte, *Scotland and the Abolition of Black Slavery*, 50–59.

43. Anstey, *The Atlantic Slave Trade and British Abolition*, 126–39, 204–33; Rice, *The Rise and Fall of Black Slavery*, 187–205.

44. Anstey, *The Atlantic Slave Trade and British Abolition*, 212–13, 218; Betty Fladeland, *Men and Brothers: Anglo-American Anti-Slavery Cooperation* (Urbana: University of Illinois Press, 1972), 11–17; Rice, *The Rise and Fall of Black Slavery*, 160–61, 186, 205.

45. Anthony Benezet, *A Caution to Great Britain and Her colonies, in a Short Representation of the Calamitous State of the Enslaved Negroes in the British Dominions* (London: James Phillips, 1785), 3.

46. Anstey, *The Atlantic Slave Trade and British Abolition*, 193.

47. Ibid., 200–233.

48. Blackburn, *The Making of New World Slavery*, 58. See also Whyte, *Scotland and the Abolition of Black Slavery*, 57–59.

49. There were only 19,500 Quakers in Britain in 1800. Walvin, *England, Slaves and Freedom*, 103.

50. Nicholas Hudson, "Britons Never Will Be Slaves," *Eighteenth-Century Studies* 34, 4 (2001): 559; Rice, *The Rise and Fall of Black Slavery*, 212–18; Walvin, *England, Slaves and Freedom*, 103–4.

51. Chris Brown, *Moral Capital: Foundations of British Abolitionism* (Chapel Hill: University of North Carolina Press, 2006), 40.

52. Separating West Indian planters from the newly independent United States also divided pro-slavery forces into two separate states. See Brown, *Moral Capital*, 453–56; Porter, *The Abolition of the Slave Trade in England*, 32; Temperley, "The Ideology of Anti-Slavery," 30.

53. Brown, *Moral Capital*, 27.

54. Ibid., 450.

55. Ibid., 424–33.

56. Blackburn, *The Making of New World Slavery*, 136–37.

57. Drescher, *Capitalism and Anti-Slavery*, 62–66, 208; James Walvin, *Questioning Slavery* (London: Routledge, 1996), 162; *England Slaves and Freedom* (Jackson: University Press of Mississippi, 1986), 18; Dale Porter, *The Abolition of the Slave Trade in England, 1784–1807* (Hamden, Conn.: Archon, 1970), 30–33.

58. Those who were responsible for the 1783 petition also played a prominent role in the new society. See Davis, *The Problem of Slavery in the Age of Revolution*, 406–18, and Walvin, *England, Slaves and Freedom*, 107–8.

59. Howard Temperley, *British Anti-Slavery 1833–1870* (London: Longman, 1972), 7.

60. Drescher, *Capitalism and Anti-Slavery*, 158.

61. Davis, *The Problem of Slavery in the Age of Revolution*, 417; Turley, *The Culture of English Anti-Slavery*, 27.

62. Clarkson's role is one of the main focal points of Adam Hochschild, *Bury the Chains: The British Struggle to Abolish Slavery* (London: Pan Books, 2005).

63. Anstey, *The Atlantic Slave Trade and British Abolition*, 254–66.

64. Drescher, *Capitalism and Anti-Slavery*, 70.

65. Harry Dickinson, *The Politics of the People in Eighteenth Century Britain* (London: St. Martin's Press, 1995), 65–88. On the conceptualization of public opinion more generally, see Thomas Holt, "The Essence of the Contract: The Articulation of Race, Gender, and Political Economy in British Emancipation Policy," in Frederick Cooper, Thomas C. Holt, and Rebecca J. Scott, eds., *Beyond Slavery: Explorations of Race, Labor, and Citizenship in Postemancipation Societies* (Chapel Hill: University of North Carolina Press, 2000), 39–42.

66. Ultimate responsibility for the petition campaign is a matter of contention. See Drescher, *Capitalism and Anti-Slavery*, 67; J. R. Oldfield, "The London Committee and Mobilization of Public Opinion Against the Slave Trade," *Historical Journal* 35, 2 (1992): 331.

67. Drescher, *Capitalism and Anti-Slavery*, 73.

68. Davis, *The Problem of Slavery in the Age of Revolution*, 421, 438–42; Drescher, *Capitalism and Anti-Slavery*, 61–62.

69. Davis, *The Problem of Slavery in the Age of Revolution*, 422.

70. Porter, *The Abolition of the Slave Trade in England*, 33–37; Walvin, *England, Slaves and Freedom*, 111.

71. The first parliamentary skirmish over the slave trade occurred in 1788 over the Slave Trade Regulation Act. See Porter, *The Abolition of the Slave Trade in England*, 37–56.

72. Dickinson, *The Politics of the People*, 65–67.

73. Drescher, *Capitalism and Anti-Slavery*, 80; see also 82, 93.

74. Thomas Clarkson, *The History of the Rise, Progress, and Accomplishment of the Abolition of the Slave-Trade by the British Parliament*, vol. 2 (1808; London: Frank Cass, 1968), 350.

75. Anstey, *The Atlantic Slave Trade and British Abolition*, 292.

76. Ibid., 430. See also Porter, *The Abolition of the Slave Trade in England*, 81–83.

77. Anstey, *The Atlantic Slave Trade and British Abolition*, 275.

78. Walvin, *England, Slaves and Freedom*, 117–19.

79. Davis, *The Problem of Slavery in the Age of Revolution*, 433–36; Walvin, *England, Slaves and Freedom*, 114.

80. James Walvin, "The Propaganda of Anti-Slavery," in James Walvin, ed., *Slavery and British Society 1776–1846* (Baton Rouge: Louisiana State University Press, 1982), 60.

81. Drescher, *Capitalism and Anti-Slavery*, 67. See also Brown, *Moral Capital*, 450.

82. This can be contrasted with earlier appraisals. See Brown, *Moral Capital*, 54–60.

83. Ibid., 228–40.

84. Porter, *The Abolition of the Slave Trade in England*, 33.

85. Anstey, *The Atlantic Slave Trade and British Abolition*, 290.

86. Cited in James Walvin, "The Public Campaign in England Against Slavery, 1787-1834," in Eltis and Walvin, eds., *The Abolition of the Atlantic Slave Trade*, 63-64.

87. See also John Oldfield, *"Chords of Freedom": Commemoration, Ritual and British Transatlantic Slavery* (Manchester: Manchester University Press, 2007), 56-81.

88. Reginald Coupland, *The British Anti-Slavery Movement* (1933; Oxford: Frank Cass, 1964). See also Ernest Howse, *Saints in Politics: The "Clapham Sect" and the Growth of Freedom* (Toronto: University of Toronto Press, 1952); Klingburg, *The Anti-Slavery Movement in England*; George Mellor, *British Imperial Trusteeship, 1783-1850* (London: Faber and Faber, 1951).

89. Eric Williams, *Capitalism and Slavery* (London: André Deutsch, 1964), 154-77.

90. Ibid., 178.

91. Williams also argued that revenues from transatlantic slavery were a key catalyst for the British industrial revolution. This argument falls outside the scope of this chapter.

92. Roger Antsey, "Capitalism and Slavery: A Critique," *Economic History Review* 21, 2 (1968): 307; C. Duncan Rice, "'Humanity Sold for Sugar!': The British Abolitionist Response to Free Trade in Slave-Grown Sugar," *Historical Journal* 13, 3 (1970): 402.

93. Seymour Drescher, *Econocide: British Slavery in the Era of Abolition* (Pittsburgh: University of Pittsburgh Press, 1977), 136. See also Brown, *Moral Capital*, 14-18; Davis, *Inhuman Bondage*, 240-44.

94. Eltis, *The Rise of African Slavery*, 59.

95. Kathleen Heasman, *Evangelicals in Action: An Appraisal of Their Social Work in the Victorian Era* (London: Geoffrey Bless, 1962), 15.

96. Anstey, *The Atlantic Slave Trade and British Abolition*, 179-83; David Turley, *The Culture of English Anti-Slavery, 1780-1866* (London: Routledge, 1991), 7-8.

97. Anstey, *The Atlantic Slave Trade and British Abolition*, 126-27; Turley, *The Culture of English Anti-Slavery*, 109.

98. Porter, *The Abolition of the Slave Trade in England*, 66; Roxann Wheeler, *The Complexion of Race: Categories of Difference in Eighteenth-Century British Culture* (Philadelphia: University of Pennsylvania Press, 2000), 254.

99. Turley, *The Culture of English Anti-Slavery*, 135. See also Brown, *Moral Capital*, 333-89.

100. Drescher, "Capitalism and the Decline of Slavery," 134-35.

101. Davis, *The Problem of Slavery in the Age of Revolution*, 428-34 (political legitimacy), 49, 63, 266 (liberal capitalism).

102. Thomas Bender, ed., *The Antislavery Debate: Capitalism and Abolitionism as a Problem in Historical Interpretation* (Berkeley: University of California Press, 1992). For a further analysis of underlying structural changes during this period, see also Joel Quirk and David Richardson, "Religion, Urbanization and Anti-Slavery Mobilization in Britain, 1787-1833," *European Journal of English Studies* 14, 3 (2010): 263-79.

103. Drescher, *Capitalism and Anti-Slavery*, 128-34.

104. Walvin, *England, Slaves and Freedom, 1776-1838*, 17.

105. Liah Greenfield, *Nationalism: Five Roads to Modernity* (Cambridge, Mass.: Harvard University Press, 1992), 7, 14, 23–86.

106. Dickinson, *The Politics of the People*, 162.

107. Brown, *Moral Capital*, 44–48, 155; Blackburn, *The Overthrow of Colonial Slavery*, 70–77.

108. Brown, *Moral Capital*, 126–28; Eric Foner, "The Meaning of Freedom in the Age of Emancipation," *Journal of American History* 81, 2 (1994): 440, 446; Hudson, "Britons Never Will Be Slaves," 563–68.

109. Eltis, *The Rise of African Slavery*, 3, 277; Foner, "The Meaning of Freedom in the Age of Emancipation," 439; Walvin, *England, Slaves and Freedom*, 26–28.

110. Davis, *The Problem of Slavery in the Age of Revolution*, 265–66.

111. Wheeler, *The Complexion of Race*, 9. See also 15–16.

112. The central importance of social membership is reflected in two inaccurate popularizations of British law that claimed, first, that slaves could attain their freedom by being baptized, and, second, that British "air was too free for a slave to breathe." See F. O. Shyllon, *Black Slaves in Britain* (London: Oxford University Press, 1974), esp. 23–25.

113. Eltis, *The Rise of African Slavery*, 57–84.

114. Brown, *Moral Capital*, 50–51.

115. Ibid., 52.

116. William Wilberforce, *An Appeal to the Religion, Justice and Humanity of the Inhabitants of the British Empire, in Behalf of the Negro Slaves in the West Indies* (London: J. Hatchard and Son, 1823), 25.

117. Benjamin Godwin, *Lectures on British Colonial Slavery* (London: J. Hatchard and Son, 1830), 2.

118. Walvin, *England, Slaves and Freedom*, 27.

119. Joseph Miller, "The Abolition of the Slave Trade and Slavery: Historical Foundations," in Doudoe Diène, ed., *From Chains to Bonds: The Slave Trade Revisited* (Paris: UNESCO, 2001), 168.

120. Brown, *Moral Capital*, 51; Miller, "The Abolition of the Slave Trade and Slavery," 167–70.

121. Quirk, *Unfinished Business*, 74.

122. Davis, *The Problem of Slavery in the Age of Revolution*, 444–45.

123. See Anstey, *The Atlantic Slave Trade and British Abolition*, 152, 293, 304–12; Brown, *Moral Capital*, 367, 372; Drescher, *Capitalism and Anti-Slavery*, 20; Stanley Engerman, "Some Implications of the Abolition of the Slave Trade," in Eltis and Walvin, eds., *The Abolition of the Atlantic Slave Trade*, 6–7.

124. Wheeler, *The Complexion of Race*, 209.

125. *Observations on the Project for Abolishing the Slave Trade, and on the Reasonableness of Attempting Some Practicable Mode of Relieving the Negroes* (London: J. Debrett, 1790), 51.

126. Anstey, *The Atlantic Slave Trade and British Abolition*, 312; Davis, *The Problem*

of Slavery in the Age of Revolution, 114; Porter, *The Abolition of the Slave Trade in England*, 64–65.

127. See Jack Ramsay, *Objections to the Abolition of the Slave Trade, with Answers* (London: James Phillips, 1788), 37–40.

128. Anstey, *The Atlantic Slave Trade and British Abolition*, 313.

129. Davis, *The Problem of Slavery in the Age of Revolution*, 102–3.

130. Anstey, *The Atlantic Slave Trade and British Abolition*, 312.

131. A 1796 bill successfully passed through a number of readings only to be defeated 74 to 70. Porter, *The Abolition of the Slave Trade in England*, 95–96.

132. Temperley, *British Anti-Slavery*, 7.

133. Anstey, *The Atlantic Slave Trade and British Abolition*, 343.

134. Drescher, *Econocide*, 100–111, 115–23; Anstey, *The Atlantic Slave Trade and British Abolition*, 343; Davis, *The Problem of Slavery in the Age of Revolution*, 440.

135. Porter, *The Abolition of the Slave Trade in England*, 131–32.

136. Anstey, *The Atlantic Slave Trade and British Abolition*, 321, 344. The votes on the three readings were 124–49, 100–42, 99–33 in favor.

137. Porter, *The Abolition of the Slave Trade in England*, 106, 124.

138. Ibid., 132.

139. It is difficult to evaluate the impact of national interest arguments. Although the abolitionists clearly treated the 1806 bill as a tactical move, other members of Parliament may not have been deceived by their public rationale. While Anstey, Porter, and Walvin claim that the bill was taken at face value, Drescher suggests that "most members of Parliament voted openly and self-consciously for the bill of 1806 as an integral step towards total abolition." Drescher, *Econocide*, 214. See also 123, 214–23.

140. Anstey, *The Atlantic Slave Trade and British Abolition*, 398.

141. Blackburn, *The Overthrow of Colonial Slavery*, 314–16.

142. The full title was the Society for the Mitigation and Gradual Abolition of Slavery Throughout the British Dominions.

143. Walvin, *England, Slaves and Freedom*, 141.

144. See Clare Midgley, *Women Against Slavery: The British Campaigns, 1780–1870* (London: Routledge, 1992).

145. William Mathieson, *British Slavery and Its Abolition, 1823–1838* (London: Longman, 1926), 138–63, 244.

146. *Substance of the Debate in the House of Commons on the 15th May, 1823, On a Motion for the Mitigation and Gradual Abolition of Slavery* (London: Dawsons, 1968).

147. Walvin, *England, Slaves and Freedom*, 154.

148. Davis, *Slavery and Human Progress*, 180–86.

149. The main starting point here is Seymour Drescher, *The Mighty Experiment: Free Labor Versus Slavery in British Emancipation* (Oxford: Oxford University Press, 2002).

150. Turley, *The Culture of English Anti-Slavery*, 38. It is by no means clear that the Parliamentarians who voted for the final bill in 1833 were totally convinced by this argument. See Drescher, *The Mighty Experiment*, 132–38, 165.

151. Walvin, *England, Slaves and Freedom,* 168.

152. Edith F. Hurwitz, *Politics and the Public Conscience: Slave Emancipation and the Abolitionist Movement in Britain* (London: Allen & Unwin, 1973), 37.

153. Walvin, "The Public Campaign in England," 76.

154. Mathieson, *British Slavery and Its Abolition,* 220.

155. Drescher, *Capitalism and Anti-Slavery,* 85, 92–94.

156. Thomas C. Holt, *The Problem of Freedom: Race, Labor, and Politics in Jamaica and Britain, 1832–1938* (Baltimore: Johns Hopkins University Press, 1992), 13–21.

157. The fact that this was a government measure is itself particularly revealing. See Drescher, *The Mighty Experiment,* 128.

158. Hurwitz, *Politics and the Public Conscience,* 65.

159. The 1833 bill also abolished slavery in Canada, Mauritius, and the Cape Colony, but not British India or Ceylon. The focus of this chapter has been the West Indies because this was the main political theater throughout the early history of British anti-slavery.

160. Temperley, *British Anti-Slavery,* 221.

161. Ibid.

162. Walvin, *England, Slaves and Freedom,* 175. See also Marcus Wood, *The Horrible Gift of Freedom: Atlantic Slavery and the Representation of Emancipation* (Athens: University of Georgia Press, 2010), 90–125.

163. Linda Colley, *Britons: Forging the Nation 1707–1837* (New Haven, Conn.: Yale University Press, 1992), 351.

Chapter 2. British Anti-Slavery and European International Society

1. See Hedley Bull, *The Anarchical Society* (London: Macmillan, 1995); Adam Watson, *The Evolution of International Society: A Comparative Historical Analysis* (London: Routledge, 1992); Martin Wight, *International Theory: The Three Traditions* (New York: Holmes & Meier, 1992) and *Systems of States* (Leicester: Leicester University Press, 1977).

2. Wight, *International Theory,* 30–48.

3. Bull, *The Anarchical Society,* 13.

4. Jacinta O'Hagan, *Conceptualizing the West in International Relations: From Spengler to Said* (Houndsmills: Palgrave, 2002), 113–15.

5. See, for example, Chris Reus-Smit, *The Moral Purpose of the State: Culture, Social Identity, and Institutional Rationality in International Relations* (Princeton, N.J.: Princeton University Press, 1999); Onuma Yasuaki, "When Was the Law of International Society Born? An Inquiry of the History of International Law from an Intercivilizational Perspective," *Journal of the History of International Law* 2 (2000): 1.

6. In this chapter I have adhered to an established convention of referring to European, rather than "Western" international society. When a larger frame of reference is required, I use the concept of a "European world," which is inclusive of European settler communities elsewhere, yet better reflects the Eurocentrism of nineteenth-century international relations.

7. See, for example, Joel Quirk, "Historical Methods," in Christian Reus-Smit and Duncan Snidal, eds., *Oxford Handbook of International Relations* (Oxford: Oxford University Press, 2008), 523–29; John Ruggie, "Territoriality and Beyond: Problematizing Modernity in International Relations," *International Organization* 47, 1 (1993): 139.

8. See, for example, Hedley Bull and Adam Watson, eds., *The Expansion of International Society* (Oxford: Clarendon Press, 1984); Paul Keal, *European Conquest and the Rights of Indigenous Peoples: The Moral Backwardness of International Society* (Cambridge: Cambridge University Press, 2003), 24–112.

9. This parallels Edward Keene, *Beyond the Anarchical Society: Grotius, Colonialism and Order in World Politics* (Cambridge: Cambridge University Press, 2002), 5–11, 22–29; Ian Clark, *Legitimacy in International Society* (Oxford: Oxford University Press, 2005), 33–50.

10. Iver B. Neumann and Jennifer M. Welsh, "The Other in European Self-Definition: An Addendum to the Literature on International Society," *Review of International Studies* 17, 4 (1991): 327; Iver B. Neumann, *Uses of the Other: "The East" in European Identity Formation* (Minneapolis: University of Minnesota Press, 1999), 39–64.

11. Brett Bowden, *The Empire of Civilization: The Evolution of an Imperial Idea* (Chicago: University of Chicago Press, 2009), 107–17; Thomas Naff, "The Ottoman Empire and the European States System," in Bull and Watson, eds., *The Expansion of International Society*, 143–69; Georg Schwarzenberger, "The Standard of Civilisation in International Law," in George W. Keeton and Georg Schwarzenberger, eds., *Current Legal Problems* (London: Stevens & Sons, 1955), 220–21.

12. Watson, *The Evolution of International Society*, 198–213.

13. Keal, *European Conquest*, 84–112; Siba N'Zatioula Grovogui, *Sovereigns, Quasi Sovereigns, and Africans* (Minneapolis: University of Minnesota Press, 1996), 11–110.

14. C. H. Alexandrowicz, *An Introduction to the History of the Law of Nations in the East Indies* (Oxford: Clarendon Press, 1967), 90–94; Onuma, "When Was the Law of International Society Born?" 33–37.

15. See John Hobson, *The Eastern Origins of Western Civilization* (Cambridge: Cambridge University Press, 2004), 135–57; John Darwin, *After Tamerlane: The Global History of Empire* (London: Penguin, 2007), 104–55.

16. Keal, *European Conquest*, 56–83; Tzvetan Todorov, *The Conquest of America: The Question of the Other* (New York: HarperPerennial, 1984), 53–62, 127–45.

17. Phillip D. Curtin, *The World and the West: The European Challenge and the Overseas Response in the Age of Empire* (Cambridge: Cambridge University Press, 2000), 3–18.

18. Curtin, *The World and the West*, 19–37; Daniel R. Headrick, *The Tools of Empire: Technology and European Imperialism in the Nineteenth Century* (Oxford: Oxford University Press, 1981); Joel Mokyr, *The Gifts of Athena: Historical Origins of the Knowledge Economy* (Princeton, N.J.: Princeton University Press, 2007).

19. Michael Adas, *Machines as the Measure of Men: Science Technology, and Ideologies of Western Dominance* (Ithaca, N.Y.: Cornell University Press, 1989), 143.

20. Bernard McGrane, *Beyond Anthropology: Society and the Other* (New York: Columbia University Press, 1989), 77; Todorov, *The Conquest of America*, 127-30.

21. Adas, *Machines as the Measure of Men*, 144-46, 194-98, 206, 272-74, 292-342.

22. See Bowden, *The Empire of Civilization*, 47-75; Patrick Brantlinger, *Dark Vanishings: Discourses on the Extinction of Primitive Races, 1800-1930* (Ithaca, N.Y.: Cornell University Press, 2003), 19-22, 170-188, 201; Gerrit Gong, *The Standard of "Civilization" in International Society* (Oxford: Clarendon Press, 1984), 55-63.

23. Antony Anghie, "Finding the Peripheries: Sovereignty and Colonialism in Nineteenth-Century International Law," *Harvard International Law Journal* 40 (1999): 12. See also Keal, *European Conquest*, 108-12; Keene, *Beyond the Anarchical Society*, 26-29.

24. Alexandrowicz, *The History of the Law of Nations*, 14-38, 96-124, 162-77, 224-37; Adam Watson, "European International Society and Its Expansion," in Bull and Watson, eds., *The Expansion of International Society*, 19-26.

25. Anghie, "Finding the Peripheries," 22-34; Edward Keene, "A Case Study of International Hierarchy: British Treaty-Making Against the Slave Trade in the Early Nineteenth Century," *International Organization* 61 (2007): 316-19; Jackson, *Quasi-States*, 38-39, 54-56.

26. Antony Anghie, "Civilization and Commerce: The Concept of Governance in Historical Perspective," *Villanova Law Review* 45 (2000): 901.

27. Jean Allain, "Slavery and the League of Nations: Ethiopia as a Civilized Nation," *Journal of the History of International Law* 8 (2006): 214-16; Bowden, *The Empire of Civilization*, 16, 116-28; Gong, *The Standard of "Civilization"*, 14-21.

28. Gong, *The Standard of "Civilization"*, 97-129; Shogo Suzuki, *Civilization and Empire: China and Japan's Encounter with European International Society* (Milton Park: Routledge, 2009), 89-176.

29. David Brion Davis, *The Problem of Slavery in the Age of Revolution; 1770-182* (Ithaca, N.Y.: Cornell University Press, 1975), 119-37; Svend E. Green-Pedersen, "Slave Demography in the Danish West Indies and the Abolition of the Slave Trade"; David Eltis and James Walvin, eds., *The Abolition of the Atlantic Slave Trade: Origins and Effects in Europe, Africa and the Americas* (Madison: University of Wisconsin Press, 1981), 231-57.

30. See Paul Kennedy, *The Rise and Fall of the Great Powers* (New York: Vintage, 1989), 151-58.

31. Leslie Bethel, *The Abolition of the Brazilian Slave Trade: Britain, Brazil and the Slave Trade Question 1807-1869* (Cambridge: Cambridge University Press, 1970), 6-12; Seymour Drescher, "The Long Goodbye: Dutch Capitalism and Antislavery in Comparative Perspective," *American Historical Review* 99, 1 (1994): 59; Pieter C. Emmer, "Abolition of the Abolished: The Illegal Dutch Slave Trade and the Mixed Courts," in Eltis and Walvin, eds., *The Abolition of the Atlantic Slave Trade*, 179; David Murray, *Odious Commerce: Britain, Spain and the Abolition of the Cuban Slave Trade* (Cambridge: Cambridge University Press, 1980), 44, 51-57.

32. Suzanne Miers, *Britain and the Ending of the Slave Trade* (New York: Africana Press, 1975), 11. See also Ian Clark, *International Legitimacy and World Society* (Oxford:

Oxford University Press, 2007), 47–58; Betty Fladeland, "Abolitionists Pressures on the Concert of Europe, 1814–1882," *Journal of Modern History* 38, 4 (1966): 357, 361, 365.

33. Seymour Drescher, *Capitalism and Antislavery: British Mobilization in Comparative Perspective* (Oxford: Oxford University Press, 1987), 93–94.

34. Fladeland, "Abolitionists Pressures on the Concert of Europe," 335–67.

35. Phillip D. Curtin, *The Image of Africa: British Ideas and Action, 1780–1850* (Madison: University of Wisconsin Press, 1964), 468–69; James Ferguson, "The Latin-American Republics and the Suppression of the Slave Trade," *Hispanic American Historical Review* 24:3 (1944): 387; Miers, *Britain and the Ending of the Slave Trade*, 40–55.

36. David Eltis, *Economic Growth and the Ending of the Transatlantic Slave Trade* (Oxford: Oxford University Press, 1987), 85–90. See also Keene, "A Case Study of International Hierarchy," 320–29.

37. R. W. Beachey, *The Slave Trade of Eastern Africa* (London: Rex Collings, 1976), 232–41; Murray, *Odious Commerce*, 104–6; Duncan Rice, *The Rise and Fall of Black Slavery in the Americas* (London: Macmillan, 1975), 229–31, 234.

38. Eltis, *Economic Growth and the Ending of the Transatlantic Slave Trade*, 97–101.

39. Ibid., 87; Bethel, *The Abolition of the Brazilian Slave Trade*, 191–93. Portugal was somewhat different here. See João Pedro Marques, *The Sounds of Silence: Nineteenth-Century Portugal and the Abolition of the Slave Trade* (New York: Berghahn, 2006), 159–87.

40. David Eltis and David Richardson, "A New Assessment of the Transatlantic Slave Trade," in David Eltis and David Richardson, eds., *Extending the Frontiers: Essays on the New Transatlantic Slave Trade Database* (New Haven, Conn.: Yale University Press, 2008), 40–41.

41. Eltis, *Economic Growth and the Ending of the Transatlantic Slave Trade*, 97–98.

42. Ibid., 97.

43. Chaim D. Kaufmann and Robert A. Pape, "Explaining Costly Moral Action: Britain's Sixty-Year Campaign Against the Atlantic Slave Trade," *International Organization* 53, 4 (1999): 636–37.

44. Eltis, *Economic Growth and the Ending of the Transatlantic Slave Trade*, 10–18, 27, 61, 82, 138–39, 204; E. Phillip LeVeen, *British Slave Trade Suppression Policies* (New York: Arno Press, 1977), 52–63.

45. Robin Blackburn, *The Overthrow of Colonial Slavery, 1776–1848* (London: Verso, 1988), 520; Eltis, *Economic Growth and the Ending of the Transatlantic Slave Trade*, 15, 106; Herbert S. Klein, *The Atlantic Slave Trade* (Cambridge: Cambridge University Press, 1999); 185–86; LeVeen, *British Slave Trade Suppression Policies*, 64–85.

46. Bethel, *The Abolition of the Brazilian Slave Trade*; Robert Conrad, *The Destruction of Brazilian Slavery, 1850–1888* (Berkeley: University of California Press, 1972), 22; Eltis, *Economic Growth and the Ending of the Transatlantic Slave Trade*, 109–12; Fladeland, "Abolitionists Pressures on the Concert of Europe"; Murray, *Odious Commerce*, 50–71.

47. Lawrence Jennings, *French Anti-Slavery: The Movement for the Abolition of Slavery in France, 1802–1848* (Cambridge: Cambridge University Press, 2000), 24–47.

48. LeVeen, *British Slave Trade Suppression Policies*, 8.

49. Bethel, *The Abolition of the Brazilian Slave Trade*, 296-99, 321-26. Jacob Ade Ajayi, *Christian Missions in Nigeria 1841-1891: The Making of a New Élite* (Evanston, Ill.: Northwestern University Press, 1965), 58-64; Howard Temperley, *British Antislavery 1833-1870* (London: Longman, 1972), 168-83.

50. Bethel, *The Abolition of the Brazilian Slave Trade*, 151-89; Marques, *The Sounds of Silence*, 99-149.

51. Bethel, *The Abolition of the Brazilian Slave Trade*, 309-63.

52. Eltis, *Economic Growth and the Ending of the Transatlantic Slave Trade*, 232-33; Klein, *The Atlantic Slave Trade*, 202-3.

53. Faced with the declining fortunes of associated slave systems, the most rational response would have been to reopen the trade, rather than taking further action to abolish slavery.

54. Camilla Townsend, "In Search of Liberty: The Efforts of the Enslaved to Attain Abolition in Ecuador, 1822-1852," in Darién Davis, ed., *Beyond Slavery: The Multilayered Legacy of Africans in Latin America and the Caribbean* (Lanham, Md.: Rowman & Littlefield, 2007), 37-53; Blackburn, *The Overthrow of Colonial Slavery*, 331-79; Herbert S. Klein, *African Slavery in Latin America and the Caribbean* (Oxford: Oxford University Press, 1986), 250-53.

55. Drescher, "The Long Goodbye," 44-69; Maarten Kluitenbrouwer, "The Dutch Case for Anti-slavery: Late and Élitist Abolitionism," in Gert Oostinde, ed., *Fifty Years Later: Antislavery, Capitalism and Modernity in the Dutch Orbit* (Leiden: KITLV Press, 1995), 67-88.

56. Drescher, "British Way, French Way," 709-34; Jennings, *French Anti-Slavery*, 229-84.

57. See, for example, Joel Quirk, *Unfinished Business: A Comparative Survey of Historical and Contemporary Slavery* (Paris: UNESCO, 2009), 78-79; Robert William Fogel, *Without Consent or Contract: The Rise and Fall of American Slavery* (New York: Norton, 1989), 238-387; Rice, *The Rise and Fall of Black Slavery*, 305-59.

58. David Brion Davis, *Slavery and Human Progress* (Oxford: Oxford University Press, 1984), 287, 297; Drescher, "British Way, French Way," 733-34; Rice, *The Rise and Fall of Black Slavery*, 376; Klein, *The Atlantic Slave Trade*, 202.

59. Robert Conrad, *The Destruction of Brazilian Slavery, 1850-1888* (Berkeley: University of California Press, 1972); Rice, *The Rise and Fall of Black Slavery*, 375-81.

60. Seymour Drescher, "Brazilian Abolition in Comparative Perspective," in Rebecca J. Scott et al., *The Abolition of Slavery and the Aftermath of Emancipation in Brazil* (Durham, N.C.: Duke University Press, 1988), 23.

61. See Steven Hahn, *The Political Worlds of Slavery and Freedom* (Cambridge, Mass.: Harvard University Press, 2009), 55-114; Peter Blanchard, *Under the Flags of Freedom: Slave Soldiers and the Wars of Independence in Spanish South America* (Pittsburgh: University of Pittsburgh Press, 2008); David Geggus, "The Arming of the Slaves in the Haitian Revolution," in Christopher Brown and Philip Morgan, eds., *Arming*

Slaves: From Classical Times to the Modern Age (New Haven, Conn.: Yale University Press, 2006), 209–52.

62. Quirk, *Unfinished Business*, 66–70, 90–91. It is important, however, not to automatically equate resistance to specific acts of enslavement with opposition to slavery as a general institution. On this general theme, see Seymour Drescher and Pieter Emmer, eds., *Who Abolished Slavery? Slave Revolts and Abolitionism* (New York: Berghahn, 2010).

63. Drescher, *Capitalism and Antislavery*, 50–66.

64. Orlando Patterson, *Slavery and Social Death: A Comparative Study* (Cambridge, Mass.: Harvard University Press, 1982), 38–51; Quirk, *Unfinished Business*, 52–53.

65. Davis, *Slavery and Human Progress*, xvi–xvii, 24, 81–82, 109–11.

66. David Eltis, *The Rise of African Slavery in the Americas* (Cambridge: Cambridge University Press, 2000), 274.

67. McGrane, *Beyond Anthropology*, 98. See also Johannes Fabian, *Time and the Other: How Anthropology Makes Its Object* (New York: Columbia University Press, 1983), 11–18, 23, 26–28, 30, 39.

68. See Bowden, *The Empire of Civilization*, 23–46; O'Hagan, *Conceptualizing the West*, 1–20.

69. One famous example of this approach is Samuel Huntington's work on the Clash of Civilizations.

70. Lucien Febvre, *A New Kind of History: From the Writings of Febvre*, ed. Peter Burke (London: Routledge, 1973), 220–21.

71. Adas, *Machines as the Measure of Men*, 199.

72. See, for example, Jean Suret-Canale, *French Colonialism in Tropical Africa, 1900–1945* (London: Hurst, 1971), 60–67; R. M. A. van Zwanenberg, "Anti-Slavery, the Ideology of 19th Century Imperialism in East Africa," *Hadith* 5 (1975): 108.

73. See Kerry Ward, *Networks of Empire: Forced Migration in the Dutch East India Company* (Cambridge: Cambridge University Press, 2009), 48–83; Marcus Vink, "The World's Oldest Trade: Dutch Slavery and Slave Trade in the Indian Ocean in the Seventeenth Century," *Journal of World History* 14 (2003): 131.

74. There is a rapidly growing literature on slavery and abolition in Africa, India, and East, Southeast, and Central Asia. In addition to works already cited, other examples include Gwyn Campbell, *An Economic History of Imperial Madagascar, 1750–1895: The Rise and Fall of an Island Empire* (Cambridge: Cambridge University Press, 2005); Gwyn Campbell, ed., *The Structure of Slavery in Indian Ocean Africa and Asia* (London: Routledge, 2004); Gwyn Campbell, Edward Alpers, and Michael Salman, eds., *Resisting Bondage in Indian Ocean Africa and Asia* (London: Routledge, 2006); Richard Allen, *Slaves, Freedmen and Indentured Laborers in Colonial Mauritius* (Cambridge: Cambridge University Press, 2005); William Gervase Clarence-Smith, *Islam and the Abolition of Slavery* (Oxford: Oxford University Press, 2006), 14–16; Richard Eaton and Indrani Chatterjee, eds., *Slavery and South Asian History* (Bloomington: Indiana University, 2006).

75. The key example here involves the predations of North African raiders on Eu-

ropean vessels and coastal settlements, but even in this case European states found it difficult to muster sufficient power to protect their citizens, leading to ameliorative policies based on ransoming captives and bribing slave raiders. See Robert Davis, *Christian Slaves, Muslim Masters: White Slavery in the Mediterranean, the Barbary Coast, and Italy, 1500-1800* (Houndsmills: Palgrave, 2004), 139-74.

76. Alice L. Conklin, "Colonialism and Human Rights, A Contradiction in Terms? The Case of France and West Africa, 1895-1914," *American Historical Review* 103, 2 (1998): 425; Eltis, *Economic Growth and the Ending of the Transatlantic Slave Trade*, 6. If strategic and economic interests had been paramount, we would also expect to encounter much greater selectivity in the application of anti-slavery ideas, with elites employing anti-slavery advocacy only in a subset of cases where it served their parochial interests. Instead, we find the Anti-Slavery Project being extended to every corner of the globe, albeit at variable rates.

77. David Eltis, *The Rise of African Slavery in the Americas* (Cambridge: Cambridge University Press, 2000), 4. This general viewpoint is echoed by many leading scholars. See David Eltis and Stanley Engerman, "Shipboard Slave Revolts and Abolition," in Seymour Drescher and Pieter Emmer, eds., *Who Abolished Slavery? Slave Revolts and Abolitionism* (New York: Berghahn, 2010), 144-47. Whether European anti-slavery can be attributed to distinctive qualms about slavery or to distinctive avenues for political mobilization is open to question. See Paul Gordon Lauren, *The Evolution of International Human Rights: Visions Seen* (Philadelphia: University of Pennsylvania Press, 1998), 38-39.

78. Sophie Bessis, *Western Supremacy: The Triumph of an Idea?* (London: Zed Books, 2003), 44-46, 68-82.

79. It is difficult to exaggerate the scale and severity of European abuses. Some relevant examples can be found in Brantlinger, *Dark Vanishings*, 46, 73, 75, 90-93, 96, 121-22, 124-10, 158; Adam Hochschild, *King Leopold's Ghost: A Story of Greed, Terror, and Heroism in Colonial Africa* (Boston: Houghton Mifflin, 1998), 225-34, 278-83; Todorov, *The Conquest of America*, 127-45.

80. Richard Price, *The Chemical Weapons Taboo* (Ithaca, N.Y.: Cornell University Press, 1997), 7.

81. Other comparable examples of "exceptional" problems were cannibalism and suttee (the burning of widows), which also feature in justifications for imperial expansion and colonial paternalism during this period.

82. Davis, *Slavery and Human Progress*, 116-29.

83. Curtin, *Image of Africa*, 27, 458-59; Edward Said, *Culture and Imperialism* (London: Vintage, 1993), 123-27.

84. Christine Bolt, *Victorian Attitudes to Race* (London: Routledge, 1971), 29-30; Vincent, "Racial Equality," 243-44.

85. Brantlinger, *Dark Vanishings*, 71-72.

86. See Marcus Wood, *The Horrible Gift of Freedom: Atlantic Slavery and the Representation of Emancipation* (Athens: University of Georgia Press, 2010), 35-89.

87. Curtin, *Image of Africa*, 138–39, 371; Seymour Drescher, *The Mighty Experiment: Free Labor Versus Slavery in British Emancipation* (Oxford: Oxford University Press, 2002), 75–87, and "The Ending of the Slave Trade and the Evolution of European Scientific Racism," *Social Science History* 14, 3 (1990): 422.

88. Bolt, *Victorian Attitudes to Race*, 75–108; Curtin, *Image of Africa*, 363–72, 384–86; David Eltis, "Abolitionist Perceptions of Society After Slavery"; James Walvin, ed., *Slavery and British Society 1776–1846* (Baton Rouge: Louisiana State University Press, 1982), 205.

89. See Adas, *Machines as the Measure of Men*, 271–342; Mike Hawkins, *Social Darwinism in European and American Thought* (Cambridge: Cambridge University Press, 1997), 184–215; Tzvetan Todorov, *On Human Diversity, Nationalism, Racism, and Exoticism in French Thought* (Cambridge, Mass.: Harvard University Press, 1993), 90–170. This racial focus first emerged in France and the United States, but Britain gradually aligned with developments elsewhere.

90. Adas, *Machines as the Measure of Men*, 199–210.

91. There is no doubt that it is easier to retain an anti-slavery policy than create one, but this should not mean that legal abolition was irrevocable or set in stone. In an environment dominated by essentialist models of human difference, the notable lack of serious attempts to officially reintroduce slavery needs to be explained, rather than assumed.

92. Bolt, *Victorian Attitudes to Race*, 109–56.

93. Adas, *Machines as the Measure of Men*, 108–27; Roxann Wheeler, *The Complexion of Race: Categories of Difference in Eighteenth-Century British Culture* (Pennsylvania: University of Pennsylvania Press, 2000), 24.

94. Frederick Cooper, *From Slaves to Squatters: Plantation Labor in Agriculture in Zanzibar and Coastal Kenya, 1890–1925* (New Haven, Conn.: Yale University Press, 1980), 32. See also Patrick Brantlinger, "Victorians and Africans: The Genealogy of the Dark Continent," *Critical Inquiry* 12:1 (1985): 166–203; Conklin, "Colonialism and Human Rights," 423.

95. Joseph Miller, "The Abolition of the Slave Trade and Slavery: Historical Foundations," in Doudoe Diéne, ed., *From Chains to Bonds: The Slave Trade Revisited* (Paris: UNESCO Publishing, 2001), 176.

96. Said, *Culture and Imperialism*, 6.

97. Gong, *The Standard of "Civilization"*, 15, 29–30, Charles Lucas, *The Partition & Colonization of Africa* (Oxford: Clarendon Press, 1922), 213–16.

98. See, for example, Ehud Toledano, *As If Silent and Absent: Bonds of Enslavement in the Islamic Middle East* (New Haven, Conn.: Yale University Press, 2007), 61–107.

99. Gong, *The Standard of "Civilization"*, 64–69; Miers, *Slavery in the Twentieth Century*, 94–96, 254–59; Jerzy Zdanowski, *Slavery in the Gulf in the First Half of the 20th Century* (Warsaw: Wydawnictwo Naukowe, 2008), 45–84.

100. Examples from an expanding literature include Thanet Aphornsuvan, "Slavery and Modernity: Freedom in the Making of Modern Siam," in David Kelly and Anthony Reid, eds., *Asian Freedoms: The Idea of Freedom in East and South*

East Asia (Cambridge: Cambridge University Press, 1998), 161–82; David Feeny, "The Decline of Property Rights in Man in Thailand, 1800-1913," *Journal of Economic History* 49, 2 (1989): 285; "The Demise of Corvee and Slavery in Thailand, 1783-1913," in Martin A. Klein, ed., *Breaking the Chains: Slavery, Bondage, and Emancipation in Modern Africa and Asia* (Madison: University of Wisconsin Press, 1993), 83–111; David Kelly, "The Chinese Search for Freedom as a Universal Value," in Kelly and Reid, eds., *Asian Freedoms*, 69–73; Bok-Rae Kim, "Korean *Nobi* Resistance Under the Chosun Dynasty (1392–1910)," *Slavery and Abolition, Special Issue, Slavery and Resistance in Africa and Asia* 25, 2 (2004): 48; Bruno Lasker, *Human Bondage in Southeast Asia* (Chapel Hill: University of North Carolina Press, 1950), 56–59: James L. Watson, "Transactions in People: The Chinese Market in Slaves, Servants and Heirs," in James L. Watson, ed., *Asian and African Systems of Slavery* (Oxford: Blackwell, 1980), 245–50.

101. The political vulnerabilities of various governments frequently had a major influence on the success of anti-slavery diplomacy. For much of the nineteenth century, Moroccan rulers were able to resist British pressure at a time when others were compelled to reach agreement, because their geopolitical position made British diplomats reluctant to press their case. This delayed major anti-slavery legislation, which followed in the wake of colonial conquest in the early twentieth century. See Mohammed Ennaji, *Serving the Master: Slavery and Society in Nineteenth-Century Morocco* (New York: St. Martin's Press, 1998), 107–24; Murray Gordon, *Slavery in the Arab World* (New York: New Amsterdam, 1987), 163–65, 171–72.

102. See Beachey, *The Slave Trade of Eastern Africa*, 20, 28–29, 38–66, 94–120, 129–30, 137–38, 163–80; Frederick Cooper, *Plantation Slavery on the East Coast of Africa* (New Haven, Conn.: Yale University Press, 1977), 270–71; Gwyn Campbell, "Madagascar and the Slave Trade, 1810–1895," *Journal of African History* 22, 2 (1981): 203; Diane Robinson-Dunn, *The Harem, Slavery, and British Imperial Culture: Anglo-Muslim Relations in the Late Nineteenth Century* (Manchester: Manchester University Press, 2006), 31–63; Martin A. Klein, "The Emancipation of Slaves in the Indian Ocean," in Gwyn Campbell, ed., *Abolition and Its Aftermath in Indian Ocean Africa and Asia* (New York: Routledge, 2005), 199–201; Gordon, *Slavery in the Arab World*, 151–207; Miers, *Britain and the Ending of the Slave Trade*, 40–55, 70–73, 77, 86–88; Toledano, *The Ottoman Slave Trade and Its Suppression*, 95–107, 115–47.

103. See Seymour Drescher, *Abolition: A History of Slavery and Antislavery* (Cambridge: Cambridge University Press, 2009), 276–77.

104. Keene, "A Case Study of International Hierarchy," 314.

105. Rough estimates of various regional networks can be found in Lovejoy, *Transformations in Slavery*, 155–58, and Patrick Manning, *Slavery and African Life: Occidental, Oriental, and African Slave Trades* (Cambridge: Cambridge University Press, 1990), 52–54, 72–83.

106. Beachey, *The Slave Trade of Eastern Africa*, 67–93, 156–62, 174–80; Ehud Toledano, *The Ottoman Slave Trade and Its Suppression: 1840-1890* (Princeton, N.J.: Princ-

eton University Press, 1982), 219–23, 228; Miers, *Slavery in the Twentieth Century*, 183–88, 262–67; Zdanowski, *Slavery in the Gulf*, 16–44.

107. Pier Larson, *Ocean of Letters: Language and Creolization in an Indian Ocean Diaspora* (Cambridge: Cambridge University Press, 2009), 40–44. See also Beachey, *The Slave Trade of Eastern Africa*, 260–62; Manning, *Slavery and African Life*, 50–54; William Gervase Clarence-Smith, "The Economics of the Indian Ocean and Red Sea Slave Trades in the 19th Century: An Overview," in William Gervase Clarence-Smith, ed., *The Economics of the Indian Ocean and Red Sea Slave Trades in the 19th Century* (London: Frank Cass, 1989), 1–20; Toledano, *As If Silent and Absent*, 10–14. For further information on the history of maritime slave trading in Africans in East Africa see Edward Alpers, "The Other Middle Passage: The African Slave Trade in the Indian Ocean," in Emma Christopher, Cassandra Pybus, and Marcus Rediker, eds., *Many Middle Passages: Forced Labour and the Making of the Modern World* (Berkeley: University of California Press, 2007), 20–38; Thomas Vernet, "Slave Trade and Slavery on the Swahili Coast," in Behnaz A. Mirzai, Ismael Musah Montana, and Paul Lovejoy, eds., *Slavery, Islam and Diaspora* (Trenton, N.J.: Africa World Press, 2009), 37–76.

108. C. W. W. Greenidge, *Slavery* (London: Allen & Unwin, 1958), 49–57; Miers, *Slavery in the Twentieth Century*, 76–78, 165–66, 183–88, 266–67; Zdanowski, *Slavery in the Gulf in the First Half of the 20th Century*, 36–44, 137–73.

109. Ehud Toledano, "Ottoman Concepts of Slavery in the Period of Reform, 1830s-1880s," in Klein, ed., *Breaking the Chains*, 47.

110. Circassian slavery was somewhat exceptional here. See Y. Hakan Erdem, *Slavery in the Ottoman Empire and Its Demise, 1800–1909* (London: Macmillan, 1996), 148–91.

111. William Ochsenwald, "Muslim-European Conflict in the Hijaz: The Slave-Trade Controversy, 1840–1895," *Middle Eastern Studies* 16, 1 (1980): 118; Toledano, *The Ottoman Slave Trade and Its Suppression*, 130–35, 203–4.

112. Gordon, *Slavery in the Arab World*, 169–71; Toledano, *As If Silent and Absent*, 108–52; *The Ottoman Slave Trade and Its Suppression*, 193–205.

113. Toledano, *The Ottoman Slave Trade and Its Suppression*, 224–48.

114. Clarence-Smith, *Islam and the Abolition of Slavery*, 108–10.

115. Kathleen Simon, *Slavery*, 2nd ed. (London: Hodder & Stoughton, 1930), 12, 26, 30–34. Simon also raises the figure of five million, framing the two million figure as conservative. Other accounts talk of hundreds of thousands. Lord Noel-Buxton, "Slavery in Abyssinia," *International Affairs* 11, 4 (1932): 512; Suzanne Miers, "Britain and the Suppression of Slavery in Ethiopia," *Slavery and Abolition* 18, 3 (1997): 257.

116. Alice Moore-Harell, "Economic and Political Aspects of the Slave Trade in Ethiopia and the Sudan in the Second Half of the Nineteenth Century," *International Journal of African Historical Studies* 32, 2/3 (1999): 416–17, 420–21.

117. Lord Noel-Buxton, *Slavery in Abyssinia* (London: Anti-Slavery and Aborigines Protection Society, 1932), 1.

118. Allain, "Slavery and the League of Nations," 219–23, 243–44; Gong, *The Standard of "Civilization,"* 124–29; Antoinette Iadarola, "Ethiopia's Admission into the

League of Nations: An Assessment of Motives," *International Journal of African Histori-cal Studies* 8, 4 (1975), 607–10.

119. There were earlier precedents to British opposition. See Iadarola, "Ethiopia's Admission into the League of Nations," 609; Miers, *Slavery in the Twentieth Century*, 254.

120. Iadarola, "Ethiopia's Admission into the League of Nations," 620.

121. Allain, "Slavery and the League of Nations," 230–35.

122. Jon Edwards, "Slavery, the Slave Trade and the Economic Reorganization of Ethiopia," *African Economic History* 11 (1982): 3–14.

123. Allain, "Slavery and the League of Nations," 237–38, 241–42; *League of Na-tions: Dispute Between Ethiopia and Italy*, C.340.M.171.1935.VII, Geneva, September 11, 1935, 46; G. C. Baravelli, *The Last Stronghold of Slavery: What Abyssinia Is* (Rome: Società Editrice Di Novissima, 1935).

124. The Italian conquest of Libya two decades earlier had been prosecuted and rationalized along similar lines, but it did not arouse the same level of condemnation, since there was then little to distinguish this conquest from others recently conducted by European powers.

125. Jonathan Derrick, *Africa's Slaves Today* (New York: Schocken Books, 1975), 150–58; Paul E. LeRoy, "Slavery in the Horn of Africa," *Horn of Africa* 2, 3 (1979): 10, 17–18; Roger Sawyer, *Slavery in the Twentieth Century* (London: Routledge, 1986), 188–90.

126. Gordon, *Slavery in the Arab World*, 223; Miers, *Slavery in the Twentieth Cen-tury*, 342.

127. Greenidge, *Slavery*, 42; Miers, *Slavery in the Twentieth Century*, 349.

128. Clarence-Smith, *Islam and the Abolition of Slavery*, 181–84.

129. *United Nations General Assembly: Sixteenth Session, Report on Debate*, 1961, 3; John Laffin, *The Arabs as Master Slavers* (Englewood, Calif.: SBS, 1982), 58–77.

130. Derrick, *Africa's Slaves Today*, 144–48; Gordon, *Slavery in the Arab World*, 225–38; Miers, *Slavery in the Twentieth Century*, 339–52; Clarence-Smith, *Islam and the Abolition of Slavery*, 114–18.

131. UN Secretary General, *Question of Slavery and the Slave Trade in all the Prac-tices and Manifestations, Including the Slavery-Like Practices of Apartheid and Colonial-ism: Note by the Secretary-General*, E/CN.4/Sub.2/326, July 19, 1972, Annex II, 1.

132. Mohammed Awad, *Report on Slavery* (New York: United Nations, 1966), 170–80; Benjamin Whitaker, *Slavery: Report Prepared by Benjamin Whitaker, Special Rappor-teur of the Sub-Commission on Prevention of Discrimination and Protection of Minorities, Updating the Report on Slavery Submitted to the Sub-Commission in 1966*, UNESCO, E/CN/Sub.2/1982?20/Rev.1, 1982.

133. Derrick, *Africa's Slaves Today*, 145–46; Gordon, *Slavery in the Arab World*, 232–34; League of Nations, *Slavery: Report of the Committee of Experts on Slavery Pro-vided for by the Assembly Resolution of September 25th, 1931*, C.618.1932.VI, Geneva, September 1, 1932, 7.

134. Hedley Bull, "The Revolt Against the West," in Bull and Watson, eds., *The Expansion of International Society*, 217–28.

135. The language of civilization and associated ideas of insider and outsider have continued to be articulated in new ideological terms. See Bowden, *The Empire of Civilization*, 161–214.

136. The most famous example here is the restoration of slavery by Napoleon in 1802, which came very early in the history of anti-slavery, and thus predated the gradual consolidation of the Anti-Slavery Project in the European world.

Chapter 3. British Anti-Slavery and European Colonialism

1. William Gervase Clarence-Smith, *Islam and the Abolition of Slavery* (Oxford: Oxford University Press, 2006), 121–23, 142–43, 187–89; Bruno Lasker, *Human Bondage in Southeast Asia* (Chapel Hill: University of North Carolina Press, 1950), 26–36, 168–269; Martin A. Klein, "The Emancipation of Slaves in the Indian Ocean," in Gwyn Campbell, ed., *Abolition and Its Aftermath in Indian Ocean Africa and Asia* (New York: Routledge, 2005), 203–5; Anthony Reid, "The Decline of Slavery in Nineteenth-Century Indonesia," in Martin A. Klein, ed., *Breaking the Chains: Slavery, Bondage, and Emancipation in Modern Africa and Asia* (Madison: University of Wisconsin Press, 1993), 69–80; Eric Tagliacozzo, *Secret Trades, Porous Borders: Smuggling and States Along a Southeast Asian Frontier, 1865–1915* (New Haven, Conn.: Yale University Press, 2005), 236–43.

2. Seymour Becker, *Russia's Protectorates in Central Asia: Bukhara and Khiva, 1865–1924* (Cambridge, Mass.: Harvard University Press, 1968), 55–57, 73–77, 86–88, 118; Clarence-Smith, *Islam and the Abolition of Slavery*, 118–20; V. G. Kiernan, *The Lords of Human Kind: European Attitudes Towards the Outside World in the Imperial Age* (London: Weidenfeld and Nicholson, 1969), 103.

3. Lasker, *Human Bondage in Southeast Asia*, 40–41; Michael Salman, *The Embarrassment of Slavery: Controversies over Bondage and Nationalism in the American Colonial Philippines* (Berkeley: University of California Press, 2001).

4. Karine Delaye, "Slavery and Colonial Representations in Indochina from the Second Half of the Nineteenth to the Early Twentieth Century," in Gwyn Campbell, ed., *The Structure of Slavery in Indian Africa and Asia* (London: Frank Cass, 2004), 129–40; Kiernan, *The Lords of Human Kind*, 94; Klein, "The Emancipation of Slaves in the Indian Ocean," 205–7; Lasker, *Human Bondage in Southeast Asia*, 59–64.

5. Lasker, *Human Bondage in Southeast Asia*, 41–56; Suzanne Miers, *Slavery in the Twentieth Century* (Walnut Creek, Calif.: Altamira Press, 2003), 30–32, 126–28, 152–53, 168, 222–34.

6. Martin A. Klein, "Introduction: Modern European Expansion and Traditional Servitude in Africa and Asia," in Klein, ed., *Breaking the Chains*, 12–14; Reid, "The Decline of Slavery in Nineteenth-Century Indonesia," 68–69.

7. Paul E. Lovejoy, *Transformations in Slavery: A History of Slavery in Africa*, 2nd ed. (Cambridge: Cambridge University Press, 2000), 238–40.

8. Howard Temperley, "The Delegalization of Slavery in British India," in Howard

Temperley, ed., *After Slavery: Emancipation and Its Discontents* (London: Frank Cass, 2000), 169–87.

9. Dennis D. Cordell, "No Liberty, Not Much Equality and Very Little Fraternity: The Mirage of Manumission in the Algerian Sahara in the Second Half of the Nineteenth Century," in Suzanne Miers and Martin A. Klein, eds., *Slavery and Colonial Rule in Africa* (London: Frank Cass, 1999), 38–56; Trevor Getz, *Slavery and Reform in West Africa: Toward Emancipation in Nineteenth-Century Senegal and the Gold Coast* (Athens: Ohio University Press, 2004), 76–79; Mohamed Mbodji, "The Abolition of Slavery in Senegal, 1820–1890: Crisis of the Rise of a New Entrepreneurial Class?" in Klein, ed., *Breaking the Chains*, 197–211.

10. Cordell, "No Liberty, Not Much Equality and Very Little Fraternity," 45; Martin A. Klein, *Slavery and Colonial Rule in French West Africa* (Cambridge: Cambridge University Press, 1998), 26–27, 34–35; Getz, *Slavery and Reform in West Africa*, 80–84; Suzanne Miers, "Slavery to Freedom in Sub-Saharan Africa: Expectations and Reality," in Temperley, ed., *After Slavery*, 238–39.

11. John Grace, *Domestic Slavery in Africa: With Particular Reference to the Sierra Leone Protectorate, 1896–1927* (London: Frederick Muller, 1975), 44–46, 49–50; Kwabena Opare-Akurang, "The Administration of the Abolition Laws, African Responses, and Post-Proclamation Slavery in the Gold Coast, 1874–1940," in Miers and Klein, eds., *Slavery and Colonial Rule in Africa*, 149.

12. See Neta C. Crawford, *Argument and Change in World Politics* (Cambridge: Cambridge University Press, 2002), 206.

13. For introductions to these topics, see Phillip D. Curtin, *The Image of Africa: British Ideas and Action, 1780–1850* (Madison: University of Wisconsin Press, 1964), 123–39; Robin Law, ed., *From Slave Trade to "Legitimate" Commerce: The Commercial Transition in Nineteenth-Century West Africa* (Cambridge: Cambridge University Press, 1995), 264–71; Felix K. Ekechí, "Studies on Missions in Africa," in Toyin Falola, ed., *African Historiography: Essays in Honour of Jacob Ade Ajayi* (Harlow: Longman, 1993), 145–65; Howard Temperley, *White Dreams, Black Africa: The Antislavery Expedition to the River Niger 1841–1842* (New Haven, Conn.: Yale University Press, 1991).

14. A. G. Hopkins, *An Economic History of West Africa* (London: Longman, 1973), 127–30, 136; Susan Martin, "Slaves Igbo Women and Palm Oil in the Nineteenth Century," in Law, ed., *From Slave Trade to "Legitimate" Commerce*, 44–46; David Northrup, "The Compatibility of the Slave and Palm Oil Trades in the Bight of Biafra," *Journal of African History* 17, 3 (1976): 358; James F. Searing, *West African Slavery and Atlantic Commerce: The Senegal River Valley, 1700–1860* (Cambridge: Cambridge University Press, 1993), 167–75.

15. Curtin, *The Image of Africa*, 428; Martin Lynn, "British Policy, Trade, and Informal Empire in the Mid-Nineteenth Century," in Andrew Porter, ed., *The Oxford History of the British Empire*, vol. 3, *The Nineteenth Century* (Oxford: Oxford University Press, 1999), 103, 106–8, 113–14.

16. Curtin, *The Image of Africa*, 125, 270–72, 301, 428–31.

17. Northrup, "The Compatibility of the Slave and Palm Oil Trades in the Bight of Biafra," 359. See also Hopkins, *An Economic History of West Africa*, 127; Robin Law, "Introduction," in Law, ed., *From Slave Trade to "Legitimate" Commerce*, 20–21; Lynn, "The West African Palm Oil Trade in the Nineteenth Century and the 'Crisis of Adaptation,'" in Law, ed., *From Slave Trade to "Legitimate" Commerce*, 60–61; Elisée Soumonni, "The Compatibility of the Slave and Palm Oil Trades in Dahomey, 1818–1858," in Law, ed., *From Slave Trade to "Legitimate" Commerce*, 82–84.

18. Paul E. Lovejoy and David Richardson, "The Initial 'Crisis of Adaptation': The Impact of British Abolition on the Atlantic Slave Trade in West Africa, 1808–1820," in Law, ed., *From Slave Trade to "Legitimate" Commerce*, 46.

19. The end of the transatlantic slave trade was a staggered process, which occurred at different times at different places. See David Eltis, "African and European Relations in the Last Century of the Transatlantic Slave Trade," in Oliver Pétré-Grenouilleau, ed., *From Slave Trade to Empire: Europe and the Colonisation of Black Africa 1780–1880s* (Milton Park: Routledge, 2004), 21–41.

20. Hopkins, *An Economic History of West Africa*, 142. See also Michael W. Doyle, *Empires* (Ithaca, N.Y.: Cornell University Press, 1986), 179–91; G. A. Hopkins, "The 'New International Economic Order' in the Nineteenth Century: Britain's First Development Plan for Africa," in Law, ed., *From Slave Trade to "Legitimate" Commerce*, 240–64; Robin Law, "The Historiography of the Commercial Transition in Nineteenth-Century West Africa," in Toyin Falola, ed., *African Historiography: Essays in Honour of Jacob Ade Ajayi* (Harlow: Longman, 1993), 95–103.

21. Gareth Austen, "Between Abolition and *Jihad*: The Asante Response to the Ending of the Atlantic Slave Trade, 1807–1896," in Law, ed., *From Slave Trade to "Legitimate" Commerce*, 100–107; Ralph A. Austen, "The Abolition of the Overseas Slave Trade: A Distorted Theme in West African History," *Journal of the Historical Society of Nigeria* 5, 2 (1970): 257; Law, "The Historiography of the Commercial Transition in Nineteenth-Century West Africa," 92–93, 101–9; Lovejoy and Richardson, "The Initial 'Crisis of Adaptation,'" 34, 52; Lynn, "The West African Palm Oil Trade in the Nineteenth Century and the 'Crisis of Adaptation,'" 57–65; Munro, *Africa and the International Economy*, 47–52.

22. Patrick Manning, *Slavery and African Life: Occidental, Oriental, and African Slave Trades* (Cambridge: Cambridge University Press, 1990), 142.

23. Lovejoy, *Transformations in Slavery*, 224–25, 250–51; Manning, *Slavery and African Life*, 109.

24. Manning, *Slavery and African Life*, 108.

25. Austen, *African Economic History*, 109–14; Munro, *Africa and the International Economy*, 45–46.

26. Frederick Cooper, *Plantation Slavery on the East Coast of Africa* (New Haven, Conn.: Yale University Press, 1977), 3–20; Lovejoy, *Transformations in Slavery*, 212–16.

27. Klein, "Introduction," 10–12; Lovejoy, *Transformations in Slavery*, 276–87; Manning, *Slavery and African Life*, 142–47.

28. See Martin A. Klein, *Islam and Imperialism in Senegal* (Edinburgh: Edinburgh University Press, 1968), 63–173; Paul E. Lovejoy, ed., *Slavery on the Frontiers of Islam* (Princeton, N.J.: Markus Wiener, 2004), chaps. 1–7; Paul E. Lovejoy, *Slavery, Commerce and Production in the Sokoto Caliphate of West Africa* (Trenton, N.J.: Africa World Press, 2005).

29. Klein, *Slavery and Colonial Rule in French West Africa*, 37–58; Lovejoy, *Transformations in Slavery*, 191–224; Claude Meillassoux, *The Anthropology of Slavery: The Womb of Iron and Gold* (London: Athlone, 1991), 44–66.

30. See Edward A. Alpers, *Ivory & Slaves in East Central Africa: Changing Patterns of International Trade in the Later Nineteenth Century* (London: Heinemann, 1975), 234–43; Murray Gordon, *Slavery in the Arab World* (New York: New Amsterdam, 1989), 151–65; Manning, *Slavery and African Life*, 136–38.

31. Cooper, *Plantation Slavery on the East Coast of Africa*; Jan-George Deutsch, *Emancipation Without Emancipation in German East Africa c. 1884–1914* (Oxford: James Currey, 2006), 17–43; A. M. H. Sheriff, "The Slave Mode of Production Along the East African Coast, 1810–1873," in John Ralph Willis, ed., *Slaves and Slavery in Muslim Africa*, vol. 2, *The Servile Estate* (London: Frank Cass, 1985), 162–78.

32. R. W. Beachey, *The Slave Trade of Eastern Africa* (London: Rex Collings, 1976), 37–66; Raymond Howell, *The Royal Navy and the Slave Trade* (London: Croom Helm, 1987), 101–2, 157–60.

33. Dennis D. Cordell, "The Delicate Balance of Force and Flight: The End of Slavery in Eastern Ubangi-Shari," in Suzanne Miers and Richard Roberts, eds., *The End of Slavery in Africa* (Madison: University of Wisconsin Press, 1988), 152–55; François Renault, "The Structures of the Slave Trade in Central African in the 19th Century," in William Gervase Clarence-Smith, ed., *The Economics of the Indian Ocean and Red Sea Slave Trades in the 19th Century* (London: Frank Cass, 1989), 146–65.

34. See Brian Stanley, "Commerce and Christianity: Providence Theory, the Missionary Movement, and the Imperialism of Free Trade, 1842–1860," *Historical Journal* 26, 1 (1983): 71–94; Adrian Hastings, *The Church in Africa, 1450–1950* (Oxford: Clarendon Press, 1994), 283–93.

35. Kevin Grant, *A Civilised Savagery: Britain and the New Slaveries in Africa, 1884–1926* (New York: Routledge 2005), 26–27; Robert Rothberg, ed., *Africa and Its Explorers: Motives, Methods and Impact* (Cambridge, Mass.: Harvard University Press, 1970).

36. Patrick Brantlinger, "Victorians and Africans: The Genealogy of the Dark Continent," *Critical Inquiry*, 12,1, (1985): 166–203; Frederick Cooper, "Conditions Analogous to Slavery: Imperialism and Free Labor Ideology in Africa," in Frederick Cooper, Thomas C. Holt, and Rebecca Scott, *Beyond Slavery: Explorations of Race, Labor, and Citizenship in Postemancipation Societies* (Chapel Hill: University of North Carolina Press, 2000), 113–16; Brian Stanley, "Commerce and Christianity," 81–84. See also Annie E. Coombes, *Reinventing Africa: Museums, Material Culture and Popular Imagination of Late Victorian and Edwardian England* (New Haven, Conn.: Yale University Press, 1994), 70, 77–81.

37. Brantlinger, "Victorians and Africans," 175; Cooper, "Conditions Analogous to Slavery," 115.

38. Phillip D. Curtin, *The World and the West: The European Challenge and the Overseas Response in the Age of Empire* (Cambridge: Cambridge University Press, 2000), 111–27; Michael Twaddle, "The Ending of Slavery in Buganda," in Miers and Roberts, eds., *The End of Slavery in Africa*, 124–41.

39. Jacob Ade Ajayi, *Christian Missions in Nigeria 1841–1891: The Making of a New Élite* (Evanston: Northwestern University Press, 1965), 105–8; Hastings, *The Church in Africa*, 309–11, 317–25.

40. Cordell, "The Delicate Balance of Force and Flight," 156–57; Klein, *Slavery and Colonial Rule in French West Africa*, 116–17; David Northrup, "The End of Slavery in the Eastern Belgian Congo," in Miers and Roberts, eds., *The End of Slavery in Africa*, 469; Don Ohadike, "The Decline of Slavery Among the Igbo People," in Miers and Roberts, eds., *The End of Slavery in Africa*, 443–44; Ahmad Alawad Sikainga, *Slaves into Workers: Emancipation and Labor in Colonial Sudan* (Austin: University of Texas Press, 1996), 27–28; Aylward Shorter, *Cross & Flag: The "White Fathers" During the Colonial Scramble* (New York: Orbis, 2006), 70–75.

41. Ajayi, *Christian Missions in Nigeria 1841–1891*, 25–44; Beachey, *The Slave Trade of Eastern Africa*, 85–93; Robert Strayer, *The Making of Mission Communities in East Africa: Anglicans and Africans in Colonial Kenya, 1875–1935* (London: Heinemann, 1978), 14–15; Howell, *The Royal Navy and the Slave Trade*, 121–22.

42. Raymond Dumett and Marion Johnson, "Britain and the Suppression of Slavery in the Gold Coast Colony, Ashanti, and the Northern Territories," in Miers and Roberts, eds., *The End of Slavery in Africa*, 78; R. M. Githige, "The Issue of Slavery: Relations Between the CMS and the State on the East African Coast Prior to 1895," *Journal of Religion in Africa* 16, 3 (1986): 161–62, 210–16; Hastings, *The Church in Africa*, 256–57; Klein, *Slavery and Colonial Rule in French West Africa*, 116–18; Lovejoy, *Transformations in Slavery*, 262–65; Roland Oliver, *The Missionary Factor in East Africa* (London: Longmans, Green and Co., 1969), 16, 26, 39; Richard Roberts and Suzanne Miers, "The End of Slavery in Africa," in Miers and Roberts, eds., *The End of Slavery in Africa*, 34–35; Sikainga, *Slaves into Workers*, 26–27.

43. Ajayi, *Christian Missions in Nigeria 1841–1891*, 118; Oliver, *The Missionary Factor in East Africa*, 49–50; Strayer, *The Making of Mission Communities in East Africa*, 37–41.

44. Ajayi, *Christian Missions in Nigeria 1841–1891*, 103–8, 165; Lovejoy, *Transformations in Slavery*, 260–67.

45. Oliver, *The Missionary Factor in East Africa*, 116; A. J. Temu, *British Protestant Missions* (London: Longman, 1972), 14, 20; Shorter, *Cross & Flag*, 64–66, 86–95.

46. Richard F. Clarke, ed., *Cardinal Lavigerie and the African Slave Trade* (1889; New York: Negro Universities Press, 1969), 328–29.

47. Brantlinger, "Victorians and Africans"; Cooper, "Conditions Analogous to Slavery," 113–16.

48. Ajayi, *Christian Missions in Nigeria 1841–1891*, 261–62; Curtin, *The Image of Africa*, 324–29; Ekechí, "Studies on Missions in Africa," 147–49.

49. Beachey, *The Slave Trade of Eastern Africa*, 222–23; Hastings, *The Church in Africa*, 254–55, 410; Suzanne Miers, *Britain and the Ending of the Slave Trade* (New York: Africana Press, 1975), 201–6; Oliver, *The Missionary Factor in East Africa*, 117–18; Shorter, *Cross & Flag*, 1–4, 63–64.

50. Clarke, *Cardinal Lavigerie and the African Slave Trade*, 126–93; Lovejoy, *Transformations in Slavery*, 266.

51. Miers, *Britain and the Ending of the Slave Trade*, 204.

52. Ibid., 236–319.

53. Doyle, *Empires*, 234–38; Bernard Porter, *Britain, Europe and the World 1850–1982: Delusions of Grandeur* (London: Allen & Unwin, 1983), 16–32.

54. John Gallagher and Ronald Robinson, "The Imperialism of Free Trade," *The Economic History Review* 6:1 (1953): 1–15. See also Robert Johnson, *British Imperialism* (Hampshire: Palgrave, 2003), 18–23; Lynn, "British Policy, Trade, and Informal Empire in the Mid-Nineteenth Century," 101–21.

55. David Mclean, "Finance and 'Informal Empire' Before the First World War," *Economic History Review* 29, 2 (1976): 291.

56. Winfried Baumgart, *Imperialism: The Idea and Reality of British and French Colonial Expansion, 1880–1914* (Oxford: Oxford University Press, 1982), 5–7; John Darwin, "Imperialism and the Victorians: The Dynamics of Territorial Expansion," *English Historical Review* 112, 447 (1997): 617; Martin Lynn, "The 'Imperialism of Free Trade' and the Case of West Africa," *Journal of Imperial and Commonwealth History* 15, 1 (1986): 23, 37.

57. Darwin, "Imperialism and the Victorians," 617–20; D. C. M. Platt, "The Imperialism of Free Trade: Some Reservations," *Economic History Review* 21, 2 (1968): 296, and "Further Objections to an 'Imperialism of Free Trade,' 1830–60," *Economic History Review* 26, 1 (1973): 71.

58. Gallagher and Robinson, "The Imperialism of Free Trade," 3, 11.

59. Doyle, *Empires*, 181–88; Lynn, "The 'Imperialism of Free Trade' and the Case of West Africa," 24–26; Miers, *Britain and the Ending of the Slave Trade*, 46–50.

60. David Eltis, *Economic Growth and the Ending of the Transatlantic Slave Trade* (Oxford: Oxford University Press, 1987), 91–94.

61. Gallagher and Robinson, "The Imperialism of Free Trade," 11.

62. Richard D. Wolff, "British Imperialism and the East African Slave Trade," *Science and Society* 36:4 (1972), 448–50; G. N. Uzoigwe, *Britain and the Conquest of Africa: The Age of Salisbury* (Ann Arbor: University of Michigan Press, 1974), 145–71.

63. John Darwin, "Globalism and Imperialism: the Global Context of British Power, 1830–1960," in Shigeru Akita, ed., *Gentlemanly Capitalism, Imperialism and Global History* (Hampshire: Palgrave, 2002), 45–48; Lynn, "The 'Imperialism of Free Trade' and the Case of West Africa," 27–37.

64. Colin Newbury, "Great Britain and the Partition of Africa, 1870–1914," in Porter, ed., *The Oxford History of the British Empire*, vol. 3, *The Nineteenth Century*, 624–25.

65. Darwin, "Imperialism and the Victorians," 630.

66. Paul Kennedy, "Continuity and Discontinuity in British Imperialism 1815–1914," in C. C. Eldridge, ed., *British Imperialism in the Nineteenth Century* (New York: St. Martin's Press, 1984), 20–38.

67. Summaries of these issues can be found in Baumgart, *Imperialism*, Doyle, *Empires*, 19–30, 141–61, 232–56, and Johnson, *British Imperialism*, 59–76. Key texts include John Gallagher, Ronald Robinson, and Alice Denny, *Africa and the Victorians: The Official Mind of Imperialism* (London: Macmillan, 1965) and P. J. Cain and A. G. Hopkins, *British Imperialism: Innovation and Expansion 1688–1914* (London: Longman, 1993).

68. G. N. Sanderson, "The European Partition of Africa: Coincidence of Conjecture?" in E. F. Penrose, ed., *European Imperialism and the Partition of Africa* (London: Frank Cass, 1975), 1–54.

69. Cordell, "The Delicate Balance of Force and Flight," 150; Toyin Falola, "The End of Slavery Among the Yoruba," in Miers and Klein, eds., *Slavery and Colonial Rule in Africa*, 235; Gordon, *Slavery in the Arab World*, 177–82; Paul E. Lovejoy and Jan S. Hogendorn, *Slow Death for Slavery: The Course of Abolition in Northern Nigeria, 1897–1936* (Cambridge: Cambridge University Press, 1993), 10–30; Suzanne Miers and Martin A. Klein, "Introduction," *Slavery and Colonial Rule in Africa*, 1; Miers and Roberts, "The End of Slavery in Africa," 19; Ohadike, "When the Slaves Left, Owners Wept," 194–95; C. N. Ubah, "Suppression of the Slave Trade in the Nigerian Emirates," *Journal of African History* 32, 3 (1991): 450.

70. Deutsch, *Emancipation Without Emancipation in German East Africa*, 102–9; Howell, *The Royal Navy and the Slave Trade*, 195–208; Miers, *Britain and the Ending of the Slave Trade*, 210–16.

71. Oliver, *The Missionary Factor in East Africa*, 149–50.

72. Adam Hochschild, *King Leopold's Ghost: A Story of Greed, Terror, and Heroism in Colonial Africa* (Boston: Houghton Mifflin, 1998), 212–13.

73. Ibid., 225–34, 280.

74. Official statements to this effect populate submissions to various League of Nations Committees on Slavery. Early examples include League of Nations, *The Question of Slavery, Memorandum by the Secretary-General*, A.25.1924.VI, Geneva, August 4, 1924; League of Nations, *The Question of Slavery: Letters from the British Government Transmitting Dispatches showing the situation with respect to Slavery in the British Colonies and Protectorates and Territories under British Mandate*, A.25(a).1924.VI, Geneva, September 15, 1925. This theme is also taken up in Gwyn Campbell, "Introduction: Slavery and other Forms of Unfree Labour in the Indian Ocean World," in Campbell, ed., *The Structure of Slavery in Indian Africa and Asia*, xxiii–xxv; Raymond E. Dumett, "Pressure Groups, Bureaucracy, and the Decision-making Process: The Case of Slavery Abolition and Colonial Expansion in the Gold Coast," *Journal of Imperial and Commonwealth History* 9, 2 (1981): 193; Richard A. Goodridge, "The Issue of Slavery in the Establishment of British Rule in Northern Cameroun to 1927," *African Economic History* 22 (1994): 22; Miers and Roberts, "The End of Slavery in Africa," 21, 28; Ismail Rashid, "'Do Dady

nor Lef me Make dem Carry me': Slave Resistance and Emancipation in Sierra Leone, 1894–1928," in Miers and Klein, eds., *Slavery and Colonial Rule in Africa*, 216.

75. Interviews and testimonies covering this period reveal a quite different picture. See Klein, *Slavery and Colonial Rule in French West Africa*, 243–46; Ann O'Hear, *Power Relations in Nigeria: Ilorin Slaves and Their Successors* (Rochester, N.Y.: University of Rochester Press, 1997), 21–45; and Marcia Wright, *Strategies of Slaves & Women: Life Stories from East/Central Africa* (London: James Currey, 1993).

76. Cordell, "No Liberty, Not Much Equality and Very Little Fraternity," 50–52; Andres Eckert, "Slavery in Colonial Cameroon, 1880s to 1930s," in Miers and Klein, eds., *Slavery and Colonial Rule in Africa*, 141; Taj Hargey, "*Festina Lente*: Slavery Policy and Practice in the Anglo-Egyptian Sudan," in Miers and Klein, eds., *Slavery and Colonial Rule in Africa*, 251, 260–61; Klein, *Slavery and Colonial Rule in French West Africa*, 97; Suzanne Miers and Michael Crowder, "The Politics of Suppression in Bechuanaland: Power Struggles and the Plight of the Basarwa in the Bamangwato Reserve, 1926–1940," in Miers and Roberts, eds., *The End of Slavery in Africa*, 180–81; Sikainga, *Slaves into Workers*, 38.

77. League of Nations, *Slavery: Report of the Advisory Committee of Experts*, Second Session, C.159.M.113. 1935. VI, Geneva, April 10, 1935, 28.

78. This strategy shared a number of features in common with earlier efforts by pro-slavery voices in the Americas to defend slavery by establishing favorable parallels between black slaves and the white working class.

79. For a snapshot of recent estimates see Joel Quirk, *Unfinished Business: A Comparative Survey of Historical and Contemporary Slavery* (Paris: UNESCO, 2009), 40–42.

80. See, for example, Cordell, "The Delicate Balance of Force and Flight," 152; Miers and Klein, "Introduction," 1–2; Miers and Roberts, "The End of Slavery in Africa," 18–21; Sikainga, *Slaves into Workers*, 44–50; Jan-George Deutsch, "The 'Freeing' of Slaves in German East Africa: The Statistical Record, 1890–1914," in Miers and Klein, eds., *Slavery and Colonial Rule in Africa*, 108; League of Nations, *Slavery: Report by the Secretary-General Presented in Accordance with the Assembly Resolution of September 21, 1929*, A.17.1930.VI, Geneva, August 11, 1930, 4; Gabriel R. Warburg, "Ideological and Practical Considerations Regarding Slavery in the Mahdist State and the Anglo-Egyptian Sudan: 1881–1918," in Paul E. Lovejoy, ed., *The Ideology of Slavery in Africa* (London: Sage, 1981), 258–59.

81. Frederick Cooper, *From Slaves to Squatters: Plantation Labor and Agriculture in Zanzibar and Coastal Kenya, 1890–1925* (New Haven, Conn.: Yale University Press, 1980), 35.

82. Dumett and Johnson, "Britain and the Suppression of Slavery in the Gold Coast Colony, Ashanti, and the Northern Territories," 82; Miers and Crowder, "The Politics of Suppression in Bechuanaland," 178; League of Nations, *Slavery: Report by the Secretary-General*, 4.

83. Lee V. Cassanelli, "The Ending of Slavery in Italian Somalia: Liberty and the Control of Labor, 1890–1935," in Miers and Roberts, eds., *The End of Slavery in Africa*,

309–10; Cordell, "The Delicate Balance of Force and Flight," 155–66; and "No Liberty, Not Much Equality and Very Little Fraternity," 44–46; James Duffy, *A Question of Slavery* (Oxford: Clarendon Press, 1967), 42, 54–59; E. Ann McDougall, "A Topsy-Turvy World: Slaves and Freed Slaves in the Mauritanian Adrar, 1910–1950," in Miers and Roberts, eds., *The End of Slavery in Africa*, 366–69; Eckert, "Slavery in Colonial Cameroon, 1880s to 1930s," 136–37; Hargey, "*Festina Lente*: Slavery Policy and Practice in the Anglo-Egyptian Sudan," 260; Allen Isaccman and Anton Rosenthal, "Slaves, Soldiers and Dependency Among the Chikunda of Mozambique, ca. 1825–1920," in Miers and Roberts, eds., *The End of Slavery in Africa*, 235–36; Klein, *Slavery and Colonial Rule in French West Africa*, 122–24; Suzanne Miers, "Slavery and the Slave Trade as International Issues in 1890–1939," in Miers and Klein, eds., *Slavery and Colonial Rule in Africa*, 20; Miers and Roberts, "The End of Slavery in Africa," 19–21; Sikainga, *Slaves into Workers*, 42–44; David Seddon, "Unfinished Business: Slavery in Saharan Africa," Howard Temperley, ed., *After Slavery: Emancipation and Its Discontents* (London: Frank Cass, 2000), 210–27.

84. Miers and Roberts, "The End of Slavery in Africa," 19–20; George Michael La Rue, "The Frontiers of Enslavement: Bagmirmi and the Trans-Saharan Slave Routes," in Lovejoy, ed., *Slavery and the Frontiers of Islam*, 48.

85. Miers and Roberts, "The End of Slavery in Africa," 21.

86. Lovejoy and Hogendorn, *Slow Death for Slavery*, 274–76; Ubah, "Suppression of the Slave Trade in the Nigerian Emirates," 448–70. In pre-colonial Africa adolescent or female slaves had often been preferred over men, but developments in this era appear to have been based primarily on a desire to conceal the trade from colonial authorities.

87. Cordell, "The Delicate Balance of Force and Flight," 165–66; Dumett and Johnson, "Britain and the Suppression of Slavery in the Gold Coast Colony, Ashanti, and the Northern Territories," 82–83; Eckert, "Slavery in Colonial Cameroon, 1880s to 1930s," 144; Goodridge, "The Issue of Slavery in the Establishment of British Rule in Northern Cameroun to 1927," 26–27; Hargey, "*Festina Lente*: Slavery Policy and Practice in the Anglo-Egyptian Sudan," 264–66; Sean O'Callaghan, *The Slave Trade Today* (New York: Crown, 1961); Ahmad Alawad Sikainga, "Slavery and Muslim Jurisprudence in Morocco," in Miers and Klein, eds., *Slavery and Colonial Rule in Africa*, 58.

88. Deutsch, "The 'Freeing' of Slaves in German East Africa," 122; Eckert, "Slavery in Colonial Cameroon, 1880s to 1930s," 140; Getz, *Slavery and Reform in West Africa*, 83; Hargey, "*Festina Lente*," 256; Lovejoy and Hogendorn, *Slow Death for Slavery*, 238–60.

89. Warburg, "Ideological and Practical Considerations Regarding Slavery," 245–50. This dynamic also contributed to further revolts after British rule had been restored. Hargey, "*Festina Lente*," 253.

90. Grace, *Domestic Slavery in Africa*, 1–6.

91. Getz, *Slavery and Reform in West Africa*, 71; Miers, "Slavery and the Slave Trade as International Issues in 1890–1939," 20.

92. Igor Kopytoff, "The Cultural Context of African Abolition," in Miers and Roberts, eds., *The End of Slavery in Africa*, 485–503; Suzanne Miers and Igor Kopytoff, "Afri-

can 'Slavery' as an Institution of Marginality," in Suzanne Miers and Igor Kopytoff, eds., *Slavery in Africa: Historical and Anthropological Perspectives* (Madison: University of Wisconsin Press, 1977), 3–81; Miers, *Slavery in the Twentieth Century*, 32. Challenges to this perspective include Paul. E. Lovejoy, "Slavery in the Context of Ideology," in Lovejoy, ed., *The Ideology of Slavery in Africa*, 11–16; Meillassoux, *The Anthropology of Slavery: The Womb of Iron and Gold*, 12–16.

93. Manning, *Slavery and African Life*, 154.

94. Ibid., 161.

95. Grant, *A Civilised Savagery*, 5; Miers, "Slavery and the Slave Trade as International Issues," 31.

96. Cordell, "No Liberty, Not Much Equality and Very Little Fraternity," 43–46; Duffy, *A Question of Slavery*, 60–101; Eckert, "Slavery in Colonial Cameroon," 136–44; Hargey, "*Festina Lente*," 251–55; Rashid, "Do Dady nor Lef me Make dem Carry me," 216–27.

97. Lovejoy and Hogendorn, *Slow Death for Slavery*, 64–97.

98. The notable exception here was German policy in East Africa, which saw colonial authorities sanction slavery and "private" slave trading, and even collect taxes on slave transactions. See Deutsch, *Emancipation Without Emancipation in German East Africa*, 97–164. Significantly, the overall slave population still experienced a major decline under this regime, pointing once again to the decisive role of slave agency in bringing slavery to an end.

99. Frederick Cooper, *Decolonization and African Society: The Labor Question in French and British Africa* (Cambridge: Cambridge University Press, 1996), 26–31; Crawford, *Argument and Change in World Politics*, 241–46; Grant, *A Civilised Savagery*, 4.

100. Miers, *Slavery in the Twentieth Century*, 216–32, 278–94.

101. Lovejoy and Hogendorn, *Slow Death for Slavery*, 278.

102. Ibid., 261–86.

103. Beachey, *The Slave Trade of Eastern Africa*, 242–59; Duffy, *A Question of Slavery*, 102–229; Dumett, "Pressure Groups, Bureaucracy, and the Decision-making Process," 193–211; Goodridge, "The Issue of Slavery in the Establishment of British Rule in Northern Cameroun to 1927," 19–36; Hargey, "*Festina Lente*," 255–66; Klein, *Slavery and Colonial Rule in French West Africa*, 16, 62–63, 126–27; Miers and Crowder, "The Politics of Suppression in Bechuanaland," 172–200; Roberts and Miers, " The End of Slavery in Africa," 24–25; Rashid, "Do Dady nor Lef me Make dem Carry me," 222–23.

104. Sikainga, *Slaves into Workers*, 100–103.

105. Kathleen Simon, *Slavery* (London: Hodder and Stoughton, 1930), 74–81.

106. Kiernan, *The Lords of Human Kind*, 203.

107. H. R. Fox Bourne, *Slavery and Its Substitutes in Africa* (London: Aborigines Protection Society, 1900), 13.

108. Raymond Leslie Buell, *The Native Problem in Africa*, vol. 1 (New York: Macmillan, 1928), 354–56, 658–59, 1043; vol. 2 (New York: Macmillan, 1928), 259–63, 321–25, 421–23; Hochschild, *King Leopold's Ghost*, 170–72; Jonathon Derrick, *Africa's Slaves Today* (New York: Schocken Books, 1975), 159–66; Grant, *A Civilised Savagery*,

22–24; Robert Johnson, *British Imperialism* (New York: Palgrave, 2003), 91–106; Michael Mason, "Working on the Railway: Forced Labor in Northern Nigeria, 1907–1912," Peter C. W. Gutkind, Robin Cohen, and Jean Copans, eds., *African Labor History* (Beverly Hills, Calif.: Sage, 1978), 56–79; Miers, *Slavery in the Twentieth Century*, 135–36; Northrup, "The End of Slavery in the Eastern Belgian Congo," 474–75.

109. David Killingray, "Labour Exploitation for Military Campaigns in British Colonial Africa," *Journal of Contemporary History* 24, 3 (1989): 483; David Killingray and James Mathews, "Beasts of Burden: British West African Carriers in the First World War," *Canadian Journal of African Studies* 13, 1/2 (1979): 6.

110. Killingray and Mathews, "Beasts of Burden," 10.

111. Alice L. Conklin, *A Mission to Civilize: The Republican Idea of Empire in France and West Africa, 1895–1930* (Stanford, Calif.: Stanford University Press, 1997), 143–73; Klein, *Slavery and Colonial Rule in French West Africa*, 216–19, 233–35; Killingray, "Labour Exploitation for Military Campaigns in British Colonial Africa," 490.

112. Cassanelli, "The Ending of Slavery in Italian Somalia," 310–11; Klein, *Slavery and Colonial Rule in French West Africa*, 74–75, 128–31, 152–53; Hargey, "*Festina Lente*," 253; Roberts and Miers, "The End of Slavery in Africa," 43–44; Manning, *Slavery and African Life*, 165; Rashid, "Do Dady nor Lef me Make dem Carry me," 220–21.

113. See, for example, *What Is Slavery?* (London: Anti-Slavery and Aborigines Protection Society, 1909), 5.

114. Grant, *A Civilised Savagery*, 168.

115. Cooper, *Decolonization and African Society*, 29; John Harris, *A Century of Emancipation* (London: Dent, 1933); Simon, *Slavery*, 144–72.

116. For a contemporary survey of labor abuses, see Buell, *The Native Problem in Africa*, vol. 1, 31, 34–38, 228, 241, 248–50, 373–76, 449–50, 498–500, 568–70; vol. 2, 16–22, 27–34, 236–38, 253–57, 321–31, 435–41, 502–7, 546–54, 567–76, 774–81, 818–36.

117. League of Nations, Convention to Suppress the Slave Trade and Slavery (1926 Slavery Convention), signed September 25, 1926, http://www.ohchr.org/english/law/slavery.htm.

118. ILO C29, Forced Labour Convention, adopted June 28, 1930, http://www.unhchr.ch/html/menu3/b/31.htm

119. Cooper, *Decolonization and African Society*, 29–31, 39–40.

120. See William Gervase Clarence-Smith, "Cocoa Plantations and Coerced Labor in the Gulf of Guinea, 1870–1914," in Klein, ed., *Breaking the Chains*, 150–70; Duffy, *A Question of Slavery*; Miers, *Slavery in the Twentieth Century*, 136–41.

121. Cooper, *Decolonization and African Society*, 34–35.

122. In the formative stages of colonialism, forced labor was frequently employed on an ad hoc basis, with limited reference to legal frameworks or guidelines.

123. Conklin, *A Mission to Civilize*, 212–45.

124. Cooper, *Decolonization and African Society*, 40–41.

125. For the problems with this formula, see Quirk, *Unfinished Business*, 60–62.

126. Cooper, *Decolonization and African Society*, 44; Linda M. Heywood, "Slavery

and Forced Labor in the Changing Political Economy of Central Angola, 1850-1949," in Miers and Roberts, eds., *The End of Slavery in Africa*, 428; Twaddle, "The Ending of Slavery in Buganda," 143.

127. Ibid., 34.

128. J. Orde Browne, *The African Labourer* (London: Oxford University Press, 1933), 133-200.

129. Buell, *The Native Problem in Africa*, vol. 1, 28-38, 224-33; Duffy, *A Question of Slavery*, 139-210.

130. Grant, *A Civilised Savagery*, 39-78; Hochschild, *King Leopold's Ghost*.

131. W. G. Clarence-Smith, "Labour Conditions in the Plantations of São Tomé and Príncipe, 1875-1914," in Michael Twaddle, ed., *The Wages of Slavery: From Chattel Slavery to Wage Labour in Africa, the Caribbean and England* (London: Frank Cass, 1993), 149-67.

132. Henry W. Nevinson, *A Modern Slavery* (London: Harper & Brothers, 1906), 13.

133. Duffy, *A Question of Slavery*, 168-229; Grant, *A Civilised Savagery*, 109-34.

Chapter 4. The Limits of Legal Abolition

1. Stanley Engerman, "Slavery, Serfdom and Other Forms of Coerced Labour: Similarities and Differences," in Michael Bush, ed., *Serfdom and Slavery: Studies in Legal Bondage* (New York: Longman, 1996), 38.

2. See, for example, Roger L. Ransom and Richard Sutch, *One Kind of Freedom: The Economic Consequences of Emancipation*, 2nd ed. (Cambridge: Cambridge University Press, 2001), 14-39.

3. Martin A. Klein, "Introduction: Modern European Expansion and Traditional Servitude in Africa and Asia," in Martin A. Klein, ed., *Breaking the Chains: Slavery, Bondage, and Emancipation in Modern Africa and Asia* (Madison: University of Wisconsin Press, 1993), 25; Igor Kopytoff and Suzanne Miers, "African 'Slavery' as an Institution of Marginality," in Suzanne Miers and Igor Kopytoff, eds., *Slavery in Africa: Historical and Anthropological Perspectives* (Madison: University of Wisconsin Press, 1977), 69-76.

4. See Frederick Cooper, *From Slaves to Squatters: Plantation Labor and Agriculture in Zanzibar and Coastal Kenya, 1890-1925* (New Haven, Conn.: Yale University Press, 1980), 32-40; Martin A. Klein, *Slavery and Colonial Rule in French West Africa* (Cambridge: Cambridge University Press, 1998), 66-68, 122-40, 178-79; Paul E. Lovejoy, *Transformations in Slavery: A History of Slavery in Africa*, 2nd ed. (Cambridge: Cambridge University Press, 2000), 252-54; Ahmad Alawad Sikainga, *Slaves into Workers: Emancipation and Labor in Colonial Sudan* (Austin: University of Texas Press, 1996), 37-38.

5. F. D. Lugard, *The Dual Mandate in British Tropical Africa*, 2nd ed. (London: Blackwood, 1923), 369, also 369-70, 373-74.

6. R. W. Beachey, *The Slave Trade of Eastern Africa* (London: Rex Collings, 1976), 204, 224; Robert Conrad, *The Destruction of Brazilian Slavery, 1850-1888* (Berkeley: University of California Press, 1972), 90-91; Paul E. Lovejoy and Jan S. Hogendorn, *Slow Death for Slavery: The Course of Abolition in Nigeria, 1897-1936* (Cambridge: Cam-

bridge University Press, 1993), 98; James Ferguson King, "The Latin-American Republics and the Suppression of the Slave Trade," *Hispanic American Historical Review* 24, 3 (1944): 388–89, 395, 405.

7. James Duffy, *A Question of Slavery* (Oxford: Clarendon Press, 1967), 38–39; Seymour Becker, *Russia's Protectorates in Central Asia: Bukhara and Khiva, 1865–1924* (Cambridge: Harvard University Press, 1968), 85–88, 118, 200; William A. Green, *British Slave Emancipation: The Sugar Colonies and the Great Experiment 1830–1865* (Oxford: Clarendon Press, 1976), 129–62; Willemina Kloosterboer, *Involuntary Labour Since the Abolition of Slavery* (Leiden: Brill, 1960), 33.

8. Klein, "Introduction," 20; Dharma Kumar, "Colonialism, Bondage, and Caste in British India," in Klein, ed., *Breaking the Chains*, 112–30; Lugard, *The Dual Mandate in British Tropical Africa*, 368–69; Suzanne Miers and Richard Roberts, "The End of Slavery in Africa," in Suzanne Miers and Richard Roberts, eds., *The End of Slavery in Africa* (Madison: University of Wisconsin Press, 1988), 12–13; Suzanne Miers, *Slavery in the Twentieth Century* (Walnut Creek, Calif.: Altamira Press, 2003), 30–31; Howard Temperley, *British Antislavery 1833–1870* (London: Longman, 1972), 93–110, and "The Delegalization of Slavery in British India," in Howard Temperley, ed., *After Slavery: Emancipation and Its Discontents* (London: Frank Cass, 2000), 169–87.

9. Robert Ross, "Emancipation and the Economy of the Cape Colony," in Michael Twaddle, ed., *The Wages of Slavery: From Chattel Slavery to Wage Labour in Africa, the Caribbean and England* (London: Frank Cass, 1993), 131.

10. Paul E. Lovejoy, "Slavery in the Context of Ideology," in Paul E. Lovejoy, ed., *The Ideology of Slavery in Africa* (London: Sage, 1981), 16–20.

11. Jonathan Derrick, *Africa's Slaves Today* (New York: Schocken, 1975), 65–68; Klein, *Slavery and Colonial Rule in French West Africa*, 237–51.

12. See Frederick Cooper, *Plantation Slavery on the East Coast of Africa* (New Haven, Conn.: Yale University Press, 1977), 212; Rebecca J. Scott, "Exploring the Meaning of Freedom: Postemancipation Societies in Comparative Perspective," *Hispanic American Historical Review* 68, 3 (1988): 423; Thomas J. Herlehy and Rodger F. Morton, "A Coastal Ex-Slave Community in the Regional and Colonial Economy of Kenya: The WaMisheri of Rabai, 1880–1963," in Miers and Roberts, eds., *The End of Slavery in Africa*, 256; Don Ohadike, "The Decline of Slavery Among the Igbo People," in Miers and Roberts, eds., *The End of Slavery in Africa*, 452.

13. See Moses Finley, *Ancient Slavery and Modern Ideology* (London: Chatto & Windus, 1980), 135–60; David Turley, *Slavery* (Oxford: Blackwell, 2000), 62–100.

14. See Seymour Drescher, *The Mighty Experiment: Free Labor Versus Slavery in British Emancipation* (Oxford: Oxford University Press, 2002), 10–33, 54–72, 106–20.

15. Adam Smith, *The Wealth of Nations* (London: Penguin, 1986), 488.

16. Drescher, *The Mighty Experiment*, 19–72.

17. For much of the twentieth century economic historians started with the assumption that slavery in the Americas was inflexible, inefficient, and archaic, but from the

1960s onward a very different picture of an adaptive, dynamic, and highly profitable slavery gradually moved to center stage. This picture has not yet had a major impression on popular impressions of slavery. See, for example, David Brion Davis, *Inhuman Bondage: The Rise and Fall of Slavery in the New World* (Oxford: Oxford University Press, 2006), 181–85, 240–43.

18. This is not simply a matter of overall economic productivity. In situations where former slaves were able to secure a great return on their labors following legal abolition, overall returns to former masters would fall even if productivity levels had remained fairly constant. See Ransom and Sutch, *One Kind of Freedom*, 4–7.

19. Drescher, *The Mighty Experiment*, 179–201; Thomas C. Holt, *The Problem of Freedom: Race, Labor, and Politics in Jamaica and Britain, 1832–1938* (Baltimore: Johns Hopkins University Press, 1992), 115–40.

20. Stanley Engerman, "Slavery, Freedom, and Sen," in Kwame Anthony Appiah and Martin Bunzl, eds., *Buying Freedom: The Ethics and Economics of Slave Redemption* (Princeton, N.J.: Princeton University Press, 2007), 89–93.

21. On the more general theme of land/labor ratios see Evsey D. Domar, "The Causes of Slavery or Serfdom: A Hypothesis," *Journal of Economic History* 30, 1 (1970): 18; Herman Nieboer, *Slavery as an Industrial System: Ethnological Researches*, 2nd ed. (The Hague: Nijhoff, 1910). For critiques of this line of argument, see Stanley L. Engerman, "Some Considerations Relating to Property Rights in Man," *Journal of Economic History* 33, 1 (1973): 56; Robert J. Steinfeld, *Coercion, Contract, and Free Labor in the Nineteenth Century* (Cambridge: Cambridge University Press, 2001), 29–84.

22. Steinfeld, *Coercion, Contract, and Free Labor*, 1–26.

23. Cooper, *From Slaves to Squatters*, 1.

24. A good, if somewhat unsystematic, starting point remains Kloosterboer, *Involuntary Labour Since the Abolition of Slavery*. See also O. Nigel Bolland, "Systems of Domination After Slavery: The Control of Land and Labor in the British West Indies After 1838," *Comparative Studies in Society and History* 23, 4 (1981): 594; W. G. Clarence-Smith, "Labour Conditions in the Plantations of São Tomé and Príncipe, 1875–1914," in Twaddle, ed., *The Wages of Slavery*, 151; Pete Daniel, *In the Shadow of Slavery: Peonage in the South, 1901–1969* (Urbana: University of Illinois Press, 1990), esp. 19–42, and "The Metamorphosis of Slavery, 1885–1900," *Journal of American History* 66 (1979): 88–99; Linda M. Heywood, "Slavery and Forced Labor in the Changing Political Economy of Central Angola, 1850–1949," in Miers and Roberts, eds., *The End of Slavery in Africa*, 427–29; Klein, *Slavery and Colonial Rule in French West Africa*, 178–79; Holt, *The Problem of Freedom*, 185, 202–4; Lovejoy and Hogendorn, *Slow Death for Slavery*, 85–88, 95–97; G. Ugo Nwokeji, "The Slave Emancipation Problematic: Igbo Society and the Colonial Equation," *Comparative Studies in Society and History* 40, 2 (1998): 340; Ohadike, "The Decline of Slavery Among the Igbo People," 446–47; Ross, "Emancipation and the Economy of the Cape Colony," 141–45; Michael Twaddle, "The Ending of Slavery in Buganda," in Miers and Roberts, eds., *The End of Slavery in Africa*, 143; David

Northrup, "The Ending of Slavery in the Eastern Belgian Congo," in Miers and Roberts, eds., *The End of Slavery in Africa*, 475.

25. Two notable examples here are the extensive use of indentured labor by the British government, and the Portuguese use of forced labor following the legal abolition of slavery.

26. Robert J. Steinfeld, *The Invention of Free Labor: The Employment Relation in English and American Law and Culture* (Chapel Hill: University of North Carolina Press, 1991) and *Coercion, Contract, and Free Labor in the Nineteenth Century*.

27. William Gervase Clarence-Smith, *Islam and the Abolition of Slavery* (Oxford: Oxford University Press, 2006), 74–76; Lovejoy, *Transformations in Slavery*, 4.

28. See, for example, Patrick Belser, *Forced Labour and Human Trafficking: Estimating the Profits* (Geneva: International Labour Office, 2005); Siddarth Kara, *Sex Trafficking: Inside the Business of Modern Slavery* (New York: Columbia University Press, 2009), 221–58.

29. See, for example, Edward A. Alpers, Gwyn Campbell, and Michael Salman, eds., *Slavery and Abolition, Special Issue, Slavery and Resistance in Africa and Asia* 25, 2 (2004); Ann O'Hear, *Power Relations in Nigeria: Ilorin Slaves and Their Successors* (Rochester, N.Y.: University of Rochester Press, 1997), 4–20.

30. See, for example, Richard Hart, *Slaves Who Abolished Slavery: Blacks in Rebellion* (Kingston: University of West Indies Press, 1985); C. L. R. James, *The Black Jaccobins: Toussaint L'Overture and the San Domingo Revolution* (London: Penguin, 2001).

31. See, for example, James H. Sweet, *Recreating Africa: Culture, Kinship and Religion in the African-Portuguese World* (Chapel Hill: University of North Carolina Press, 2003); Paul E. Lovejoy and David Trotman, eds., *Trans-Atlantic Dimensions of the Ethnicity in the African Diaspora* (London: Continuum, 2003).

32. Scott, "Exploring the Meaning of Freedom," 425.

33. Richard Roberts and Martin A. Klein, "The Banamba Slave Exodus of 1905 and the Decline of Slavery in the Western Sudan," *Journal of African History* 21, 3 (1980): 375; Richard Roberts, "The End of Slavery in the French Soudan, 1905–1914," in Miers and Roberts, eds., *The End of Slavery in Africa*, 282.

34. See, for example, Davis, *Inhuman Bondage*, 326; Klein, *Slavery and Colonial Rule in French West Africa*, 74–75, 129–31, 216–19, 235–36; Sikainga, *Slaves into Workers* (Austin: University of Texas Press, 1996), 60, 65, 68, 106.

35. Jan S. Hogendorn and Paul E. Lovejoy, "The Reform of Slavery in Early Colonial Northern Nigeria," in Miers and Roberts, eds., *The End of Slavery in Africa*, 398–99; Kristan Mann, "Owners, Slaves and the Struggle for Labour in the Commercial Transition at Lagos," in Robin Law, ed., *From Slave Trade to "Legitimate" Commerce: The Commercial Transition in Nineteenth Century West Africa* (Cambridge: Cambridge University Press, 1995), 153–64; Patrick Manning, *Slavery and African Life: Occidental, Oriental, and African Slave Trades* (Cambridge: Cambridge University Press, 1990), 162–63.

36. Martin A. Klein, "Slave Resistance and Slave Emancipation in Coastal Guinea," in Miers and Roberts, eds., *The End of Slavery in Africa*, 205; Clarence-Smith, "Labour

Conditions in the Plantations of São Tomé and Príncipe," 150; Rebecca J. Scott, "Defining the Boundaries of Freedom in the World of Cane: Cuba, Brazil, and Louisiana After Emancipation," *American Historical Review* 99, 1 (1994): 73, 76.

37. Holt, *The Problem of Freedom*, 64, 151–52, 170; Temperley, *British Antislavery*, 115–16.

38. Manning, *Slavery and African Life*, 163–64; O'Hear, *Power Relations in Nigeria*, 12–15, 82; Urs Peter Ruf, *Ending Slavery: Hierarchy, Dependency and Gender in Central Mauritania* (Bielefeld: Transcript Verlag, 1999), 35, 136–38; Sikainga, *Slaves into Workers*, 21–24, 51, 54–57, 83, 112–21; Richard Roberts and Suzanne Miers, "The End of Slavery in Africa," in Miers and Roberts, eds., *The End of Slavery in Africa*, 38–40.

39. See, for example, Catherine Coquery-Vidrovitch, "Women, Marriage and Slavery in Sub-Saharan Africa," in Gwyn Campbell, Suzanne Miers, and Joseph C. Miller, eds., *Women and Slavery: Africa, the Indian Ocean World, and the Medieval North Atlantic* (Athens: Ohio University Press, 2007), 43–58.

40. See Klein, *Slavery and Colonial Rule in French West Africa*, 136; Lovejoy and Hogendorn, *Slow Death for Slavery*, 111–26; Sikainga, *Slaves into Workers*, 112–21.

41. Dennis D. Cordell, "No Liberty, Not Much Equality and Very Little Fraternity: The Mirage of Manumission in the Algerian Sahara in the Second Half of the Nineteenth Century," in Suzanne Miers and Martin A. Klein, eds., *Slavery and Colonial Rule in Africa* (London: Frank Cass, 1999), 51–52; Sikainga, *Slaves into Workers*, 112–15. Eve M. Troutt Powell, *A Different Shade of Colonialism: Egypt, Great Britain, and the Mastery of the Sudan* (Berkeley: University of California Press, 2003), 1–4.

42. C. W. W. Greenidge, *Slavery* (London: Allen & Unwin, 1958), 94. See also Lugard, *The Dual Mandate in British Tropical Africa*, 385–88.

43. Greenidge, *Slavery*, 94–104; Miers, *Slavery in the Twentieth Century*, 434–35.

44. For contemporary examples, see Monika Satya Kalra, "Forced Marriage: Rwanda's Secret Revealed," *U.C. Davis Journal of International Law and Policy* 7 (2001): 197; Hannana Siddiqui, "The Ties That Bind: The New Slavery: Forced Marriage," *Index on Censorship* 29, 1 (2000): 50; Elizabeth Warner, "Behind the Wedding Veil: Child Marriage as a Form of Trafficking in Girls," *American University Journal of Gender, Social Policy and the Law* 12 (2004): 233.

45. Scott, "Exploring the Meaning of Freedom," 421.

46. See, for example, League of Nations, *Slavery: Report of the Advisory Committee of Experts*, 3rd (extraordinary) Session, League of Nations, C. 189(i).M.145. 1936.VI, Geneva, 15th May 1936, 24, *Slavery: Report of the Advisory Committee of Experts*, 2nd Session, League of Nations, C.159.M.113.1935.VI, Geneva, April 10, 1935, 10.

47. In particular, see Mohamed Awad, *Report on Slavery* (New York: United Nations, 1966); League of Nations, *Slavery: Report of the Advisory Committee of Experts*, 3rd (extraordinary) Session.

48. David Northrup, *Indentured Labor in the Age of Imperialism, 1834–1922* (Cambridge: Cambridge University Press, 1995), 4–6.

49. See Richard B. Allen, *Slaves, Freedmen and Indentured Laborers in Colonial Mau-*

ritius (Cambridge: Cambridge University Press, 1999); Marina Carter, "The Transition from Slave to Indentured Labour in Mauritius," in Twaddle, ed., *The Wages of Slavery*, 115–30; Rosemarijin Hoefte, *In Place of Slavery: A Social History of British Indian and Javanese Laborers in Suriname* (Gainesville: University Press of Florida, 1998); Evelyn Hu-Dehart, "Chinese Coolie Labour in Cuba in the Nineteenth Century: Free Labour or Neo-Slavery," in Twaddle, ed., *The Wages of Slavery*, 70–85; Arnold J. Meagher, *The Coolie Trade: The Traffic in Chinese Laborers to Latin America 1847–1874* (Philadelphia: Xlibris, 2008); Northrup, *Indentured Labor in the Age of Imperialism*, 43–79; Jane Sampson, *Imperial Benevolence: Making British Authority in the Pacific Islands* (Honolulu: University of Hawai'i Press, 1998), 115–29.

50. Northrup, *Indentured Labor in the Age of Imperialism*, 157.

51. See Duffy, *A Question of Slavery*, 21–22, 42–43, 83, 168–210; Suzanne Miers, *Britain and the Ending of the Slave Trade* (New York: Africana Press, 1975), 28–30; and *Slavery in the Twentieth Century*, 19, 48–51; Miers and Roberts, "The End of Slavery in Africa," 14–15; Northrup, *Indentured Labor in the Age of Imperialism*, 26–27, 50; Elisée Soumonni, "The Compatibility of the Slave and Palm Oil Trades in Dahomey, 1818–1858," in Law, ed., *From Slave Trade to "Legitimate" Commerce*, 86–88. The Dutch were also involved, but to a lesser extent.

52. Consul Cambell to the Earl of Malmesbury, August 2, 1858, National Archives, Kew, UK, FO 541/13.

53. See, for example, Ibrahim K. Sundiata, *From Slaving to Neoslavery: The Bight of Biafra and Fernando Po in the Era of Abolition, 1827–1930* (Madison: University of Wisconsin Press, 1996); Duffy, *A Question of Slavery*, esp. 66–68; Clarence-Smith, "Labour Conditions in the Plantations of São Tomé and Príncipe," 149–50.

54. David Eltis, "Labour and Coercion in the English Atlantic from the Seventeenth to the Early Twentieth Century," in Twaddle, ed., *The Wages of Slavery*, 211.

55. Northrup, *Indentured Labor in the Age of Imperialism*, 43–79, esp. 78.

56. Hugh Tickner, *A New System of Slavery: The Export of Indian Labour Overseas 1830–1920* (London: Oxford University Press, 1974), 117–18.

57. Northrup, *Indentured Labor in the Age of Imperialism*, 5–7, 104–13; Tickner, *A New System of Slavery*, 177.

58. Duffy, *A Question of Slavery*, 83, 97–101, 156–59, 211–12; Clarence-Smith, "Labour Conditions in the Plantations of São Tomé and Príncipe," 151, 157–60; Tickner, *A New System of Slavery*, 186–95.

59. Duffy, *A Question of Slavery*, 15–20; Tickner, *A New System of Slavery*, 220.

60. Northrup, *Indentured Labor in the Age of Imperialism*, 129–38; Nicholas Thomas, "Colonial Conversions: Difference Hierarchy, and History in Early Twentieth Century Evangelical Propaganda," *Comparative Studies in Society and History* 34, 2 (1992): 382.

61. William A. Green, "Emancipation to Indenture: A Question of Imperial Morality," *Journal of British Studies* 22, 2 (1983): 98; Meagher, *The Coolie Trade*, 274–94; Sampson, *Imperial Benevolence*, 116–22; Tickner, *A New System of Slavery*, 103.

62. Duffy, *A Question of Slavery*, 159–60; Temperley, *British Antislavery*, 124–27, 130–33; Tickner, *A New System of Slavery*, 236–39, 278.

63. There was a period directly after British emancipation in 1834 where abolitionists successfully campaigned for the trade to be halted, but they were not able to maintain this prohibition, and once the trade had been restarted it continued until the early twentieth century, with a further bout of scandals in the 1870s limiting non-British involvement in migration from India.

64. Northrup, *Indentured Labor in the Age of Imperialism*, 113–20.

65. Holt, *The Problem of Freedom*, 201.

66. Tickner, *A New System of Slavery*, 288, 314, 334–46, 374.

67. Linda M. Heywood, "Slavery and Forced Labor in the Changing Political Economy of Central Angola, 1850–1949," in Miers and Roberts, eds., *The End of Slavery in Africa*, 428; Ohadike, "The Decline of Slavery Among the Igbo People," 450; Scott, "Defining the Boundaries of Freedom in the World of Cane," 80.

68. See Green, *British Slave Emancipation*, 295–26; Rebecca J. Scott, "Fault Lines, Color Lines, and Party Lines: Race, Labor and Collective Action in Louisiana and Cuba, 1862–1912," in Frederick Cooper, Thomas C. Holt, and Rebecca J. Scott, *Beyond Slavery: Explorations of Race, Labor, and Citizenship in Postemancipation Societies* (Chapel Hill: University of North Carolina Press, 2000), 61–106, and "Defining the Boundaries of Freedom in the World of Cane," 77–78.

Chapter 5. Defining Slavery in All Its Forms

1. See, for example, Kevin Bales, *New Slavery: A Reference Handbook* (Santa Barbara, Calif.: ABC-CLIO, 2000), xiv; Gwyn Campbell, "Introduction: Slavery and Other Forms of Unfree Labour in the Indian Ocean World," in Gwyn Campbell, ed., *The Structure of Slavery in Indian Africa and Asia* (London: Frank Cass, 2004), vii–viii; Indrani Chatterjee, *Gender, Slavery and Law in Colonial India* (Oxford: Oxford University Press, 1999), 1–5.

2. Frederick Cooper, Thomas C. Holt, and Rebecca J. Scott, *Beyond Slavery: Explorations of Race, Labor, and Citizenship in Postemancipation Societies* (Chapel Hill: University of North Carolina Press, 2000), 6.

3. See, for example, Joseph C. Miller, *Slavery and Slaving in World History: A Bibliography*, vol. 1, *1900–1991*, vol. 2, *1992–1996* (New York: M.E. Sharpe, 1999). More recent editions have been published in the journal *Slavery and Abolition*.

4. Jean Allain, *The Slavery Conventions: The Travaux Préparatoires of the 1926 League of Nations Convention and the 1956 United Nations Convention* (Leiden: Nijhoff, 2008), 31. A related resolution specifically concerned with Ethiopia was not taken up.

5. See League of Nations, *The Question of Slavery*, A.18.1923.VI, Geneva, August 10, 1923, and *The Question of Slavery*, A.25.1924.VI, Geneva, August 4, 1924.

6. See Kevin Grant, *A Civilised Savagery: Britain and the New Slaveries in Africa, 1884–1926* (New York: Routledge 2005), 159–16; Suzanne Miers, *Slavery in the Twentieth Century* (Walnut Creek, Calif.: Altamira Press, 2003), 100–116; Claude Welch,

"Defining Contemporary Forms of Slavery: Updating a Venerable NGO," *Human Rights Quarterly* 31, 1 (2009): 87–89.

7. For further information on the drafting of the 1926 Convention see Allain, *The Slavery Conventions*, 31–166.

8. Jean Allain, "The Definition of Slavery in International Law," *Howard Law Journal* 52 (2009): 247.

9. Ibid., 247–51; Allain, *The Slavery Conventions*, 70–79.

10. League of Nations, Convention to Suppress the Slave Trade and Slavery (1926 Slavery Convention), signed September 25, 1926, http://www.ohchr.org/english/law/slavery.htm.

11. Allain, *The Slavery Conventions*, 12–17.

12. See ibid., 39–79, 101–24; Grant, *A Civilised Savagery*, 159–16; Miers, *Slavery in the Twentieth Century*, 121–30.

13. Orlando Patterson, *Slavery and Social Death: A Comparative Study* (Cambridge, Mass.: Harvard University Press, 1982), 21–27.

14. According to Weissbrodt and Anti-Slavery International, the "Slavery Convention covered not only domestic slavery but also the other forms of slavery listed in the Report of the Temporary Slavery Commission." While a tenuous link can be established here, there is little evidence to suggest it meant much in practice, as the 1926 Convention has been consistently understood to refer to "classical" slavery, and there were few subsequent references to this addendum until its recent rediscovery. David Weissbrodt and Anti-Slavery International, *Abolishing Slavery and Its Contemporary Forms* (New York: United Nations, 2002), 5.

15. C. W. W. Greenidge, *Slavery* (London: Allen & Unwin, 1958), 23.

16. Kathleen Simon, *Slavery* (London: Hodder and Stoughton, 1930), 4.

17. Ibid., 135.

18. Peonage is not an easy term to define. In some cases, it can be used to describe cases of debt-bondage, in others, a type of serfdom. Weissbrodt and Anti-Slavery International, *Abolishing Slavery and Its Contemporary Forms*, 11–12.

19. Simon, *Slavery*, 135–94. For an additional perspective from this period, see John Harris, *A Century of Emancipation* (London: Dent, 1933), 236–62. Unlike Simon, Harris tends to merge various categories of bondage, and he also gives substantial billing to related practices and institutions in his historical survey of the century after 1833.

20. Ibid., 135.

21. League of Nations, *Slavery*, C.618.1932.VI, 3. See also Miers, *Slavery in the Twentieth Century*, 197–232; Welch, "Defining Contemporary Forms of Slavery," 90–92.

22. Miers, *Slavery in the Twentieth Century*, 198–99.

23. *Slavery*, C.159.M.113.1935.V1, Annex 1, 23.

24. *Slavery*, C.618.1932.VI, 22 (my emphasis).

25. During the 1930s, the British Empire was disproportionately represented in League reports, thanks to the aforementioned efforts of George Maxwell.

26. For more information on these issues, see Seymour Drescher, *Abolition: A History of Slavery and Antislavery* (Cambridge: Cambridge University Press, 2009), 415–55; Joel Quirk, *Unfinished Business: A Comparative Survey of Historical and Contemporary Slavery* (Paris: UNESCO, 2009), 96–98.

27. John Harris, *Slavery Trading in China* (London: Anti-Slavery Society, 1930), and *A Century of Emancipation*, 238–40; Simon, *Slavery*, 97–114; Greenidge, *Slavery*, 105–16.

28. See Miers, *Slavery in the Twentieth Century*, 157–61, 283–86; Sarah Paddle, "The Limits of Sympathy: International Feminists and the Chinese 'Slave Girl' Campaigns of the 1920s and 1930s," *Journal of Colonialism and Colonial History* 4, 3 (2003): 1–22; Pauline Pui-Ting Poon, "The Well-Being of Purchased Female Domestic Servants (*Mui Tsai*) in Hong Kong in the Early Twentieth Century," in Gwyn Campbell, Suzanne Miers, and Joseph Miller, eds., *Children in Slavery Through the Ages* (Athens: Ohio University Press, 2009), 152–65.

29. *Slavery*, C.159.M.113.1935.V1, 9.

30. By the 1950s the only region where slavery was widely known to be legal was the Arabian peninsula. For a survey of the state of knowledge in this period see Greenidge, *Slavery*.

31. Joel Quirk, "Ending Slavery in All Its Forms: Legal Abolition and Effective Emancipation in Historical Perspective," *International Journal of Human Rights* 13, 4 (2008): 529–54.

32. Allain, *The Slavery Conventions*, 171–203; M. Cherif Bassiouni, "Enslavement as an International Crime," *New York University Journal of International Law and Politics* 23 (1991): 478–80.

33. Supplementary Convention on the Abolition of Slavery, the Slave Trade, and Institutions and Practices Similar to Slavery, 226 U.N.T.S. 3, *entered into force* April 30, 1957, http://www.ohchr.org/english/law/slavetrade.htm.

34. Ibid. (my emphasis).

35. These are defined by the Convention in the following terms: (a) Debt bondage, that is to say, the status or condition arising from a pledge by a debtor of his personal services or of those of a person under his control as security for a debt, if the value of those services as reasonably assessed is not applied towards the liquidation of the debt or the length and nature of those services are not respectively limited and defined. (b) Serfdom, that is to say, the condition or status of a tenant who is by law, custom or agreement bound to live and labour on land belonging to another person and to render some determinate service to such other person, whether for reward or not, and is not free to change his status. (c) Any institution or practice whereby: (i) A woman, without the right to refuse, is promised or given in marriage on payment of a consideration in money or in kind to her parents, guardian, family or any other person or group; or (ii) The husband of a woman, his family, or his clan, has the right to transfer her to another person for value received or otherwise; or (iii) A woman on the death of her husband is

liable to be inherited by another person. (d) Any institution or practice whereby a child or young person under the age of 18 years, is delivered by either or both of his natural parents or by his guardian to another person, whether for reward or not, with a view to the exploitation of the child or young person or of his labor.

36. On the relationship between "servitude" and "practices similar to slavery" see Jean Allain, "On the Curious Disappearance of Human Servitude from General International Law," *Journal of the History of International Law* 11 (2009): 303–32.

37. For a fuller account of these issues see Miers, *Slavery in the Twentieth Century*, 317–38.

38. Ibid., 319–20. See also William Korey, *NGOs and the Universal Declaration of Human Rights: "A Curious Grapevine"* (New York: St. Martin's, 1998), 119–21.

39. Miers, *Slavery in the Twentieth Century*, 324–25. Greenidge attributed the Peruvian government's actions to the offense caused by the publication of a report on forms of servitude in Latin America by Poblete Troncoso, a member of the Committee. C. W. W. Greenidge, *Slavery at the United Nations* (London: Headley Brothers, 1953), 10.

40. The Committee also recommended the establishment of a protocol formally transferring the 1926 Convention to the United Nations, which was duly enacted in 1953.

41. Miers, *Slavery in the Twentieth Century*, 320–22.

42. Allain, *The Slavery Conventions*, esp. 207–335, and "The Definition of Slavery in International Law," 266–73; Welch, "Defining Contemporary Forms of Slavery," 95–101.

43. Patrick Montgomery, *The Anti-Slavery Society in 1973* (London: Anti-Slavery Society, 1973), 1.

44. Mohammed Awad, *Report on Slavery* (New York: United Nations, 1966). For an earlier version, see Mohammed Awad, *Slavery: Report of the Special Rapporteur on Slavery Appointed Under Council Resolution 960*, United Nations, Economic and Social Council, E/4056, May 27, 1965.

45. This was by no means the only forum available to address these major political issues during this period. See, for example, Audie Klotz, *Norms in International Relations: The Struggle Against Apartheid* (Ithaca, N.Y.: Cornell University Press, 1995), 39–54.

46. Benjamin Whitaker, *Slavery: Report Prepared by Benjamin Whitaker, Special Rapporteur of the Sub-Commission on Prevention of Discrimination and Protection of Minorities, Updating the Report on Slavery Submitted to the Sub-Commission in 1966*, United Nations, Economic and Social Council, E/CN/Sub.2/1982?20/Rev.1, 1982, 10. See also Jean Allain, "The Legal Regime of Slavery and Its Obfuscation by the Term of Art: 'Slavery-Like Practice,'" paper on file with author.

47. There is some ambiguity here, in that references to the "slavery-like practices of apartheid and colonialism" have included both general statements about the nature of political authority and more specific statements concerned with specific labor practices occurring under these regimes. See Whitaker, *Slavery*, 10–11; Roger Sawyer, *Slavery in the Twentieth Century* (London: Routledge, 1986), 53–76.

48. Working Group on Slavery, *Report of the Working Group on Slavery on Its First Session*, United Nations Economic and Social Council, E/CN.4/Sub.2/AC.2/3, August 28, 1975, 4.

49. Ibid.

50. Ibid.

51. Working Group on Contemporary Forms of Slavery, *Report of the Working Group on Contemporary Forms of Slavery on Its Thirteenth Session*, United Nations Economic and Social Council, E/CN.4/Sub.2/1988/32, August 22, 1988, 5.

52. Kevin Bales, *Ending Slavery: How We Free Today's Slaves* (Berkeley: University of California Press, 2007), 142–43; Welch, "Defining Contemporary Forms of Slavery," 115–21.

53. This has recently evolved into the UN Voluntary Fund on Contemporary Forms of Slavery.

54. Welch, "Defining Contemporary Forms of Slavery," 125–26.

55. Working Group on Slavery, *Report of the Working Group on Slavery on Its Twelfth Session*, United Nations Economic and Social Council, E/CN.4/Sub.2/1987/25, August 28, 1987, 26.

56. Working Group on Slavery, *Report of the Working Group on Slavery on Its Ninth Session*, United Nations Economic and Social Council, E/CN.4/Sub.2/1983/27/Corn.1, August 21, 1983, 11.

57. See, for example, Kevin Bales, "Throwaway People," *Index on Censorship* 29/1 (2000): 36–45; Gary E. McCuen, ed., *Modern Slavery and the Global Economy* (Hudson, Wis.: Gary E. McCuen, 1998); Andrew Cockburn, "21st Century Slaves," *National Geographic* 204, 3 (September 2003): 2–26; Christien van den Anker, ed., *The Political Economy of the New Slavery* (Hampshire: Palgrave, 2004).

58. Ole Wæver, "Securitization and Desecuritization," in Ronnie Lipscutz, ed., *On Security* (New York: Columbia University Press, 1995), 65.

59. UN Secretary General, *Question of Slavery and the Slave Trade in All Their Practices and Manifestations, Including the Slavery-Like Practices of Apartheid and Colonialism: Statement Submitted by the Following Non-Governmental Organizations in Consultative Status with the Economic and Social Council, Category II*, E/CN.4/Sub.2/NGO.47, August 15, 1972, 2. See also Benjamin Whitaker, *Updating of the Report on Slavery Submitted to the Sub-Commission in 1966: Report by Mr. Benjamin Whitaker, Special Rapporteur*, E/CN.4/Sub.2/1982/20/add.1, July 7, 1982, 18.

60. This practice dates back at least as far as the Ancient Greeks, who "used the term 'slavery' to describe the tyrannical governments of their neighbors." David Brion Davis, *The Problem of Slavery in Western Culture* (Ithaca, N.Y.: Cornell University Press, 1966), 69.

61. See Eric Foner, "The Meaning of Freedom in the Age of Emancipation," *Journal of American History* 81, 2 (1994): 440–51; David Roediger, "Race, Labor and Gender in the Languages of Antebellum Social Protest," in Stanley L. Engerman, ed., *Terms of Labor: Slavery, Serfdom, and Free Labor* (Stanford, Calif.: Stanford University Press, 1999), 168.

62. John Boli and George Thomas, "INGOs and the Organization of World Cut-lure," in John Boli and George Thomas, eds., *Constructing World Culture: International Nongovernmental Organizations Since 1875* (Stanford, Calif.: Stanford University Press, 1999), 20–48; Thomas Risse and Kathryn Sikkink, "The Socialization of International Human Rights Norms into Domestic Practices: Introduction," in Thomas Risse, Stephen Ropp, and Kathryn Sikkink, eds., *The Power of Human Rights: International Norms and Domestic Change* (Cambridge: Cambridge University Press, 1999), 19–22.

63. Clifford Bob, *The Marketing of Rebellion: Insurgents, Media and International Activism* (Cambridge: Cambridge University Press, 2005), 14–53; Welch, "Defining Contemporary Forms of Slavery," 112–14.

64. For a useful survey of recent developments, see Bales, *Ending Slavery*.

65. See Jean Allain, "Clarifying the Definition of 'Slavery' in International Law," *Melbourne Journal of International Law* 10, 1 (2009): 246–57, and "*Rantsev v. Cyprus and Russia*: The European Court of Human Rights and Trafficking as Slavery," *Human Rights Law Review* 10, 3 (2010): 546–57; Helen Duffy, "*Hadijatou Mani Koraou v. Niger*: Slavery Unveiled by the ECOWAS Court," *Human Rights Law Review* 9, 1 (2009): 151–70.

66. See, for example, Anker, *The Political Economy of the New Slavery*; Gilbert King, *Women, Child for Sale: The New Slave Trade in the 21st Century* (New York: Chamberlain, 2004); *Ethan B. Kapstein*, "The New Global Slave Trade," *Foreign Affairs* 85, 6 (2006): 103–15.

67. Kevin Bales, *Disposable People: New Slavery in the Global Economy* (Berkeley: University of California Press, 1999), 12. Variations in these categories also appear in Bales's more recent work. See Kevin Bales, Zoe Trodd, Alex Kent Williamson, *Modern Slavery: The Secret World of 27 Million People* (Oxford: One World, 2009), 27–34.

68. Claude Meillassoux, *The Anthropology of Slavery: The Womb of Iron and Gold* (London: Athlone, 1991).

69. Richard Hellie, *Slavery in Russia 1450–1725* (Chicago: University of Chicago Press, 1982).

70. The one notable exception here is Mauritania, where Bales briefly discusses the failure to end slavery under French colonial rule. This lack of engagement with the history of slavery outside the Americas is a common feature of recent works. See Joel Quirk, "Uncomfortable Silences: Contemporary Slavery and the 'Lessons' of History," in Alison Brysk and Austin Choi-Fitzpatrick, eds., *Human Trafficking and Human Rights: Rethinking Contemporary Slavery* (Philadelphia: University of Pennsylvania Press, forthcoming).

71. Bales, *Disposable People*, 19–20.

72. Grant, *A Civilised Savagery*, 1–37. Other examples include Roger N. Baldwin, ed., *A New Slavery: Forced Labor: The Communist Betrayal of Human Rights* (New York: Oceana, 1953), Henry Nevinson, *A Modern Slavery* (London: Harper, 1906).

73. Kevin Bales, *Understanding Global Slavery: A Reader* (Berkeley: University of California Press, 2005), 91. This definition of slavery is held to be equally applicable to both historical and contemporary slavery, but it does not deal adequately with (among

other things) the noncommercial functions slaves performed in many historical slave systems.

74. Bales, *Disposable People*, 5.

75. Bales, *Understanding Global Slavery*, 183–86.

76. In *Disposable People*, the figure given for the subcontinent was 15 to 20 million. While Bales has retained his overall figure of 27 million, different estimates for individual countries and regions have appeared in his published works at various points over the last decade.

Chapter 6. "Classical" Slavery and Descent-Based Discrimination

1. C. W. W Greenidge, *Slavery To-Day: Measures for Its Abolition* (London: Anti-Slavery Society, 1948), 5.

2. Further examples of anecdotal claims include Benjamin Whitaker, *Updating of the Report on Slavery Submitted to the Sub-Commission in 1966: Report by Mr. Benjamin Whitaker, Special Rapporteur*, E/CN.4/Sub.2/1982/20/add.1, July 7, 1982; Ronald Segal, *Islam's Black Slaves: A History of Africa's Other Black Diaspora* (London: Atlantic, 2001), 199–204; John Laffin, *The Arabs as Master Slavers* (Englewood, N.J.: SBS, 1982), 5–7.

3. E. Ann McDougal, "The Practice of *Rachat* in French West Africa," in Kwame Anthony Appiah and Martin Bunzl, eds., *Buying Freedom: The Ethics and Economics of Slave Redemption* (Princeton, N.J.: Princeton University Press, 2007), 169. See also Robert Maughum, *The Slaves of Timbuktu* (London: Longman, Greeno, 1961), esp. 174–77, 201–7, 217–20.

4. UN Secretary General, *Question of Slavery and the Slave Trade in All Their Practices and Manifestations, Including the Slavery-Like Practices of Apartheid and Colonialism. Note by the Secretary-General. Annex II. Reply Received from the International Criminal Police Organization (Interpol)*, E/CN.4/Sub.2/XXV/CRP.1, August 8, 1972, 2.

5. Roger Sawyer, *Slavery in the Twentieth Century* (London: Routledge, 1986), 27.

6. Anti-Slavery Society, *United Nations Commission of Human Rights: Statement on Behalf of the Anti-Slavery Society for the Protection of Human Rights*, March 7, 1968, 1, National Archives, Kew, United Kingdom, FCO 61/220.

7. "'Lamentable' Record of UN on Slavery," *The Guardian*, January 12, 1968, 4; Suzanne Miers, *Slavery in the Twentieth Century* (Walnut Creek, Calif.: Altamira Press, 2003), 375.

8. Sawyer, *Slavery in the Twentieth Century*, 14.

9. Anti-Slavery Society, *The Anti-Slavery Society: Its Task Today* (London: Headley Brothers, 1966), 1–24.

10. Anti-Slavery Society, *Statement on Behalf of the Anti-Slavery Society*, 3.

11. Martin A. Klein, *Slavery and Colonial Rule in French West Africa* (Cambridge: Cambridge University Press, 1998), 194. David Seddon also cites a 200,000 figure, but for Mauritania alone. David Seddon, "Unfinished Business: Slavery in Saharan Africa," in Howard Temperley, ed., *After Slavery: Emancipation and Its Discontents* (London: Frank Cass, 2000), 228.

12. Jonathon Derrick, *Africa's Slaves Today* (New York: Schocken, 1975), 16.

13. Ibid., 21.

14. Ibid., 30.

15. Ibid., 80.

16. Seddon, "Unfinished Business," 228.

17. See Janet Hoskins, "Slaves, Brides and Other 'Gifts': Resistance, Marriage and Rank in Eastern Indonesia," *Slavery and Abolition*, Special Issue, *Slavery and Resistance in Africa and Asia* 25, 2 (2004): 92, 96–106; Klein, *Slavery and Colonial Rule in French West Africa*, 237–51; Paul E. Lovejoy and Jan S. Hogendorn, *Slow Death for Slavery: The Course of Abolition in Nigeria, 1897–1936* (Cambridge: Cambridge University Press, 1993), 30, 262; Claude Meillassoux, *The Anthropology of Slavery: The Womb of Iron and Gold* (London: Athlone, 1991), 66, 120, 318; Don C. Ohadike, "When the Slaves Left, Owners Wept: Entrepreneurs and Emancipation Among the Igbo People," in Suzanne Miers and Martin A. Klein, eds., *Slavery and Colonial Rule in Africa* (London: Frank Cass, 1999), 202–3; Ahmad Alawad Sikainga, *Slaves into Workers: Emancipation and Labor in Colonial Sudan* (Austin: University of Texas Press, 1996), 166–72, 187; Amendra Kumar Thakur, *Slavery in Arunachal Pradesh* (New Delhi: Mittal Publications, 2003), 102–7, 150–66.

18. Klein, *Slavery and Colonial Rule in French West Africa*, 238.

19. Martin A. Klein, "Slave Descent and Social Status in Sahara and Sudan," in Benedetta Rossi, ed., *Reconfiguring Slavery: West African Trajectories* (Liverpool: University of Liverpool Press, 2009), 26.

20. Ibid., 41.

21. See, for example, chaps. 5–9 in Rossi, ed., *Reconfiguring Slavery*; Baz Lecocq, "The Bellah Question: Slave Emancipation, Race, and Social Categories in Late Twentieth Century Northern Mali," *Canadian Journal of African Studies* 39, 1 (2005): 42–67; Mirjam de Bruijn and Lotte Pelckmans, "Facing Dilemmas: Former Fulbe Slaves in Modern Mali," *Canadian Journal of African Studies* 39, 1 (2005): 69–95; Catherine Ver-Eecke, "The Slave Experience in Adamawa: Past and Present Perspectives from Yola (Nigeria)," *Cahiers d'Études Africaines* 34, 133–35 (1994): 23–53.

22. Samuel Cotton, *Silent Terror: A Journey into Contemporary African Slavery* (New York: Harlem River Press, 1998), 30–31; Amnesty International, *Mauritania: A Future Free from Slavery?* (London: Amnesty International, 2002), 5, http://web.amnesty.org/library/pdf/AFR380032002ENGLISH/$File/AFR3800302.pdf.

23. Zekeria Ould Ahmed Salem, "Bare-Foot Activists: Transformations in the Haratine Movement in Mauritania," in Stephen Ellis and Ineke van Kessel, eds., *Movers and Shakers: Social Movements in Africa* (Leiden: Brill, 2009), 164–66.

24. John Mercer, *Slavery in Mauritania Today* (Edinburgh: Human Rights Group, 1982), 10–12; Sawyer, *Slavery in the Twentieth Century*, 22–23.

25. See Martin A. Klein, "Slavery and French Rule in the Sahara," in Miers and Klein, eds., *Slavery and Colonial Rule in Africa*, 82–85; E. Ann McDougall, "A Topsy-Turvy World: Slaves and Freed Slaves in the Mauritanian Adrar, 1910–1950," in Suzanne

Miers and Richard Roberts, eds., *The End of Slavery in Africa* (Madison: University of Wisconsin Press, 1988).

26. Abdel Wedoud Ould Cheikh, cited in Klein, "Slavery and French Rule in the Sahara," 73.

27. Klein, "Slavery and French Rule in the Sahara," 80–82; McDougal, "The Practice of *Rachat* in French West Africa," 166–76.

28. Ron Parker, "The Senegal-Mauritania Conflict of 1989: A Fragile Equilibrium," *Journal of Modern African Studies* 29, 1 (1991): 155; Anthony G. Pazzanita, "Mauritania's Foreign Policy: The Search for Protection," *Journal of Modern African Studies* 30, 2 (1992): 281; Janet Fleischman, *Mauritania's Campaign of Terror: State-Sponsored Repression of Black Africans* (New York: Human Rights Watch/Africa, 1994).

29. Philip D. Curtin, "Jihad in West Africa: Early Phases and Inter-Relations in Mauritania and Senegal," *Journal of African History* 12, 1 (1971): 11; Raymond M. Taylor, "Warriors, Tributaries, Blood Money and Political Transformation in Nineteenth-Century Mauritania," *Journal of African History* 36, 3 (1995): 419.

30. Mercer, *Slavery in Mauritania Today*, 7–8; Sawyer, *Slavery in the Twentieth Century*, 19.

31. Urs Peter Ruf, *Ending Slavery: Hierarchy, Dependency and Gender in Central Mauritania* (Bielefeld: Transcript Verlag, 1999), 9; Salem, "Bare-Foot Activists," 158–59; *SOS-Slavery, Report Year 2001*, 4–5, www.liberationafrique.org/IMG/doc/SOS_Esclaves _rap01_Angl.doc.

32. Mercer, *Slavery in Mauritania Today*, 1.

33. Kevin Bales, *Understanding Global Slavery: A Reader* (Berkeley: University of California Press, 2005), 185.

34. This figure appears in Elinor Burkett, "God Created Me to Be a Slave," *New York Times Magazine*, October 12, 1997; Cotton, *Silent Terror*, 131–34; David Hecht, "Virtual Slavery," *New Republic*, May 12, 1997; American Anti-Slavery Group, *Slavery Today: The Global Tragedy* (Boston: American Anti-Slavery Group, 2000), 14–15; *SOS-Slavery, Report Year 2001*, 5. Walter E. Williams, "Black Slavery Survives," *Human Events* 57, 3 (January 22, 2001). In many cases, the 90,000 figure has been reproduced without any of its original qualifications.

35. The 2004 Trafficking in Persons report states that "Although slavery was officially outlawed in 1980, vestiges of slavery remain, particularly in remote areas of the country, flowing from ancestral master-slave relationships inherited from one generation to the next. This relationship, though one of unequal status, can be likened, at times, to that of family, with the physical needs of the slave provided for, even into old age, in exchange for work performed. Instances of traditional slavery—defined as not receiving payment for work performed and being prohibited from leaving one's situation—reportedly exist, but are becoming less frequent as the population becomes increasingly less nomadic and more urbanized." U.S. Department of State, *Trafficking in Persons Report, June 2004*, 66, http://www.state.gov/documents/organization/34158.pdf.

36. Mark Bossuyt, *Slavery and Slave-Like Practices: Question of Slavery and the Slave

Trade in all their Practices and Manifestations, Including the Slavery-Like Practices of Apartheid and Colonialism, Report of the Mission to Mauritania, E/CN.4/sub.2/1984/23, July 2, 1984, 8.

37. American Anti-Slavery Group, *Slavery Today: The Global Tragedy*, 14.

38. Kevin Bales, *Disposable People: New Slavery in the Global Economy* (Berkeley: University of California Press, 1999), 86; Fleischman, *Mauritania's Campaign of Terror*, 85, *SOS-Slavery, Report Year 2001*, 5.

39. Burkett, "God Created Me to Be a Slave," 56. A similar story is recounted in Elizabeth Bryant, "Faces of Globalization: Mauritania Slavery," *Washington Times*, August 27, 2004.

40. Cotton, *Silent Terror*, 118–19.

41. Bossuyt, *Slavery and Slave-Like Practices*, 6.

42. Anti-Slavery International, *Slavery in Mauritania: Report on Field Research* (London: Anti-Slavery International, 1992), 1.

43. Bales, *Disposable People*, 107.

44. Ruf, *Ending Slavery*, 78.

45. Salem, "Bare-Foot Activists," 173–77.

46. Ibid., 10.

47. Alongside this theme is the ever-present language of race. See Chris Simpson, "Mauritania's Victims of the Race Divide," *BBC News*, August 29, 2001, http://news.bbc.co.uk/2/hi/africa/1515054.stm.

48. Human Rights Watch, *Caste Discrimination; A Global Concern: A Report by Human Rights Watch for the United Nations World Conference Against Racism, Racial Discrimination, Xenophobia and Related Intolerance, Durban, South Africa, September 2001* (New York: Human Rights Watch, 2001), http://www.hrw.org/reports/2001/globalcaste/caste0801-03.htm#P131_16327.

49. Hecht, "Virtual Slavery."

50. *Mauritania: A Future Free From Slavery?* 39.

51. Garba Diallo, "Mauritania: The Other Apartheid?" *Current African Issues* 16 (Nordiska Afrikainstitutet, 1993), 6–48.

52. "Independent UN Expert Urges Mauritania to do More to end Slavery Practices," November 4, 2009, UN News Desk, http://www.un.org/apps/news/story.asp?NewsID=32836&Cr=slavery&Cr1

53. Burkett, "God Created Me to Be a Slave," 57.

54. See, for example, Cotton, *Silent Terror*; Segal, *Islam's Black Slaves*; E. Benjamin Skinner, *A Crime So Monstrous* (Edinburgh: Mainstream Publishing, 2008), 128.

55. Galy Kadir Abdelkader, ed., *Slavery in Niger: Historical, Legal and Contemporary Perspectives* (London: Anti-Slavery International & Association Timidira, 2004), http://www.antislavery.org/homepage/resources/PDF/Full%20English%20Slavery%20in%20Niger.pdf.

56. Ali R. Sékou and Saidou Abdoulkarimou, "The Legacy of Slavery in Niger," in Beate Andreas and Patrick Belser, eds., *Forced Labor: Coercion and Exploitation in the Private Economy* (Boulder, Colo.: Lynne Reinner, 2009), 78, 86.

57. Ibid., 88.

58. Sékou and Abdoulkarimou, "The Legacy of Slavery in Niger," 74. See also "Still with Us," *Economist*, March 9, 2005; "Testimony: Former Niger Slave," *BBC News*, November 3, 2004, http://news.bbc.co.uk/1/hi/world/africa/3972669.stm.

59. "Drama as Niger Slaves Are Freed," *BBC News*, December 19, 2003, http://news .bbc.co.uk/1/hi/world/africa/3334099.stm.

60. "Niger Cancels 'Free-Slave' Event," *BBC News*, March 5, 2005, http://news.bbc. co.uk/1/hi/world/africa/4321699.stm.

61. Jeevan Vasagar, "Cry Freedom, Quietly," *The Guardian*, May 10, 2005, http:// www.guardian.co.uk/elsewhere/journalist/story/0,1480553,00.html.

62. Sékou and Abdoulkarimou, "The Legacy of Slavery in Niger," 75; "March to Free Niger's Slave Pair," *BBC News*, May 19, 2005, http://news.bbc.co.uk/1/hi/world/ africa/4562219.stm.

63. See Jean Allain, Case Note: *Mani v. Niger, American Journal of International Law*, 103, 2, (2009): 311–16; Helen Duffy, '*Hadijatou Mani Koraou v. Niger*: Slavery Unveiled by the ECOWAS Court," *Human Rights Law Review* 9, 1 (2009): 155.

64. International Labour Office, *A Global Alliance Against Forced Labour, Global Report Under the Follow-up to the ILO Declaration on Fundamental Principles and Rights at Work* (Geneva: International Labour Office, 2005), 42–44, http://www.ilo.org/dyn/ declaris/DECLARATIONWEB.DOWNLOAD_BLOB?Var_DocumentID=5059, 43.

65. Ibid., 42.

66. Ibid., 43.

67. Patrick Manning, *Slavery and African Life: Occidental, Oriental, and African Slave Trades* (Cambridge: Cambridge University Press, 1990).

68. *Abducted and Abused: Renewed Conflict in Northern Uganda* (New York: Human Rights Watch/Africa, 2003), http://www.hrw.org/reports/2003/uganda0703/ uganda0703.pdf; *Uganda, "Breaking God's Commands": The Destruction of Childhood by the Lord's Resistance Army* (New York: Amnesty International, 1997); Louise Taylor, *"We'll Kill You if You Cry": Sexual Violence in the Sierra Leone Conflict* (New York: Human Rights Watch, 2003), http://hrw.org/reports/2003/sierraleone/sierleon0103.pdf; Randall Fegley, "Bound to Violence: Uganda's Child Soldiers as Slaves," in Jay Spaulding and Stephanie Beswick, eds., *African Systems of Slavery* (Trenton: Africa World Press, 2010), 203–28; Human Rights Watch, *"The Guns Are in the Bushes": Continuing Abuses in Liberia, A Human Rights Watch Briefing Paper* (New York: Human Rights Watch, 2003), http://hrw.org/backgrounder/africa/liberia0104.pdf.

69. The issue of slave soldiers in the Sudan is explored by Douglass H. Johnson, "Sudanese Military Slavery from the Eighteenth to the Twentieth Century," in Léone Archer, ed., *Slavery and Other Forms of Unfree Labour* (London: Routledge, 1988), 142–56.

70. See Mansour Khalid, *War and Peace in Sudan: A Tale of Two Countries* (London: Kegan Paul, 2003), 133–61; Ann Mosely Lesch, *Sudan: Contested National Identities* (Bloomington: Indiana University Press, 1998), 45–58.

71. Millard Burr, *Working Document II: Quantifying Genocide in Southern Sudan*

and the Nuba Mountains 1983–1998, U.S. Committee for Refugees, December 1998, http://www.refugees.org/news/crisis/sudan.pdf.

72. U.S. Department of State, *Slavery, Abduction and Forced Servitude in Sudan, Report of the International Eminent Persons Group* (Washington, D.C.: U.S. Department of State, Bureau of African Affairs, 2002), www.state.gov/p/af/rls/rpt/10445.htm, 10. In December 2001 the government of Sudan and the SPLA agreed to receive a visit by an international mission to investigate slavery and forced servitude. The group was comprised of experts from France, Italy, Norway, the UK, and the United States.

73. *God, Oil and Country: Changing the Logic of War in Sudan* (Brussels: International Crisis Group Press, 2002); Jok Madut Jok, *Sudan: Race, Religion, and Violence* (Oxford: Oneworld, 2007), 185–211.

74. Human Rights Watch, *Civilian Devastation, Abuses by All Parties in the War in Southern Sudan* (New York: Human Rights Watch/Africa, 1993), http://www.hrw.org/reports/1993/sudan/; U.S. Department of State, *Slavery, Abduction and Forced Servitude in Sudan*, 9. This point is also highlighted by David Hoile, "Sudan, Propaganda and Distortion: Allegations of Slavery and Slavery-Related Practices: An Open Letter to Baroness Cox and Christian Solidarity International," Politics File, 5 (London: Sudan Foundation, 1997), 1–10.

75. Jok Madut Jok, *War and Slavery in Sudan* (Philadelphia: University of Pennsylvania Press, 2001), 2–5, 12; Richard Lobban, "Slavery in the Sudan Since 1989," *Arab Studies Quarterly* 23, 2 (2001): 32; U.S. Department of State, *Slavery, Abduction and Forced Servitude in Sudan*, 8, 18, 21.

76. A depressing catalogue of these issues is provided in a series of UN missions. See, for example, Emmanuel Akwei Addo, *Report of the Independent Expert on the Situation of Human Rights in the Sudan*, E/CN.4/2005/11, February 28, 2005; Gerhart Baum, *Situation of Human Rights in the Sudan: Report of the Special Rapporteur*, E/CN.4/2003/42, January 6, 2003; Gerhart Baum, *Situation of Human Rights in the Sudan: Report of the Special Rapporteur*, E/CN.4/2002/46, January 23, 2002; Gáspár Bíró, *Situation of Human Rights in the Sudan: Report of the Special Rapporteur*, E/CN.4/1997/58, February 3, 1997; Gáspár Bíró, *Situation of Human Rights in the Sudan: Report of the Special Rapporteur*, E/CN.4/1998/66, January 30, 1998.

77. Human Rights Watch, *Children in Sudan: Slaves, Street Children and Child Soldiers* (New York: Human Rights Watch/Africa, 1995), http://www.hrw.org/reports/1995/Sudan.htm.

78. *Sudan: Who Will Answer for the Crimes?* (New York: Amnesty International, 2005), http://web.amnesty.org/library/pdf/AFR540062005ENGLISH/$File/AFR5400605.pdf.

79. Amir H. Idris, *Sudan's Civil War: Slavery, Race and Formational Identities* (Lewiston, N.Y.: Edwin Mellen Press, 2001).

80. Lesch, *Sudan*, 15–21.

81. Khalid, *War and Peace in Sudan*, 4–16; Alice Moore-Harell, "Economic and Po-

litical Aspects of the Slave Trade in Ethiopia and the Sudan in the Second Half of the Nineteenth Century," *International Journal of African Historical Studies* 32, 2/3 (1999): 407; Sikainga, *Slaves into Workers*, 1–35.

82. This does not mean, however, that the Egyptian role was irrelevant. See Eve M. Troutt Powell, *A Different Shade of Colonialism: Egypt, Great Britain, and the Mastery of the Sudan* (Berkeley: University of California Press, 2003).

83. Khalid, *War and Peace in Sudan*, 18–23.

84. Lesch, *Sudan*, 32.

85. Jok, *War and Slavery in Sudan*, 90–98; Idris, *Sudan's Civil War*, 54–71; Sikainga, *Slaves into Workers*, 65–71.

86. Taj Hargey, "*Festina Lente*: Slavery Policy and Practice in the Anglo-Egyptian Sudan," in Miers and Klein, eds., *Slavery and Colonial Rule in Africa*, 255–67.

87. Khalid, *War and Peace in Sudan*, 41–60.

88. Idris, *Sudan's Civil War*, 20–26.

89. Jok, *Sudan*, 49–80.

90. Khalid, *War and Peace in Sudan*, 281–313.

91. Jok, *War and Slavery in Sudan*, 21.

92. A useful synopsis is provided by Peter Verney, *Slavery in Sudan* (London: Sudan Update and Anti-Slavery International, 1997).

93. Francis Bok and Edward Tivnan, *Escape from Slavery, The True Story of My Ten Years in Captivity: And My Journey to Freedom in America* (New York: St. Martin's Press, 2003); Mende Nazer and Damien Lewis, *Slave: The True Story of a Girl's Lost Childhood and Her Fight for Survival* (London: Virago Press, 2004).

94. This in turn reflects the larger importance attached to Sudanese politics among religious groups in the United States. See Allen D. Hertzke, *Freeing God's Children: The Unlikely Alliance for Global Human Rights* (Lantham, Md.: Rowman & Littlefield, 2004), 237–300.

95. Jok Madut Jok, "Slavery and Slave Redemption in Sudan," in Kwame Appiah and Martin Bunzl, eds., *Buying Freedom: The Ethics and Economics of Slave Redemption* (Princeton, N.J.: Princeton University Press, 2007), 143–47.

96. See Human Rights Watch, *Slavery and Slave Redemption in the Sudan, Human Rights Watch Backgrounder* (New York: Human Rights Watch, 2002), http://www.hrw.org/backgrounder/africa/sudanupdate.htm; Richard Miniter, "The False Promise of Slave Redemption," *Atlantic Monthly* (July 1999): 63–70; Peter Verney, "Redemption by Numbers," *Index on Censorship* 1 (2000), 60–64; Mike Dotteridge, "Dollars and Sense," *New Internationalist: The Burden of Slavery* 333 (2001): 16; Declan Walsh, "Scam in Sudan: An Elaborate Hoax Involving Fake African Slaves and Less-Than-Honest Interpreters Is Duping Concerned Westerners," *Independent*, February 24, 2002, http://news.independent.co.uk/World/Africa/story.jsp?story=139416.

97. U.S. Department of State, *Slavery, Abduction and Forced Servitude in Sudan*, 41–42. See also Hertzke, *Freeing God's Children*, 250–57.

98. Anti-Slavery International, *Is There Slavery in Sudan?* (London: Anti-Slavery International, 2001), 7, http://www.antislavery.org/homepage/resources/isthereslavery-insudanreport.pdf; Skinner, *A Crime So Monstrous*, 112–18.

99. Rift Valley Institute, *The Sudan Abduction and Slavery Project*, Rift Valley Institute, http://www.riftvalley.net/?view=abductee. See also Jok, "Slavery and Slave Redemption in Sudan," 152–53, and "Appendix: 'They Call Us Animals, Testimonials of Abductees and Slaves and Sudan," in Appiah and Bunzl, eds., *Buying Freedom*, 258–67.

100. "Forced Labour and Slavery in Sudan," Submission to the Working Group on Contemporary Forms of Slavery (London: Anti-Slavery International, 2003), http://www.antislavery.org/archive/submission/submission2003–sudan.htm; U.S. Department of State, *Slavery, Abduction and Forced Servitude in Sudan*, 29–32.

101. According to Jok, slave raiding ending in 2001, but some other reports speak of later raids. Jok, "Slavery and Slave Redemption in Sudan," 150.

102. Sudan Comprehensive Peace Agreement (CPA), January 9, 2005, Institute for Security Studies, http://www.iss.org.za/AF/profiles/Sudan/darfur/cpaprov.htm.

103. Jok, "Slavery and Slave Redemption in Sudan," 150–57; Skinner, *A Crime So Monstrous*, 122–29.

104. Darfur Consortium, *Abductions, Sexual Slavery and Forced Labour in Darfur* (Kampala: Darfur Consortium, 2009), 3, http://www.antislavery.org/includes/documents/cm_docs/2009/d/darfur.pdf.

105. J. Millard Burr and Robert O. Collins, *Africa's Thirty Years War: Libya, Chad and the Sudan, 1963–1993* (Oxford: Westview Press, 1999), 55–73, 190–206, 232–51; R. S. O'Fahey, *State and Society in Dār Fūr* (London: Hurst, 1980), esp. 8–13.

106. Jok, *Sudan*, 115–55.

107. See Human Rights Watch, *Darfur Destroyed: Ethnic Cleansing by Government and Militia Forces in Western Sudan* (New York: Human Rights Watch, 2004), http://hrw.org/reports/2004/sudan0504/sudan0504.pdf.

108. See Amnesty International, *Darfur: Rape as a Weapon of War: Sexual Violence and Its Consequences* (London: Amnesty International, 2004), http://web.amnesty.org/library/pdf/AFR540762004ENGLISH/$File/AFR5407604.pdf; Médecins sans Frontières, *The Crushing Burden of Rape: Sexual Violence in Darfur* (Médecins sans Frontières, 2005), http://www.artsenzondergrenzen.nl/usermedia/files/Report%20Sexual%20Violence%20march%202005.pdf; Human Rights Watch, *Sexual Violence and Its Consequences Among Displaced Persons in Darfur and Chad* (New York: Human Rights Watch, 2005), http://hrw.org/backgrounder/africa/darfur0505/darfur0405.pdf.

109. *Abductions, Sexual Slavery and Forced Labour in Darfur*, Mike Pflanz, "Darfur Civilians Seized as Slaves by Sudan," *The Telegraph*, December 16, 2008, military'http://www.telegraph.co.uk/news/worldnews/africaandindianocean/sudan/3795607/Darfur-civilians-seized-as-slaves-by-Sudan-military.html.

110. Alex Maroya, "Rethinking the Nation-State from the Frontier," *Millennium* 32, 2 (2003): 267.

111. In recent times, the Mauritanian government has repeatedly prosecuted anti-

slavery activists for tarnishing its international reputation. See, for example, Bryant, "Faces of Globalization: Mauritania Slavery"; Amnesty International, *Mauritania: A Future Free from Slavery?* 2–3.

Chapter 7. Slaves to Debt

1. International Labour Conference, *Stopping Forced Labour, Global Report Under the Follow-up to the ILO Declaration on Fundamental Principles and Rights at Work*, International Labour Conference, 89th Session, 2001, 32, http://www.ilo.org/dyn/declaris/DECLARATIONWEB.DOWNLOAD_BLOB?Var_DocumentID=1578.

2. See Judith Spicksley "Debt and Enslavement: Towards an Understanding of the Relationship," paper presented at Debt and Slavery, Indian Ocean World Centre, McGill University, Montreal, May 9–11, 2009.

3. Gwyn Campbell, "Introduction: Slavery and Other Forms of Unfree Labour in the Indian Ocean World," in Gwyn Campbell, ed., *The Structure of Slavery in Indian Africa and Asia* (London: Frank Cass, 2004), xiii–xiv, xvii; Richard Hellie, *Slavery in Russia 1450–1725* (Chicago: University of Chicago Press, 1982), 33, 41–44; Salim Kidwai, "Sultans, Eunuchs and Domestics: New Forms of Bondage in Medieval India," in Utsa Patnaik and Manjari Dingwaney, eds., *Chains of Servitude: Bondage and Slavery in India* (Madras: Sangam, 1985); Bok-Rae Kim, "Korean Nobi Resistance Under the Chosun Dynasty (1392–1910)," *Slavery and Abolition*, Special Issue, *Slavery and Resistance in Africa and Asia* 25, 2 (2004): 48; Orlando Patterson, *Slavery and Social Death: A Comparative Study* (Cambridge, Mass.: Harvard University Press, 1982), 124–26; Alan Winnington, *The Slaves of the Cool Mountains: The Ancient Social Conditions and Changes Now in Progress on the Remote South-Western Borders of China* (London: Lawrence & Wishard, 1959), 88–89.

4. Peter Boomgaard, "Human Capital, Slavery and Low Rates of Economic and Population Growth in Indonesia, 1600–1910," in Campbell, ed., *The Structure of Slavery in Indian Africa and Asia*, 87–88; David Feeny, "The Demise of Corvee and Slavery in Thailand, 1783–1913," in Martin A. Klein, ed., *Breaking the Chains: Slavery, Bondage, and Emancipation in Modern Africa and Asia* (Madison: University of Wisconsin Press, 1993), 83–111; M. I. Finley, "Between Slavery and Freedom," *Comparative Studies in Society and History* 6, 3 (1964): 233; Orlando Patterson, *Freedom* (New York: Basic, 1991), 57–58, 66–67, 208–9.

5. See Indrani Chatterjee, "Abolition by Denial: The South Asian example," in Gwyn Campbell, ed., *Abolition and Its Aftermath in Indian Ocean Africa and Asia* (New York: Routledge, 2005), 152–53; Jean Allain, "The Definition of Slavery in International Law," *Howard Law Journal* 52 (2009): 251.

6. Krishna Upadhyaya, "Bonded Labour in South Asia: India, Nepal and Pakistan," in Christien van den Anker, ed., *The Political Economy of the New Slavery* (Hampshire: Palgrave, 2004), 118–36. See also Kevin Bales, *Disposable People: New Slavery in the Global Economy* (Berkeley: University of California Press, 1999), 9; Human Rights Watch, *Small Change: Bonded Child Labor in India's Silk Industry* (New York: Human Rights Watch, 2003), 18, 46, 50, http://www.hrw.org/reports/2003/india/india 0103.pdf.

7. A useful starting point here remains Judith Ennew, *Debt Bondage: A Survey* (London: Anti-Slavery Society, 1981).

8. Gwyn Campbell, "Introduction: Slavery and Other Forms of Unfree Labour in the Indian Ocean World"; Martin A. Klein, "The Emancipation of Slaves in the Indian Ocean," in Campbell, ed., *Abolition and Its Aftermath in Indian Ocean Africa and Asia*, 203–11; Bruno Lasker, *Human Bondage in Southeast Asia* (Chapel Hill: University of South Carolina Press, 1950), 113–68.

9. Anthony Reid, "Introduction: Slavery and Bondage in Southeast Asian History" in Anthony Reid, ed., *Slavery, Bondage and Dependency in Southeast Asia*, (St Lucia: University of Queensland Press, 1983), 10. See also Andrew Turton, "Thai Institutions of Slavery," in James L. Watson, ed., *Asian and African Systems of Slavery* (Oxford: Blackwell, 1980), 262–67.

10. M. L. Bush, *Servitude in Modern Times* (Cambridge: Polity Press, 2000), 40; Lasker, *Human Bondage in Southeast Asia*, 154–63.

11. Willemina Kloosterboer, *Involuntary Labour Since the Abolition of Slavery* (Leiden: Brill, 1960), 98.

12. See, for example, Elizabeth Dore, "Debt Peonage in Granada, Nicaragua, 1870–1930: Labor in a Noncapitalist Transition," *Hispanic American Historical Review* 83, 3 (2003): 52; Ennew, *Debt Bondage*, 11–16; Alan Knight, "Mexican Peonage: What Was It and Why Was It?" *Journal of Latin American Studies* 18 (1986): 41–74, and "Debt Bondage in Latin America," in Léone Archer, ed., *Slavery and Other Forms of Unfree Labour* (London: Routledge, 1988), 102–17. While bonded labor in Latin America does not continue on the same scale as the Indian subcontinent, it would be premature to conclude that the problems involved are confined to the past. See, for example, Eduardo Bedoya, Alvaro Bedoya, and Patrick Belser, "Debt Bondage and Ethnic Discrimination in Latin America," in Beate Andreas and Patrick Belser, eds., *Forced Labor: Coercion and Exploitation in the Private Economy* (Boulder, Colo.: Lynne Rienner, 2009), 35–50.

13. Patterson, *Freedom*.

14. See, for example, David Kelly and Anthony Reid, eds., *Asian Freedoms: The Idea of Freedom in East and South East Asia* (Cambridge: Cambridge University Press, 1998).

15. Campbell, "Introduction," xxii–xxiii. See also Richard Eaton, "Introduction," in Indrani Chatterjee and Richard Eaton, eds., *Slavery and South Asian History* (Bloomington: Indiana University Press, 2006), 2–9.

16. Ibid., xxiii.

17. Dharma Kumar, "Colonialism, Bondage and Caste in British India," in Klein, ed., *Breaking the Chains*, 115.

18. Gyan Prakesh, *Bonded Histories: Genealogies of Labor Servitude in Colonial India* (Cambridge: Cambridge University Press, 1990), 3–4. For a critique, see Prabhu P. Mohapatra, "From Contract to Status: Or How Law Shaped Labour Relations in Colonial India, 1780–1880," in Jan Breman, Isabelle Guérin, and Aseem Prakash, eds., *India's Unfree Workforce: Of Bondage Old and New* (New Delhi: Oxford University Press, 2009), 116–21.

19. Prakesh, *Bonded Histories*, 83.

20. Ibid., 140–82.

21. See Peter Robb, "Meanings of Labour in Indian Social Context," in Peter Robb, ed., *Dalit Movements and the Meanings of Labour in India* (Oxford: Oxford University Press, 1993), 1–66.

22. On this point, see Robb's critique of Prakesh; Robb, "Meanings of Labour in Indian Social Context," 26–51.

23. Howard Temperley, "The Delegalization of Slavery in British India," in Howard Temperley, ed., *After Slavery: Emancipation and Its Discontents* (London: Frank Cass, 2000), 177. See also William Gervase Clarence-Smith, *Islam and the Abolition of Slavery* (Oxford: Oxford University Press, 2006), 14–15.

24. Chatterjee, "Abolition by Denial," 154–55.

25. Ralph A. Austen, "The Nineteenth Century Islamic Slave Trade from East Africa (Swahili and Rea Sea Coasts): A Tentative Census," in William Gervase Clarence-Smith, ed., *The Economics of the Indian Ocean and Red Sea Slave Trades in the 19th Century* (London: Frank Cass, 1989), 29, 32; Boomgaard, "Human Capital, Slavery and Low Rates of Economic and Population Growth in Indonesia," 91; Kidwai, "Sultans, Eunuchs and Domestics," 85–86.

26. In this context, slave trading appears to have involved a disproportionate number of women and children (of both sexes). Indrani Chatterjee, *Gender, Slavery and Law in Colonial India* (Oxford: Oxford University Press, 1999), 11.

27. See Anupama Rao, *The Caste Question: Dalits and the Politics of Modern India* (Berkeley: University of California Press, 2009), 39–80.

28. Kumar, "Colonialism, Bondage and Caste in British India," 116–17; Benedicte Hjejle, "Slavery and Agricultural Bondage in South India in the Nineteenth Century," *Scandinavian Economic History Review* 15, 1–2 (1967): 71.

29. Chatterjee, "Abolition by Denial," 151.

30. Temperley, "The Delegalization of Slavery in British India," 173–80; Jacques Pouchepadass, "After Slavery: Unfree Rural Labour in Post-1843 Eastern India," in Breman, Guérin, and Prakash, eds., *India's Unfree Workforce*, 24–25.

31. See, for example, S. K. Singh, *Bonded Labour and the Law* (New Delhi: Deep & Deep, 1994), 7–12.

32. Chatterjee, *Gender, Slavery and Law in Colonial India*, 177–84.

33. Ibid., 176–213; Manjari Dingwaney, "Unredeemed Promises: The Law and Servitude," in Utsa Patnaik and Manjari Dingwaney, eds., *Chains of Servitude: Bondage and Slavery in India* (Madras: Sangam, 1985), 298–314; Temperley, "The Delegalization of Slavery in British India," 181–83.

34. Chatterjee, *Gender, Slavery and Law in Colonial India*, 213–14; Dingwaney, "Unredeemed Promises," 311–12.

35. Hjejle, "Slavery and Agricultural Bondage in South India in the Nineteenth Century," 98–100; Pouchepadass, "After Slavery," 27–29; Rish Pal Nainta, *Bonded Labour in India: A Socio-Legal Study* (New Delhi: Aph, 1997), 24–25; K. T. Rammohan, "Modern Bondage: Atiyaayma in Post Abolition Malabar," in Breman, Guérin, and Prakash, eds.,

India's Unfree Workforce, 70–71, 76–78, 93; Temperley, "The Delegalization of Slavery in British India," 183–86.

36. Chatterjee, *Gender, Slavery and Law in Colonial India*, 213–14.

37. Klein, "The Emancipation of Slaves in the Indian Ocean," 202–3; Kumar, "Colonialism, Bondage and Caste in British India," 121.

38. Kumar, "Colonialism, Bondage and Caste in British India," 125.

39. V. C. P. Chaudhary, K. P. Jayaswal, and P. P. Singh, eds., *Unclassified Class Oppression Under the Crown: An Archival Probe in Indo-Nepalese Relation on Slavery* (Patna: Rahul Press, 1991), 1–52, 65–84; Keya Dasgupta, "Plantation labour in the Brahmaputra Valley," in Campbell, ed., *Abolition and Its Aftermath in Indian Ocean Africa and Asia*, 169–79; Dingwaney, "Unredeemed Promises," 314–24; V. G. Kiernan, *The Lord of Human Kind: European Attitudes Towards the Outside World in the Imperial Age* (London: Weidenfeld and Nicolson, 1969), 60–61; Tanika Sarkar, "Bondage in the Colonial Context," in Patnaik and Dingwaney, eds., *Chains of Servitude*, 114–22.

40. See Dingwaney, "Unredeemed Promises," 313; Hjejle, "Slavery and Agricultural Bondage in South India in the Nineteenth Century," 100–102, 122–24; Kumar, "Colonialism, Bondage and Caste in British India," 121–22; Sarkar, "Bondage in the Colonial Context," 98, 108–14; Singh, *Bonded Labour and the Law*, 12; Temperley, "The Delegalization of Slavery in British India," 183.

41. Dingwaney, "Unredeemed Promises," 313; Hjejle, "Slavery and Agricultural Bondage in South India in the Nineteenth Century," 100–102, 122–24; Kumar, "Colonialism, Bondage and Caste in British India," 121–22; Sarkar, "Bondage in the Colonial Context," 98, 108–14; Singh, *Bonded Labour and the Law*, 12; Temperley, "The Delegalization of Slavery in British India," 183.

42. Pouchepadass, "After Slavery," 29–30. See also Bush, *Servitude in Modern Times*, 216.

43. Chaudhary, *Unclassified Class Oppression Under the Crown*, 85–150.

44. Amendra Kumar Thakur, *Slavery in Arunachal Pradesh* (New Delhi: Mittal, 2003).

45. Prakash, *Bonded Histories*, 160, 184.

46. See Chatterjee, "Abolition by Denial," 157–61; Robin Jeffrey, ed., *People, Princes and Paramount Power: Society and Politics in the Indian Princely States* (Delhi: Oxford University Press, 1978).

47. Suzanne Miers, *Slavery in the Twentieth Century* (Walnut Creek, Calif.: Altamira Press, 2003), 126–27, 29, 282–83.

48. Clarence-Smith, *Islam and the Abolition of Slavery*, 182.

49. United Nations Treaty Collection, as of February 5, 2002, Office of the United Nations High Commissioner for Human Rights, http://www.unhchr.ch/html/menu3/b/treaty4.htm. The later date for India and Pakistan details the point of ratification.

50. Supplementary Convention on the Abolition of Slavery, the Slave Trade, and Institutions and Practices Similar to Slavery, 226 U.N.T.S. 3, *entered into force* April 30, 1957, http://www.ohchr.org/english/law/slavetrade.htm.

51. These laws do not operate in isolation. Many other pieces of legislation indirectly

cover many of the abuses associated with bonded labor, involving issues such as wages, borrowing, contracts, violence, and child labor. These legal instruments often have a longer pedigree, but they have rarely been coherently applied to bonded labor. See Lakshmidhar Mishra, *Burden of Bondage: An Enquiry into the Affairs of the Bonded Quarry Mine Workers of Faridabad* (New Delhi: Manak Publications, 1997), 22–43; National Commission on Labour, *Report of the Second National Commission on Labour* (Delhi: Jaina, 2002), ch. 6, http://www.indialabourarchives.org; Aine Smith, "Child Labor: The Pakistani Effort to End a Scourge upon Humanity: Is It Enough?" *San Diego International Law Journal* 6 (2005): 475; Anti-Slavery International, *This Menace of Bonded Labour: Debt Bondage in Pakistan* (London: Anti-Slavery International, 1996), 20–21; Singh, *Bonded Labour and the Law*, 70–80; Lee Tucker, "Child Slaves in Modern India: The Bonded Labor Problem," *Human Rights Quarterly* 19, 3 (1997): 583–87, 591–93; Uday Kumar Varma, "State-Sponsored Interventions in India," in G. K. Lieten, Ravi Srivastava, and Sukhadeo Thorat, eds., *Small Hands in South Asia: Child Labour in Perspective* (New Delhi: Manohar, 2004), 226–34.

52. Bales, *Disposable People*, 186–92; Farhad Karim, *Contemporary Forms of Slavery in Pakistan* (New York: Human Rights Watch, 1995); Anti-Slavery International, *This Menace of Bonded Labour*, 22–24.

53. Shubhankar Dam, "Lawmaking Beyond Lawmakers: Understanding The Little Right and the Great Wrong (Analyzing the Legitimacy of the Nature of Judicial Lawmaking in India's Constitutional Dynamic)," *Tulane Journal of International and Comparative Law* 13, 109 (2005): 110.

54. See National Centre, *Bonded Labour and Its Abolition*, vol. 1, *Report*; vol. 2, *Documents*, Part I, *Statutes, Reports and Circulars*, Part II, *Case Material* (New Delhi, National Centre for Human Settlement and Environment, 1990); Nainta, *Bonded Labour in India*, 111–37; Singh, *Bonded Labour and the Law*, 220–43. Two detailed, if overlapping, case studies are provided by Mahaveer Jain, *Bonded Labour: Justice Through Judiciary* (New Delhi: Manak, 1997), and Mishra, *Burden of Bondage*.

55. Ravi S. Srivastava, *Bonded Labour in India: Its Incidence and Pattern* (Geneva: ILO, 2005), 1, 6–7, 32–35.

56. Lakshmidhar Mishra, *A Perspective Plan to Eliminate Forced Labour in India* (Geneva: International Labour Office, 2001), 10–11; Human Rights Watch, *Small Change*, 68–70; Srivastava, *Bonded Labour in India*, 32–33.

57. M. R. Anderson, "Work Constructed: Ideological Origins of Labour Law in British India to 1918," in Robb, ed., *Dalit Movements and the Meanings of Labour in India*, 105–10; Dingwaney, "Unredeemed Promises," 324–33; Nainta, *Bonded Labour in India*, 28–40; S. K. Singh, *Bonded Labour and the Law*, 85–89.

58. Human Rights Watch, *Small Change*, 46, 68–70; Singh, *Bonded Labour and the Law*, 250–51; Human Rights Watch, *The Small Hands of Slavery: Bonded Child Labor in India* (New York: Human Rights Watch/Asia, 1996); Tucker, "Child Slaves in Modern India," 583–87.

59. National Centre, *Bonded Labour and Its Abolition*, vol. 1, 3.

60. Ibid., vol. 2, 3–8.

61. Ibid., vol. 2, 3.

62. Srivastava, *Bonded Labour in India*, 3–4.

63. Human Rights Watch, *Small Change*, 70. See also Bales, *Disposable People*, 217–18.

64. Mishra, *A Perspective Plan to Eliminate Forced Labour in India*, 10; Srivastava, *Bonded Labour in India*, 7; Human Rights Watch, *Small Change*, 45; Anti-Slavery International, *This Menace of Bonded Labour*, 15, 29; Upadhyaya, "Bonded Labour in South Asia," 133–34.

65. Jain, *Bonded Labour*, 77; R. Vidyasgar, "Debt-Bondage in South Arcot District: A Case Study of Agricultural Labourers in Handloom Weavers," in Patnaik and Dingwaney, eds., *Chains of Servitude*, 149.

66. National Centre, *Bonded Labour and Its Abolition*, vol. 2, Part I, 9–11, 19.

67. National Labour Institute, *Identification and Rehabilitation of Bonded Labour: Report of a National Seminar* (New Delhi: Kalpana Printing House, 1983), 19; Human Rights Watch, *Small Change*, 46–47; Mishra, *A Perspective Plan to Eliminate Forced Labour in India*, 10; Singh, *Bonded Labour and the Law*, 140–50; Tucker, "Child Slaves in Modern India," 58.

68. Nainta, *Bonded Labour in India*, 104–7; Srivastava, *Bonded Labour in India*, 33; Human Rights Watch, *Small Change*, 73; Tucker, "Child Slaves in Modern India," 627.

69. See Singh, *Bonded Labour and the Law*, 125–38.

70. This should not be construed as a blanket endorsement of existing development programs, which come with their own attendant problems. See, for example, Karin Kapadia, ed., *The Violence of Development: The Politics of Identity, Gender and Social Inequalities in India* (London: Zed Books, 2002).

71. Nainta, *Bonded Labour in India*, 107.

72. Singh, *Bonded Labour and the Law*, 15–20; *The Enslavement of Dalit and Indigenous Communities in India, Nepal and Pakistan Through Debt Bondage*, UN Sub-Commission on the Promotion and Protection of Human Rights, Submission by Anti-Slavery International, February 2001, 2–5.

73. The attendant dangers of legal abolition without effective rehabilitation were recently demonstrated in Nepal. See Kevin Bales, *Ending Slavery: How We Free Today's Slaves* (Berkeley: University of California Press, 2007), 98–108.

74. Krishna Upadhyaya, *Poverty, Discrimination and Slavery: The Reality of Bonded Labour in India, Nepal and Pakistan* (London: Anti-Slavery International, 2008), 18. See also Srivastava, *Bonded Labour in India*, 6.

75. Human Rights Watch, *Small Change*, 46.

76. Nainta, *Bonded Labour in India*, 94–95.

77. Ibid., 104.

78. See Aly Ercelawn and Muhammad Nauman, *Bonded Labour in Pakistan* (Working Paper, Pakistan Institute of Labour Education and Research, 2001), 14–17, http://

www.ilo.org/dyn/declaris/DECLARATIONWEB.DOWNLOAD_BLOB?Var_Docu
mentID=1545; Upadhyaya, *Poverty, Discrimination and Slavery*, 20–22.

79. Bales, *Ending Slavery*, 36–46, 62–70; Srivastava, *Bonded Labour in India*, 18, 33–35.

80. Bales, Disposable People, 227–29; Mishra, *A Perspective Plan to Eliminate Forced Labour in India*, 19; Human Rights Watch, *Small Change*, 51–52; Tucker, "Child Slaves in Modern India," 626.

81. Human Rights Watch, *Small Change*, 71.

82. See Lakshmidhar Mishra *Annotated Bibliography on Forced/Bonded Labour in India* (Geneva: International Labour Office, 2002); *Slavery, Indentured Labour and Bonded Labour: A Bibliography*, Patnaik and Dingwaney, eds., *Chains of Servitude: Bondage and Slavery in India*, 348–66.

83. See, for example, G. V. Chitnis, *Forced Labour in India* (Bombay: All-India Trade Union Congress, 1954), 2–8.

84. Jan Breman and Isabelle Guérin, "On Bondage: Old and New," in Breman, Guérin, and Prakash, eds., *India's Unfree Workforce*, 2–5; Nainta, *Bonded Labour in India*, 50–52.

85. See Srivastava, *Bonded Labour in India*; National Commission on Labour, *Report of the Second National Commission on Labour*.

86. Srivastava, *Bonded Labour in India*, 12, and "Conceptualizing Continuity and Change in Emerging Forms of Labour Bondage in India," in Breman, Guérin, and Prakash , eds., *India's Unfree Workforce*, 136–37. See also Upadhyaya, "Bonded Labour in South Asia," 126–27.

87. National Commission on Labour, *Report of the Second National Commission on Labour*, chap. 7, 271.

88. Ibid., chap. 7, 269.

89. ILO, *A Global Alliance Against Forced Labour, Global Report Under the Follow-up to the ILO Declaration on Fundamental Principles and Rights at Work* (Geneva: ILO, 2005), 31, http://www.ilo.org/dyn/declaris/DECLARATIONWEB.DOWNLOAD_BLOB?Var_DocumentID=5059.

90. Jayoti Gupta, "Himalayan Polyandry: Bondage Among Women in Jaunsar Bawar," in Patnaik and Dingwaney, eds., *Chains of Servitude*, 258–81; Siddarth Kara, *Sex Trafficking: Inside the Business of Modern Slavery* (New York: Columbia University Press, 2009), 45–82.

91. Asian Development Bank, *Combating Trafficking of Women and Children in South Asia: Regional Synthesis Paper for Bangladesh, India, and Nepal* (Manila: Asian Development Bank, 2003), 67, http://www.adb.org/Documents/Books/Combating_Trafficking/Regional_Synthesis_ Paper.pdf; Upadhyaya, "Bonded Labour in South Asia," 131.

92. National Labour Institute, *National Survey on the Incidence of Bonded Labour* (New Delhi: National Labour Institute, 1979), 29.

93. See, for example, Adam Robertson and Shisham Mishra, *Forced to Plough: Bonded Labour in Nepal's Agricultural Economy* (London/Kathmandu: Anti-Slavery International and Informal Sector Service Centre, 1997), 15–21.

94. Tucker, "Child Slaves in Modern India," 573.

95. See Amnesty International, *Children in Bondage: Slaves of the Subcontinent* (London: Anti-Slavery International, 1989); Lieten, Srivastava, and Thorat, eds., *Small Hands in South Asia*.

96. Human Rights Watch, *Small Change*, 53–61; Tucker, "Child Slaves in Modern India," 623–27.

97. Archana Mehendale, "Realities of Child Labour and Contextualizing the Legal Strategy: A Case Study of India," in Lieten, Srivastava, and Thorat, eds., *Small Hands in South Asia*, 249–54; Smith, "Child Labor," 475–87.

98. Bernard D'Mello, "Child Labour in a Buyer-Driven Global Commodity Chain," in Lieten, Srivastava, and Thorat, eds., *Small Hands in South Asia*, 320–22; Peter Lee-Wright, *Child Slaves* (London: Earthscan, 1990), 19–24, 35–36, 46–53.

99. Mehendale, "Realities of Child Labour and Contextualizing the Legal Strategy," 258–59; Upadhyaya, "Bonded Labour in South Asia," 129–30. See also Richard Falk, "Interpreting the Interaction of Global Markets and Human Rights," in Alison Brysk, ed., *Globalization and Human Rights* (Berkeley: University of California Press, 2002), 65–69; David Kinley and Junko Tadaki, "From Talk to Walk: The Emergence of Human Rights Responsibilities for Corporations at International Law," *Virginia Journal of International Law* 44 (2004): 931.

100. Upadhyaya, "Bonded Labour in South Asia," 135.

101. Human Rights Watch, *Caste Discrimination: A Global Concern, A Report by Human Rights Watch for the United Nations World Conference Against Racism, Racial Discrimination, Xenophobia and Related Intolerance* (Durban: Human Rights Watch, 2001), http://www.hrw.org/reports/2001/globalcaste/.

102. Rao, *The Caste Question*, 241–64.

103. A number of commentators have suggested that bonded labor has recently slipped down the political agenda after an earlier period of prominence. See Human Rights Watch, *Small Change*, 6–7, 45, 58; Upadhyaya, "Bonded Labour in South Asia: India, Nepal and Pakistan," 133.

Chapter 8. Trafficked into Slavery

1. Edward J. Bristow, *Prostitution and Prejudice: The Jewish Fight Against White Slavery* (Oxford: Clarendon Press, 1982), 41.

2. Ibid., 34–38.

3. See Jane Jordan, *Josephine Butler* (London: John Murray, 2002).

4. Annemieke van Drenth and Francisca de Haan, *The Rise of Caring Power: Elizabeth Fry and Josephine Butler in Britain and the Netherlands* (Amsterdam: Amsterdam University Press, 1999), 106–7.

5. David J. Langum, *Crossing over the Line: Legislating Morality and the Mann Act* (Chicago: University of Chicago Press, 1994), 34.

6. Edward J. Bristow, *Vice and Vigilance: Purity Movements in Britain Since 1700* (Dublin: Gill and Macmillan, 1977).

7. Kathleen Barry, *Female Sexual Slavery* (Englewood Cliffs, N.J.: Prentice-Hall, 1979), 10; Frederick K. Grittner, *White Slavery: Myth Ideology and American Law* (New York: Garland, 1990), 66–67, 75.

8. Grittner, *White Slavery*, 132–33; Ethan A. Nadelmann, "Global Prohibition Regimes: The Evolution of Norms in International Society," *International Organization*, 44, 4 (1990): 515; Petra De Vries, "Colonial Nation: The Dutch Campaign Against the Traffic in Women in the Early Twentieth Century," *Social & Legal Studies* 14, 1 (2005): 55.

9. See, for example, Donna J. Guy, *White Slavery and Mothers Alive and Dead: The Troubled Meeting of Sex, Gender, Public Health, and Progress in Latin America* (Lincoln: University of Nebraska Press, 2000), esp. 74–75; and Judith R. Walkowitz, "Male Vice and Feminist Virtue: Feminism and the Politics of Prostitution in Nineteenth Century Britain," *History Workshop* 13 (1982): 85.

10. Margit Stange, *Wives, White Slaves and the Market in Women* (Baltimore: John Hopkins University Press, 1998).

11. Walkowitz, "Male Vice and Feminist Virtue," 89.

12. Barry, *Female Sexual Slavery*, 27–28; De Vries, "Colonial Nation," 54; George L. Mosse, *Nationalism and Sexuality: Middle-Class Morality and Sexual Norms in Modern Europe* (Madison: University of Wisconsin Press, 1985), 90.

13. Eileen Scully, "Pre-Cold War Traffic in Sexual Labor and Its Foes: Some Contemporary Lessons," in David Kyle and Rey Koslowski, eds., *Global Human Smuggling: Comparative Perspectives* (Baltimore: Johns Hopkins University Press, 2001), 84–85. William Wilberforce also occupied a dual role at the head of two major campaigns: anti-slavery and anti-vice. See van Drenth and de Haan, *The Rise of Caring Power*, 33–36.

14. Grittner, *White Slavery*, 69–74, 95, 130–31; Philippa Levine, "The White Slave Trade and the British Empire," in Louis A. Knafla, ed., *Crime, Gender and Sexuality in Criminal Prosecutions*, Criminal Justice History 17 (Westport, Conn.: Greenwood Press, 2002), 136.

15. Ernest A. Bell, "A White Slave Clearing House: A White Slave's Own Story," in Ernest A. Bell, ed., *Fighting the Traffic in Young Girls or The War on the White Slave Trade* (Nashville, Tenn.: Southwestern Company, 1910), 75.

16. Stange, *Wives, White Slaves and the Market in Women*, 76. See also Christopher Diffee, "Sex and the City: The White Slavery Scare and Social Governance in the Progressive Era," *American Quarterly* 57, 2 (2005): 411; Grittner, *White Slavery*, 15–32, 107–23.

17. Jacqueline Berman, "(Un)Popular Strangers and Crises (Un)Bounded: Discourses of Sex-Trafficking, the European Political Community and the Panicked State of the Modern State," *European Journal of International Relations* 9, 1 (2003): 61.

18. Mosse, *Nationalism and Sexuality*, 9. See also Ann Laura Stoler, *Race and the Education of Desire: Foucault's History of Sexuality and the Colonial Order of Things* (Durham, N.C.: Duke University Press, 1995), 134–36.

19. See Anna Davin, "Imperialism and Motherhood," *History Workshop* 5 (1976): 9.

20. International Agreement for the Suppression of the "White Slave Traffic," May 18,

1904, University of Minnesota Human Rights Library, Article One, http://www1.umn
.edu/humanrts/instree/whiteslavetraffic1904.html. See also Nora V. Demleitner, "Forced
Prostitution: Naming an International Offense," *Fordham International Law Journal* 18
(1994): 167; Stephanie Farrior, "The International Law on Trafficking in Women and
Children for Prostitution: Making It Live Up to Its Potential," *Harvard Human Rights
Journal* 10 (1997): 216; Nadelmann, "Global Prohibition Regimes," 515.

21. Philippa Levine, "The White Slave Trade and the British Empire," 136–37.

22. Guy, *White Slavery and Mothers Alive and Dead*, 74.

23. This only scratches the surface of a series of complex issues. Throughout this
period, we find discussion of intra-European deviants and "anomalies" whose behavior
and standing posed a problem for imperial ideals. When European women purposely
migrated to Asia or the Middle East to work as prostitutes, they were harshly denounced
as traitors to both their nation and their race. See Stoler, *Race and the Education of Desire*, 95–136.

24. Wendy Chapkis, *Live Sex Acts: Women Performing Erotic Labour* (London: Cas-
sell, 1997), 44–45; De Vries, "Colonial Nation," 47–49; Grittner, *White Slavery*, 69, 95;
Levine, "The White Slave Trade and the British Empire," 137–38; Scully, "Pre-Cold War
Traffic in Sexual Labor and Its Foes," 89–90.

25. Jo Doezema, "Loose Women or Lost Women? The Re-Emergence of the Myth
of White Slavery in Contemporary Discourse of Trafficking in Women," *Gender Issues*
18, 1 (2000): 26.

26. See, for example, Barry, *Female Sexual Slavery*, 14–38.

27. De Vries, "Colonial Nation," 41.

28. De Vries, "Colonial Nation," 41; Langum, *Crossing over the Line*, 35.

29. Scully, "Pre-Cold War Traffic in Sexual Labor and Its Foes," 87.

30. Bristow, *Prostitution and Prejudice*, 34; Julia Martínez, "Trafficking in Women
and Children Across the China Sea," in Emma Christopher, Cassandra Pybus, and Marcus Rediker, eds., *Many Middle Passages: Forced Labour and the Making of the Modern
World* (Berkeley: University of California Press, 2007), 204–21; Scully, "Pre-Cold War
Traffic in Sexual Labor and Its Foes," 83–93; Eric Tagliacozzo, *Secret Trades, Porous Borders: Smuggling and States Along a Southeast Asian Frontier, 1865–1915* (New Haven,
Conn.: Yale University Press, 2005), 230–58.

31. Commission of Enquiry into Traffic in Women and Children in the East, Report
to the Council, League of Nations, Geneva, December 10, 1932, C.849.M.393.1932.IV,
Traffic in Women and Children: Work of the Bandoeng Conference, League of Nations,
Geneva, December 20, 1937, C.516.M357.1937.IV.

32. Commission of Enquiry into Traffic in Women and Children in the East, Report,
62.

33. John Dillon, *From Dance Hall to White Slavery* (New York: Padell, 1942); Sean
O'Callaghan, *The White Slave Trade* (London: New English Library, 1965).

34. Bristow, *Prostitution and Prejudice*, 44–45; De Vries, "Colonial Nation," 40;
Grittner, *White Slavery*, 166.

35. See, for example, Nora V. Demleitner, "The Law at a Crossroads: The Construction of Migrant Women Trafficked into Prostitution," in David Kyle and Rey Koslowski, eds., *Global Human Smuggling: Comparative Perspectives* (Baltimore: Johns Hopkins University Press, 2001), 261; Frank Laczko, "Introduction," in Frank Laczko and Elzbieta Gozdziak, eds., *Data and Research on Human Trafficking: A Global Survey* (Geneva: International Organization for Migration, 2005), 10-11, http://www.iom.int//DOCU MENTS/PUBLICATION/EN/Data_and_Research_on_Human_Trafficking.pdf.

36. Laura María Agustín, *Sex at the Margins: Migration, Labour Markets and the Rescue Industry* (London: Zed Books, 2007), 6-7, 127-28; Elaine Pearson, *Human Traffic, Human Rights: Redefining Victim Protection* (London: Anti-Slavery International, 2002), 32-33.

37. More comprehensive evaluations can be found in Farrior, "The International Law on Trafficking in Women and Children for Prostitution," 217-21; Demleitner, "Forced Prostitution," 172-75.

38. See Elizabeth Bruch, "Models Wanted: The Search for an Effective Response to Human Trafficking," *Stanford Journal of International Law* 40 (2004): 11; Demleitner, "Forced Prostitution," 172-79; David Weissbrodt and Anti-Slavery International, *Abolishing Slavery and Its Contemporary Forms* (New York: United Nations, 2002), 16-41.

39. See, for example, Pearson, *Human Traffic, Human Rights*, 65, 87, 119-20, 173, 187, 199.

40. This process is by no means complete. See Dina Francesca Haynes, "Used, Abused, Arrested and Deported: Extending Immigration Benefits to Protect the Victims of Trafficking and to Secure the Prosecution of Traffickers," *Human Rights Quarterly* 26, 2 (2004): esp. 234-36.

41. Jyoti Sanghera, "Unpacking the Trafficking Discourse," in Kamala Kempadoo, Jyoti Sanghera, and Bandana Pattanaik, eds., *Trafficking and Prostitution Reconsidered: New Perspectives on Migration, Sex Work, and Human Rights* (Boulder, Colo.: Paradigm, 2005), 16.

42. Fara Gold, "Redefining the Slave Trade: The Current Trends in the International Trafficking of Women," *University of Miami International and Comparative Law Review* 11 (2003): 105.

43. Protocol to Prevent, Suppress and Punish Trafficking in Persons Especially Women and Children, supplementing the United Nations Convention against Transnational Organized Crime, Office of the United Nations High Commission for Human Rights, 2000, http://www.ohchr.org/english/law/protocoltraffic.htm.

44. Anne Gallagher, "Human Rights and the New UN Protocols on Trafficking and Migrant Smuggling: A Preliminary Analysis," *Human Rights Quarterly* 23, 4 (2001): 975.

45. United Nations Convention Against Transnational Organized Crime, United Nations Crime and Justice Information Network, http://www.uncjin.org/Documents/Conventions/dcatoc/final_documents_2/convention_eng.pdf.

46. Gallagher, "Human Rights and the New UN Protocols on Trafficking and Migrant Smuggling," 976.

47. Barry, *Female Sexual Slavery*, 5.

48. Mallika Dutt, "Bibliography," in Kathleen Barry, Charlotte Bunch, and Shirley Castley, eds., *International Feminism: Networking Against Female Sexual Slavery: Global Feminist Workshop to Organize Against Traffic in Women* (New York: International Women's Tribune Centre, 1984), 110–18.

49. For a sympathetic analysis of the methodological issues involved, see Patrick Belser and Michaelle de Cock, "Improving Forced Labor Statistics," in Beate Andreas and Patrick Belser, eds., *Forced Labor: Coercion and Exploitation in the Private Economy* (Boulder, Colo.: Lynne Rienner, 2009), 173–94.

50. Thomas M. Steinfatt, Simon Baker, and Allan Beesey, "Measuring the Number of Trafficked Women in Cambodia: Part I of a Series." Paper presented at conference The Human Rights Challenge of Globalization in Asia-Pacific-US, Honolulu, November 13–15, 2002; Chandre Gould, *Selling Sex in Cape Town: Sex Work and Human Trafficking in a South African City* (Pretoria: Institute for Security Studies, 2008); Jerry Markon, "Human Trafficking Evokes Outrage, Little Evidence: U.S. Estimates Thousands of Victims, But Efforts to Find Them Fall Short," *Washington Post*, September 23, 2007; Nick Davies, "Inquiry Fails to Find Single Trafficker Who Forced Anybody into Prostitution," *The Guardian*, October 20, 2009.

51. Guri Tyldum and Anette Brunovskis, "Describing the Unobserved: Methodological Challenges in Empirical Studies on Human Trafficking," in Laczko and Gozdziak, eds., *Data and Research on Human Trafficking*, 17–18.

52. Agustín, *Sex at the Margins*, 37. See also Kamala Kempadoo, "Introduction: Globalizing Sex Workers' Rights," in Kamala Kempadoo and Jo Doezema, eds., *Global Sex Workers, Rights Resistance and Redefinition* (New York: Routledge, 1998), 15.

53. See Doezema, "Loose Women or Lost Women?" 32–33; Kamala Kempadoo, "From Moral Panic to Global Justice: Changing Perspectives on Trafficking," in Kempadoo, Sanghera, and Pattanaik, eds., *Trafficking and Prostitution Reconsidered*, xix–xxi; Alison Murray, "Debt-Bondage and Trafficking: Don't Believe the Hype," in Kempadoo and Doezema, eds., *Global Sex Workers, Rights Resistance and Redefinition*, 51–64.

54. See Laczko and Gozdziak, eds., *Data and Research on Human Trafficking*.

55. Liz Kelly, *Fertile Fields: Trafficking in Persons in Central Asia* (Vienna: International Organization for Migration, 2005), 40, 42, 47–48, http://www.iom.int//DOCUMENTS/PUBLICATION/EN/Fertile_Fields.pdf.

56. Ibid., 44.

57. Ibid., 49–50.

58. The number of international migrants has been estimated at 175 million, far exceeding figures concerned with human trafficking and contemporary forms of slavery. Lauren B. Engle, *The World in Motion: Short Essays on Migration and Gender* (Geneva: International Organization for Migration, 2005), 17.

59. UNICEF, *Trafficking in Human Beings, Especially Women and Children, in Africa* (Florence: UNICEF Innocenti Research Centre, 2003), 11, 13–14, 15, 17, http://www

.unicef.org/media/files/insight8e.pdf. See also Kathleen Fitzgibbon, "Modern-Day Slavery? The scope of trafficking in persons in Africa," *African Security Review* 12, 1 (2003), http://www.iss.co.za/Pubs/ASR/12No1/EFitz.html.

60. David Ould, Claire Jordan, Rebecca Reynolds, and Lacey Loftin, *The Cocoa Industry in West Africa: A History of Exploitation* (London: Anti-Slavery International, 2004), 3, 51–53, http://www.antislavery.org/homepage/resources/cocoa%20report%20 2004.pdf; David Ould, "Trafficking and International Law," in Christien van den Anker, ed., *The Political Economy of the New Slavery* (Hampshire: Palgrave, 2004), 65.

61. UNICEF, *Child Trafficking in West Africa: Policy Responses* (Florence: UNICEF Innocenti Research Centre, 2002), 6, http://www.unicef-icdc.org/publications/pdf/insight7.pdf; Ould et al., *The Cocoa Industry in West Africa*, 50–51.

62. Aderanti Adepoju, "Review of Research and Data on Human Trafficking in sub-Saharan Africa," in Laczko and Gozdziak, eds., *Data and Research on Human Trafficking*, 77; Jonathan Cohen, *Togo Borderline Slavery: Child Trafficking in Togo* (New York: Human Rights Watch, 2003), http://www.hrw.org/reports/2003/togo0403/togo0403 .pdf.

63. Kevin Bales, *Ending Slavery: How We Free Today's Slaves* (Berkeley: University of California Press, 2007), 184–96; Ould et al., *The Cocoa Industry in West Africa*, 54–65; Thanh-Dam Truong, *Poverty, Gender and Human Trafficking in Sub-Saharan Africa: Rethinking Best Practices in Migration Management* (Paris: UNESCO, 2005), 62–67, 100–108.

64. Adepoju, "Review of Research and Data on Human Trafficking in Sub-Saharan Africa," 76–80; Siddarth Kara, *Sex Trafficking: Inside the Business of Modern Slavery* (New York: Columbia University Press, 2009), 86–92.

65. See Asian Development Bank, *Combating Trafficking of Women and Children in South Asia: Regional Synthesis Paper for Bangladesh, India, and Nepal* (Manila: Asian Development Bank, 2003), http://www.adb.org/Documents/Books/Combating_Trafficking/Regional_Synthesis_ Paper.pdf; Jeannine Guthrie, *Rape for Profit, Trafficking of Nepali Girls and Women to India's Brothels* (New York: Human Rights Watch/Asia, 1995), http://www.hrw.org/reports/pdfs/c/crd/india957.pdf; Sankar Sen, ed., *A Report on Trafficking in Women and Children in India, 2002–2003* (New Delhi: National Human Rights Commission, 2004), http://www.ashanet.org/focusgroups/sanctuary/articles/ ReportonTrafficking.pdf. For a more skeptical view, see John Frederick, "The Myth of Nepal-to-India Sex Trafficking: Its Creation, Its Maintenance, and Its Influence on Anti-trafficking Interventions," in Kempadoo, Sanghera, and Pattanaik, eds., *Trafficking and Prostitution Reconsidered.*

66. Sen, *A Report on Trafficking in Women and Children in India*, 14.

67. Ibid., 17; see also 50–80, 82.

68. Ibid., 19, 34.

69. Engle, *The World in Motion*, 57–58, 66–67; Kara, *Sex Trafficking*, 5–11.

70. Not all debts take the same form; see Agustín, *Sex at the Margins*, 30–35.

71. See, for example, *Combating Trafficking of Women and Children in South Asia*, 47–51, 55–57; Engle, *The World in Motion*, chap. 2; Ronaldo Munck, *Globalization and Labour: The New Great Transformation* (London: Zed Books, 2002), 74–75; Valentine M. Moghadam, "The 'Feminization of Poverty' and Women's Human Rights," SHS Papers in Women's Studies (Paris: UNESCO, 2005); Bharati Sadasivam, "The Impact of Structural Adjustment on Women: A Governance and Human Rights Agenda," *Human Rights Quarterly* 19, 3 (1997): 630. For a critique see Agustín, *Sex at the Margins*, 23–26.

72. Alison Brysk, "Introduction: Transnational Threats and Opportunities," in Alison Brysk, ed., *Globalization and Human Rights* (Berkeley: University of California Press, 2002), 21.

73. See Seyla Benhabib, *The Rights of Others: Aliens, Residents and Citizens* (Cambridge: Cambridge University Press, 2004); Andrew Linklater, *Men and Citizens in the Theory of International Relations*, 2nd ed. (London: Macmillan, 1990).

74. Peter Andreas, "The Transformation of Migrant Smuggling Across the U.S.-Mexican Border," in Kyle and Koslowski, eds., *Global Human Smuggling*, 107–22; Khalid Koser, "The Smuggling of Asylum Seekers into Western Europe; Contradictions, Conundrums, and Dilemmas," in Kyle and Koslowski, eds., *Global Human Smuggling*, 58–72.

75. On this point, it is important not to equate all criminal elements with elaborate criminal organizations. See Berman, "(Un)Popular Strangers and Crises (Un)Bounded," 52–55; James O. Finckenauer, "Russian Transnational Organized Crime and Human Trafficking," in Kyle and Koslowski, eds., *Global Human Smuggling*; Sanghera, "Unpacking the Trafficking Discourse," 15–16; Nandita Sharma, "Anti-Trafficking Rhetoric and the Making of a Global Apartheid," *NWSA Journal* 17, 3 (2005): 94.

76. Widney Brown and Joe Saunders, eds., *Bad Dreams: Exploitation and Abuse of Migrant Workers in Saudi Arabia* (New York: Human Rights Watch, 2004), 8, 11–14, http://hrw.org/reports/2004/saudi0704/saudi0704.pdf. The systematic abuse of migrant workers has also been identified as a new global trend. See Bridget Anderson, *Doing the Dirty Work: The Global Politics of Domestic Labour* (London: Zed Books, 2000); Toby Shelley, *Exploited: Migrant Labour in the New Global Economy* (London: Zed Books, 2007).

77. Ibid., 80.

78. Munck, *Globalization and Labour*, 113.

79. Ulrich Beck, *The Brave New World of Work* (Cambridge: Polity Press, 2000), chap. 1, 6.

80. Kevin Bales and Ron Soodalter, *The Slave Next Door: Human Trafficking and Slavery in America Today* (Berkeley: University of California Press, 2009), 223–25; Anna Marie Gallagher, "Triply Exploited: Female Victims of Trafficking Networks: Strategies for Pursuing Protection and Legal Status in Countries of Destination," *Georgetown Immigration Law Journal* 19, 1 (2004): 99; Tala Hartsough, "Asylum for Trafficked Women: Escape Strategies Beyond the T Visa," *Hastings Women's Law Journal* (2002): 77; Haynes, "Used, Abused, Arrested and Deported," 221–72.

81. Berman, "(Un)Popular Strangers and Crises (Un)Bounded," 40, 50–53; Doezema, "Loose Women or Lost Women," 31; Frederick, "The Myth of Nepal-to-India Sex Trafficking," 128–29; Gretchen Soderlund, "Running from the Rescuers: New U.S. Crusades Against Sex Trafficking and the Rhetoric of Abolition," *NWSA Journal* 17, 3 (2005): 81, 83.

82. Melissa Ditmore, "Trafficking in Lives: How Ideology Shapes Policy," in Kempadoo, Sanghera, and Pattanaik, eds., *Trafficking and Prostitution Reconsidered*, 109; Gallagher, "Human Rights and the New UN Protocols on Trafficking and Migrant Smuggling," 983.

83. Bruch, "Models Wanted," 1–45; Wendy Chapkis, "Trafficking, Migration and the Law: Protection Innocents, Punishing Immigrants," *Gender & Society* 17, 6 (2003): esp. 930; Jo Doezema, "Forced to Choose: Beyond the Voluntary v. Forced Prostitution Dichotomy," in Kempadoo and Doezema, eds., *Global Sex Workers, Rights Resistance and Redefinition*, 43–47.

84. See Chapkis, *Live Sex Acts*, 11–32, 53–57; Soderlund, "Running from the Rescuers," 70–72; Kate Sutherland, "Work, Sex, and Sex-Work: Competing Feminist Discourses on the International Sex Trade," *Osgoode Hall Law Journal* (2004): 139; Joyce Outshoorn, "The Political Debates on Prostitution and Trafficking of Women," *Social Politics: International Studies in Gender, State and Society* 12, 1 (2005): 141. A more general starting point is provided by Joyce Outshoorn, ed., *The Politics of Prostitution: Women's Movements, Democratic States and the Globalization of Sex Commerce* (Cambridge: Cambridge University Press, 2004).

85. Ditmore, "Trafficking in Lives," 111–14; Gallagher, "Human Rights and the New UN Protocols on Trafficking and Migrant Smuggling," 1002–3; Outshoorn, "The Political Debates on Prostitution and Trafficking of Women," 148–52.

86. See Chapkis, *Live Sex Acts*, 46–53; Soderlund, "Running from the Rescuers," 65–68, 74, 79–83.

87. Marjolein van der Veen, "Beyond Slavery and Capitalism: Producing Class Difference in the Sex Industry," in J. K. Gibson-Graham, Stephen A. Resnick, and Richard D. Wolff, eds., *Class and Its Others* (Minneapolis: University of Minnesota Press, 2000), 126.

88. Chapkis, *Live Sex Acts*, 131–40, 155–79.

89. See Sheila Jeffreys, *The Industrial Vagina: The Political Economy of the Global Sex Trade* (London: Routledge: 2009), 15–37; Catherine A. MacKinnon, *Are Women Human? And Other International Dialogues* (Cambridge, Mass.: Harvard University Press, 2006), 247–58; Janice G. Raymond, "Prostitution on Demand: Legalizing the Buyers as Sexual Consumers," *Violence Against Women* 10, 10 (2004): 1163. This is part of a special issue of the journal entitled "The Case Against the Legalization of Prostitution." Following historical precedent, religious groups have played a major role in campaigning against trafficking, and tend to align to this perspective. See Allen D. Hertzke, *Freeing God's Children: The Unlikely Alliance for Global Human Rights* (Lantham, Md.: Rowman & Littlefield, 2004), 315–35.

90. Jeffreys, *The Industrial Vagina*, 203–7.

91. Ratna Kapur, "Travel Plans: Border Crossings and the Rights of Transnational Migrants," *Harvard Human Rights Journal* 18 (2005): 114.

92. See, for example, Agustín, *Sex at the Margins*; Berman, "(Un)Popular Strangers and Crises (Un)Bounded"; Julia O'Connell Davidson, *Children in the Global Sex Trade* (Cambridge: Polity, 2005); Julia O'Connell Davidson and Bridget Anderson, "The Trouble with 'Trafficking,'" in Christien van den Anker and Jeroen Doomernick, eds., *Trafficking and Women's Rights* (Houndsmills: Palgrave, 2006), 11–26; Jeroen Doomernick, "Migration and Security: The Wrong End of the Stick?" in van den Anker, ed., *The Political Economy of the New Slavery*; Kempadoo, "From Moral Panic to Global Justice," vii–xxxiv.

93. Haynes, "Used, Abused, Arrested and Deported," 229. See also Soderlund, "Running from the Rescuers," 75–79.

94. Sharma, "Anti-Trafficking Rhetoric and the Making of a Global Apartheid," 91.

95. Earlier versions of the report offered clear estimates of numbers of trafficking victims (in 2007, the estimate given was 800,000 people being annually trafficked across national borders, with millions more being trafficked within countries), but the latest report avoids making similar claims, and instead uses figures from the International Labour Organization. U.S. Department of State, *Trafficking in Persons Report, June 2010*, http://www.state.gov/documents/organization/142979.pdf.

96. Bales and Soodalter, *The Slave Next Door*, 99–116; E. Benjamin Skinner, *A Crime So Monstrous* (Edinburgh: Mainstream, 2008), 40, 68–69, 73–77, 200, 215, 231, 289–96.

97. One major alternative to trafficking comes from the International Labour Organization, which has tended to organize its work around forced labor rather than human trafficking.

Conclusion: Contemporary Slavery in the Shadow of History

1. See, for example, Chuck Stetson, ed., *Creating the Better Hour: Lessons from William Wilberforce* (Macon, Ga.: Stroud & Hall, 2007); Danny Smith, ed., *Slavery: Now and Then* (Eastbourne: Kingsway, 2007).

2. See James Lee Ray, "The Abolition of Slavery and the End of International War," *International Organization* 43, 3 (1989): 405–39.

3. See, for example, Margaret Keck and Kathryn Sikkink, *Activists Beyond Borders: Advocacy Networks in International Politics* (Ithaca, N.Y.: Cornell University Press, 1998), 8–32; Audie Klotz, "Transnational Activism and Global Transformations: The Anti-Apartheid and Abolitionist Experiences," *European Journal of International Relations* 8, 1 (2002): 49–76.

4. See, for example, Lynn Hunt, *Inventing Human Rights: A History* (New York: Norton, 2007), 66–69; Micheline R. Ishay, *The History of Human Rights: From Ancient Times to the Globalization Era*, 2nd ed. (Berkeley: University of California Press, 2008), 110–15.

5. Keck and Sikkink, *Activists Beyond Borders*, 27.

6. For a further analysis of various ways of combating contemporary forms of slavery, see Joel Quirk, *Unfinished Business: A Comparative Survey of Historical and Contemporary Slavery* (Paris: UNESCO, 2009), 113–20.

7. See, for example, Kevin Bales, *Disposable People: New Slavery in the Global Economy* (Berkeley: University of California Press, 1999).

Acknowledgments

This book has been under construction since 2001. The early stages of the writing process took place at the Australian National University in Canberra, where I had the good fortune to encounter many talented teachers and colleagues. I would like to especially express my gratitude to Chris Reus-Smit, head of the Department of International Relations, for helping mold a project that regularly threatened to collapse under its own weight. Among the many scholars in Canberra who offered support, I would also like to especially thank André Broome, Michelle Burgis, Malcom Cook, Thuy Do, Greg Fry, Nicky George, Ayla Göl, Sarah Graham, Paul Keal, Stuart Harris, Craig Meer, Heather Rae, Wynne Russell, Len Seabrooke, Yongjin Zhang, and Tianbiao Zhu. It has been a great privilege to have such excellent role models, both intellectual and personal. Particular thanks are also owed to Darshan Vigneswaran and Shogo Suzuki, who have borne the brunt of a steady stream of excessive tirades, peculiar digressions, and numerous repetitions. I would also like to express my gratitude to Amelia Twiss and David and Rebecca Bramwell-King for their extended hospitality during a research trip to London in 2003. During my time at ANU, I also benefited tremendously from years of encouragement and assistance from Anna Rajander. Thank you.

Various elements of the book have been presented at a number of conferences and lectures. I would like to express my gratitude for the valuable feedback and encouragement I received from audiences at the Australian National University, University of Cambridge, l'Università G. d'Annunzio, University of Hull, University of Liverpool, University of Oxford, University of Pennsylvania, University of Saint Andrews, University of Southern California, and Witwatersrand University. I would also like to especially thank Peter Agree, Bert Lockwood, and three anonymous reviewers for helping bring the final product to press, and to also thank Barbara Combes for her invaluable assistance in helping edit and refine numerous drafts over the years.

At the University of Hull, I would like to especially thank David Richardson, Director of the Wilberforce Institute for the study of Slavery and Emancipation, for helping to fill numerous gaps in my understanding of the history of slavery and abolition. Being based at a specialized slavery institute has been a tremendous privilege, as I have been able to learn from many experts on various aspects of historical and contemporary slavery. I would also like to express my individual thanks to Kevin Bales, Richard Burchill, Nicholas Evans, Mike Feintuck, Douglas Hamilton, Gerry Johnstone, and Judith Spicksley for their valuable instruction and assistance over the years. The most significant debt I have incurred at Hull is to Stacey Sommerdyk, who has offered invaluable support, insight and humor. Thank you.

Finally, I would like to express my deepest gratitude to my parents, Pat Quirk and June Forbes, who have offered decades of guidance, encouragement, tolerance, and support.

When it comes to analytical frameworks, historical expertise, and underlying starting points, this book is also especially indebted to Kevin Bales, Hedley Bull, Frederick Cooper, Seymour Drescher, David Eltis, Suzanne Miers, Paul Lovejoy, and Orlando Patterson.

As is always the case in such matters, all errors and omissions are my own.

CPSIA information can be obtained at www.ICGtesting.com
Printed in the USA
BVOW05s2228140514

353339BV00001B/1/P